JIM DOUGHERTY'S GUIDE TO
BOWHUNTING DEER

By Jim Dougherty

Edited by Jack Lewis

DBI BOOKS, INC.

DEDICATION
For my Dad, one of those stars up there.
The nicest man I've ever known

EDITORIAL DIRECTOR

Jack Lewis

ART DIRECTOR

Rueselle Gilbert

PRODUCTION DIRECTOR

Sonya Kaiser

COPY EDITOR

Julie T. Rieman

PRODUCTION COORDINATOR

Russ Thurman

PHOTO SERVICES

Lori Morrison

LITHOGRAPHIC SERVICES

Gallant Graphics

PUBLISHER

Sheldon L. Factor

Produced by

GALLANT CHARGER

OUTDOOR GROUP

ISBN: 0-87349-148-3

Library of Congress Catalog Card Number: 92-81319

CONTENTS

INTRODUCTION

This is a book about deer hunting — deer hunting with bow and arrow. It is not a book of never-before revealed secrets for catching truckloads of giant bucks. While there have been volumes of good advice based on scientific knowledge and practical application that have helped us all to understand hunting big deer, there *never* has been a guaranteed formula for big deer success.

For sure, we know more about deer today than we did in the Fifties, when I started bowhunting, just as we know more about our planet and the universe that surrounds us. Increased knowledge is inevitable as man digs into everything.

I took up archery in the early 1950s, because hunting with a bow had an appeal to me that I hardly understood then and cannot explain now. One should bear in mind that in the Fifties, hardly anyone did it. There was scarce opportunity to bowhunt at all.

Time changes all things. Bowhunting for deer today is a major outdoor pursuit, a proper use of a natural, in some cases, phenomenally increasing resource that offers opportunity ten times greater today than when I began!

In the years that have passed, I have improved as a bowhunter, been involved actively in the sport both as vocation and avocation at all levels. Through it all, I have been, as most all of us are, just another bowhunter looking for a deer.

I try to hunt big deer wherever I am. I try hard, but truly big deer only come along on rare occasions. Big deer are the things of which dreams are born.

Looking for a deer, enjoying all the subtle multi-colored elements of fall that go with the experience is what bowhunting really is about. The fanatical obsession with big bucks, in my experience, has caused men to lose families, friendships, reputations and credibility.

It seems to be a natural trait of man to over-engineer everything. It is no different in his pursuit of deer. I hunt deer with a bow because I love it for many varied reasons. While I shoot a compound bow today, and employ the use of some of the equipment "advances" that have come along in the forty years I have chased deer, I have found that much of what we see, hear, and read today about the materials necessary to success are, in fact, unnecessary results of that tendency to over-engineer.

Hunting is a personal thing. The pursuit and the selection of tools we use in the chase are equally a matter of personal taste. I have no axe to grind with anyone who bowhunts in terms of tactics or equipment, as long as they subscribe to the rules of the land, the law and fair chase. All that being said, this is simply a book about bowhunting for deer.

Jim Dougherty
Tulsa, Oklahoma

CHAPTER 1

BOWHUNTING TODAY

The Animal Rights Fanatics Now Are The Sport's Greatest Enemy

Bowhunting for deer, or any game animal, is being threatened. While not actually new, the threat has intensified in the 1990s.

*Young Jim Dougherty
gained a deep appreciation
for the outdoors and wildlife
while bowhunting California.*

I HAVE been thinking about the differentiation between hunting as a right or as a privilege.

Today, more than ever, I think any hunting, but especially bowhunting, is a right. I didn't start out feeling that way. In the beginning of my bowhunting life, we didn't have many places to bowhunt for big game—deer were the issue—in California, nor were there many folks who wanted to hunt them with a bow. Back then we were just fighting for the opportunity to do it.

In terms of that era's population base, "sportsmen," (that's what we all were called then) made up a reasonable percentage of that base. Admittedly, bowhunters were a minority struggling for identity. The beginning was pretty tough. The population percentage equation, as far as California is concerned, has been pretty well eroded. Too many people moved there, habitat vanished and realism gave way to...well, you get the picture.

Anyhow, back then, bowhunters had to kick and scratch pretty hard at public hearings for the privilege of bowhunting at all. Special opportunities like ten-day pre-seasons for the two major deer general seasons came first. Special archery-only hunts were earned in a manner best described as hand-to-

hand combat. Quite frankly, we were considered a rather strange breed, armed as we were with slim, light weapons that did nothing more than: "Throw a spear only slightly better than the hand of a child could propel it." We were called, by that same ballistically unoriented orator, "Barbarians."

I was about 16 years old and it upset me. The attitude was hard to understand. In those days, I could take my shotgun and hunt anything in feathers virtually anywhere simply by asking permission. What is hard to realize now, is that then, in the Fifties, California was just one fine piece of country with more types of game, and habitat, than one could properly begin to say grace over. I found it a contradiction that, having become really interested in archery—bowhunting being the subliminal reason, though I didn't understand all of that then, and much of what I was to come to understand hadn't been invented—that a lot of people didn't think we should practice our sport for reasons that were never even close to properly explained. Not much has changed there.

I spent a great deal of time in my formative years at public hearings where eloquent speakers argued on behalf of our young sport, lobbied and, yes, pleaded for bowhunting opportunity. What was happening in California then was not at all

Bowhunting has changed a lot since Jim (center) took this doe in 1953 while hunting with his dad (right) and Doug Kittredge.

unique. Indeed, the same scenario was being played out across the land, though some states were making better progress. Most game departments at that point were not convinced bowhunting tackle was effective for big game. "What," asked one, "in the hell is wrong with gun powder?"

I suppose, if you look at how that tackle has evolved, forty years ago it did appear archaic. But, a few decades back, nobody knew how it would look today. The point, if there is one, is moot. There were then, fortunately, people who knew that what we used worked quite well. In fact, in the hands of a competent user, the bow and arrows of then were equal with what we have today.

Bowhunters initially fought for the privilege to hunt, proving the sport's worth as we went along on every color shade of the game management spectrum. It took awhile. We still have our enemies, but we have earned the *right* to bowhunt.

Is bowhunting different today? Certainly. There's an obvious new look to our equipment. Though it generally works in the same manner, it is easier to use, more efficient and better made. The simple ink mark on the face side of a hand-crafted yew wood bow that served as a reference point for elevation has given way to micro-adjustable bow sights. Sinew backing

has been replaced with synthetic fibers that gave way to fiberglass—a substance that improved almost annually. Straight or reflex limb designs evolved into smooth recurves that stored more energy, shot faster and felt better—designs that were possible because of fiberglass technology.

No matter how far back you go, though it might rankle today's "traditionalists," every bowmaker everywhere always tried to make his bows shoot faster, and every archer stood in line to buy them. Nothing really has changed.

The late Fred Bear was the father of modern bowhunting. He did more than any other individual to pioneer it properly. It is necessary to add that the vision of Glenn St. Charles, who founded the Pope & Young Club, had an incalculable impact on how bowhunting was perceived eventually by the game departments we were trying to convince. And, it is perfectly correct to say that today we are almost right back where we started.

This, if you have been around for as long as I have, can be truly upsetting!

In the interim forty or so years, bowhunters have proved themselves, their equipment and their minor impact position on the resource. In terms of man hours of recreation versus the

Without question, Fred Bear was the father of modern bowhunting. Here he takes time to share his experiences with two young bowhunters.

resources impacted, we really don't take much, while paying a lot of bills. For sure, the resource impact has changed. It's greater than it used to be, but what isn't, considering how many more people there are doing everything. Cars and habitat decimation have a greater impact on wildlife than any hunting persuasion, singly or combined, ever will generate.

We, as hunters, pay for the wildlife's habitat preservation and protection. Hunting is no longer a privilege, it is a right that we have well earned. We hunters have earned the right to hunt.

I know some who will disagree, still contending hunting is a privilege. Fine. It doesn't matter. What does matter is that anyone today who wants to hunt or fish again wears the cloak of the barbarian in the minds of too many folks who truly believe that Bambi, Thumper and Flower hold regularly scheduled tea parties. Some who aren't so anthromorphistically radical just believe their cats should be allowed to vote.

None of these people I have met—there has been a number—ever purchase a Federal duck or habitat improvement stamp. Few check off the deductible box for a buck or two on their state income tax forms earmarked for non-game wildlife, while many apply for, receive and destroy limited hunt applications in the La-La Land belief they have "saved a life." All they have done is interrupt scientifically ordered management by contributing to the ill-health of the critter they are so magnanimously attempting to save. It's a sad state of affairs getting worse.

It's the anti-hunters you say? Not really.

Anti-hunters are not our real problem. Oh, they are a pain alright. They disagree with what we want to do. We find that offensive to our sense of what's right and get all carried away with it, missing the real point. It's not anti-hunters who pose the real threat, but animal rights extremists who threaten both hunters, non-hunters, and the anti-hunters. There are a lot of big dollars involved here, mucho millions!—as these extremists insist exploitation of any form of animal life is wrong! No pets. No eggs. No milk or leather. No white rat medical science. No horse racing. No seeing-eye or drug-detection dogs. No zoos, no aquariums, no furs, no steaks. No guinea pigs, no field trials, no Thanksgiving turkey or Sunday chicken dinner. No nothing.

"A boy is a dog, is a rat, is a pig." Think about that line from PETA's Ingrid Newkirk for awhile.

In spite of this inane attitude, bowhunting today is relatively healthy. We have excellent seasons, superb equipment and a following large enough to be considered a political force. We are better at it or more successful, because we have more whitetail deer, antelope, elk and turkeys, for instance, than ever before.

I believe our opportunities will increase if we can keep the radicals in check, which won't be easy.

More important to our success will be our attitude, our appearance and demeanor in the public eye. We have to present the proper face to the non-hunting public. They could control our destiny. Only we can insure it.

CHAPTER 2

THE BOW

From A Crude Tool To Today's Fancy Compounds, The Bow Really Hasn't Changed Much!

W AY BACK in man's history, one of our short, stocky ancestors sought — and found — a better way to protect himself and collect dinner. It's imagined, in a moment of deep contemplation, he bent a stout tree limb, attached a thin length of hide between the straining tips, and created the bow. Maybe it happened that way, maybe not, but somewhere, somehow, it happened.

In the hundreds of thousands of years that passed, not much came along to change the basic design of this tool that could propel an arrow — a miniature spear — farther, faster and more accurately than man could throw it. Bows today are obviously more efficient than those first efforts and, certainly, as in the case of compounds, different in appearance. But, overall, they still work pretty much the same.

THE LONGBOW

That first bent stick evolved into the longbow. The refinements of its design are credited primarily to the English. More battles have been won and more warriors slain in combat by the longbow than by any other weapon in warfare — so far! Constructed today from combined laminates of wood and fiberglass — modern processes that have increased its efficiencies — the longbow still is in use, largely unchanged in overall design from that used for hunting and war for thousands of years.

The first "real bow" I ever had was a longbow, a straight lemonwood bow by York Archery. This was back in the mid-1940s; the company that made it still is in existence today. I guess I should say that was my first commercial bow. My dad had made me several of the traditional bent-stick, backyard models that parents have been making forever. I remember that he used cat gut taken from his tennis racquet for the bowstring, and that he even hand-fletched arrows from the

Jim Dougherty enjoyed hunting with recurve bows for more than twenty years. Shooting instinctively, he successfully harvested hundreds of game animals throughout the world.

During the 1960s, Dougherty (left) and famed bowhunter Doug Walker (third from left) were shooting and hunting companions. All these bows are recurves made by Bear.

bamboo hedge in our yard. He glued and wrapped the feathers — usually from the wing of a duck — with considerable effort.

I find it interesting now to reflect on that effort. My dad was not an archer then, and for all I know, had little if any knowledge about bows and arrows. It was just one of those very special things that dads do for their sons.

I don't recall if the presentation of the York bow was on a special occasion like a birthday, but I remember how sleek and real it was, and how beautiful were the set of steel-tipped target arrows with bright red-dip, black-cresting and barred feathers. The appeal of that first bow and set of arrows is something that I have never gotten over.

Some years later, I met Doug Kittredge. Kittredge had established a fine custom-arrow business and had just opened what was to become the famous Kittredge Bow Hut in South Pasadena, California. I was a skinny high school kid. He had graduated from the same school, incidentally. I was caught up in the romance and mystery of bows; Kittredge was an experienced, big-league archer who had won tournaments, and successfully shot some game. We got along well, and I went to work for him, starting out on a part-time, after-school basis. My avocation led to full-time vocation evolving into a life-long way of life.

In that era — the mid-Fifties — archery was entering a boom period. My idols were men like Fred Bear who had made his first bow, a long bow, in 1927. By the time I got involved, Bear was one of the leading manufacturers of archery equipment along with Ben Pearson.

Howard Hill, then a resident of California, started archery fires burning in thousands of hearts with his trick shooting exhibitions and the release of his movie, *Tembo.*

These men, as well as Kittredge, Doug Easton, Jack Howard, Hugh Rich and others — men who had won tournaments but, more importantly to me, had succeeded in the hunting fields — set a fire in me that has never, for a moment, flickered low.

THE RECURVE

While Howard Hill shot a longbow, Fred Bear was experimenting, designing and producing recurves. Pearson was a longbow — or semi-recurve — shooter, though his company was in the design/development race with Bear.

Recurve design was not new, the concept being credited to the Turks, Chinese and others thousands of years before. What the recurve did was store more energy, smooth out the force-draw curve as the bow was drawn and impart that increased energy to the arrow. Its looks appealed to many as did its shorter, more maneuverable and comfortable length.

Bow design did not change significantly over the next dozen or so years. Raw materials, primarily technology-improved fiberglass, allowed bowmakers to gain more in terms of performance, but the bow, as it appeared to the eye, remained much the same. I shot in competition, and hunted with recurve bows for better than twenty-six years, as did the rest of the archery fraternity.

We seem to forget at times — especially with *high-speed* compound bows so much in the limelight — that everything being done in the hunting field today already had been done with the recurve or longbow. No matter how much longer I might live, I never will take as much game with a compound — some of it of significant size and challenge — as I have with a recurve. Others will, some already have, but the point is moot. In spite of what we have today — better, more efficient tackle, perhaps, in terms of ballistic capabilities — in the hands of a good bowhunter, they are not necessarily better tools than the bow Fred Bear used to take his first deer in 1935.

THE COMPOUND

Holless W. Allen of Billings, Missouri, designed the compound bow in the mid-1960s. Its arrival created a hubbub of no small proportion in the archery community. Convinced his innovation had merit, Allen attempted to interest the major

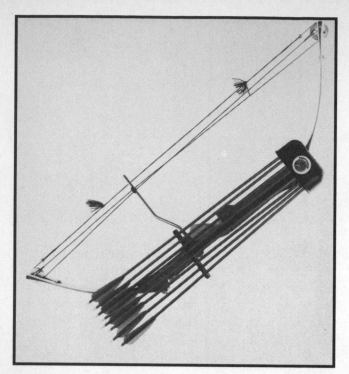

The side-mounted, detachable bow quiver with its four to eight arrow capacity is the favorite with most bowhunters.

favor by the buying public. Without exception, the "Big Guys" all passed. Many, of course, rued the day.

Time has proved Allen's concept acceptable. The public, admittedly after some years of doubt, generally embraced the compound, but certainly not everyone cheered its arrival. Its explosion on the archery/bowhunting scene was met with harangue and denial, leading to a controversy that perhaps never will be stilled.

That, as far as a dialogue on equipment evolution is concerned, is a pity, but not important. There are those who prefer blondes to brunettes, or dry flies to live minnows. Debates and differences are a part of our way of life. I think today's equipment debates among bowhunters are unnecessary, and harmful for the well being of bowhunting, considering the far greater threats we face. But back in the mid-Sixties, they seemed truly important to some

In the beginning, the compound was not really considered a bow. It offended the sense of tradition held by most archers of that era. Some claimed it was no more than a mechanical catapult. Others were specifically more derogatory, and the compound met with stiff resistance.

After being rejected by the industry majors, Allen looked elsewhere and found someone who believed in his concept. It really wasn't Allen who pioneered the compound's eventual climb to prominence. It was a custom recurve bowmaker from Burbank, California, who saw the potential, embraced Allen's idea and went for it. That man was Tom Jennings.

I've known Jennings from the days when I was that skinny high school kid. I shot his custom-built recurves, the Citations, for years. I admired him then, and do today. While Allen was indeed the inventor, Jennings was the doer. The man—and the company who evolved—changed the face of archery, a face that hadn't changed in several thousand years.

While longbows and recurves are simplistic in appearance, they are difficult to learn to use; requiring dedicated and disciplined practice to develop real proficiency. The com-

bow manufacturers in its production. He had no success. I know what he went up against, because I then was with one of the firms that turned him down. What Allen had was a terrible looking contraption that defiled everything traditional bowmakers held dear. While they might have admitted the concept worked, they doubted it would ever be received with

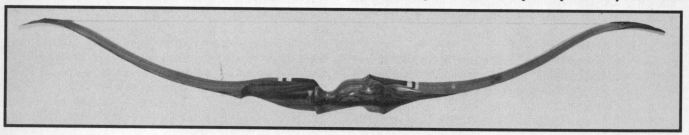

Martins' Super Diablo is one of the most popular production recurves. It's made of Zebra wood. Maple stripe adds strength.

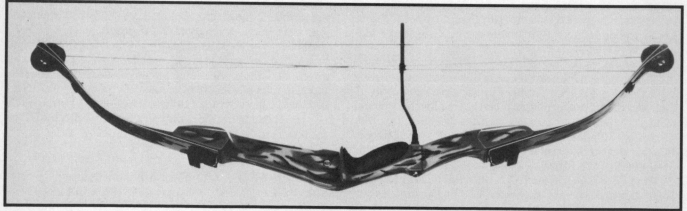

Hoyt's ProVantage handle riser is popular with both bowhunters and target archers because of its forgiving performance.

There are many ways to buy a bow, arrows and all the gear for bowhunting. However, the best place is at a pro shop. A lot of money and headaches will be saved by getting the proper gear at the beginning. Here, Dougherty (left) helps a customer at Jim Dougherty Archery in Tulsa, Oklahoma.

Every archer is built different. That's why each archer needs to be properly fitted with the right bow. That is best done at a proven archery pro shop.

pound, even though it looks more complicated, is much easier to master. This is due to the let-off, the reduction from the peak or true drawing weight to the holding weight. In most of today's models this reduces the drawing weight by fifty to sixty-five percent.

As an example, if the bow pulls fifty pounds at peak weight, the shooter is only holding twenty-five pounds — or less — at full draw. The advantage is obvious. With "traditional" bows, the full drawing weight is achieved as the bow is pulled. As the weight builds, the shooter has to strain to develop and hold the bow's energy. With the mechanical advantage of the compound, the eccentric wheels, or cams, "roll over," and stored energy is achieved when the bow is partially drawn. Once it

"breaks over," the archer can concentrate on aiming while holding less weight.

It took time for the compound to become widely accepted. For years, it wasn't a legal hunting bow in many states. Slowly this changed — as did the compound. Innovators increased its performance, simplified its mechanics and streamlined its appearance.

Bowhunting would not be nearly as popular today without the compound. It has made shooting a bow easier, a point that irritates some hard-core traditionalists. Certainly, the mechanics of the compound, and its high-tech look contradicts the undeniable romance associated with traditional longbow and recurve designs.

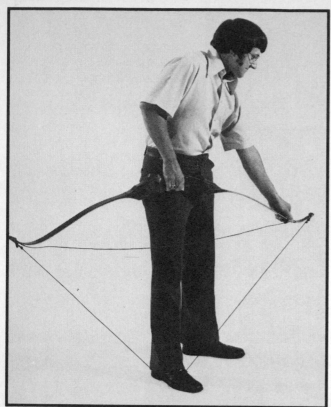

Recurve and longbow shooters should always use a simple bowstringer when installing or removing a bowstring. Not only is it easier and safer, it will also prevent limb twist.

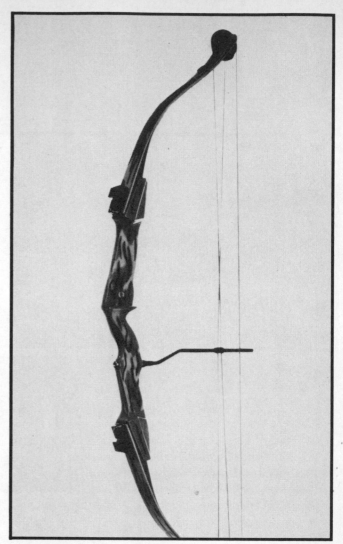

For the last five years, the Hoyt USA's Spectra handle riser design has been Dougherty's favorite for all-around hunting.

I sympathize to some extent with the traditionalist point of view. Deep down, I always will love the simplicity of a recurve's delicate lines, but progress has always been an unstoppable motivation of man, and the evolution of the compound, like it or not, has improved bowhunting equipment and opportunity.

The most positive way to perceive its advantage has to do simply with numbers. The increased number of new bowhunters for whom the compound made bowhunting possible — easier, if you like — and interesting. Our very numbers today are what make bowhunting a positive force in a changing society where hunting is no longer a way of life and rabid animal rights activists run rampant. Do it the way you choose — longbow, recurve or compound — remembering that the force of our numbers is the key to being able to do it at all.

Archery is different today. Like it or not, it is. As the compound evolved through the late 1970s into the 1980s, becoming more acceptable and more efficient, a rash of components — some call them gimmicks — materialized to increase shooting performance. Increased arrow speed created a demand for better bowsights. Arrow shaft manufacturers such as Easton developed shaft sizes more compatible to the compounds.

Pete Shepley, the bright engineer who founded PSE, added many sound concepts to compound bow development and pioneered the overdraw system. Not new to archery, overdraws could be found on recurves as far back as the Fifties. While it never met with much acceptance with recurves, the system was particularly effective on compounds. Their use has truly revolutionized outdoor competitive archery.

Release aids have become commonplace. Releases are not new, either. The Turks and Chinese used thumb rings thousands of years ago to achieve a crisp, clean release from their ultra-short, heavyweight bows of laminated horn and sinew; bows whose performance has remained unequaled by modern recurve bowmakers.

Has the evolution of the compound with its faster arrow speed and easier-to-master potential been good or bad for bowhunting? Personally, I think it has been good, though there are arguments to the contrary. I leave the debate to those who do not see the real problems facing bowhunters today. It — the compound and its accoutrements — is here to stay. This cold, hard fact of life should be recognized and accepted. We should turn our attention elsewhere.

In today's social climate, those of us who choose to hunt, fish or trap by whatever legal means are being looked upon more and more as barely human relics of another age, unfit to mingle with gentle society. What we do, many contend, should be eliminated. Thus, we need to stand together, united in a real fight for our way of life.

I use a compound today. I don't hunt differently now just because this bow is a little faster or easier to shoot. Nothing I shoot dies any deader, but I probably shoot them a little better; more accurately. I think that's a plus.

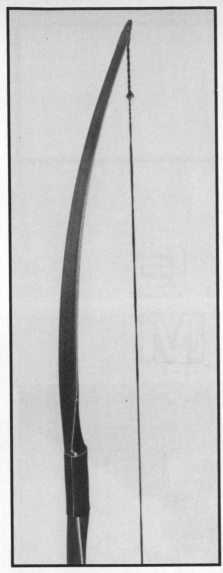

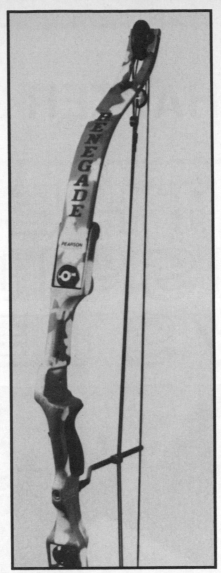

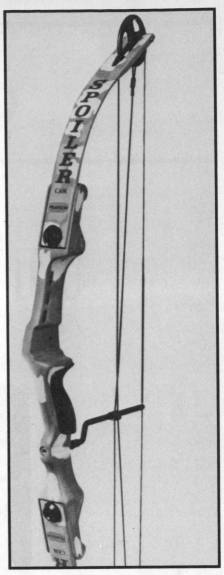

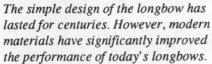

The simple design of the longbow has lasted for centuries. However, modern materials have significantly improved the performance of today's longbows.

The longer Pearson Renegade is the ideal bow for both release and finger shooters. It is also a quiet performer.

Pearson's Spoiler is a super fast, high performance bow that is extremely popular with western hunters who must face longer range hunting conditions.

The real challenge of bowhunting is being able to outsmart an animal under fair chase conditions — up close and personal. Letting the hype of improved ballistics alter the basics of good bowhunting is a mistake. And, it is mostly hype. Our bows today are only slightly faster than those we used twenty years ago. Bowhunters still have to do it the old-fashioned way: work hard, get inside the effective range and shoot a good arrow.

SELECTING THE RIGHT BOW

The recommended bow weights for big game have not varied much over the years. A minimum of forty pounds is the legal requirement for hunting deer in most places. With properly matched arrows for maximum performance and, more important, the right broadhead, this forty-pounder will get the job done.

Heavier weights are better, though, especially for the downward angle of tree stand shots. Shoot the heaviest weight you can handle comfortably. This is an age-old rule that hasn't

changed. Also, shoot the same hunting tackle all year — same weight bow and arrows — for big or small game.

If you plan on hunting bigger game than deer, increased bow/arrow weight combinations are called for and, again, the right selection of a broadhead. I shoot between sixty-five- to seventy-pound bows all the time. For me, this weight range with recurves and compounds has effectively handled big game for thirty-five years. My only exception was in Africa where I went to an eighty-pound recurve to shoot a Cape buffalo. It worked just fine.

I strongly recommend that beginners in archery and bowhunting take the following suggestion to heart: When it comes time to purchase your equipment, go to an archery pro shop to get outfitted. Let the pros fit you. Let them determine the right combination of bow, arrows and accessories that will provide you with room to "grow into a bow."

Professional help in selecting properly balanced, matched equipment is worth ten times what you might imagine you'll save by purchasing from another source.

CHAPTER 3

THE MISSILE SYSTEM

Hand filing and honing is a must to keep traditional-style broadheads in hunting shape.

The Combination Of Shaft, Fletching And Arrowhead Is All-Important To Bowhunting Success

Kelly Dougherty checks the fletching on his hunting arrow. Bright fletching helps in seeing arrow once it is released.

THE ARROW must match the bow weight and draw-length combination of the archer. Further, with today's wide variety of bows, proper arrow selection is more involved than in the good, old days of simple recurve and longbows. Shooting an incorrect arrow in the world's best bow will not give you the accuracy you expect. The arrow and the bow have to match.

An arrow is made up of the following components: shaft, nock, fletching, insert and point. Shaft materials today are much different than in the old days. Then we had wood (Port Orford cedar), aluminum and fiberglass. Today there are carbon and graphite shafts and those made of aluminum/carbon composition. The variety of shaft sizes also has increased dramatically. I prefer aluminum shafts by Easton because of their combined strength and the precise engineering controls used in their manufacture. So do other bowhunters. About ninety-two percent of them use Easton aluminum shafts, according to one recent survey.

The late Doug Easton introduced the aluminum arrow in 1939. At that time, it was considered a radical departure from tradition, but it soon became the number one arrow shaft in the world.

In selecting the right shaft, point type and weight also must be considered, as well as the task you have in mind. A lighter, faster shaft may be what you want for practice and competition, but in my opinion, a heavier shaft weight is best for hunting big game. Admittedly, the lighter, thin-walled shafts flatten the arrow's trajectory, which makes hitting targets at longer ranges easier — but not by much.

Each bow-weight to arrow-length combination is provided with several shaft size options with Easton aluminum arrows. These options are designated as follows: UltraLite, SuperLite, Lite and Standard Aluminum. Easton shafts are marked with a four digit size code, ie: 2117. The first two digits, 21, represent the outside diameter to the closest sixty-fourths of an inch. The second two digits, 17, represent the wall thickness in thousandths of an inch.

UltraLites are purely target sizes. SuperLites, which are shafts with wall thicknesses of .014 and .013 are dual purpose, though favored for target shooting. Lite Aluminum, covering sizes .015 and .016, and Standard .017, .018, .019 represent the largest use among bowhunters, though some SuperLite sizes are gaining rapid popularity. Easton provides a thoroughly detailed catalog and periodic updates of their technical bulletins. They are available by contacting: Easton Aluminum, 5040 W. Harold Gatty Dr., Salt Lake City, UT 84116.

Overall, the heavier shaft is going to penetrate better and more deeply on game. The larger the animal, the more important this becomes. You'll also need this power when hunting from a tree stand. While the distance is usually closer, the downward angle means the arrow is going to hit high on the animal.

Deep, complete penetration is needed for maximum blood trails. Yes, I have seen game taken effectively with lighter arrow combinations. But I still hold to one point of view: If you want to stop 'em, you've got to whomp 'em. Heavier shafts, with the proper broadheads, give me optimum hunting performance.

Since the introduction of smokeless gunpowder or perhaps even before, big-game riflemen have had a wagonload of ballistic theories to kick around at campfires and on barstools. When it comes to calibers, sectional densities, muzzle velocities or bullet configurations for big-game hunting, the rifleman can get himself embroiled in never-ending debates. With bowhunters, much the same takes place, although there is a great deal less to talk about on a variety basis. After all, we still

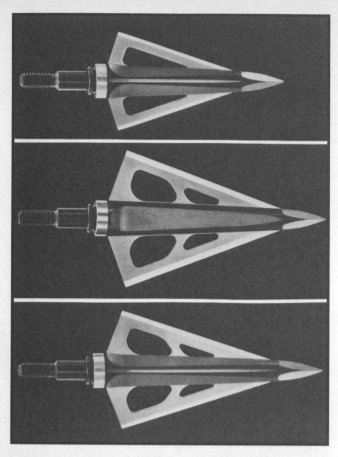

The Thunderhead 125 Broadhead (top) is a favorite choice for a lot of deer hunters. The head has a chisel tip, heavy razor-sharp blades and a sound aerodynamic design. These Thunderhead broadheads are from New Archery Products.

are limited to a relatively primitive piece of equipment, and regardless of all the modern advancements, it will not replace the .270 Winchester cartridge. While advances continue to be made in archery equipment technology, the bow is destined to remain a close-range, one-on-one tool.

While there have been significant increases in arrow velocities, things still are pretty much identical hunting-wise, whether the hunter uses a recurve, straight bow or compound.

So, what is all this leading up to? I suppose I've simply reached a point where I'm getting somewhat concerned about all the theorizing I've been exposed to around those campfires for the last few seasons, especially regarding the question of what type of equipment it takes to consistently put really big, big game on the ground. In one man's opinion, a great deal of it is just pure hogwash!

In my own opinion, it takes just about the same things that have been required for the last thirty years to down big game: bows of adequate weight, which means on the heavy side, and heavy arrows with extremely sharp, durable broadheads. There is hardly anything mysterious about that.

To the bowhunter, comparisons of field experiences should be interesting and informative, but they also will be full of subtle variables that make precise, equal evaluations impossible. No outdoor experience offers the statistic security of a

laboratory test. However, they do provide ammunition for formulating positive attitudes about adequate equipment.

Big-game animals such as elk, moose, caribou and the larger bears, are solidly constructed animals with thicker hair or fur, denser skins and larger bones than your average river-bottom whitetail or rimrock muley. African big-game species are even bigger and tougher. On the so-called Dark Continent, the medium-size game is huge, the big stuff awesome.

With more and more bowhunters taking longer and more exotic hunting trips, even safaris where they will be confronted with strange animals of unfamiliar construction and temperament, critters with onerous dispositions and constitutions like tanks, some words need to be said about what it really takes to put such creatures in a horizontal position.

The purpose of this is not to take potshots at compound bows, which I use myself, or most of the plethora of new "high velocity" equipment on the market. It is intended to provide you with some opinions, based on practical application, of the best marriage of equipment for the successful pursuit of bigger game.

What is meant by bigger game? The favorite big-game animal hunted in this country is the whitetail deer, yet the average bow-killed whitetail will probably stand soaking wet at 135 pounds. The average elk will better than triple that, while a run-of-the-mill moose will blow the springs plumb off the scales. Caribou probably fall into the five-hundred-pound range, give or take the type and maturity of the animal. All in all, the comparison on body size alone leaves a few gaps in hunting experience, if you happen to be an Oklahoma whitetail hunter planning on making tracks for the Alaskan Peninsula.

I have been in and around a great deal of "laboratory"-type programs where velocities and penetrations were measured on a variety of substances in hopes of arriving at worthwhile data as it relates to penetration on big-game animals. While I realize useful information can be obtained from these programs, to me a gelatin block or foam blob in no way resembles a high-strung, muscle-tensed, ready-to-explode bull elk,—or a jackrabbit, for that matter.

Personally, I don't feel the increased velocities of today's compound bows coupled with the new, lighter-weight shafts, regardless of composition, are the total cure-all often claimed. For sure, faster makes hitting the mark easier simply by reducing the guesswork associated with distance calculations, and while it is fashionable today to cite kinetic energy values as the key to optimum bow/arrow big game set-ups, I find the discussions sometimes a bit clinical.

A live-weight 135-pound whitetail deer can offer a target in a relaxed, soft mode or a fully wired, muscle-tensed, ready-to-explode bundle of much firmer tissue, and there are a considerable number of variables in-between. At the same distance and angle, each of these two whitetails suggests a separate set of requirements from the arrow. The "soft" target demands less than the firm. The latter fights the arrow's energy with its own reactionary friction requiring much more energy to subdue it. Given that we'd all prefer the soft scenario experience suggests that a fifty/fifty ratio can be expected, particularly when hunting whitetail deer. Therefore, conscientious selection of adequate arrow weight values is a must to meet the variables of field conditions. Just hitting them is only the first step.

Many seasons ago, while hunting with a prototype Ben

Easton XX75 SuperLite arrows, surveys show, are the world's most popular shafts with bowhunters. Doug Easton developed the aluminum arrow in 1939. It took time for hunters to accept, however the Easton arrow soon became the industry standard.

Pearson compound, I did a fair amount of jouncing about the country in the course of late season business. During that season, I had the opportunity to shoot several deer with a couple of new arrow combinations of lighter overall weights than I was accustomed to using. While the results were adequate, I was not in awe of the total performance. In not one case did my combination achieve complete penetration on broadside shots, something that I had come to expect as being routine.

Concerned by this marginal performance, I wanted to check it further, so with a fast bow/light arrow setup, I met my long-time hunting companion, George Wright, in California. Our mission was to proceed to the finest testing ground I know of, Catalina Island, where a big island billy goat is about the size of a nice whitetail deer. While constitutions are different, both are hell for tough, and hard to convince that their time has come. We started out shooting exactly the same equipment, sixty-seven-pound bows, light, thin-wall arrow shafts and a variety of razor-insert-type broadheads.

On the first afternoon, suffering from negotiating cliffs that I once had scampered over, I punched my first goat, a medium-sized billy. He was downhill at somewhere around thirty yards. My reaction at the sound of the arrow impact was that I had caught the center of the shoulder blades and penetration had not taken place. In reality, I had hit it in the center of the engine room and the goat expired, but I was not pleased with the results.

George Wright and I had a carte blanche situation on pig hunting in this area, as the pigs were decimating a hard-fought landscape program. In the interest of science balanced with a desire for pork roasts, we waded into the abundance of pigs with something close to abandon. In the course of two days of hunting, we did put some meat on the ground, lightly sprinkled with a few more goats. However, with but one exception, we did not get complete penetration on a single animal. The exception was a smallish boar that I took at twenty yards with a four-blade Satellite, and the boar did a header where he stood.

Admittedly, we collected what we shot, but the animals were of smallish size and frail when compared to a big buck, a bull moose or a stump-ripping grizzly bear, critters I feel would not take kindly to the indignity of being vaccinated by lightweight projectiles. Sufficiently annoyed, such beasts have a tendency to want to step on you.

Overall, our week-long hunting/testing provided the conclusion that the lighter weight arrows, when tipped with insert-style heads with conical point designs, apparently lost some energy, and did not deliver the type of penetration performance we prefer. Since then, more measured investigations have suggested energy losses of up to twenty-five percent when comparing the conical or rounded-point configuration to traditional broadhead designs. This, combined with lighter overall arrow weight, does reduce performance on game.

When I was in Africa, I scrambled around for the most part armed with as heavy a recurve bow as I could shoot all day —

There seems to be an endless variety of broadheads for the serious deer hunter to consider. Selecting the right hunting broadhead is important since it is the arrow's business end.

monster mountain goat in his home state. He told me the heavy hair raised hell with his auxiliary blades and seriously affected penetration. For my goats, I will remove my bleeder blades. First-hand advice is valuable information.

My favorite varmint rifle is the .222 magnum, but I don't recommend shooting deer with it. I have a tack-driving .243 that would roll up a deer like a beach ball, but I wouldn't shoot a moose with it. Most bowhunters today also are, or were, rifle hunters. For them such comparisons will make sense. Why then consider the equivalent "varmint-size" arrow combination on a critter that will shake the earth if you knock him down?

Certainly, bowhunting equipment has changed in the last twenty-plus years. But the fundamentals of bowhunting have not. Regardless of the bow design we choose, we must still shoot it well. We must get close enough for optimum accuracy and the shaft must strike with as much authority as can possibly be mustered. That, my friends, is the name of the game.

NOCKS

The arrow nock is vital to accurate arrow flight. Always check each nock on every arrow you buy or make for perfect, concentric alignment. Off-center nocks will cause horrendous shooting problems. I once completely missed a buck whitetail at ten yards due to a crooked nock that caused the arrow to shoot at least a foot high.

You can check nocks for alignment simply by spinning the arrow in a vertical position or rolling it on a smooth flat surface where you can eye-ball it up close for mis-alignment. Nock-to-bowstring fit is also important. A bowhunter's nocks should fit the string snugly enough to not fall off the string when held horizontally and the string tapped smartly or jiggled. New string materials like FastFlite oftentimes result in smaller diameter strings creating proper fit problems. Larger diameter center serving material on the bowstring can help fit, as can changing nock styles to designs with smaller throats. I prefer the Plasti Nock by AAE and find it gives me good fit on most strings with a minimum of modification.

Nock position in relation to fletching is also important. Today, with the wide range of shoot-through arrow rests in favor, nock rotation is required to provide fletching clearance. Popular rests like the TM Hunter, Star Hunter, Bo Doddle as well as many others — particularly on overdraws — demand attention regarding nock position. If you are in doubt as to how to do it or are experiencing arrow flight problems, the best advice is to seek help from a good technician at a pro shop.

FLETCHING

The only purpose of fletching is to steer and stabilize your arrow during flight. There's straight fletching, which runs straight down the shaft; off-set fletching, set on the shaft at a slight angle; and helical fletching that wraps around the shaft. Off-set and helical fletching make the arrow spin during flight.

For hunting with broadheads you *need* helical fletching. It prevents or greatly reduces "planing" which is air resistance pushing against the broadhead blades. As you increase the size of the broadhead, the more helical spin is needed to keep

about sixty-five pounds and the heaviest shaft I could get to fly right. Long-range trajectory was not my problem — it was getting close enough to pop 'em where I wanted.

This equipment was okay for game up to wildebeest size. Beyond that, I went to a bigger seventy-five-pound bow and 2219 shafts, a combination that took a year's hard training to work up to. Even so, there were moments when I felt seriously underpowered. I have a piece of dried Cape buffalo hide in my den that measures three-quarters-inch thick. In its dried-out state you can't drive a nail through it.

Marv Clyncke of Colorado — in my opinion, one of the best and toughest bowhunters in this country — shot a the arrow on a straight course.

Helical, at the same time, may cause an arrow to fly slower than straight or off-set fletching. However, inasmuch as accuracy is the objective, any difference — even slight — is meaningless if the arrow is not flying properly. There's plenty of debate, as in all areas of equipment, as to whether the spiral should twist right or left. Dwight Schuh offers his opinion in his comprehensive, *Bowhunter's Encyclopedia:* "Convention has always said that a right-handed shooter should fletch his arrows with a right helical twist and lefties should fletch with a left helical twist. I've never found it makes much difference which way vanes are twisted and most authorities I've talked with agree."

Might be, but Chuck Adams, in *The Complete Guide to Bowhunting Deer,* thinks differently: "A fine point of fletching that many archery perfectionists pay attention to is whether fletching spirals to the left or to the right around an arrow. This is especially important with plastic vanes, which do not flatten out if they bump a bow in flight.

"For the best accuracy, a right-handed shooter should select vanes that spiral from left to right when viewed from the rear of the arrow. For a left-handed shooter, vanes should spiral from right to left. By doing so, vanes more perfectly clear an arrow rest and wobble less as they leave the bow."

As it relates to synthetic vanes, I agree with Adams. From my experience, I don't believe it makes much of a difference with feathers. However, if you feel it will give you an extra edge, fine.

What about fletching materials? Are feathers superior to plastic? There are pros and cons to each. Dave Holt, in *Balanced Bowhunting,* says feathered fletch is faster off the bow. "A feathered arrow starts out faster, because the feathers weigh less (by about thirty grains), but they cause more resistance while moving through the air."

Holt has an illustration in his book that shows the feathered arrow and vaned arrow about even at thirty-five yards, but the vaned arrow is out in front as the two arrows near sixty yards.

"But in my opinion," Holt says, "there is not enough difference between feathers and vanes regarding arrow speed to make this a consideration when choosing the type of fletching material to be used on hunting arrows."

For almost forty years my fletching preference always has been feathers. I tend to believe they recover and stabilize a hunting arrow a bit better. They are more forgiving under the variety of shooting conditions — discounting weather — do not require elaborate arrow rests for excellent flight, and I believe they tend to recover faster if a bad release is jinxed under pressure, or if you have to shoot from an unorthodox position.

Feathers are not as tough as synthetic vanes — they're somewhat fragile by comparison — and do not withstand inclimate weather as well. Foul conditions notwithstanding, day in and day out, under all the conditions I've faced, I shoot them in complete confidence. You can treat feathers for wet weather with applications of dry fly spray which has a silicone base, or use Bohning's Dri-Tite and ScotchGard. Applications should be light; too much will stiffen the fletch.

My preference leans to five-inch helical fletching with either three or four feathers. There is no need for four five-inch feathers as far as stability is concerned. I use them simply because they are easier to see in flight, and I use bright colors for the same reason. Up to thirty yards, both the three- and the

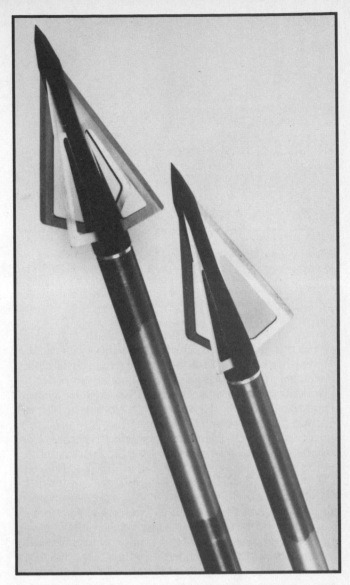

Insert blade style heads have become popular with many bowhunters. Author believes the chisel-type point is a must.

four-fletch hit in the same place. Beyond that, the increased drag of the fourth feather becomes noticeable. Shorter feathers in four-fletch would reduce this drag effect and still provide the visibility I desire. Being able to see the arrow in flight is important. Knowing where the arrow struck is an essential key in how we handle and follow up our hits to recover game.

FIELD POINTS

The arrowhead or point most used for hunting practice is the field point. This point in standard weights and diameters will match or closely approximate the weights of most broadheads and arrow shafts on the market. Select a field

Easton constantly updates its arrow shaft technical bulletins to keep archers fully informed of the newest developments.

point that is as close as possible to the weight of your preferred hunting head. In most cases you can hit it right on the money; if not, stay on the heavy side. Field points are perfect for practicing at standard target butts of hay or straw, synthetic matts like the Stanley Hips line of ethafoam, Dale Morrell's Eternity target matts and 3-D animals. They are not nearly so good for my favorite form of practice, which is just wandering around stump shooting . For this I use the Zwickey Judo.

BROADHEADS

Regardless of the fact that all we seem to hear today is "which bow is the fastest?", the question has little to do with being a good bowhunter. In one man's opinion, that simply means speed doesn't matter a helluva lot. Successful bowhunters have been getting by just fine for a lot more years than "fast bows" have been around.

A better question would be: Which broadhead is best, or which bow is the quietest? Neither question has a finite answer, but if you are seriously interested in being a good bowhunter, the first question is much more germane to success. The important issue is how effective are your arrowheads.

To my mind, the concern with bow speed has been grossly overemphasized when it comes to bowhunting. Bow speed — arrow velocity, actually — really hasn't mattered all that much when it comes to being a competent, successful bowhunter. A quiet bow is infinitely more valuable in my book than the highly acclaimed, widely advertised "fast" bow. None of which are very quiet, admittedly.

Reasonable arrow speed is an aid in bowhunting. It always has been, but today's obsession with speed alone seems to have shifted proper bowhunting technique and ethics out of synch with reality. When it gets down to brass tacks, the most important item of equipment in the bowhunter's arsenal is the hunting head selected for the business end of the arrow. There's a gob of them to choose from today. More are showing up all the time — about a dozen new models each year — in an already glutted market.

Some of them are fine though not revolutionary in design

concept, while others are nothing more than gimmick products that prey on naive consumers by touting performance claims that are ridiculous horse puckey.

Overall, in "hunting heads," basic designs are similar. Ferrules featuring milled slots accommodate pre-sharpened blades locked in place by compression locks at the trailing end. Just how well these blades and slots are designed and manufactured dictates how well the blades stay in place at impact and facilitate penetration. Design of the point is extremely crucial. Blade thickness is obviously important to strength and strength is essential to good performance. In addition to the modern hunting head, there is the true broadhead, most often referred to today as the "traditional" hunting head, a designation I consider appropriate — and a design I consider superior.

Simply described, these are spear-type points that begin cutting immediately on impact, maximizing the efforts of the arrow's energy. As a general rule, insert blade-style hunting heads do not do this as well.

Hunting heads can be tricky to tune for accurate shooting, and some say broadheads are much more difficult. I disagree that one is more difficult than another save for the extremely heavy, wide models of each which require greater attention to proper shaft selection versus bow weight and fletching at the beginning.

A careful selection of arrow shaft and fletching is required to make any style head shoot right. It can be a chore to get everything just so, but it's the premier requirement to conscientious bowhunting. Different configurations in hunting heads produce varied flight characteristics, all of which can be controlled properly with attention to detail. For instance, vented blades are controlled more easily than a similar sized head without vents. Solid blades catch more air and try to run away in flight.

It logically follows that big, wide heads are harder to get flying properly than skinny, narrow heads. That's why there are so many little heads out there today enjoying popularity. It's easier to make them go where you want them to.

The evolution of little, tiny broadheads began — as do most things that impact the sport — on the target range where competitive accuracy and targets placed in ridiculous positions challenge equipment rather than true hunting/shooting skills. Admittedly, they do challenge individual excellence among archers who play that game.

There's nothing wrong with this, if you are just going to shoot hard-to-see, tough-to-hit targets. Carrying it over to the big-game fields with tiny arrows and teeny-weeny heads — and the attitude that no shot is too difficult — strikes me as irresponsible.

Poor head-to-shaft alignment and inadequate fletching are the most common problems in achieving good arrow flight with any style of adequately sized hunting point. Insufficient fletching without enough wrap or spiral (helical) is the biggest cause of wayward hunting arrow flight. Screw-in heads, which takes in all the insert types, are sometimes out of alignment due either to the threading on the head, or the in-shaft insert. Bad threads are the most common cause.

Each arrow should be checked carefully for perfect point/shaft alignment, no matter what hunting head style you prefer. Once aligned properly, they should be marked to match the corresponding arrow if you plan on removing them from the shaft for any reason.

Crooked nocks comprises another culprit. A misaligned nock can make an arrow do some really wild things. It's easy to spin-check both point and nock alignment; make sure you do.

Mans' incessant search for the easier way continues to go hog wild. The quest has affected virtually everything we do, and hunters have long been guilty of embracing new things that promise an easier, more successful hunt. This includes even bowhunters whose tenet at the onset was: "We do it the hard way."

It's human nature and I can't knock it. I'm as guilty as anyone. If I weren't, I'd be hunting with rocks or a spear, but then, if I switched to a spear from a rock, I'd be guilty again.

Advances in archery equipment have given us bows that are easier to shoot. Admittedly, these bows require less effort than traditional recurves or longbows, which really makes them — and the shooter — actually more efficient. This is probably good. Most folks won't or can't — for any number of reasons — work hard enough at the training, so the easier, more efficient tool used in the field increases the odds for success and, more importantly, a clean kill.

People who hunt, will hunt. Some work hard at perfecting shooting skills, but most don't. I would just as soon that those who don't practice, hunt with the easier-to-use bow that increases their odds for solid, positive hits than use a bow over which they have only marginal control. The problem is that only about thirty-percent of the bowhunting population has any real contact with those of us who live and breathe this game. Yet, in that Big Computer Print-Out in the Sky, where license sales and total numbers are counted up, the Know-Nothing guy from Someplace, USA means just as much to the total as PSE's Pete Shepley. As long as Know-Nothing is going to be out there anyhow, as a recognized, counted part of the total, I'd rather he be equipped with one of Shepley's bows over which he has control and confidence.

What I can't accept is the mentality that sometimes is seen in selecting hunting heads. Some demand heads that shoot better, not heads that kill better. Others want cheap heads: "Give me those. I'll probably miss or lose 'em anyhow."

I simply cannot understand or accept the rationale behind saving an extra five bucks on this most essential piece of equipment, yet the same guy won't blink an eye or ask the price when purchasing a box of ammo for his deer rifle which he probably hasn't sighted in eithcr.

The Zwickey Black Diamond hunting head has been around for as long as I can remember, the Bear Razorhead for almost the same length of time. Other broadheads of the same proven design that have followed more recently include the Bohning Blazer, the Magnus I and II, the Satellite Titan and Hoyt's Bow Bullet and Top Cut. These are the type of heads I would pick if I had to make the one shot that would save my life, defend my wife or simply to tag an animal.

This is not to say that the insert-blade "hunting heads" are not good. On the contrary, most of them are well designed, tough, aerodynamically sound, proven performers. Good examples, in my opinion, are the Thunderhead 125s, Bob Barrie's Rocky Mountain Razors, the Satellite Mag 125s, and the Thunderhead 150 two-blade. In all of the insert-style hunting heads, I prefer three-blade designs which just seem easier to tune for perfect flight. Sales figures indicate these are the preferred configuration nationwide.

Broadheads, or hunting heads, do not shoot like field points regardless of the fact they weigh the same. This goes back to the steerage problems mentioned earlier. For most people not into the finer intricacies of tuning bows — and most aren't — getting them to shoot the same is tough. As a general rule, they can't.

Chuck Adams gets his broadheads shooting into the same hole as his practice points, but, Adams is one of the finest archery technicians I know, thoroughly involved and knowledgeable in terms of archery ballistics. He's the rare exception to Mr. Average Bowhunter who never will get nearly as involved in hunting arrow accuracy; a few might, but most won't or don't take the time. That's sad, too bad, but true.

Get your bow tuned in tight with field points for year-round practice, then re-sight in with the actual broadhead or hunting head you have selected for the field. Don't get caught up in worrying about wrecking a few. Wreck 'em, dull them up. It's the best investment you will ever make. I talk to hundreds of people every year who haven't checked out their hunting arrow flight thinking they will shoot the same because they weigh the same. Don't believe it, unless you know it.

If you opt for the insert blade heads, select those with stainless steel blades at least .015-inch thick, preferably thicker. Hunting heads that push before they cut lose significant downrange energy on impact. The bigger the game — thicker hide, hair and flesh — the greater the negative impact this energy loss has on penetration. With deer-size game, this loss is not enough to lose any sleep over, but, if big stuff like elk or moose is in your plans, increasing bow and arrow weight certainly will help.

I have been bowhunting for a long time, with no accurate knowledge of the numbers of big-game animals I have shot and seen shot with every type head you might imagine. This does provide bias. Mine is based on honest personal observation that you cannot beat the traditional broadhead design for best results under the widest range of conditions.

Some broadheads require hand sharpening. This is an art that takes time and practice, but not a helluva lot more time once you get the knack of it than assembling a dozen hunting heads.

Use adequate fletching in helical configuration with sufficient shaft weight to deliver the best downrange energy load. While we need accuracy, we do not need to be concerned with shooting tight four-arrow groups on game. One is just fine! Pick heads that are solidly constructed, capable of busting through bone and holding up as they go on through.

Stay away from gimmicks with swiveling or pop-out blades. Pay attention to guys like the Wensel Brothers, Fred Asbell, Chuck Adams and Marv Clyncke, as well as the folks that were there before us: Ben Pearson, Fred Bear, Art Young and Saxton Pope. They knew what it took to get the job done.

There are folks out there who will delight in taking me and my prejudice in this regard to task. I will hear from some who praise gimmick heads and vapor trail speed. They will cap their remarks — mostly unkind — with a gospel account of a 213-pound, sixteen-point whitetail buck killed deader than a rock at seventy-seven yards. Perhaps someone will even send me a photo of an elephant slain with similar stuff.

I will be envious of the sixteen pointer, and marvel at the stupidity of the elephant killer — but it won't change convictions carefully gathered through almost forty years of experience one damn bit!

CHAPTER 4

A MATTER OF NEED

There Are All Sorts Of Doo-Dads To Hang On Your Bow And Your Person

Jim likes to travel light when he's bowhunting, taking just enough equipment to enjoy the hunt and get the job done. However, a lot of bowhunters today load themselves and their bows down with every gadget on the market. But how important are accessories?

I N RECENT years, there have been many booms in the outdoor world. Perhaps most dramatic has been the evolution of bass fishing, which went from a peaceful pastime of Hula Poppers in lily pads to high-technology baits and tournaments worth hundreds of thousands of dollars.

A similar explosion has occurred in archery—it's called bowhunting. It is staggering to review the extraordinary amount of equipment and accessories available to the bowhunter, especially for those seeking whitetails. In the area of equipment development—plus the marketing of secrets on How To Bag The Big Ones—the whitetail has generated a mega-industry accompanied by considerable hysteria.

I find these things of extreme interest, because I pursue all of my outdoor/hunting avocations in depth, frequently to the depths of deep indebtedness. The garage, attic, spare rooms and closets of my home resemble entire pages from the catalogs of Bass Pro Shop, Cabela's and the entire product offering of Remington and Hoyt. I have the latest in Boron Flipp'n Sticks, buffered duck loads and Gore-Tex garments, while the baby—who's now an adult—wears last year's waders.

Heavily featured among my paraphernalia—for everything from waterfowling to frog-gigging—is equipment dedicated to the pursuit and taking of big whitetail deer. Addicted to the phenomenon of the whitetail boom, my sons and I have been in the chase for years—prior to the explosion.

These products are designed to outsmart in order to kill a four-legged beast with a brain roughly the size of a tennis ball, that runs around the woods with a bunch of pointy little things on his head. If the truth would out, it is these pointed things that cause all the anxiety. If deer didn't have them, probably no one would bother. But they do, and sometimes they are huge!

There are those who profess to be totally unimpressed with *trophies*, those who don't give a damn for horns and some who claim they're immune. I'm sure this is true right up until the time they see one. Then, if the sight of a stately buck doesn't cause their breath to run shallow and their knees to tremble, I suggest they take themselves promptly from the woods. They should go home and tidy up their personal affairs, paying close attention that the insurance premiums are paid to date. Someone then should get them off to the family plot, informing them along the way that they are obviously dead.

The whitetail is definitely a phenomenon. While there are elements of it we may not care for, the phenomenon—especially the central character—is here to stay, and we should consider ourselves fortunate. I get a kick out of most of it; after all, what other excuse could we offer for playing around in tree tops after we've grown up?

I find it interesting that there are as many tree stands sold as there are species and quantities of trees in which to place them. It boggles my mind that there is an industry entirely devoted to the collection of deer pee; that there are folks who derive their hourly wage by pouring it into little bottles. I read with interest the hundreds of thousands of words on the hunting of trophy bucks and the harvesting of same. I am amazed that there is a rapidly expanding market for whitetail antlers, both fallen and attached to the original skull plate, for amounts that at the least have to be considered large. I am dumbfounded by the number of trophy bucks, often in a mounted condition, that are stolen for the obvious purpose of selling them to someone else!

In perusing journals on the subject, I often find myself reviewing advertisements by outfitters offering mighty bucks

Here's a way of getting above big bucks. Tripod stands are easy and fast to set up. They're comfortable and effective.

and the fees for same. I find I could avail myself of a Boone & Crockett buck for a cost comparable to the purchase of my own MX missile. A Pope & Young buck goes for slightly less.

Sporting catalogs collectively detail more inventory elements for a successful field campaign than that catalog of armament available to the Joint Chiefs of Staff.

There are sights for bows that compensate for the downward angle of the shot from a tree, with lights the color of your choice. There are camouflage patterns that Nature herself has not had time to invent. There's a multitude of tree-climbing devices that allow you to climb to nose-bleed heights—these obviate the need for camo, but make safety ropes a marvelous idea. At a recent show, I saw a rearview mirror designed to be placed in a tree, thereby making it unnecessary to turn your head—honest! There are clocks you can affix to trees in the forest with trip wires. These are intended to advise you of the exact time, day or night, when the whitetail passes. It seems that if the spot looked good enough to place a clock, it would look equally good as a place to hunt, thus, you could observe what time the deer passed during daylight hour and shoot him in the process. Knowing that he comes at 2:45 a.m. does not fit into the time frame my game department has set aside for me to hunt.

There are deer feeders—legal in some states—with automatic timers. At the appointed hour, the timer sets off a signal. Sounding on the order of an air raid siren and simultaneously broadcasting a bushel of corn upon the land. I have an acquaintance who has perfected the art of making *mock scrapes,* thereby throwing big bucks into a turmoil as they dash about looking for love in all the wrong places. This, to me, seems fair, but I have been reluctant to try it for fear that someone might see me scraping the ground under an overhanging live oak, pouring stuff into it from a little bottle, then climbing the nearest tree. It would confirm the already firm suggestion that I am strange.

OVERDRAWS

Overdraws have become quite the rage in recent years. This device is really just an extended shooting shelf that moves the arrow rest closer to the shooter. The purpose of an overdraw is to let you shoot a shorter arrow at a faster speed. Since the arrow is shorter, you can use a lighter weight arrow as less spine is needed to maintain proper flight.

At first glance, the overdraw system makes sense. By increasing the arrow's speed you flatten trajectory, which gives you more accuracy at longer distances. But many have found the overdraw difficult to shoot accurately because of increased torque which can result in more left-right arrow movement. There are other drawbacks. With an overdraw, the broadhead is drawn behind the bow hand. This is the main contributor to torque, to achieve the proper — that means accurate — flight.

Even though most overdraws are designed with safety for the archer in mind, there have been some nasty accidents attributed to overdraws. Depending on the configuration, overdraws can shorten arrow length in mere fractions up to around six inches. For folks with extremely long draws in excess of thirty-one inches, a short overdraw, reducing arrow length by two to three inches, may be advantageous in obtaining a good bow-to-arrow match-up. Longer overdraws — the ones designed with arrow speed foremost in mind — offer that speed as the obvious primary advantage. There are drawbacks, in my opinion, however, that obviate the speed advantage. I believe it takes an extremely good archer to shoot a long overdraw well. Overdraws require shorter fletching, while clearance between bowstring and arrow rest or the back end of the overdraw actually is greatly reduced.

Most arrow rests compatible with good overdraw performance are noisy. Inasmuch as most overdraw bows are heavyweights, this factor added to the sound of even admittedly superb functional rests dramatically increases bow noise.

Left and right margin of error, the result of torque, can be exaggerated under in-the-field shooting conditions where perfect, square-up shooting form can be tough to accomplish. Left and right errors suggest an increased possibility of poor hits.

Since I prefer the heavier broadhead, I need the additional fletching, and I'm more than willing to give up super fast, shorter, lightweight arrows for the consistent stopping power I get from the heftier arrow.

Obviously, my preference in hunting bows doesn't include an overdraw, though many bowhunters believe in their advantages. I would suggest, for example, that they might be more practical for mule deer than whitetails; longer ranges, less sound impact perhaps.

ARROW RESTS

Arrow rests seem such a simple piece of equipment that their importance often is overlooked by the bowhunting newcomer. Think about it: The rest is the last point of arrow contact with the bow once the arrow is released. You can do all the right things in bow and arrow selection, but if the arrow gets a shaky send-off, you're going to have fits. Bows don't often come with suitable arrow rests; they're usually one-piece jobs made of rubber or plastic.

In selecting an arrow rest, look for one that will cause as little interference with the shaft and fletching as possible, and is durable and quiet. The shaft must ride smoothly on the rest when the bow is drawn, then glide off the rest when the arrow is released. The fletching must pass the rest with only minimal contact.

Like all accessories, there are plenty of arrow rests to leave you confused. There are rests with springs, levers, plungers, flippers and launcher arms, and some with these in combination. While several are excellent when shooting in ideal conditions such as at the archery range, they won't stand up in the field.

Don't select a rest that is too delicate or too difficult to adjust. If you select a spring-type rest, make sure it won't bend

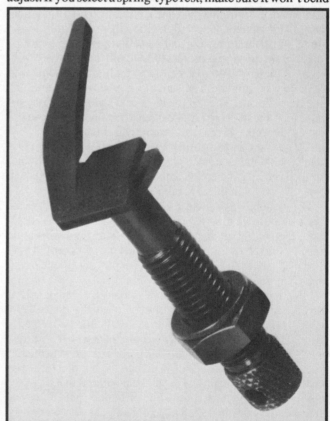

Dougherty prefers the easy-to-tune Centerest when he uses feather fletching on his hunting arrows. The dependable, simple rest is from New Archery Products Corporation.

When using plastic fletching, it is best to use an arrow rest like the Centerest flipper from New Archery Products.

or break easily. Plunger-type rests can freeze up in cold weather or become sluggish, so look for quality. Also, not all arrow rests can be used on overdraws and you'll have to be careful in selecting a rest if you use a mechanical release—the arrow reacts differently than when released with your fingers. Again, ask a lot of questions of the pros at the archery shop.

After having tried several different types of arrow rests, I prefer the Hoyt Hunter or Centerest, because they are quiet, dependable and simple. I use the Centerest on bows with risers cut past center and the Hoyt on standard-handle risers.

ARROW HOLDERS

Arrow holders are helpful but can be misused. This small attachment holds the arrow on the rest so you don't have to sit for long periods with your finger holding the arrow in place. When the arrow is drawn, the holder automatically detaches and flips out of the way. They are not intended to hold the arrow in place while hiking—something new bowhunters are prone to do. They are handy for tree stand and blind hunting.

STABLILIZERS

Stabilizers are weighted extension bars attached to the front of the bow below the grip. They do two things: reduce the shock and twist of the bow when the arrow is released, and help absorb the noise that vibrates through the bow. You'll often see lengthy stabilizers on bows used for target competition. Hunting stabilizers are much shorter primarily for maneuverabilty.

Stabilizers can be as simple as a solid weight that screws into the bow on the back side below the bow grip, the standard mounting on almost all bows. Or it can be as high-tech as those like the Saunders Torque Tamer that incorporates rubber baffles as shock absorbers, or the Neutralizer that is loaded with mercury. There are many configurations in between. On average, they will add approximately three-fourths of a pound to your overall bow weight. Many archers prefer them for the vertical balance they offer, as well.

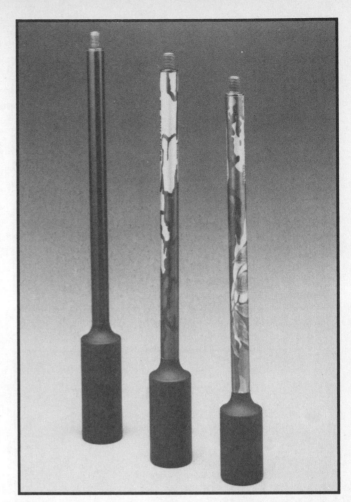

Stabilizers reduce shock when the arrow is released. They also diminish noise by absorbing vibrations.These Easton Enhancer stabilizers come in black, Trebark and Realtree.

TABS, GLOVES AND RELEASE AIDS

The act of physically letting go of the arrow—the release or loose—is, in my opinion, the single most difficult act of shooting a bow.

For years, when armed with the conventional longbow or recurve, the fingers were protected with a shooting glove. This was necessary, because these heavy bows placed all their draw weight on the fingers. The shooting gloves were called "finger stalls." They fully covered the three fingers of the drawing hand, index to third.

The shooting tab is a simple device: a small pad held between the fingers and the string. It is available in a variety of materials. When shooting with my fingers, I have always preferred the tab for its simplicity and freedom.

With the increasing development of compounds—especially those designed for speed—the overall length of the bow has become shorter. This causes a higher degree of string angle at the nock point/finger position, and increased finger pinch. These bows are extremely difficult to shoot because of the high degree of compression placed on the fingers. The modern mechanical release solves this problem.

The mechanical snaps on the string and is activated by

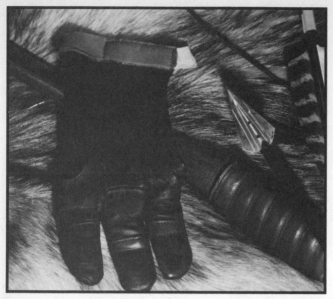

Standard shooting gloves are favored by traditional archers.

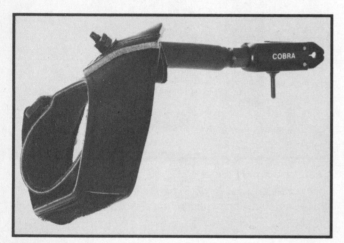

Caliper-style releases rarely malfunction and are extremely quiet. The releases are available in wrist and concho styles.

I've killed with a compound, I used a release. I shot them exactly where I wanted. And though I've had some glitches, overall, the mechanical release has performed well.

Like all equipment, there are many different styles of mechanical releases. Do not buy one without a "hands on" review to determine which one best fits you and your shooting style. Again, face to face shopping with qualified pros in a specialty shop is sound advice.

In closing on this subject, I strongly recommend you learn to shoot both ways: with and without a release, regardless of the bow you choose. Trust me, there will be times when it will pay off.

STRING SILENCERS—QUIET BOWS

All bows make noise when released. Compounds make far more noise than longbows or recurves. Compounds with overdraws are horrendously noisy by comparison. A bowhunter's first concern when setting up a hunting bow is to get it quiet. No bow is faster than an animal, so having a quiet bow is much more important than arrow speed.

All parts on a compound, and there are many, should be detailed for solid fit. Arrow rests, sight windows and arrow shelves should be covered with soft material. This will elimi-

String silencers like the "puff" (top) are a must for serious bowhunters. Fast Flight cables will also accept mini-muff string silencers (below) which further reduce bow noise.

simply pressing or pulling a triggering device with the index, little finger or thumb. Since they only hold generally less than a quarter-inch of the string, pinch is eliminated. Gone is the excessive finger pressure, and they go off on demand, creating the perfect release. Mechanical releases are in vogue today. I guess as many as fifty percent of today's archers use them on compounds, and that will increase.

Are they effective for the bowhunter? Yes, but they have their drawbacks. They can be awkward to use—even with experience—when hustling for a second shot. But, in reality, second shot opportunities are rather rare. With a good deal of practice, they can be mastered to achieve reasonable speed.

The mechanical release has become a necessary piece of my equipment. With many of today's bows that I shoot, I find I cannot shoot good arrows with my fingers. But I can shoot perfect arrows with a release. And, if one remains cool under hunting pressure—always a potential problem—and thinks out the shot, the release can be deadly. The last seventeen deer

nate "clicks" should you tap the bow with an arrow.

String silencers are a must on any bow. I have found that acrylic puff-ball-types seem best overall for reducing string noise, although it is never totally eliminated. Padding where the string hits the limbs on recurves is another important, noise-eliminating detail that should not be ignored. Handles on most compound risers today snap on. They should be removed and filled with silicone or some similar agent. This fills the voids and keeps them tight. All nuts and bolts on accessory items should be tightened. Some will require glue to prevent them from becoming loose with continued shooting.

QUIVERS

Quivers come in two groups: those that attach to your hip, shoulder or back; and those that are attached to your bow. The

Bow quivers must be of solid construction to reduce any arrow rattle. They must also be deep enough to cover the cutting blades of broadheads.

The lightweight recurve bow and St. Charles-style quiver for broadheads were popular through the Fifties and Sixties.

bow quiver has become the most popular with bowhunters.

The main features to look for in a quiver are how well it protects the arrows, how tight it holds them, and how quiet it is. Note the main feature is protection of the arrowhead—and you! There are countless injuries each year, many of them serious, caused by broadheads. The quiver should, above all, safely keep your arrows where you want them.

Quivers come in leather, vinyl and polar fleece. There even are models that combine a quiver and pouches with a full-size pack such as the popular Cat Quiver by Rancho Safari.

For the active bowhunter, the attached bow quiver is the most popular. It puts your arrows where you can see them, giving you an extra edge in getting your bow into action for those second and third arrows. The bow quiver does add weight to the bow and tends to pull the bow slightly off balance, something you overcome with practice.

Some bow quivers are nothing more than an arrow holder. They are not too solid and do not hold arrows tightly and quietly when the bow is shot, but they do transport the arrows safely to the hunting stand or blind where they can be removed and hung up close at hand.

A hunter who prefers to leave his bow quiver in place at all times should select a quiver designed for silent, permanent and solid mounting. Good examples are the Pegasus 11 from Sagittarius, the PSE Uni-System series and the Side-Locks from Hoyt USA. There are, of course, many others, but this will give you the idea.

Hip quivers are experiencing a return to popularity due primarily to the increased physical weight of today's bows; fully rigged, many weigh as much as six pounds. All of them, like blonds or brunettes, are a matter of personal taste. Whatever you choose, I recommend that you keep safe construction foremost in mind when it comes to how your razor-sharp broadheads are covered.

Most popular bow quivers are detachable, which allows them to be removed quickly. This is a popular feature with tree stand hunters.

TREE STANDS

Sooner or later you're going to hunt from a tree stand, and many of you will find it is the best way to hunt some game, mostly whitetails. Before you go rushing off to purchase a tree stand, check the laws of the area where you'll be hunting.

There are some restrictions in a few states. There are all kinds of tree stands to pick from to meet your own hunting and comfort needs. There are climbing tree stands, non-climbing tree stands and those you put up permanently such as tripod stands.

Climbing tree stands are designed for use on trees that have fairly straight trunks without branches. By using the lever-gripping action of the tree stand, you inch your way up the tree and then set the stand in place. Sounds easy—and it almost is—but you'd best be in good physical shape.

The non-climbing tree stands are carried up trees that have

Using natural surroundings helps this bowhunter blend into the environment, giving him a real edge when it comes to outwitting deer. Remember, a safety harness is important.

Hunting from a tree stand requires good techniques. This hunter forgot to position the stand so he'd be hidden. He also forgot a safety harness, a must when using a tree stand.

limbs stout enough to support your weight. These stands usually are larger than climbing tree stands, which gives you a little more luxury once they're in place, but you also have to carry the thing to and up the tree. The tree climbing part can be eliminated with those models that come with a folding ladder that extends the platform part of the stand up the tree for securing. There also are handy platforms designed to be wedged between two tree trunks.

Permanent tree stands are most often made of materials you can get at any hardware and lumber store; however, there are some prefabricated kits on the market. This type of stand, for the most part, is larger and sturdier than portable stands. For most bowhunters, permanent stands, while sounding great, aren't something they can use simply because they don't have a place to put one.

Here are some things to consider when selecting a tree stand. Make sure it's built well. Check all welds and other stress areas. Will the thing hold your weight, plus your bow and equipment? Don't buy a cheap stand that will collapse the first time you lean to one side. How well can it be secured to the tree? How long will it take you to set up and take down? Is it big enough to sit on comfortably and accommodate your

Successful game calling requires more than mastering techniques. Hunters must be ready to shoot and be totally camouflaged.

equipment easily? Is the foot platform designed to insure firm footing, or will it send you sliding when it's touched by the least bit of moisture? Is the seat big enough to comfortably hold your seat? Remember, you could be there awhile. While you don't have to spend big bucks to get a good-quality tree stand, you shouldn't cheat yourself on this item.

When you purchase your tree stand, get a safety harness at the same time. Perching yourself on a platform eight to nine feet off the ground is dangerous. The simplest solution to tree stand accidents is some form of safety harness, or even a stout rope. It doesn't have to be elaborate, but you should have something. If you don't want to use a safety harness or rope, don't use a tree stand. I have talked to guys who disdain them for reasons ranging from misinterpreted machismo to a slightly more rational, "They get in my way." They needn't get in your way and, in fact, they don't. What they do is save you from serious injury.

CALLS

Calling up wildlife is one of the most rewarding aspects of bowhunting. To have a buck, predator or turkey respond to your call is a grand part of the hunting adventure. As rewarding as calling is, it also can be frustrating. It takes practice and patience to develop the right techniques. Fortunately, calling up game today is a lot easier than when I first started in the brush-covered hills of Southern California. There are some excellent cassette tapes on the market that will speed your understanding of how to call in game.

There are calls that imitate rutting bucks and forlorn does, bucks that are fighting, bucks that are looking. There are elk bugles, varmint calls and mouse squeakers that will attract animals looking for lunch. There are flappers which imitate a turkey flying down and box calls which sound just like an old hen. While it takes some effort to learn how to call in wildlife, it's well worth the time.

But again, basic wildlife skills—being where game is located, concealing yourself, et al.—are the keys to success.

CAMOUFLAGE

I got my first camouflage suit in the early Fifties. It was a one-piece jump suit of Marine Corps issue that a friend of my uncle's had worn on Tarawa during WWII. I thought it was super cool and extremely effective, as I waged my own war on

Matching background cover and camo are important for a bowhunter using a tree stand. A face mask or camo paint will eliminate facial glare.

This snow camouflaged outfit helps the bowhunter blend into the white background while breaking up his outline.

geese in the rice and barley fields of California's Sacramento and San Joaquin Valleys. It was "super cool," because nobody then had any camo clothing.

That is no longer the case! Today there is a smorgasbord of camo patterns on the market with more, I am sure, to come. The camo suit has become the bowhunter's trademark. Camo clothing does not make the human form instantly invisible to wild animals, though I constantly see folks who, by their behavior, seem to think otherwise.

There is one simple rule for picking a camo pattern or patterns depending on how many varied places in terms of terrain you will hunt: the pattern must blend with the surroundings. Certainly, this seems elementary. If you are hunting on the ground, large, blotchy irregular patterns of the proper color work best. Trebark will not work well on the Oklahoma prairie, but it's fine in the blackjack oak thickets adjacent to that prairie.

When you think camo patterns, think about background. What is it that you are trying to blend into? Tree stand hunters should think in terms of background cover, too, and as the leaves fall throughout the season, the more solid patterns should be shifted to lighter-shaded, broken shapes in an attempt to reduce the human silhouette. Quiet material should be a serious consideration: a man-made material, such as brushed cotton, wool or fleece.

Patterns I have found to be highly effective in the last few seasons include: Trebark with leaves; Mirage in the spring and fall colors; RealTree during the early fall seasons for tree stands; Predator, mostly the brown, but they are all good; and vertical tiger stripe in a gray/black/brown finish.

Did I name them all? Hardly, and there are others equally effective. The patterns listed have blended well and met the

Camouflage head nets reduce glare from bowhunter's face.

conditions in places I hunt all across the country, and yes, I take them all with me when I go hunting.

Movement or the lack of it is the key to getting game in a close-range situation. Blending as well as possible simply helps disguise movement. Just the other day, my youngest son set an interesting example. Darrall spotted several whitetails feeding adjacent to a prominent creek and used the creek to begin his stalk. By the time he got up to the deer they had fed out onto the open blue stem prairie. Darrall's camo was a close match to the yellow ochre and burnt sienna hues of the winter grass slashed with hints of gray and rich brown. He closed from two hundred to forty yards — no simple feat when dealing with whitetails — and was rewarded with a reasonable

shot. No cigar, but the game is in getting the chance.

The most overlooked area when it comes to personal camo is the face. If you are hunting at ground level, something has to be done about that shining face and eyes Mom thought so doggone precious.

Option one is face paint. Most people who use it don't use enough; a few token streaks are not sufficient. Smear it on with gusto, leaving enough breaks to provide contrast.

A solid dark color also will stand out, appearing as out of place in the woods as your bare face. Mix the colors if you're feeling creative; just get covered. Face masks are a good choice if you're not into goo. Spando-Flage is an excellent, form-fitting choice available in several colors. Head nets are okay, though I do not like the loose fit which distracts my vision somewhat as well as interfering mentally with my anchor point when I shoot. Don't forget the hands; an application of face paint or camo gloves will eliminate the glare they cause. Remember, you will move your hands more than any other visible part of your body when you are ready to shoot. Camouflage is certainly no cure-all to close-range success, but a valuable aid that, properly employed, will help you get a shot.

SCENTS

Bowhunters probably have more impact on the scent market than any one element of the outdoor hunting accessory consumer. Bowhunters are just plain scent crazy, purchasing all matters of scent, scent aids or scent and odor eliminators in astronomical quantities, swearing on them as being just as important as their bows. If you're a bowhunter, you will use some form of scent or scent-eliminating product, if for no other reason than your mind telling you to grasp at anything that suggests help.

I break scent products into the following categories: cover scents, attractors and the odor eliminators. Skunk scent remains a popular covering agent with bowhunters nation-wide. I personally have never liked it. It's too damn disgusting for my money, though I know a lot of bowhunters who swear by it. I believe that it should be used sparingly.

Earth scent is used widely and regarded highly by many successful bowhunters. Natural scents like cedar, apple,

Camo Dust and Wind Whiffer by Game Tracker can be used to camo a bowhunter's skin, plus, when squirted into the air, it effectively indicates the direction the wind is blowing

Milligan Brand's Buck Buster II is an all season, natural tarsal gland lure formulated to attract the hardy mule deer.

acorn as well as skunk and earth have their followings as do such potions as Russell Hull's Cover Up and the newer Nature's Essence, an interesting concoction that suggests a mingled variety to my nose.

I do not believe that any cover scent will fool a mature deer. The human body emits too many varied and alarming odors, all of which spell danger to educated animals. Such concoctions can help, and they might provide a certain element of confusion, thereby providing that extra second needed for a shot.

Depending on any scent as a total shield is foolhardy. Covering or masking scents are truly most effective for blind or stand hunters who remain in a fixed location. Still hunters, by necessity, always should work into the wind which obviates the scent's value, though using some cover scent seems to have become a routine to which we all adhere.

In the West, the pungent sage can be broken and placed in a plastic bag with clothing to help in masking odor. I almost always wear rubber-bottomed boots in order to cut down my own scent line in going to stands or blinds, and some type of cover scent such as fox on coon as a garnish to the boots and pants can't hurt.

Odor eliminators are much in vogue today, and if care is taken with the hunter's clothes at the onset, attempting to purify or neutralize body odor with the special soaps, liquid and powdered products available certainly can work toward success.

Some formulas claim to eliminate human scent. As a practical matter, that has to be a blue-sky scenario dreamed up by an advertising account exec who never met a wild deer. It may be, as we sniff each other with our dull olfactory senses, that indeed we appear fresh as a new rain breeze. To a deer, whose nose is no less than ten times better than ours, we always will stink of danger. The joys of the campfire and outdoor cooking permeate our clothing, as does gasoline when we fill up the truck and put onions in the chili. All of these elements combine to make us smell like what we are. Care should be exercised in keeping the clothes we wear afield separated, but as a practical matter, we seldom do.

It is that ten-times-better ultra sense of smell that works to our advantage when the attractor scents are employed. These are designed to bring the critters to you, and many of them work extremely well. Scent always has been the number one weapon of the trapper, since wild animals live by their noses. Beaver trapping opened the West, with scent from beaver castor the means.

Deer react to attractor scent out of curiosity, the need to feed, the hierarchy of the herd and the rut or a combination of these elements. Unquestionably, the rut of the whitetail deer is first when it comes to utilizing scents for success. Scent during the rut can be dispersed in many fashions. The most effective method I have used on whitetail bucks is the laying of a scent line, or lines, that will bring a trailing buck past my tree stand. Boot pads treated with scent are one method of laying a trail.

I prefer to use a drag, a saturated cloth that I pull across the ground behind me as I walk the route. In the area of my stand, where I have proper shooting lanes, I will either hang a scent-impregnated rag, or most often a plastic 35mm film cannister filled with scent-saturated cotton. I can simply freshen the cannisters from time to time and close them up when I leave the area.

Scents are not magic. They can really work when things are right, and I have shot more than a few nice bucks that were following my laid-out scent lines. I also have seen scents spook deer, mostly does, as well as be ignored completely by bucks that obviously were looking for action.

There is no guarantee, but in the fall whitetail woods, when things start to pop, you can bet I'll be thinking about how and where to play the scent game. As a point of information, the scents I have had the best results with are Scrape-Mate by Sure-Kill, and Milligan Brand Rut Stuff and Buck Buster. For eliminators, Scent Shield products seem as effective as can be expected.

RANGEFINDERS

Rangefinders have become increasingly popular with today's "modernized" bowhunter. Considered "gimmicky" by many, they have a place in harmony with today's equipment and its accompanying attitude about long-distance shooting. I feel that, if the archer is going to try the long-range, sometimes irresponsible shot and has the time to use it, a rangefinder can make the difference in not a hit or a miss but perhaps a good hit versus a marginal one.

There are some excellent rangefinders designed specifically for archers. The Ranging TLR75 is perhaps the easiest to use for in-the-field shots with its Thru-Lens readout, as

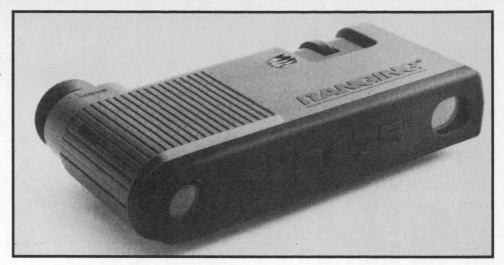

The Ranging TLR-75 features Thru-Lens Readout. It quickly determines shooting distances.

opposed to external dials that require focusing, then taking it off the subject to read the distance.

While they will be used for long shots under spot-and-stalk conditions — open country where distance can be damned deceiving — I see their application more practically employed from tree stands or blinds to familiarize distances to adjacent landmarks. The information then is stored in the mind and the rangefinder tucked away. Estimation distance in the woods is a tricky prospect that requires a great deal of combined natural aptitude and practice.

I guess I have been thinking of things in ten-yard increments all my bowhunting life, so estimating range accurately for shooting situations has become fairly easy for me. While I have shot animals at what would have to be considered long range, those shots were taken when there was a certain sense of "feeling good" about the entire setup at the onset. As a practical matter, ninety percent of the big game animals I have shot over the years have been well inside forty yards. A range-finder can be useful in your walk-about practice sessions where just plain stump shooting is excellent training. Pick a spot, estimate the range and shoot it accordingly, then use your rangefinder to check yourself. Over time, your ability to quickly figure distance inside of reasonable bow range can become second nature.

STRING TRACKERS

Most commonly referred to today as game trackers for the Michigan based company that brought them to the public eye, string trackers work on the same principle as a closed-face spinning reel for fishing. Lightweight line is attached to the point end of the arrow, and peels off the spool which is attached to the stabilizer mount hole on the back of the bow.

These trackers are considered quite handy under certain close-range shooting conditions, especially with bear and turkey hunters. They can be invaluable where tracking conditions are horrid in swamps or high grass, or when hunting for bears which produce notoriously poor blood trails, or turkeys which have a tendency not only to flee quickly with little blood trail but also to fly, making them almost impossible to track. Deer are encountered in the same tough tracking conditions, too.

The advantage of a string tracker becomes obvious, and I have used them with pleasant results. On the down side, they

The Professional Tracking Unit from The Game Tracker contains 2500 feet of seventeen-pound test nylon line.

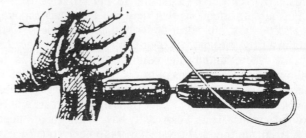

The hunting stabilizer is designed with a special mounting hole that permits the attaching of a Game Tracker line unit.

increase arrow drag beyond twenty yards which negatively affects arrow flight. The whirring line playing off the spool is noisy; not a good thing when dealing with high-strung animals with explosive evasive tactics and reactions.

Depending on the particular conditions — and the game in question — string trackers can be a worthy consideration or a negative factor.

BOWSIGHTS

Today, bowhunters can choose from an overwhelming

The Accra Fast Track sight features small pins that can be positioned close together. It's favored for today's fast bows.

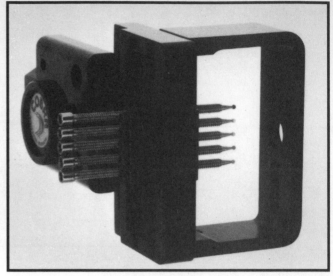

Hunting bowsights should be of rugged construction with prominent pins that are easy to locate for quick, sure shots.

Bowsights will face rough treatment during a hunt. They must have a solid design and a pin protector is important.

selection of hunting bowsights and bowsight accessories. While the options are varied, the function of the sight — to position the arrow's impact point — has not changed since someone first stuck something in his bow to serve as a point of reference.

The multiple pin sight, in its many forms, remains the runaway preference with today's bowhunters. Sight pins are positioned at incremental yardages — usually ten yards — and most often are color coded simply to remind the shooter to think. For instance, I use three Saunders T-Dots pins because of their great ability to gather ambient light: green, fifteen yards; red, twenty-five yards; orange, thirty-five yards.

For hunting situations that may call for longer shooting distances — elk, mule deer or caribou, for example — I will sight in a fifty-yard pin. Knowing my "point-on" range, that distance where holding the point dead on the mark is the optimum distance in terms of arrow arc, gives me one more reference. As a practical matter, this point-on range with most bow/arrow combinations I have shot over the years will be sixty-five yards. Thus, I can easily have five sight positions.

A fixed, multiple sight system works quickly, often necessary in any hunting situation. To make it work well, the shooter must be able to think quickly in terms of actual yardage, and understand the ballistics of his bow/arrow combination. For example, if a shot is offered at thirty yards, I quickly position my twenty-five-yard pin exactly where I want to hit, then raise it until the deer is bracketed by the twenty-five- and thirty-five, yard pins.

Today's faster bows have reduced error margins considerably from bows of years past. If I'm holding solidly on a proper spot on the deer, a slight miscalculation still puts the arrow in the boiler room. While tournaments are won today with an almost zero margin of error in terms of tiny "X" rings in the bullseye, I can get the job perfectly done with an error margin of several inches. Whitetail hunting is generally close-range work. With today's faster bow, I know many whitetail hunters who use only one pin; a great many mule deer guys get by just fine with two.

Any hunting sight must be of solid construction to withstand the accidental hard knocks, the juggling abuse of normal wear and tear, as well as the vibrations caused by just plain shooting.

The amount of vibration movement within the entire bow system is truly hard to imagine. Just recently, I viewed a technical film produced by Don Rabska with Easton. Shot at a rate of 4000 frames per second, it graphically displayed in this ultra-slow motion the amount of movement associated with shooting an arrow. Everything moves!

A pin protector, a wrap-around shield outside the pins, is a must. I'll contradict that by stating I don't use one usually. For some reason, the sight picture presented while looking through the box-like opening bugs me. To eliminate this distraction, I mount my sight on the face side of the bow where the riser, cables and string serve as a relatively reliable protective perimeter. For hunting, this shortening of my sight plane has no negatives, protects my sight and eliminates my personal bug-a-boo.

There are many aperture configurations available today, with cross-hairs quite popular. Set in the manner of multiple pins, they work the same, with the vertical wire aiding in quick alignment. They have some drawbacks, as many models have thin, dark wires that can be almost impossible to pick up quickly in low light or a cluttered woods background. The best cross-hair models, in my opinion, have neon-like clear plastic pins in fluorescent colors that gather light in the manner of the Saunders T-Dots. The Fisher Sight by AAE also is a good example, as are similar models from Cobra and PSE.

Pendulum or "tree sights" offer an aperture style that is growing in popularity. These are designed simply to compensate for the downward angle of the shot by swinging upward as the angle increases from the dead-on range — usually around thirty yards, depending on the height used to sight in — to the point-blank range of approximately ten yards.

Lighted sight pins, either battery-operated or fiber optic, are an aid to low-light shooting conditions, as are certain styles of battery-operated miniature floodlights that illuminate the sight pins with a red, amber or green light.

It should be pointed out, of course, that the use of any electronic aid in sights or other bow/arrow accessories is illegal in some states. Further, the Pope & Young Club does not consider their use proper under the rules of fair chase and will not accept entries into the bowhunting records for game animals taken with any bow or arrow supported by any electronic device.

The peep sight, simply a rear sight installed on the bowstring, comes in a multitude of variations.

Peep sights simply force the shooter to come to exactly the same position every time with the drawing hand. As a training aid, I believe they are invaluable in establishing a good shooting regimen for the sight shooter, but the drawback is in low light situations. If I hear it once each season, I hear it fifty times: "I had him right there, and couldn't see through my damn peep." Such sights are a matter of personal choice. Unquestionably, you can shoot better with a peep, but there undoubtedly will be a time when it eats your lunch. I have enough things go wrong without adding to the possibilities and do not use a peep.

Each year we see additional entries into the bowsight and sight accessory market, and to discuss them all would take an entire book in itself. It is safe to say, however, that the multiple pin sight of quality manufacture and components will continue to be the hunting sight of choice.

ARMGUARDS

The primary function of the armguard is to protect against the whipping effect of the bowstring on the bare skin of the bow arm. That's an obvious advantage, but for the bowhunter, an armguard provides another valuable service by keeping loose or bulky clothing out of the string's forward path which, if hit, can cause erratic arrow flight.

Recurve and longbow shooters are more prone to hit their

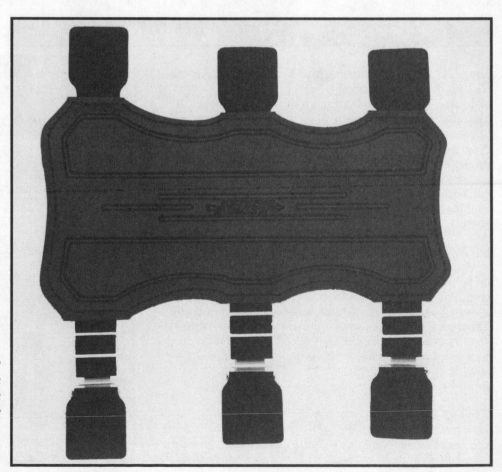

Armguards do more than just protect the arm. They serve a vital function in keeping a hunter's heavy clothing away from the bow string's path.

arm or clothing when shooting bare-bow or "instinctive," the term used to describe shooting without a sight.

Instinctive compound shooters have the same problem. It's caused by canting the bow to align the arrow under the eye. Shooting with a bowsight, the bow in a perfectly vertical position, I never hit my arm, but I do when I practice my instinctive shooting technique, something I do regularly.

There's a wide variety of armguards from which to choose, but the three-strap full forearm style guard is best for keeping clothing tucked neatly out of the way of the string's path when hunting.

BOW SLINGS

The bow sling is designed simply to keep the archer from dropping or losing control of the bow at the moment of release. It serves a practice function by allowing the archer to develop a loose, comfortable bow hand as opposed to a power grip. There is a great deal of forward thrust in today's bows that can literally make the bow jump from the hand. Your shooting style will dictate whether or not a bow sling is required on your hunting bow.

Bow slings, in several designs, give the archer a bit of an edge while shooting. They also can prevent a shooter from dropping his bow. This is a Golden Key-Futura Bow-Mate.

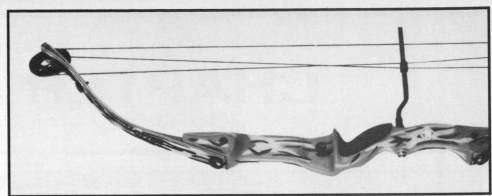

Hoyt's Super Slam FastFlite features Super Slam riser, FastGlass laminated limbs and AIM Fast Flight system. A hunter also can choose Hoyt's SpeedCam, Energy Wheel or ControlCams. The Super Slam FastFlite is available in camouflage and target colors.

BOW CAMO

I can remember the days when one could hardly sell a factory-camouflaged hunting bow. That was in the recurve era, twenty-plus years ago.

When I worked for Ben Pearson Archery, we came out with nice factory-camouflaged bows several times, as did other major manufacturers. The consumers didn't want them. I suspect it had to do with a suspicion that we were covering something up.

I just never understood it, since those non-camo bows would leave the retail stores and be camouflaged at home within hours. Today, probably ninty-five percent of the compound hunting bows bought are equipped with a factory-installed camo finish, and, of course, there are a bunch of patterns from which to choose.

It truly doesn't matter what camo finish you have on a bow, but it does matter whether the bow has a non-glare surface. Bows without factory camo can be covered with camo tape, camo bow sleeves or spray-painted with easily removable camo paint available at most archery pro shops.

I always enjoyed putting on my own camo finish with two or three colors of camo paint and a few natural leaves to use as templates. The style-conscious bowhunter today can match his bow, arrows and accessories to his selection of camouflage clothing, right down to his boots.

The highly touted, high-tech equipment of today is superior to that of a decade ago, but not nearly so much so as many would have you believe. It's my opinion that there is entirely too much emphasis being placed on equipment and not nearly enough on the basic skills of bowhunting. It doesn't matter whether your bow shoots an arrow at 180 feet per second or 245 feet per second. What matters is that you are clever enough to get close enough to do it right. What matters is that you become a bowhunter, rather than an archer.

Clothing like this Polar Fleece outfit from Day One has become popular with bowhunters. To really be ready for the field, hunter should have a camouflaged bow.

CHAPTER 5

Bowhunting equipment must be properly tuned to reach its full potential. But that's not enough. Mental tuning is also vital. Dougherty, with thousands of hours of hunting to his credit, has mastered the challenges of equipment and mental tuning.

TUNING: BOWS, ARROWS & SELF

Mental Attitude And Practice Have As Much To Do With Success As Equipment

For many years, Dougherty has kept his bow skills tuned during the deer off-season by hunting varmints like coyote.

S UCCESSFULLY MOVING through the maze of bows and arrows and accessories on the market today can be as challenging as tracking a mule deer in blowing snow at night. Once you've made your bow selection and balanced it with arrows and broadheads — remember, there needs to be a proper balance of bow, arrow and broadhead — it's time to tune your bow for the hunt.

Bow tuning can be as difficult as you want to make it. If you decide you want a bow with all the racy arrow rests, overdraws and accessories designed primarily for high-speed performance, then you've got a tuning challenge. It can be complicated.

On the other hand, if you want a bow you can take to the field and hunt with, a bow that's as simple and efficient as possible, then you won't have a difficult time tuning it.

You're going to run into more problems tuning if you try developing a super-fast setup with ultra-light arrows and heavy bows — stuff which, quite frankly, I don't think is necessary. The more you put on a bow, the more can go wrong.

This also means you'll have more things to remember to do correctly when you're shooting. Sometimes you have to do things in a helluva hurry. Under hunting conditions, things are much different than on the target range.

All the bells and whistles that are often put on a bow can interfere with a difficult shot such as when you're down on one knee, bent over or with the bow canted. You're not always going to get ideal shooting positions when hunting, and using all the gizmos is, in my mind, a handicap.

Weather and terrain factors also add to the challenge. When you add a lot of intricate moving parts to your bow, you're just increasing the chance for problems; freeze ups, dust, mud and your own elevated pulse rate can interfere.

The bow and arrow setups I use are suitable for the beginner and advanced hunter. There really are two compound bow selections you can make, but I'll use Hoyt bows as an example. The Hoyt Super Slam Extreme, with its energy wheels, is an

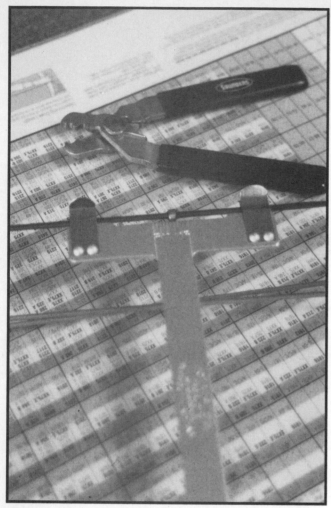

When tuning a bow, nocking pliers and a bow square are required to properly position the nock on the bow's string.

line adjustments and it doesn't do anything but hold the arrow. When I shoot, I get perfect arrow flight. The rest shoots feathers better than vanes from my experience. It doesn't have any moving parts that need to be tinkered with, and when one wears out, I pull the cap off and stick on a replacement. It's trouble free and gets the job done. If you prefer vanes, the Center Right Flipper is an ideal choice.

I make sure my tiller is adjusted for my own shooting style. This is something normally done at a pro shop, which is again the place to start to insure you get the right setup. Have them teach you so you can do it yourself.

In tuning my bow, I spend most of my time finding, then eliminating or reducing noise. I really emphasize getting my bow quiet. Animals have acute hearing and many — especially deer — are spring-loaded to react to the slightest noise. No matter how fast your bow is, sound travels faster — 1,008 feet per second. And the noise you think is just a soft squeak sounds like a freight train to deer.

When I work on reducing noise, I think about the quiet recurve. When they went off, they just went *thump*. It's difficult to obtain that level of silence with today's compound bows, but you can get close. I experiment with the position of string silencers, moving them up and down the string to find

ideal bow to shoot with your fingers because it is fairly long, but you also can shoot it with a release.

The Hoyt Spectra FastFlite with speed cams has a more radical pull since it is shorter and cams are not as smooth as wheels. Because of the higher string angle, I can't shoot it efficiently with my fingers. So I set it up to shoot with a mechanical release.

Regardless which bow you choose, you have to be able to shoot consistently good arrows. Except for using a release, I set both bows up the same. If I use a sight, I pick a solid, well-constructed model with as few moving parts as possible—just enough to get the job done. I want to be able to adjust it, then lock it down so it doesn't move. I mount my sights permanently. I don't want to worry about the sight that can be removed. I want it on my bow as solid as a rock, and I check it frequently to be sure it is.

I want my arrow rest to be solid and simple. Most of today's bows have what is called a shoot-through handle or broadhead tunnel; they're offset for center-shot. This provides for overdraw attachments. As soon as you put an overdraw on your bow, you've got to make an arrow rest selection from umpteen different types. Most of these rests have a lot of moving parts, are more difficult to tune and usually noisy.

I set my bows today with a center-rest made by New Archery Products. It's long enough for left and right center-

Nock location is critical. Its placement is best done at a pro shop where the bow can be tuned to your shooting style.

where they reduce the most vibration. Sometimes it takes two sets. I put Neet MiniMufflers on my FastFlite cables. I make sure I don't have any loose parts on my bow. I tighten all nuts and bolts on accessories, the limbs and quiver bracket, and Loctite them in place.

I also make sure the handle is tight. I've found some of them make a great amount of noise. Most bows have a stick-on handle made of hard plastic which moves just a bit when an arrow is shot, creating a slight click.

The quickest way to find out if a handle is making noise is to remove it and shoot the bow. You'll probably find you've reduced the noise level. I fill the handles with silicone and reattach them to the bow.

When you nock an arrow in a hurry, there's a good chance you'll click it against the arrow rest or sight window. I put self-adhesive fleece above and below my arrow rest to eliminate noise.

There's a lot of fancy equipment designed to help tune bows. I don't use much of it. The bow square is really all you need. I check the tiller, place the nocking point, eyeball the center-shot/arrow position and I'm ready to start sighting in.

That's it. I don't do anything else to prepare my bow for hunting. I don't use a stabilizer, preferring to carry and shoot a bow that's as light as I can get it and still take advantage of its design.

Tuning a bow is easy, unless you want to make it complicated by adding a batch of accessories. Often each accessory must be tuned in balance with another. Adjusting one may mean readjusting a different accessory, which may...well, you get the idea.

What usually happens when someone gets caught up in adding every fancy toy that comes on the market is it becomes a never-ending process. I can understand a guy wanting to improve his chances of success while hunting, but in my opinion, intricate accessories are not the answer. Developing hunting skills, along with properly balanced equipment, is what makes you a successful bowhunter.

Once I've set up my bow, I start shooting. Tuning a bow is not something you do all at once. You'll continue to make fine adjustments as you practice. If I can't get my arrows to fly perfectly straight when I start practicing, I will paper tune them. But I don't need to often.

If you do decide to paper tune, here's how to keep the

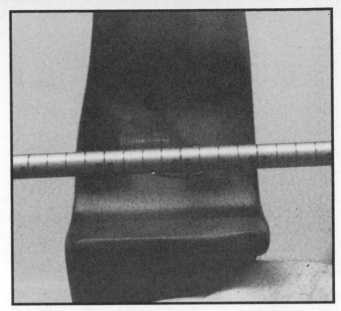

You must first determine your correct draw length before selecting an arrow shaft size to match your bow's weight.

process simple. The purpose of paper tuning is to determine how your bow is sending the arrow to the target. It will quickly show you whether your arrows are flying left or right, high or low. Then you can make adjustments to straighten the arrow's flight.

Start with a cardboard box at least two feet square. Cut a window in one side and tape a single sheet of newspaper over the opening. Place the box in front of your target butt, just far enough away so the arrow will pass completely through the paper. From ten feet away, shoot an arrow through the paper window, then examine the hole. The ideal arrow flight will leave only a round hole in the paper with some small cuts made by the fletching.

If there are some angled tears in the paper, then the arrow is not flying straight and adjustments need to be made. If the tear in the paper is above the hole, the arrow passed through the paper tail-high; a tear below the hole, of course, means a tail-

Proper arrow shaft size is the first step to archery accuracy. Easton has a lot of detailed information to aid in selection.

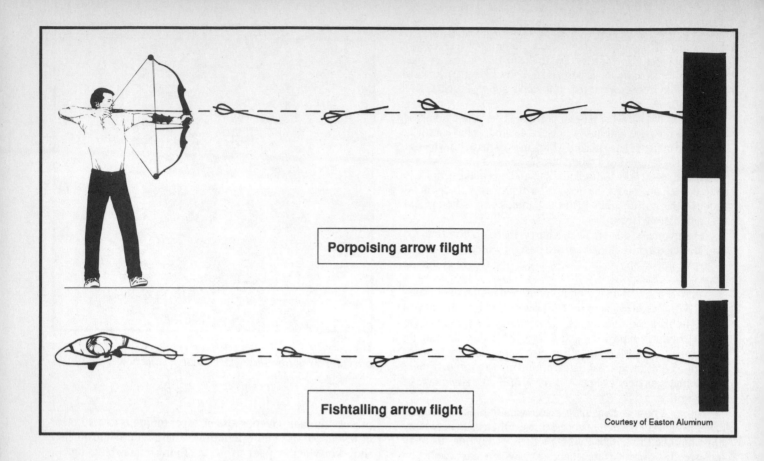

Porpoising arrow flight

Fishtailing arrow flight

Courtesy of Easton Aluminum

low arrow. Move your nocking point down for high tail. For tail-low arrows, move the point up.

Once you've moved the nocking point, shoot another set of arrows, making additional adjustments to the nocking point until your arrows are making only a round hole with slight tears where the fletching passed through.

If the arrow tears the paper to the left or right of the hole, then you have a fishtailing problem. If the tear is to the left, you need to adjust your arrow rest, moving it to the left. If the tear is to the right, move the rest to the right (for right-handed shooters.). Again, make the adjustment a little at a time until your arrows are passing through the paper cleanly.

You may and probably will have both a porpoising and fishtailing problem. Solve porpoising first, then fishtailing. If you still can't get your arrows to fly straight after several adjustments, you may have to make some other changes. You may have to change your arrow rest, change the arrow you're shooting or change the arrowhead. Bow, arrow and head must be balanced. Perhaps some weight adjustment would help and that would best be done at a pro shop. Again, paper tuning, if you have to do it, is simple. Just take your time.

I schedule my practicing to prepare myself both physically and mentally for the hunting season. Usually I have taken a layoff from shooting at the end of December when the season has closed. If I'm going to bowhunt spring turkey, I start practicing in March. If not, I don't start shooting until June. Then I pick up a bow and shoot a few arrows a day, just getting familiar with the bow again. I usually shoot all my bows at a seventy-pound draw weight, but I start practicing at sixty to sixty-five pounds. Just like most folks, my muscles have

gotten loose, my fingers have become soft and I'm not ready to jump into the game at full speed. If I did, I'd just get sore and wouldn't shoot as well.

I shoot for a month at the lighter draw weights before I start cranking things up. I may use the same bow with two different arrow sizes. I work up to where I'm shooting every day. I go out every morning and shoot twenty-five to thirty arrows before breakfast, concentrating on shooting good arrows, not getting in a hurry. I've learned it's better to shoot twenty or thirty good arrows, taking a break between every five or so to think about it, rather than shooting fifty or sixty arrows real fast. I usually shoot another set in the evening. I'm also fine-tuning my bow during this time. I'm listening carefully to isolate noise and double checking to make sure everything remains tight.

After a few weeks, I've worked my way up to seventy pounds or so; wherever the bow/arrow combination and I are most comfortably accurate. My muscles are firmed up and it feels good. Then I move to a range where I can shoot at greater distances. Most guys can only set up a backyard range of fifteen to twenty yards. That doesn't matter, because in the beginning you're just getting the feel of the bow, and getting into the groove of shooting.

This is also when I start looking in around the woods. I carry the same bow and arrow setup I use for hunting, except I have Judo points instead of broadheads on my arrows. I just start shooting as I move through the woods. I shoot at leaves and trees. I shoot a lot of arrows under field conditions. I shoot through narrow woods openings, at shadows and grass clumps, from different positions. I'm just getting used to shooting the

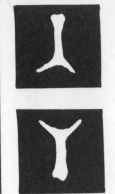

The arrowhead creates a small rip when it passes through the paper. The fletching enlarges the hole when it hits the paper.

Moving the nocking point on the bowstring will eliminate the up and down, porpoising, flight of the arrow. This will cause the arrow to present a tail-right or tail-left rip when it passes through the paper.

Arrows that are not tuned will usually show both porpoising and fishtailing problems when they pass through the paper. This arrow's pattern shows it is tail-high and to the right.

Its not difficult to determine if an arrow is properly tuned. It will leave a clean hole through the paper without jagged edges.

way it's really going to be when the season starts. This helps in fine-tuning my range estimation, too.

In addition to helping me physically, these stump shooting trips get me ready mentally. If I can look at a shadow on the side of a hill and put an arrow into it, walk along and pick out a leaf and hit it or make a twenty-yard shot on a squirrel it's clicking, and I know I'm getting in the right mental and physical groove.

Many people make the mistake of doing all their practicing at the range. By getting out in the woods, you start to get everything tuned. If you've been away from the woods for a long time, you loose your step. You don't walk right and it takes a few days to get back in the groove. You don't take in details as well. The first few days you might be looking for deer signs, but can't find them. As your mental skills become sharper, you start to see things that were there all along. Seeing things, really seeing them, is an art that has to be developed, then refreshed.

Depending on where you're going to be hunting — and the weather and terrain — you may have to devote a lot more time to getting into good physical shape. Face it, if you're going to the mountains of Colorado or Wyoming from the flatlands of South Dakota or Oklahoma, you need to put aside the time and be motivated to get ready physically. If you don't, your hunt could be extremely disappointing.

A guy who is in good physical shape has a tremendous edge over those who, after the first few hours or days, are so exhausted they've lost their hunting edge. This is supposed to be fun. Remember?

I could relate a hundred stories of guys who quit after the first few days. They just couldn't take it physically or mentally. I remember one trip to British Columbia with Chuck Adams and another gent. Adams was all over that goat mountain. The other guy, who was the same age as Adams, was through the first day. He was a basket case. He stayed around camp hoping a moose would wander by. After the third day, the mountain had pretty much crunched me, too. I had wrecked my knee. But Adams went up that mountain every day and killed a goat. He was in great condition and the mountain didn't stop him. I can guarantee, of the three of us, Adams got the most enjoyment out of that trip.

It's common to underestimate the physical demands of bowhunting. Talk to some outfitters and you'll hear some real horror stories of guys who become a total mess in the woods, because of poor physical shape. And a lot of it's mental. There are a lot of people who go hunting who are in good physical shape, but are not mentally prepared to deal with rugged country, primitive settings or the vast isolation.

The entire tuning process of equipment and mind is really simple. Over-engineering your equipment as a shortcut to success is not the answer. Shooting in sterile range conditions does not develop a hunting situation mind-set. The most successful bowhunters you hear about are really hunters who happen to use a bow as their preferred tool.

The charm of bowhunting is the challenge it offers by doing it in a more simplistic way. The most successful hunters always have been, perhaps, better woodsman than they were technical archers, though complete familiarity with the capabilities of their equipment and knowing their limitations are important elements of their success.

In recent years, many of the camps I've frequented are full of technical equipment dialogue and product. I've seen hundreds of valuable scouting or hunting hours wasted on retuning, resighting, reworking and reengineering. I'll shoot my practice Judo-tipped arrows a few times while sneaking about at mid-day, seeking out the answers as to what the bucks are doing.

Unless I do something stupid like cut a bowstring or drop the bow out of a tree, I know my equipment is ready to go to work when I am.

Between-Seasons Practice Is A Must For The Serious Pursuer Of Trophy Bucks

Charles Reneau (left) and Jim Dougherty display two bare-bow forms. For quick moving shots, Dougherty uses high anchor under the eye for fast pointing. Taking moving game requires a lot of skill, skill that is honed during many practice sessions.

PRACTICE IS important! I'm a bowhunter rather than a technical or tournament archer, and for me, practice with a bow and arrow is just a means to an end. Once I'm in the groove and I'm shooting real well, I then practice just enough to remain in the groove.

I usually start practicing seriously sometime in June or July. By this time, I've had a layoff. I may not even have carried a bow since spring turkey hunting or carp shooting season. I start a routine of shooting every day, taking it easy at first. I want to get back in the groove, and get familiar with the bow, again. I don't crank the bow up to my full hunting weight of around seventy pounds. Since I haven't been shooting for awhile, I back the bow off to sixty or sixty-five pounds. Your own experience and age will determine how fast you work up to your hunting draw weight.

I have a setup at home that's good up to thirty yards, which is adequate for most practice required. I like synthetic target matts, because arrows can be pulled out of this material easily. Target matts like the Eternity or Pro Shop II designs will stop anything that shoots but eliminate the grunt and grind required to pull the arrows out. That can be an exercise even with the field points I use for practice at this stage.

I usually shoot at plain targets and pick an imaginary spot to hit. Most of the synthetic targets have some type of facing on them, but I usually just pick a spot on which I can concentrate. I also like to shoot at full-size animal faces like the Ames all-weather targets. When I've developed good form, arrow flight and release, with everything working right, I start practicing with broadheads. I shoot at Stanley Hips ethafoam targets with their replaceable cores. I'm looking to determine where my broadheads shoot so I can make any minor adjustments. Once I'm satisfied I'm getting good broadhead flight, everything's ready for hunting season.

Practicing with broadheads is important. They are going to shoot differently than your field points. With field points you have an almost perfectly aerodynamic arrow. When you add broadheads, you've added wings to the tip. In most cases, as I've said, these two arrows will not fly the same. By practicing with broadheads, you'll be able to make the fine adjustments necessary for perfect broadhead flight.

I know there are those who don't want to practice with broadheads, because the heads are rather expensive. Yes, you may damage a few dollars worth of broadheads or use up some blades, but so what! The bottom line is that your broadhead is the single most important piece of equipment you've got. It's what kills the critter. If you must sacrifice a few broadheads to know where they shoot, then that's what you do. You can resharpen some replaceable blades if you want to go to that much trouble. Conventional heads like a Bear Razorhead, a Zwickey Black Diamond or the Magnus I and II are normally

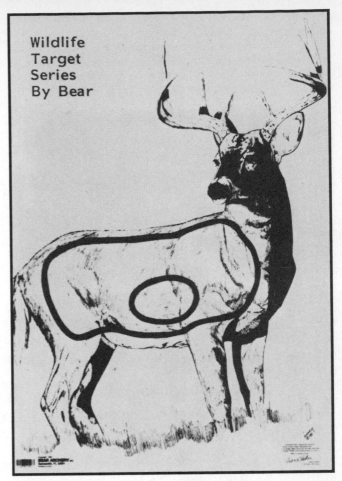

This fine-looking mule deer target from Bear Archery can tolerate a lot of arrows as the bowhunter develops his skill.

Sometimes shots don't go where you intended. Practicing translates to a lot more game taken and fewer lost arrows.

resharpened anyway. Regardless, you've got to practice with these broadheads.

Range practice or tournament shooting seems to dictate that each shot is taken under almost perfect body-position conditions. Some range setups are a bit more demanding, but, generally, shots are taken with an eye to proper form and posture. This is all well and good, if just shooting, or winning awards is the objective. Practice for hunting situations needs a bit more thought.

I've mentioned that I do a lot of stump shooting as I feel it's a superb conditioning method and it gets me in the field. With imagination, you can duplicate almost any hunting situation shot under real conditions. I like that.

For the most part, I use a bow sight. However, the live target and conditions will not allow one to use the proper body position a bow sight demands. To shoot a bow sight correctly, the bow must be in a perfectly vertical position, as canting it from horizontal will alter the arrow impact point.

There are times, especially if you are on the ground, when vertical bow position is not possible. I practice for these opportunities by coming to a higher, closer to and under-my-eye anchor point, canting the bow in the bare-bow or instinctive posture and ignoring the sight pins.

It works for me largely, I suspect, because I still shoot bare bow sometimes and have done so for many years. A release shooter who never learns to shoot with his fingers is making a mistake. A sight shooter who never learns to shoot without one can be equally lost when a golden opportunity comes along. Too many bowhunters spend all their time on the range, practicing to take game under those "proper" procedures. I have met archers afield who never have shot an arrow from their knees let alone more awkward angles. Practicing different shooting styles and positions is a must, in my opinion.

I always try to get within forty yards, with the perfect range anything inside of twenty-five yards. At that range, taking almost any animal should be considered a cinch.

There are times, depending on what you're hunting and the conditions, when you may be offered a longer shot. If I feel good about the setup, I don't have a problem shooting at something fifty yards out, even farther, occasionally. I judge distances well; I know my equipment; and I know where to hold. I can hit almost as well at fifty yards as I can at twenty.

However, unless one has developed his shooting skills and mental edge, a bowhunter never should shoot beyond what he knows to be his most effective range. Of the last sixty deer I have taken with a bow, only seven were beyond forty yards. Most were well inside of twenty-five yards, some, even within ten. Bowhunting, to my mind, is a game designed to be played inside of forty yards. That's how I try to do it.

When I'm shooting well at twenty, thirty, thirty-five and forty yards, all my arrows are going to be grouping well on the target. At fifty yards, they won't be as tight, but I'm going to have them where I want them. When I know I am shooting well, it gives me the confidence to take longer shots when hunting. Good shooting is largely mental. If it feels right, I do it.

Until a person gains that type of skill and confidence, he has no business attempting the longer shots on game, regardless of a "once in a lifetime opportunity." I actually spend ten times more hours target practicing in my backyard at the shorter distances than I do at the longer ranges. I know if I'm shooting well up close, I'll be alright.

Another way to hone your skills is to use true-life silhouette targets. When you place them in a natural environment, you're really looking at what you expect to see during the hunt. These are really good for practice, especially if you place the target in such a way that it forces you to make a challenging shot because of the angle, the lighting, or the position from which you must shoot. Then you're getting some excellent practice.

These life-size, life-like targets are especially good for developing distance-judging skills. Most hunters misjudge distance mainly because they misjudge the size of the animal. Of course, range-finders can help solve this problem, but all of us really need to learn to judge distance by eye. When

Mid-day practice sessions in camp will help keep a hunter fine-tuned and mentally ready.

Practicing with 3-D targets, placed at angles expected in the field, is an excellent way to fine tune shooting skills.

One of the most popular archery sports today is 3-D shooting. The targets are life-size and are placed at unknown distances. The sport presents a lot of enjoyable challenges, but is marginal as serious bowhunting practice.

hunting from a tree stand or blind, one can establish the distance to certain landmarks. However, when you're still hunting, you have to be able to judge distance quickly.

The big rage in some archery tournaments, and for bowhunting practice today, is the 3-D animal round, using life-like, full-body targets. They are a great deal of fun with a huge following. The original intent of the 3-D round, as set several years ago by the International Bowhunters Organization (IBO) of which I was an original board member, was to offer a competitive round based on sound bowhunting principles.

That concept has largely gone out the window. Unmarked distances demanded a need for greater bow speed to compensate for poor range estimation. As a result, faster bows with extra-heavy arrow weights, lighter arrows and overdraws became the norm. The original concept of sane bowhunting practice under normal conditions was long gone. That's fine. The 3-D game is neat, but it's a game. Bowhunting is serious!

Today, 3-D targets are often set under conditions that offer few, if any, honest, even sane, shots. Super-heavy, hot setups prevail. On the last range I looked at, I doubted whether there was more than a handful of targets I could get to trajectory-wise with my hunting bow. At 240 feet per second, it's not fast and flat enough to play the game, but it sure works fine in the real world. The extra-heavy bows of eighty or ninety pounds, commonplace on the 3-D range, have spawned a hunting mentality for some that says no shot is too far or too difficult. This is an irresponsible attitude.

A heavy bow, when one is standing flat-footed and pulling with a great deal of bow arm movement and grunting, is one thing on the range. It is quite another in the woods, shooting from a tree stand at an awkward angle. This year, one young fellow on our Oklahoma deer lease learned the hard way. Unable to pull his bow after several attempts, with a nice buck before him, he over-exerted and propelled himself from his stand. His injuries were not severe.

That is not a rare scenario. I have seen and heard of many similar incidents. If you want to play top-score 3-D in the off-season, and bowhunt, too, work up two separate setups,—one for the game, the other for hunting.

The ideal hunting bow is one you can pull easily from any position with a minimum amount of movement. The motion involved under usual close-range hunting situations, either at ground level or from an elevated position, is one of bowhunting's major disadvantages.

The peripheral vision of deer is designed to afford them certain protection from attacking predators, including bowhunters. Smooth, careful, slow-motion drawing of a bow that can be handled comfortably will get you more shots at unalarmed game than the effort required to pull heavy weight bows.

Overall, when you consider that the average whitetail taken by bowhunters is inside of twenty yards, where its ability to see and sense danger is at its maximum, the conclusion has to be that finesse obviously counts for a great deal more than awkwardly controlled power.

CHAPTER 6

HOW & WHEN TO SHOOT

This Is Not 3-D. It Is Real! It's Different!

AS IMPORTANT as pre-hunting season practice may be, when it comes down to the real thing, when you actually are shooting at a live animal, it's a lot different.

First, conditions are not the same. The target now is not an inert object with scoring rings or a replica of a buck positioned down a well defined path over which your arrow will fly before you walk, to score and recover it. This target is real.

Most likely you will not have the time you're used to for getting set up for the shot. The bantering of your shooting friends — pressure though that might be — is not the same kind of pressure. If you miss or make a poor hit on the range, there's always the next target. None of the shooting conditions you experience on the range create the same cotton-mouthed, heart-thumping emotion you encounter with real animals.

Shooting for real is different. Doing it right is not easy.

Shooting opportunities when hunting will fall into three angle possibilities: front-on, broadside or angling away, all obviously in various degrees. Further, the angle of attack also will vary from below center, level broadside or from above. The most common whitetail angle will be from above, as in tree stands, while the stalking still hunter can be faced with any of the other possibilities.

Understanding animal anatomy is precious information here. On the 3-D-target range, it's common to find incorrect heart/lung placement on the target. They often are far too low and forward to be correct. In looking at a live game animal, I quickly try to break its body position down in horizontal thirds in order to identify and concentrate on the lower third as either the point of impact, depending on the angle (from below to above horizontal), or the point of exit. My objective always

Here's perfect arrow placement. Dougherty's arrow hit tight behind the shoulder, angling away. The Anticosti Island whitetail made three jumps after ground-level stalking shot.

is a double lung hit, though these are not always possible, and other angle options work just as well. A steep quartering-away shot, for instance, might not offer both lungs, but will make one lung and the liver vulnerable. Elevated stands offer a false sense of vital target zone simply because we are looking at more deer. For this reason, I always try to set my tree stands as low as possible in order to keep the angle of impact or attack as level as possible.

When coming to full draw on a deer or any big game animal, my setup always starts below the animal's brisket, then moves up inside the front leg. This position, tight to, or farther behind in a horizontal line is determined by the animal's posture. My thought process is homing in not only on where the arrow will hit, but just as important, where it will come out.

I do not alter the sight picture setup, of coming from below, in any shooting scenario. I believe this is the result of missing too many deer in my early years from tree stands.

The ideal method for quick, precise shooting action is to begin exactly on the target, aim and shoot. However, the motion required to do this usually negates a dead-on start. A pistol shooter from a draw-and-shoot posture comes up to the target. Most riflemen, unless shooting from a rest, come down, while shotgunners come the closest simply by beginning from behind, on the same level, and swinging through.

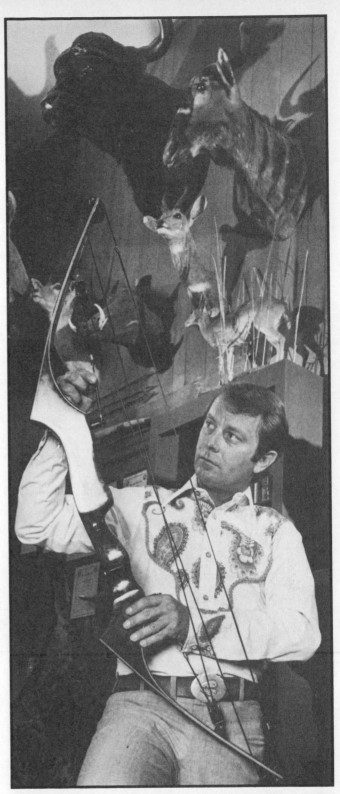

Dougherty's first compound bow, the Pearson Model 250, changed his shooting style, but not technique. Behind are a few of the many animals he has taken with the bow.

Getting a chance for a shot at a trophy buck takes a lot of work. Here's the perfect shooting angle on a big mule deer.

None of this has anything to do with shooting a bow, though perhaps the shotgunner's stance is the best comparison to an instinctive bow-shooting technique.

With today's trend to heavy bows that require extra leverage to present them, the tendency always will be to come down

This deer presents an excellent opportunity for a shot. The buck's attention is diverted and he is broadside to the bowhunter.

on the target area from above. The simple mechanics of pulling the bow already have the shooter in that position. In the adrenalin rush that goes with it, the tendency to get on target quickly — too high — and release too soon are signifi-

Here's a new bowhunter with her first deer. The placement of the arrow is important, regardless of the size of the deer.

cant factors in the number one excuse for missing: "I shot over it!"

Even though I might have to start my bow above a level line of sight to the target, depending on its weight, my body position, the routine of settling in low and coming up restricts the natural tendency to rush and (hopefully) reminds me to think things through. There almost always is more time available to do it than we realize.

If you're hunting deer from a tree stand, the perspective is going to be different. You're really seeing more of the animal than you want to see. When you're at ground level, you can easily break the animal down into thirds and determine where you should shoot. But when you see the same animal from an elevated position, you see more of his back and more of the overall radius of the animal. There really is more of the animal than you need to be concentrating on.

This causes many hunters to aim too high. That's a mistake, because what you're looking at, an extra twenty-five percent, is above the vital zone. So, from an elevated position, concentrate on the lower twenty-percent of what you're seeing. That's where the vital organs are and that's where you want your arrow to penetrate.

Shooting low or, most certainly, in the lower third of the animal, is important, especially if we're talking about white-tails; they are explosive and wired to spring away at the slightest noise. Your bow will make noise. Mine does, and I spend a great deal of time in creating a quiet bow.

If you're in a tree stand fifteen yards away and ten feet high, and you don't aim low enough, chances are the arrow will pass over the deer's back. Why? As soon as you release the arrow, the deer will react to the noise. He's going to get out of there. He's going to start to drop his body in order to make his first jump. That's when your arrow arrives and clears the deer's back. By aiming low, you increase your chances of putting the arrow in a vital area, instead of shooting over its back.

There are also a lot of shots you shouldn't take. During my last trip to New Mexico, I passed up a good bull elk, because I couldn't get the shot I wanted. I could have hit him, but not in the right place for a sure kill. I want to put the animal down. That means waiting for the right shot, and not shooting if I

Dougherty has hunted a lot to develop his savvy. Here, a younger Dougherty perches in a tree, awaiting a trophy deer. High-angle shooting requires different point of aim.

The shooting distance is right. However, the shooting angle is poor. A conscientious bowhunter will not take this shot.

don't have it. If I don't think I can put the arrow where I want, then I don't take the shot. You should think about where the point is going to go when the arrow hits. In your mind's eye, think of the course of the arrow through the critter. I want a shot with an angle that will put the point forward of the diaphragm. That means the point will penetrate the chest cavity. It's going to hit the liver, lungs or the heart. That's what I'm looking for and that animal is going down!

In the case of the elk in New Mexico, all I could see was the paunch and rear legs at twenty-five yards. The target area on that elk was bigger than a whole deer, but I really didn't have anything vital to shoot. I could have shot him in the big middle, but the chances of recovering him with a paunch shot would have been poor.

My second alternative was to punch him through both hams. Such ham shots can be deadly, but they are chancy, unreliable, and best passed for a better angle. I've killed big game with ham hits, but never on purpose.

I never take a straight head-on shot. Oh, I guess one could, if the animal was five feet away and it was a matter of life or death. With elk or deer, unless you hit him right under the chin and break his neck — a luck shot — the only place you've got to shoot is where the throat joins the brisket. That's not much to aim at, plus there's a good chance the arrow will deflect left or right, underneath the shoulder. This could mean a long-term fatal wound which isn't going to do anybody any good. Don't take such shots. With a bow and arrow, they're irresponsible!

Here's a one-shot opportunity with no second prize. Point of aim, lead, release and the follow-through all have to be right.

WHEN TO SHOOT

Personally, I think the most irresponsible shot on a deer, one that is chanced frequently by inexperienced, excited hunters, is the straight down shot that often is offered from a tree stand. Obviously, this usually is a close-range, point-blank opportunity. It looks too good to be true; the fish-in-the-barrel syndrome in living color. It's hard to pass up, but the shot most often is directed straight down between the shoulders which, from above, provides the greatest protection to the chest cavity in terms of muscle and bone. If the shot does succeed in penetrating the chest cavity, it is doubtful whether it will exit, there being too much energy loss to penetrate the brisket.

The resulting high hit/no exit situation virtually guarantees there will be no easy way to find blood trails for a considerable distance, if at all. In thick cover, high grass, et al, such a deer might be impossible to locate. The general idea with such shots is to break the deer's spine. This is an absolute long-shot, and the odds are truly against it.

Imitating "The Master's" shooting style, Dougherty tries the late Fred Bear's personal bow. Bear's instinctive shooting style was developed during his many years of bowhunting.

Dougherty often uses four-fletch on hunting arrows. They are easier to see during flight.

If such a shot is taken, it should be directed much farther back, toward the end of the rib cage with an eye to taking out the liver and to the right or left of dead-center to avoid the spine, while making complete penetration. Here, the knowledge of the animal's anatomy becomes important. Overall, I strongly suggest that such shots not be taken. A deer that close is in your pocket. Let it move to a location that improves your angle and your chances for a hit in the engine room.

Always try to wait until a deer's attention or line of sight is diverted from your position. Even from an elevated stand, the slightest movement often is detected. Deer are aware of what's going on above them, and this is more true it appears, with each new generation.

Just the other day, my son, Holt, ran into a classic example. It was late in the season and he hadn't had many days of hunting opportunity, much less a chance. He was hunting one of my favorite stands and it looked like a dry run, until late in the morning. It was well after normal movement at this spot, when an old dry doe appeared, coming from the opposite direction one would expect. Conditions were dead still. Holt could hear the deer before he saw it and when he moved slightly, the cagey old gal picked up just enough of something to become suspicious. For awhile, it was a stand-off.

Reassured finally, she began to move again on a quartering course, close but in the scant, bleak cover of late December, Holt dared not swing to full draw. Glancing nervously ahead, he picked out a large tree behind which the doe would pass. When her vision was obscured, he drew. The slight noise of his arrow on the rest, perhaps the rustle of his clothing stopped her in her tracks, chest fully exposed at fifty feet. Heart shot, she was down in three long jumps. Experience paid off here. An attempt at drawing quickly, even though the deer was close, probably would have met with failure. Holt had been dealt similar cards before.

MOVING SHOTS

For moving game, the process is much the same as with animals that are standing still. The sight picture is the same. The thought process as to where the arrow is going to hit and where the point is going to pass through is the same. Then it's just a matter of swinging the bow in a nice smooth rhythm. Either it feels right or it doesn't.

A good rule of thumb is to lead twice as far in front of the animal as you think you should. Despite all the hype about speed, even an arrow traveling at 250 feet per second is really quite slow. More to the point, bows with super-fast setups — overdraws, for instance — delicate arrow rests, ad infinitum, are not designed for the layover, or canting of the bow required to make the quick moving shoot. Such bows are designed for the static, perfectly proportioned draw-and-shoot position. Quick shots are really a finger shooter's shot, although they can be performed with a release. I have done so, as have quite a few of my bowhunting acquaintances. It's simply a matter of practice, and few bowhunters practice it.

I've made some great moving shots. With some, I knew I'd done everything right. Others were probably pure luck. For every moving shot I've made, I've passed up dozens. It has to feel right!

When I was younger, I took a lot of moving shots. I got lots of practice on jackrabbits. The first deer I ever shot with a bow and arrow was running right to left at about twenty yards. The year was 1952. I was hunting a piece of real estate Doug Kittredge and I called "The Mansion," an abandoned palatial estate of some two hundred acres in the foothills that butted up against Southern California's San Gabriel Mountains, right at the end of Lake Street in what is now Altadena.

I'd been to the top of a bordering ridge that morning and loosed, in vain, some wooden shafts at sleek gray mule deer. I was a frustrated, tired and thirsty lad of 15, walking carelessly down a trail through the orange grove when a big doe leaped from the grass, hell bent for less cluttered country.

In spite of my lack of attention, I was able to make a quick draw and release delayed only for the fraction of a second it took to allow for a lead. The thought was still clear, that I must keep swinging the bow in a follow-through motion. Long hours of practice on jackrabbits and thrown objects paid off!

My shooting style is a result of the way I hunt. When I'm not hunting from a stand or blind, I'm walking or observing from vantage points. Once I locate an animal suitable for a

These two does present excellent shooting profiles. Inexperienced bowhunters, however, will often miss such a shot because they think it an easy one and they fail to concentrate on utilizing those sound shooting techniques.

stalk, I plan a one-on-one hunt that will bring me well inside forty yards. Think of the animals that are hunted this way: Sheep, mountain goat, mule deer, elk, moose, caribou, javelina and boar are stalked either individually or in groups. You can expect a chance for a moving shot at close range under these conditions. Your odds for good hits are excellent if you have practiced and feel mentally confident.

Shooting a bow and arrow at moving game is much easier for folks who have had experience with shotguns. The two are much alike. A shotgunner points more than he aims while concentrating on the target. When all feels right, the shooter fires. The method is much the same with a bow.

The archer must swing the arrow — again, a blurred line under the eye along a tracking path — through and ahead of a spot on the animal. If the motion is stopped, the arrow will miss the spot. Lead and follow-through always must be maintained. Just as with shooting at stationary game, the oft discussed invisible spot on the animal must be the mark you shoot at, not the entire animal. If the right spot is not there, or the right "feel" is missing, one simply should not shoot.

Using a bowsight for moving shots is difficult. It can be done, but it takes thousands of arrows to master the technique. The bowhunter who uses a sight is better off not using it during moving shots, and should go back to the instinctive technique I've mentioned. By canting the bow, the sight is shifted to one side and the shot can be made by tracking the animal in a smooth motion with the arrow under your eye.

Good practice for moving shots can be conducted with an old tire and a piece of cardboard in the center for a target. Roll it uphill, downhill and on the level, taking a few shots in each situation. You'll be surprised how difficult it is to hit at first, but you'll soon learn the proper lead and follow-through techniques. Taking moving game requires being close, a smooth follow-through, proper lead, a lot of practice and solid concentration.

As mentioned earlier, the most valuable practice for me is stump shooting. Once I've really gotten myself back into shooting shape, I also can fine-tune my shooting skills. It's at this time I feel everything comes together for me, just walking around, taking potshots, honing my shooting and scouting for deer.

Wandering through an area, I take a shot at a shadow next to a tree, a stump tucked behind a bush, a leaf highlighted along a trail or a flower on the side of a hill.

Since I don't know how far these targets are, it forces me to judge the distance. I shoot and try to mesh all my gears. It's really a great test to see whether they are working. I like this best, short of having small game to hunt.

When I lived in California, I spent hours, year-round, hunting ground squirrels, cottontails and jackrabbits. Here in Oklahoma, we don't have as much of a small-game opportunity, so I stump shoot when I'm scouting. The two efforts complement each other, putting me in touch with the woods and, my bow.

Picking An Outfitter: Some Viable Tips For Happy Results

Jim Dougherty has hunted all over the globe, including a good bit in Africa. He feels some U.S. outfitters would do well to take a few lessons from some of the professionals on the so-called Dark Continent. They can meet the hunter's every need.

In recent years, I have seen it happen with disenchanting frequency: hunters returning shocked and angry from the shuffling treatment they received on an expensive outing that turned sour. Actually, they may not realize even now that the hunt was sour from the beginning.

Fortunately, we have a fine contingent of professional outfitters available to us throughout the U.S., and the mysteriously enchanting lands to the north and south of our borders. We are likewise blessed with a great many reputable booking agents/consultants who will help guide us through the interesting red tape attached to some of the more exotic places of interest. But they are only as good as you are in pursuit of their capabilities. Put another way, the only dumb question is the one that isn't asked.

Anything worth doing is worth doing right. Booking a hunt is no exception. Planning, which includes initial contact, needs to begin early, like a year or so in advance. The best outfitters book early; in most cases a year in advance. Initial contact should be with a personal letter. Form letters, which any outfitter will quickly realize as containing less than genuine interest, tend to be set aside in favor of more sincere inquiries. At the beginning, bowhunters should always make

Good outfitters take care so clients never complain about the amount, quality of food.

it plain how they intend to hunt and inquire as to the outfitter's experience with bowhunters.

In addition to the fact that good outfitters book early, there is another important reason for getting a head start. In today's game management scene, hunts for some species are becoming more tightly controlled. This means limited license availability, drawings for tags, deadlines and a certain degree of necessary, but sometimes confusing red tape.

The outfitter will understand the requirements for his area. In many cases, he will handle the process for you. Certainly, he will give you proper advice. After you have made the initial contact by letter and pretty much arrived at a decision, contact the outfitter by phone and go over your questions on a one-to-

one basis. It will give you both a good feeling for each other.

Always ask the outfitter for references, several of them. Follow up on the references by phone. It's easier to get a real feel for an opinion in a conversation than in a letter. It is also difficult to get a timely reply by mail and it is an inconvenience to the person to whom you are writing. Have your pertinent questions prepared so as not to take up too much time.

You will want to know about the country hunted and the outfitter's ability, his equipment and accommodations. Poor equipment means downtime — your downtime. Good help and assistants usually mean a smooth, professional operation. Feel comfortable in making these inquiries; it is, after all, your money.

While the facilities are rustic in many a hunting camp, they are adequate. Shelter, food and transportation action are a must to meet the requirements of the hunter.

Always let an outfitter know if you require anything special in terms of service; special diets, for instance, or an inability to do a lot of climbing. Get the details worked out up front. Surprises in camp are not good.

Find out how the outfitter wants to conduct your hunt and what the options are. You'll need to know whether it will be tree stand hunting or hard days with lots of walking. Plan accordingly.

If you are going on a hunt that requires a major amount of physical effort, do everything you can to get in shape. Too many times flatlanders, arriving for a Western highcountry hunt, are nowhere near ready for the physical effort involved. This is costly in terms of effective time in the field.

While no outfitter will expect you to be totally able to keep in perfect step with him or his guides, he'd like you to be able to keep him in sight. Altitude is a problem that requires several days of acclimation for some. Being a physical basket case is a waste of everybody's time. How long it takes the individual to get used to 10,000 feet or more altitude depends upon many factors, but especially one's general overall physical condition.

All of these elements need to be discussed with your outfitter in advance, as well as with the references you contact. It's always been just as important to me to know whether or not a hunter had a good time, as much as whether he shot anything.

Outfitters and their guides are not super-human. They cannot control the weather, they have no control over our ability when the hard-earned chance arrives. They cannot — as far as I know — use voodoo or pull rabbits out of hats.

I have heard hunters bitch about a rotten hunt, because they didn't kill something. The fact that they missed six shots seemed irrelevant...it was the outfitter's fault!

Any hunt can falter because of bad weather. Those are simply the breaks. I have been on many outfitted hunts when I didn't shoot something. Sometimes I never had a chance, other times I elected not to take the opportunity and there were the times I missed. That's what hunting is all about. If killing is all you're interested in, go to a game farm.

Good outfitters and their staff do their damndest to see that the client has an enjoyable experience. They try hard for success. After all, the client's success is their best endorsement. No question, sometimes things go wrong, but they don't like it any better than we do.

From the beginning, the ball is in the hunter's court when researching and selecting an area and an outfitter for a bowhunting adventure. If you follow these few simple tips, you should be pleased with the outcome.

CHAPTER 7

THOUGHTS ON SCOUTING

A Lot Of Advance Learning Can Make The Difference When The Season Opens

Adjacent to a poplar thicket, this scrape reveals a pattern. The author is scouting for the right place with a good tree for his tree stand. This is a tough chore in skimpy woods.

S COUTING: Observing. Gathering information. Reconnoitering, i.e., To spy.
To a deer hunter, this definition simply means trying to understand what's going on now or later. Put another way, it's an exercise in paying attention.

Sometimes, I think I look around and pay attention pretty well. Most of the time, as careful as I like to think I am, I know I miss something.

The importance of scouting — a simple act of careful observation — cannot be ignored. Year after year, there are successful bowhunters, no matter the geographic area from which we come, who walk to a different set of drums. They always are a beat beyond the range of those of us who are average hunters.

Truth is, these hunters are not superhuman, but extremely detail-oriented men and women when it comes to deer hunting. They understand the need for an intimate knowledge of the terrain and animals they hunt. They thrive on the tactical aspects of the game.

A consistently successful trophy deer hunter may well spend more time scouting than hunting. Finding a good area for deer takes less effort and knowledge than finding a big buck hangout. It's all a matter of how hard you want to play. How hard — and for how long. Trophy deer hunters realize this.

Locating big deer takes more effort, along with a greater

Finding concentrations of deer is not difficult. Finding the proper location to set up a stand or blind is the real challenge.

understanding of what big deer are all about, than any other form of big-game hunting. Simply put, your reward will be in direct proportion to the effort expended, though there is no guarantee you will be rewarded at all, if nothing less than big bucks comprise your objective.

Before I talk more about scouting, let me make an observation or two about hunting for big bucks. First, if you are really serious about it, you have to have almost fanatical dedication and self-discipline. Next, you have to have a great deal more than an ordinary amount of hunting time. Further, you have to have a hunting area where genetics and longevity work toward producing "big" deer; albeit, *big* is relative to the geographics and sub-species hunted.

For example, it is not expected you will be able to harvest Pope & Young-class bucks consistently in central Pennsylvania. Deer there simply don't live long enough. A few might, but that's what they are: few. Next, you have to be extremely expert in understanding deer and deer behavior. Last, you have to be more than just a little bit lucky.

For the record, I fall short in most of these listed categories. However, at any level, deer hunting is deer hunting and scouting is the key to consistent success. Recently, my youngest son proved its importance. He took a nice nine-point whitetail on opening day only because he put in a great deal of time in pre-season scouting on a ranch we hadn't hunted before. He started by marking likely spots on a topographical map, then walked the ground extensively. It was tough, dry, late summer with cement-hard ground.

He studied the contour breaks that suggested natural travel routes. He pin-pointed seasonal food sources while scouting on foot, and located one fence line crossing that indicated recent travel: slight scuff marks on the rock-hard ground; a few strands of deer hair.

Then, just before opening day, it rained. Son Darrall dashed down there two evenings in a row and located fresh sign where he was sure it should be. He selected his tree stand location and collected the buck on opening evening.

He left work at 4 p.m., made the seventy-minute drive and shot the buck at 6:45. He did it right. He put in his time and homework, and believed in his scouting strategy. It paid off. He's been finding his own hunting places since he was 12. He's really getting pretty good at it.

Darrall made a commitment to a new place, which obviously required some extra effort. But old, favorite, familiar places require the same treatment, for deer adjust their habits to meet current conditions. A good stand of mast-bearing oak may be barren from one season to another. Water sources dry up, movement changes. Pressure increases from habitat loss. Poaching is a serious consideration in deer movement and a steadily increasing factor in big buck loss. More good areas go downhill as a result of poaching than you can possibly imagine. This is more true with whitetails than any other deer.

Scouting can be done in several ways. Year-round scouting is best. Keeping tabs on the deer herd for twelve months can't be beat. Sure, some folks can't — they don't live close enough to the hunting area. Here are several points to consider.

YEAR-ROUND OBSERVATION

Observing deer around the calendar can be perfect if you live in close proximity to their habitat, or within comfortable striking range so you can be in that vicinity on a regular basis.

This helps to keep you up-to-date on everything that affects herd movement in this area. You know how the seasonal food sources look, where the water is and where it will be later. You can locate summer gangs of bachelor bucks and keep tabs on them, discovering what impact the creeping crush of civilization might have.

JUST VISITING

Get to know the local folks. These include farmers, mail carriers, cowboys, herdsmen, oil pumpers, gas station people, the local game warden and, yeah, the fellow behind the bar in the *cantina* most preferred by the resident outdoor crowd. You learn a little by listening, a lot more when you make friends.

On a south Texas stream bank, signs of earlier bowhunters are discovered by an archer carrying modern equipment.

For a lady who wouldn't walk across the street to shoot the world's biggest whitetail, Sue is exceptional at spotting deer. We see some truly nice deer this way. I get a solid feel for what's happening, and it puts me in the proper mindset for October.

Of course, there are other ways and places to do the same thing, away from the truck and martinis. You have to go where you have to go, any way you can get there. In the West, for mule deer, I might do the same thing with a day pack, the spotting scope and a canteen. Just water, thank you.

SPOTLIGHTING

For openers, "spotlighting" is a term that carries a nasty innuendo. However, use of a spotlight is a legal way to observe deer in many areas. Checking local regulations is prudent. It also is an effective way to census deer.

I have spotlighted under legal circumstances many times with law enforcement personnel. One thing is for sure: It can reveal some incredible nocturnal deer that we probably never would see any other way.

Noted Canadian longbow hunter Dave Richardson ponders trophy whitetail discovered while scouting with the author.

JUST DRIVING

Cruise the right roads. Follow them after a fresh rain to pick up new tracks. Drive them in the magic very early and very late hours when movement is at its peak. It's easy to locate good deer areas from the road. After that, it's up to you and your own charm to gain access on the other side of the right-of-way fence. Don't be surprised if the warden stops you. That's probably how you will meet him. The rest is up to you.

SITTIN' AND LOOKIN'

A tactic that can't be beat once you're on the ground is simply to sit and watch. This requires good vantage points, quality optics, patience enough to enjoy the scenery and a pretty fair knowledge of where to look — and when.

My wife and I scout this way in the late summer, when it's getting close to hunting time. We might have fished a bit through the late afternoon, but as the shadows start to stretch, we have a few places where I like to park and set up the spotting scope. With a pair of good binoculars apiece, a chilled martini mixed on the pick-up tail gate and a few munchies, we get to the business of looking for deer; mostly bucks, of course, but just counting up deer is good fun.

The trophy whitetail that made this huge scrape field-dressed at 212 pounds. It was heaviest whitetail taken by Dougherty.

LONG DISTANCE

This type of scouting goes a bit hand-in-hand with "visiting." Not quite face to face, it's a matter of keeping in touch via the phone with the friends you have developed along the scouting trail. It's a fine way to keep information and friendships up to date.

Altogether, I prefer the get-out-and-walk-around method of scouting. I always think in terms of food zones, either as the place to hunt or the routes to and from. I prefer established travel routes. Deer traveling with a sense of purpose, though lolly-gagging along, offer excellent hunting patterns. Deer in feed zones are the best. Intent on foraging, they eventually will provide the best shot opportunity.

When I find the right hunting zone, it becomes a matter of deciding whether it can be hunted effectively without blowing the location. It's much easier to find deer concentrations than it is to find a proper spot for a blind or stand within that area. If it's not there, don't force it. Back off and look for an alternative.

The best thing about scouting — if you do enough of it — is the comfortable feeling it gives you with your hunting area. If you believe in your ability to pick the right spot, success is just a matter of sticking to the plan.

Dougherty has often used a motor bike to quickly reach several hunting areas in a day. Once he walks the area, scouting for likely setups, he rides to another location.

CHAPTER 8

WHICH IS THE TOUGHEST?

In the never-ending quest for the perfect deer hunt and the ideal trophy, an outfitter/guide can prove to be invaluable.

ABOUT A MILLION years ago, we're told, primitive deer drifted across the great land bridge that joined Asia to the New World, along with the early sheep and many other predecessors of our present big-game species. Just as the sheep evolved into four distinct species, the deer evolved into two distinct groups, continuing to subdivide until they slowly covered what is now North America.

Today, their wide-spread geographic distribution has made deer the most populous big-game animal on our continent. Biologically there are currently eleven classifications of mule deer/blacktail and seventeen North American whitetail groups. There are thirty-eight, including subtropical species of South America.

As a category, deer are so plentiful that anyone with even a slight outdoor notion has a good opportunity to see them in the wild just about anywhere. For the big-game hunter, they are made to order: plentiful numbers, easily accessible and economically feasible. Most "big-game hunters" are deer hunters, period.

Deer cause more pulses to quicken, energy and dollars to be expended, stories to be told and shirttails to be cut off than all other big-game critters combined. No animal can be hunted successfully in so many different ways or places, provide such a variety of fine eating, keep more taxidermists in business or cause more folks to clutch up than a respectable deer, and as far as I am concerned, any deer is "respectable." Some are just bigger!

To most folks, deer are deer. Percentage-wise, few of the total number of deer hunters pursue both mule deer and whitetail. Fewer still hunt blacktails and a goodly portion have heard never of a Coues, the sprightly desert whitetail, or the remote Sitka blacktail, all individual categories of deer recognized by the Boone and Crockett and Pope & Young Clubs.

Five North American Species Each Offer Their Own Challenges

Collecting a mule deer that is large enough to be recorded in The Book is one of today's toughest bowhunting tasks.

They are all deer to be sure, but each has its own distinct appearance, environmental requirements, habitat preference and whims of nature and temperament geared to remind us frequently of our human frailties.

Each of the most huntable three — whitetail, mule deer and blacktail — is a special product of its environment. The mule deer ranges over relatively open country, covering some distance from summer to winter, while the whitetail lives and dies in a closer, more intimate relationship with its home ground. The mule deer is easier to locate visually than the whitetail because of its living quarters, but the pattern of a whitetail buck can be determined with a great deal of exactness. A hunter can pinpoint where he will be, sooner or later, yet not actually see him beforehand.

As hunters are inclined to do, we make comparisons — call it arguing — about the biggest, best, smartest or tastiest deer

The whitetail (Odocoileus virginianus), the most hunted deer in North America, is also the most talked about. Countless hours have been devoted to the merits of the whitetail versus all other deer, especially the mule deer. Which is the tougher deer?

species. To the Easterner, the whitetail is king; nothing is sharper, more magnificent or tougher to hunt. He thinks the mule deer is stupid, a big-eared clod that stands around in the open inviting termination.

Northwesterners make good cases for the secretive black-tail, a close cousin to the big-bodied Rocky Mountain mule deer, a look-alike that runs somewhat smaller and favors the thick canyons of Washington, Oregon and the northern portions of California. How these opinions that the mule deer is stupid originated escapes me. Any animal that has been around for thousands upon thousands of years, taking the worst that man and beast can throw at him, generally holding his own in the process, *isn't* stupid. The hunter who claims he is, hasn't hunted him overly much and has been lucky when he connected.

Are whitetails smarter than mule deer? It takes a whitetail buck scoring 125 inches to make the Pope & Young Club record book; it takes a mule deer of 145. Both are probably equal in age, health, experience and brains. If this is the case, why then are there 3288 typical whitetails listed in the third edition of the Pope & Young record book and only 863 mulies? These ratios — almost exactly four to one — suggest

that perhaps it's the other way around.

Actually, it has nothing to do with one being smarter than the other. *Odocoileus virginianus* — the whitetail deer — does not possess superior intellect, although we sometimes seem inclined to lay credit for almost supernatural powers at its feet. The reasons for the differences are quite simple:

First, more people — a bodaciously overwhelming percentage — hunt whitetails than mule deer. Second, in most states whitetail seasons are much longer in duration than those for mule deer and bag limits are substantially larger. Third, the seasons for whitetail include the rut, a period of time when big bucks — and little ones — are more vulnerable. (Fewer mule deer seasons include the rut period.) Fourth, and this is important, whitetails are much easier, physically, to hunt.

And finally, from Canada to Mexico and over all the U.S. in between, there are more whitetail deer than all the other species combined. That, when wrapped up with reasons one through four, accounts for that skewed four-to-one ratio.

That ratio, I am willing to bet, will become even greater as time goes on. For example, at the midpoint of the Pope & Young Club's eighteenth biannual recording period, ending December 31, 1991, there had been entered for that twelve-

To find the Columbian blacktail, bowhunters must travel to Washington, Oregon, California and British Columbia.

month period: twenty-two Columbian blacktail deer, 145 mule deer, 1068 whitetail deer, eight Coues and thirteen Sitka blacktails. As glaring as the difference is, it has nothing to do with individual deer species' brainpower; only circumstance.

It is not fair to suggest mule deer are dumb in comparison to whitetails, but it happens all the time. It is not fair to suggest a camp meat pole laden with tasty young venison cooling in whispering high-country aspens is proof of species ignorance, but it is a common suggestion. This status has nothing to do with brain power; instead, it has to do with the age class of the most commonly shot mule deer buck, the yearling fork-horn. Such juvenile, velvety-antlered deer are relatively easy in August and September.

I have hardly ever been in a whitetail camp that could not have its branches similarly laden with bucks — easier to collect, in my opinion — of the same age class. In fact, most do, but few claim the juveniles to have been "dumb." Perish the thought! They are whitetails! I don't understand it.

Unquestionably, whitetail deer are the most talked about, romanticized and commercialized of our big game. If you want people to sit up and pay attention to you, just come up with a new twist in hunting the whitetail. It is also without question that whitetails are our most widely distributed, prolific and pursued big-game resource. For sheer numbers of hardcore fans, the whitetail has the muley beat hands down. That doesn't win any arguments, but with all those aficionados

hitting the woods each sweet and crispy fall, the whitetail doesn't lack for good press.

If we delete Alaska and Hawaii from the conversation, thirty-one of our states are whitetail range only. Seventeen states support mule deer, but ten of those also have whitetail herds.

While I don't have exact figures, there's no question that the whitetail population roaming the U.S. outnumbers mule deer dramatically. Small wonder they generate such enthusiasm. One argument mule deer proponents offer is that, if a person is to have a chance at a trophy rack, he has to have access to that deer population. In other words, with so many whitetails available, it has to be easier to put one into the records. Statistically, I suppose, that's a good argument.

But what's the real answer? Well, I'll tell you what I think. We have many more bowhunters hunting healthy whitetail herds. More importantly, there is more whitetail information available than ever before. Through a variety of vehicles — clinics, seminars, articles, books, videos and even television programs — people are being educated as to how to hunt good bucks. If you think that hasn't helped, you haven't been paying attention. It all has made whitetail hunting for big bucks ten times more understandable than it was ten years ago. That doesn't mean you'll harvest one, but you have a better chance.

So, you have the following ingredients: more whitetail habitat, more whitetail deer, longer whitetail seasons, more whitetail hunters and better hunter education/understanding. Also, the whitetail is more adaptable to living and flourishing in close proximity to man.

Deer are deer when it comes time to hunt them. Your strategies should be based on the country, time of year and weather rather than the animal's supposed intelligence level.

I have found it quite difficult to stalk whitetails. I think this is primarily because the country in which I have hunted them has not lent itself to stalking. Most whitetail hunting is done in the fall when the leaves are knee-deep and noisy, when the woods are so nearly bare as to reduce cover. This is not as conducive to stalking mule deer in the aspen patches of a Colorado August. Certainly, there are exceptions. Deer are found most everywhere and some whitetails live in a lot of swell places for the stalking bowhunter, but most of them do not.

I have hunted mule deer in the desert, where the cover was mesquite and greasewood and the ground sunbaked sand, where there were so few rocky areas that the deer hooves did not wear down and they pranced about on toes that grew for inches and curled up like slippers on an elf. You don't take up the trail and stalk mulies in that stuff. You lay in wait for them the same as most whitetail hunters do.

The similarities between mule deer and blacktails are many. In appearance, they differ little. Blacktails are generally smaller than the Rocky Mountain mule deer, but not much different than a good many of the mule deer subspecies whose ranges adjoin theirs. California's Pacific Coast and Inyo mule deer on which I cut most of my hunting teeth are small deer. A big one may dress out at around 110 pounds, if the coastal type. They are somewhat bigger inland. They are dark in color with prominent markings.

Because the range of the mule deer has been expanding, the legitimate blacktail boundaries have been changed from time to time by the record keeping bodies to insure that sufficient

The small Sitka is one of the toughest blacktail deer to hunt. These does on Alaska's Afognak Island enjoy a few minutes in the rare sunshine.

separation is maintained for purity's sake. They will interbreed.

While the blacktail is most often a small deer, as one moves farther up the coast they tend to get somewhat larger. Most of my blacktail hunting has been done in Northern California and lower Oregon. I have found they cannot be hunted, for the most part, as I would hunt muleys in Colorado or Arizona, with a lot of looking and stalking in the more open range.

The farther north one travels in blacktail country, from Northern California through western Oregon into the damp coastal forests of Washington, the tougher hunting them gets. It's a matter of changing habitat and terrain.

Blacktails in Oregon and Washington, as a rule, cannot be hunted as effectively by spot-and-stalk strategy, except around heavily timbered clearcut areas and old burns. The country is just too dense, the deer too secretive. Rattling, and/or bleat calling in tandem is the technique employed by consistently successful hunters.

In the West, bowhunting for deer starts early in the year, as early as mid-July in some places. Colorado bowhunting starts in late August and most Western bowhunting seasons are in full swing by the first of September.

What a hunter experiences at that time of year is a far cry from what he is used to if he's a whitetailer, born and bred along the Eastern shore. He's hunting big bucks traveling together, most still carrying racks in full velvet and spending a good deal of time in the open. They are creatures of the high lonesome, coming off a hard winter and a summer of plenty.

Their temperament is that of a gentleman who would like to spend the summer taking things easy. Take care that this impression does not lull you into a false sense of security. Check back with him in November, if you care to take notes on personality adjustments.

I have spent many summer months with whitetails, and their metabolisms and attitudes are much different from what they will be when the first frost of fall lays its carpet. In fact, they act surprisingly like mule deer during the same period of time.

During late summer on into early fall, right up to hunting season's opening day around October 1, whitetail deer are perhaps more vulnerable to pattern hunting than any other time. The bucks most often will be in the company of others, taking things easy and sunning their headgear as it matures. It's the quiet time for the whitetail, as it is the muley, days away from the changing weather that will stir in him the inbred knowledge that life will change and times will get tougher.

Now is the time, if you do your homework properly — a lot of late summer scouting — when your chances of putting together a pattern of consistent behavior are excellent. At no other time will you be able to hunt a whitetail in a more relaxed frame of mind.

When it comes to hunting the various species, I have definite preferences. For whitetails, I can enjoy the game of figuring out where they will be and setting up for them.

For me, still-hunting or stalking them is not very effective. I will see a good many deer on these jaunts — southern ends of north-bound beasts — but I will not bring many to bag. I do not think it is because I am inadequate as a still hunter. I think it's because the country is against me during that time of year. I'm inclined to see the whitetail as a more explosive critter, less inclined to stand about when anything signals danger.

But it certainly can be done. As an example, in 1988, I shot eight whitetails from the ground, still hunting, walking around on both feet. It was simply one of those years when everything was going along just right.

Two of the deer were taken on Anticosti Island where still hunting is the accepted way, and the real estate is perfectly suited for the style. They were both nice bucks. Three of them expired in Texas on one of those huge, lightly hunted ranches where the whitetails were, quite honestly, a little bit less supercharged than those we're all used to seeing. The remaining three deer were taken in Oklahoma, a place where such events should not be expected to happen more than once in every third blue moon. Since then, I have shot two others from the ground, one from a blind (not quite the same thing), the other on a little spot-and-stalk routine.

Locating a good buck and putting a stalk on him is about as much fun as my heart can stand. It is my favorite way of hunting mule deer — easing slowly through the country in keeping with normal animal movement patterns, stopping frequently to look things over carefully. This is a challenge worthy of any bowhunter, taking advantage of the high ground and looking for hour upon hour, searching out the pockets where the bucks feed, putting them to bed and trying to come up with a stalk.

Much blacktail/muley country allows this type of hunting and there are, of course, similar whitetail places, but not many. The ground cover is right for careful footwork; there is cover to hide in, get behind, and use for your approach.

My experience with blacktail deer is not nearly as extensive as with whitetails or mule deer. What that experience has suggested is a strong similarity between blacktails and muleys, however. Both seek and prefer rough country. The prime blacktail habitat I have experienced is steep, dense and gnarly. While many deer are present, few are seen. Dwight Schuh, one of our better bowhunters, told me that if he saw one or two bucks a day, it was an extremely good day.

Blacktails can be called and rattled much more effectively than mule deer. In recent years, many bowhunters have perfected these techniques which have had much to do with the increased numbers of big bucks being taken today.

Looking at the situation from every perspective, the mule deer is certainly no less intelligent than the whitetail, and definitely not easier to hunt. Actually, they are more difficult simply because of the places they live. A record-class mule deer is one of our most magnificent of big-game animals, symbolic of what was and what is left of our great Western wilderness. What the record books suggest is gospel. Does that make them the toughest deer to hunt? Not really. We haven't talked about the Coues.

My experience with Coues deer is not extensive. I have a lot of friends with a great deal more. However, I have done just enough to know that on the easiest, best day ever hunted this species was damned tough!

Chuck Adams, whose overall big-game experience has as much depth as anyone is likely to accumulate, claims his attemps for a Coues buck was the toughest, most exasperating hunt of his life. Fred Asbell, who I consider among the best

There are not a lot Coues deer in the record book. The tiny deer, according to Dougherty, is the toughest deer to hunt with a bow. He has the frustrated memories to prove it!

bowhunters that ever will walk this land, just shakes his head, and Bill Krenz, one of the few bowhunters to have harvested all of our deer species, grins in a funny way when he thinks back on his record class Coues buck. You can see the aggravating frustration mixed with the pride of accomplishment in his eyes.

Coues are small, sleek, gray, diminutive critters, and this little subspecies whitetail lives in a terribly inhospitable land that generally is just downright difficult for bowhunting. It's spot-and-stalk for the most part, across open, loose, rolling rock, and noisy side hills. Lots of this terrain is nasty and steep with desert plant life that rips, tears and stabs.

Altogether, most folks quit, because they aren't having any fun. Coues deer hunting has to be done in the right frame of mind, on a par with not caring too much if you are getting your tail kicked. You have to accept it going in.

I never have met a man who's killed a Coues deer buck with a bow who didn't honestly admit to more than a smidgen of luck. I have shot at four Coues deer in my life, two standing, two running. The two that were standing were running by the time my arrow was halfway down the road. I came much closer to the two runners, and actually got a handful of hair off one. I kept it for a long time in a plastic bag until I finally threw it out. There's no sense beating up on yourself.

Altogether, statistically and as a practical matter, the Coues deer is undeniably the toughest of the deer to bowhunt. Take it from a guy who never has killed one.

Better yet, ask the ones who have!

CHAPTER 9

WHAT TO TAKE ON A HUNT

Traveling Light Is Important, But Don't Forget Tools For The Job

Dougherty believes a successful bowhunter needs to know what to take and what not to take on a hunt. He travels as light as possible, given the weather conditions and terrain.

IN AN EARLIER chapter, I discussed accessories in some detail, sometimes a bit tongue in cheek, since there are so darn many of them. My intent was to try to focus your attention on the matter of hunting deer with a bow, to cause the reader to think about being a bowhunter rather than an ultra-sophisticated bowshooter. There is a difference.

It's pretty obvious, I guess, if you paid attention, that I am inclined to keep my shooting equipment as simple and, therefore, trouble-free as possible. In the long haul, it will pay off. However, the trend today leans heavily toward intricate accessories that are designed to increase shooting performance, and they work, no question about it. The problem is that a lot of bowhunters are going to feel totally inept and unprepared

Before packing, Dougherty spreads his equipment out for a final check. Gear that might be damaged from moisture is carefully wrapped in plastic.

A pair of quality binoculars are a must for a serious hunter. The bow is an excellent stabilizer while glassing for deer.

without such accessories. If you have such a problem, let me give you a bit of advice on the subject. Understand your shooting equipment intimately. Know how to fix anything that can go wrong and have the materials necessary to fix it in the field or camp yourself. This might seem to be an unnecessary comment, but I have seen it happen so many times. I have seen a man's hunt ruined because of a minor equipment flaw, a broken part, a missing screw. When you're a long way from Nowhereville without what you need, you are a dead duck!

So, with the shooting equipment's possible problems taken care of and set aside, let's think about what else you should take along on a day's hunt, whether for the whitetails you might be chasing a few miles from home, or a mule deer a thousand miles away.

I like to hunt with a day pack. Mine is fairly large. Counting pockets, it has a 2800 cubic-inch capacity. The first consideration is that it be waterproof, not just water repellant! I also prefer the quiet finish of material like Polar Fleece or Polartuff, and yes, you can find these materials in waterproof packs. The large capacity provides plenty of storage room. I don't fill it up to start, but I can stuff my jacket in it when it's too warm to wear late in the day, for example. The pockets give me room for organizing my necessities; most will remain there all season wherever I might go. Here's how it's set-up.

UPPER LEFT POCKET: Mini-Mag flashlight with fresh batteries; one set of spare batteries; roll of fluorescent orange surveyor's tape; twenty-five feet of 150-pound nylon rope with clinch clip at one end; a Truangle R-4 broadhead sharpener; and my wind check powder bottle.

LOWER LEFT HAND POCKET: Compact Nikon 35mm camera and an extra roll of film. Camera is wrapped in a large camo bandana inside a zip-lock storage bag. The pocket also carries a compact emergency-style space blanket that folds down to overall size of about four inches long, two inches wide; spare cap for CenterRest; a varmint call; diaphragm call and compass.

Dougherty carries a number of cutting tools while hunting, including a sharpening aid, dressing knife and folding saw.

RIGHT HAND POCKET: Arm guard; spare release aid; spare finger tab (depending on what bow I might be carrying, I'm prepared); deer grunt call; six-inch single-cut mill bastard file; sheath knife and sharpening steel; butane cigarette lighter, two Zwickey Judo points; and my folding saw.

CENTER OUTER POCKET: Game Tracker DeLuxe model safety belt; two screw-in style bow hangers; two one-gallon size zip-lock storage bags; glove for bow hand; scents in plastic bag.

MAIN COMPARTMENT: Folded Kool-Dri two-piece bib-style camo rain suit compressed, that fits flat across the bottom of my day pack; wool stocking cap; pair of medium-weight gloves; one-pint water bottle.

The main compartment is basically empty, allowing me room for extra clothes, snacks, the deer's heart and liver (in zip-lock bags) if I get lucky, and I often put in a full-size 35mm camera with telephoto lens.

I carry my binoculars, — Bausch & Lomb compacts — around my neck. A Leatherman tool, which is unbelievably handy, is in a sheath on my belt. As mentioned, most of these items are in the pack year-round.

Occasionally, there will be a few minor changes but the nuts and bolts stuff is always there. Altogether, it weighs about five pounds — without the big camera. I might not always wear the pack, but it will be close at hand, locked in my truck box not far from my hunting spot. Everything I need is there, and properly organized.

This is an especially good system for long hunting days with plenty of room for a lunch, if you plan on waiting out a buck or decide to hit the top of a distant mule deer ridge some ways from camp. If I want, I can put in a 1 1/2-pound down pack-style sleeping bag. With the space blanket, I can make out pretty well should I get caught out.

There are occasions when I convert to one of Rancho Safari's Catquivers. The Catquiver III has a day pack of almost equal size and it allows me to carry more than the four arrows I normally carry in a bow quiver. If the weather is rainy and bad, I can remove my bow quiver and put all my feather-fletched arrows inside the quiver's protective shroud. The Catquiver II has less capacity, yet still provides me with plenty of room for the most important items I need to carry on a walk-around hunt.

One of the main reasons I prefer a day pack is to keep from having my pants and jacket pockets full of lumpy, jangling odds and ends. Such day pack items can be shimmed with the gloves, stocking cap and what have you to eliminate any

Powder filled squeeze bottles are the most effective way to read wind currents. Dougherty uses Puff 'N Glo powder.

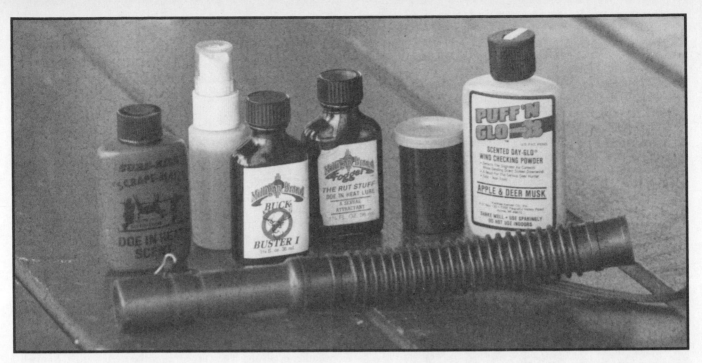

These are aids Dougherty takes on a hunt. They're designed to attract deer and to prevent the deer from sensing the hunter.

rattles. Such a pack always has plenty of extra room and is comfortable to wear provided you have made sure the shoulder straps are properly padded and adjustable. Some styles have hip belts for extra-heavy loads.

In stalking situations, I can remove the day pack easily, if I need to slip through brush or under low branches. It's a good system, allowing plenty of flexibility in carting around all the things we shouldn't be without in the field.

The items carried in a day pack or fanny pack are obvious necessities. Hopefully, you will need your knife and sharpening steel several times during the season. That's one example.

Carrying a spare tab or release makes good sense, if you have ever lost one. I was once on a hunt with a guy who lost two. You might not want to tote along the weight of a water bottle. That judgment depends on the conditions and the individual. Over the years, though, I have found all the items mentioned easy to pack and nice to have handy.

A serious consideration in planning what you need on a hunt concerns the clothing you will wear, from head to foot. This is vitally important when dealing with cold or wet weather conditions. It can rain any time, of course. The high country of the West during mule deer and elk archery season is famous for its almost daily late afternoon thunderstorms. An easily tucked away set of good rainwear can prove to be a true blessing.

Cold weather is the toughest on most hunters. Shooting a bow under extremely cold conditions can be really difficult. The act of drawing and shooting is much easier with a comfortable body temperature and loose muscles. Archery really is a muscle game, and when shivering cold or wet, our muscles do not respond well to the call for sudden action.

Having been miserable on many hunts, I eventually got everything pretty well figured out. Thus, I have some recommendations on what types of clothing you might want to consider taking along. The number one rule is: Always

consider what it will take to handle the worst possible weather that might be expected in the time frame and place you will be hunting.

In selecting bowhunting clothing, consider quality first. A few extra bucks up front might make you flinch at the onset, but there's a definite payback over the long haul. Comfort is important, of course, but quiet material is another top consideration for either stand hunting or stalking. Today, we have a great selection of soft, quiet, durable materials, as well as a host of camouflage patterns from which to choose.

Speaking of camo patterns for a moment, here's a thought to take into account. Early in the season when there is still plenty of cover, tree stand hunters actually can get away with just about any of the fine camo patterns available. Later, when all the leaves have fallen, it's a different matter. Darker designs are going to appear as alien blobs against a clear winter sky, easily noticeable to suspicious late-season deer. Lighter, more broken patterns are the answer now. Styles like ASAT, Predator and even some of the snow camo patterns blend into the sparse background much better. For stalking, color shades that match the terrain in the large, broken pattern elements blend well.

One of the most important clothing items is what you put on your feet. I have seen some really uncomfortable disasters as a result of ignoring top quality footwear. Sure, good boots are expensive, but a good pair will give you many seasons of reliable service. I have several pairs of boots that have served me well for a decade; amortizing their original high dollar cost over ten years is a solid investment. It's lot better than you'll get from a new pickup truck!

Mild weather footwear selection isn't nearly as critical in terms of comfort as what you put on your feet when it gets downright cold. For hunting conditions that do not require excellent gripping soles — high-country mule deer, sheep or goats, for example — I have always preferred soft rubber soles

This is Dougherty's quick dispenser of scent. In an empty film canister, he places cotton and adds a scent. When it is needed, he hangs the canister in a tree and removes the cap.

on my boots, or the flexible leather soles of my moccasins. Sure-footed Vibram soles are great for clambering over rocks where a slip could be dangerous in the high country, but they are difficult to slip around in without sounding exactly like a human being trying to slip around.

Keeping your feet comfortable in mild weather isn't hard in a well fitting pair of boots or the lightweight hunting shoes so popular today, provided they have sturdy ankle and arch support.

It is different, though, when the weather turns around and gets breath-fogging cold; when your hunting strategy is devoted to one-place tactics like tree stands where there is no protection from the cold that comes at you from everywhere and always seems to start at your feet. You quickly become aware of your toes.

There are a lot of really fine cold weather boots on the market. The problem with most of them is weight and bulk. If you have to walk in them for any distance, your feet will begin to sweat. Once on the stand, motionless feet begin to chill as the accumulated moisture cools. It doesn't take long for your toes to react and send complaining messages to the rest of your body.

Another thing that bothers me about oversize boots on tree stands is the lack of feel because of the bulk. No matter how familiar with a tree stand you might be, your toes are always thinking subconsciously about contact with the edges. In bulky boots, this edge-attitude can be lost and that can be dangerous.

I have come up with a pretty fair solution to cold weather stand hunting. I walk in wearing a pair of lightly insulated rubber-bottom boots, which helps in minimizing my scent line. When I arrive at the stand's location, I remove the boots and place them in a plastic bag, effectively sealing off their scent. I then put on a fresh pair of dry wool socks and a pair of custom-made sheepskin-lined moccasins that are slightly oversize. I keep them well oiled and waxed, which seals off moisture penetration. Soft as a baby blanket, they are soundless. I don't make any noise in them when shifting my feet on those glorious frosty fall mornings that are oftentimes as still as death, and my toes can feel exactly where they are.

When temperatures get seriously cold, I drop air-activated heat packs in each moccasin. I use the Grabber brand, which offers a specially designed toe pack that sticks in position on the sock. My feet haven't been cold on a stand in quite a few seasons. They help me stay longer on tough days in relative comfort, maximizing my chances for a shot.

No matter what style of boot you choose, I'd recommend you take a look at adding some of these heat-pack warmers to your list of supplies. Besides the toe warmers, heat packs are available in pocket models for the hands. They're usually good for three to five hours. Larger style warmers generally designed for sleeping bags I have found really effective when positioned at the small of the back on dreadfully cold mornings. Keeping your kidney area warm is another step to cold weather comfort. They are among the items added to my list of day pack essentials as the season progresses.

Like bulky insulated boots, too much heavy clothing on a

A pistol-grip plastic bottle is a quick and effective way to dispense scents. Be sure to pack carefully to prevent leakage.

walk to your stand on a frosty morning can be counter-productive by overheating you in short order.

Dress as lightly as you can for the walk. Carry your warm outer layers separately and put them on after you reach your hunting location, first taking a moment to cool off.

One of the greatest heat dispensers is your head. If the weather is not too tough, try to avoid wearing your hat on the trip to the stand. Overheating when walking to a stand is a potentially dangerous situation that could result in a vulnerable, run-down condition that triggers winter colds, flu and even hypothermia. Stay comfortable when going to your stand. Walk slowly and allow for some cool-down time when you get there. With appropriate heavy clothing, prepare to meet the conditions once you have arrived.

You have probably heard a hundred times about layering your clothing. Believe this excellent advice, which is exactly what we are talking about on this walking to your stand business. Layer it on, layer it off. What you don't need goes in the day pack.

There are a couple of more items that go in to my day pack when I am off on a hunt that's more exotic than a close-to-the-truck trek or local deer camp. One is a minor first-aid kit consisting of a few gauze compresses, a roll of adhesive tape, a small bottle of iodine, some aspirin, a folded piece of aluminum foil and a few bullion cubes. These items handle quick-fix first aid for a cut, a minor pain reliever, bullion cubes if I am stuck someplace with nothing at all to eat. All of this is tucked into a zip-lock bagged tin cup I can use to heat water

for the bullion. On several occasions, this has been really handy stuff to have along.

In a 35mm plastic film cannister, I store several fish hooks, a few split shot, a couple of all-purpose fishing flies and a length of six-pound monofilament line. Actually emergency stuff, it has provided welcome pleasure on many hunts when I stumbled across a tiny stream or out of the way beaver pond and became tantalized with what might be living there. A pair of eight- to ten-inch brook trout baked on the coals of a small mid-day fire in the tinfoil makes for a memorable day. Every time I do it, though, I wish for a bit of salt. I guess I should add some to the kit.

Each and every one of you will have to make a list of what seems important for the type of hunting you plan to do. My list might seem long, but it's simple, covering essentials without any real frills. Altogether, I suspect we might all carry too much afield. Admittedly, there are some things I could do without. On the other hand, it's easy enough to store them in a day pack, which I enjoy having with me.

On more than one occasion I've had something in my day pack that a bowhunting buddy needed: the adhesive tape, something with which to mark a blood trail, a piece of rope or the solution to a very dull knife.

All of this is a matter of individual preference. Years ago, a bow, a few arrows, flint, steel and a handful of corn meal was enough for our continent's original bowhunters, but that's no fun. Toys for Boys — the essential ones — are much more exciting!

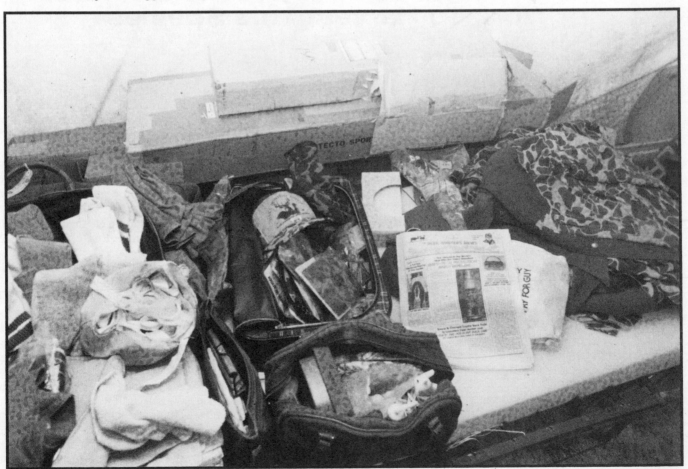

Yes, there must be a kitchen sink in there somewhere. Most hunters take too much gear to the field, most of it unnecessary.

CHAPTER 10

MULE DEER: A STUDY IN TOUGH

He's Hardy And Savvy. Plan On Hard Work To Harvest This Species

AS MENTIONED, I began my deer bowhunting career in Southern California. We hunted mule deer, one of the seven or eight generally recognized sub-species. Products of their environment — thick chaparral, manzanita, chemise and scrub and live oak — they were quite small in stature. We didn't realize how small, until we began expanding our bowhunting horizons to Arizona, Utah, Idaho and Nevada where an average buck tipped the scales at twice the weight, some almost triple, of those we had taken in our home environs.

There were a lot of deer in Southern California then. There also were substantial herds in the other states mentioned. Heavy-beamed old-timers with spreads in excess of twenty-nine inches were common sights, interspersed with run-of-the-mill twenty-two to twenty-four inchers. These seemed highly acceptable to us, but wouldn't rate even an idle glance from the locals, bow kill or otherwise.

It's safe to state things are not the same big buck-wise these days. Habitat decimation is the major cause, though poor management resulting in overkill in the beginning led to the decline in trophy mule deer. Not that there are not areas with good bucks still available, and it should be stated that response to the problem led to a change in management strategies. Still, the days of seeing dozens of high, wide-racked muleys in relatively easy to reach places are over.

As mentioned in another chapter, statistically the odds of collecting a Pope & Young-class mule deer today are ex-

tremely long. While the Coues deer may well be the toughest to actually take, the percentage of book heads seen and tried for is significantly higher than are true trophy bucks in mule deer country today.

Given all this rather dismal news, it is, strangely enough, the bowhunter who probably still has the best chance to take a good mule deer. This is based on the timing of most archery mule deer seasons — late August to early September — when the deer are frequenting more open summer range. Generally, they travel in bachelor groups, according to size, though mixed age classes are common enough. More or less following established movement patterns, they will maintain these until they shed their glistening velvet, and the commotion pressures of October gun season send them to scattered hiding. They are as relaxed — within reason — as they ever will be.

One factor regarding the increasing odds of collecting a record class mule deer is worth noting. The issue of velvet-covered antlers is one over which the Pope & Young Club has anguished for years. The established criteria for measuring dictates hard, polished antlers as set by the Boone & Crockett Club, the rules of which have been followed largely by P&Y. Today, Pope & Young accepts mule deer with velvet antlers in a separate category.

This concession — which as a board member, I fought for personally — seems only just when we consider the time of year during which most mule deer are taken by bowmen. That it has made sense in terms of entries is pointed out at the mid-

Here is an outstanding mule deer buck. Deer like this are among the most difficult of all bowhunting trophies to collect.

point of the current eighteenth recording period, December 31, 1991, wherein seventy-two typical velvet muleys have been entered, but a velvet trophy cannot be accepted as the all-time world record. It must be stripped.

It's a fine step, in my opinion, allowing us to accept outstanding trophies without penalty; trophies that certainly epitomize what late-summer mule deer hunting is all about.

Emphasis on managing mule deer has changed the way we have to go about it. Simply driving out West and purchasing an over-the-counter license on the way to the high country is almost a thing of the past. In Colorado, bowhunters still can buy over-the-counter licenses, though I suspect the days are numbered. Pre-season applications for limited, controlled or general licenses are the order today. Each year, the application forms from various states become increasingly involved. You

have to fill them out properly, send them in early — and cross your fingers.

I suggest it still is not difficult to obtain a non-resident mule deer tag and load up for the West, expecting a reasonable chance to shoot a small buck or doe. For many, that's more than enough incentive for an enjoyable hunting trip. Big bucks are another story.

Young bucks and doe/fawn family groups can be found at easily accessible levels of the summer range, frequenting shaded aspen groves adjacent to sage flats, willow-shrouded creeks and adjacent to summer alfalfa farming. The occasional big deer or two might be around, though the first suggestion of sudden hunting pressures will move them quickly.

Big bucks — the biggest and best — are going to be found at the higher elevations, in isolated out-of-the-way niches

This is perfect mule deer country. The terrain is open with clusters of thick cover. There's a lot of rugged country to explore.

where they can spend the summer in lazy contemplation as their antlers finish out and dry in the clear summer air. These bucks take physical effort to locate, careful reconnoitering to close with — and not much pressure to spook out of the country!

To me, the absolute epitomy of bowhunting is in stalking mule deer: watching them from afar, setting a game plan and moving on them along the course of their normal routine in hopes of intercepting or dealing with a buck, or making it one-on-one when he beds in a spot that makes him appear vulnerable to a careful approach.

This is a game of cat and mouse filled with dry-mouth anticipation where a successful outcome is solely up to you. It requires quiet clothes and boots, stocking feet over the last fifty yards, careful, up-close scrutiny through good optics. Sometimes, the closer you get, the harder they are to see, and a great deal of patience is required. I have shot several bucks in their beds under settings like that. Such successful stalks rank high in my memory of bowhunting victories.

Teamwork can play a big role in successfully stalking mule deer. An observer positioned to signal from the across the canyon — a terrain factor so common in mule deer country — can direct the stalker. The latter loses perspective after circling. His teammate can signal that he should move right or left, press or sit. With experience, such teamwork becomes a deadly tactic and one of my favorites.

One of the best proven techniques for mule deer — more

often associated with whitetails — is tree stand hunting. Savvy bowhunters have found that packing along a portable stand is likely to be as effective as the bow. Many of the West's premier outfitters, who have the luxury of large tracts of property under their control, hunt tree stand almost exclusively with dynamite results.

Having the benefit of careful scouting, they know their deer and what they are doing. It allows them to manage the hunting pressure carefully, keeps deer disturbance to a minimum and puts on the ground a high percentage of the good bucks we hear about today. Freelance hunters can do the same, and more and more are, with similar results.

Water is a premium consideration in late August mule deer hunting. I have an acquaintance who has taken four record class mule deer in the last four seasons from portable tree stands that were positioned to cover water sources. He used to be a dyed-in-the-wool spot and stalker, a game he claims he misses, but, as he pointed out, "These are hard results to beat!"

One thing is for sure: The tree stand will give you the best shooting opportunity, for slipping around on muley is a tough game. Even when you have done it pretty well, something probably will go wrong. Another deer spots you, a rock slips, the wind swirls. Any of these can alert the deer, offering the hunter only a quick chance in the split-second moment of indecision. When you have both feet on the ground, shots on these big-eared rascals are frequently on the long side. I have shot a ton of them at between fifty and sixty yards. Being able

Most mule deer bowhunting seasons in the Western states occur when bucks are still wearing velvet-covered antlers.

to judge distance quickly and possessing the familiarity and confidence to make longer shots is something newcomers to mule deer hunting should consider in their pre-hunt planning and practice.

Mule deer habitat being what it is — open country with vast sage flats, open side hills adjacent to stands of aspen or clumps of conifer — scouting for them is really a long-range looking situation rather than the careful walk-and-look-closely scouting routine employed for the whitetail. In summer, deer follow the declining shadows of morning and the stretch of afternoon as they move out to feed. Thus, they are quite easy to locate, which affords insight as to good hunting locations. In this situation, one actually sees the deer, whereas with much whitetail country, you might be hunting a buck you've never seen, simply by sign alone.

It takes a mule deer scoring a minimum of 145 inches to make the Pope & Young records, a score of 185 to make Boone & Crockett. When mule deer are in the velvet, their antlers often look much bigger than they actually are. Deer also are slimmer in appearance in summer coats, which adds to the illusion.

When trying to size up a trophy deer, remember that his main beams must at least equal in width the tips of his ears with a height that appears to be close to one-half the spread. That's ballpark, but you can bet that anything less will fall short.

Obviously, there are other considerations, not counting the eye guard or brow point, which needs to be considered in sizing up the rest. The muley must have four points to a side, counting the main beam. For a long while, I had the highest scoring three-point mule deer on the records. A buck that was missing one point on both sides, he scored in the mid-150s. With G-4s present that equaled what he had, he would have been a 175-class buck.

As a rule, a three-pointer will not make the book. Incidentally, there is some confusion on how antler points are counted in the West. A buck in Utah referred to as a four-point is really a ten-point by eastern count. In the West, for reasons known only to the keepers of tradition, I guess, only the top points on the side with the most are counted. In the eastern part of the country, we count them all, which I think makes a great deal more sense. My three-point is actually an eight-pointer. Beginning with the brow points he has four on a side, the tip of the main beam always counting as a point.

Good mule deer hunting is not restricted to what we commonly call the West, meaning the states I mentioned earlier, along with New Mexico. Washington and Oregon have excellent mule deer on their eastern slopes. Nebraska has muleys, as does Kansas. We have a few in western Oklahoma and the last one I shot was on a river-bottom deer drive in South Dakota.

Mule deer and whitetail ranges overlap from eastern Colorado across Nebraska into the Dakotas with an increasing

Tree stands in high mountain quaking aspen groves have become popular with hunters seeking the hardy mule deer.

Using techniques and patience that made him famous, Fred Bear stalked this record-class mule deer in the early Sixties.

incidence of interbreeding. I'm told the whitetail is dominate in these cases, which is probably another thorn in the mule deer's struggle. I have seen mixed mule deer and whitetail herds on alfalfa fields in Idaho where years ago no one knew what a whitetail was. The same is true for Colorado. Conditions today favor the whitetail, a deer I truly love, though I hate to see him pushing in on the mule deer.

Of all the ways I have hunted mule deer, the still hunt/drive combination has been one of the most effective. The country has to be right. Relatively level benches covered with aspen are good examples of the type of terrain to push at mid-day on bedded deer.

Arizona's Kiabab Plateau was a perfect place for this technique when I hunted there in the Sixties. It would still work there today, I'm sure.

Topo maps are an important aid in laying out the campaign which requires a group of sneaking still hunters who slip along, looking for a shot. A group of standers waits at points where flushed deer are expected.

This is kind of an any-deer-is-okay hunt, good for family and group hunt vacations where mom and the kids get involved. Sure, there's always the chance a big buck might be involved. He'll come flying out of there, looking as big as a horse, running right over someone in the process. They make for great campfire conversation.

Still hunters actually move with the wind on these semi-drives, while the standers have to be on the downwind side.

It's difficult to push big bucks this way, another reason not to expect one. It's not so difficult, though, to move younger, less experienced deer. Driving whitetails in the same manner is a common practice, and it is equally effective on mule deer. It's well worth a try.

If you feel especially tough, there are some fine mule deer opportunities available in late season or in post-season hunts. Idaho has several prime winter hunts. Arizona's late season, which offers bowhunters mule deer, Coues deer and javelina in the same terrain, is excellent.

Winter hunts like Idaho's can be demanding. Steep snow-covered mountains and extremely cold temperatures make them an exercise in teeth-gritting tenacity. Your chances for seeing some exceptional deer, however, are outstanding. Big solitary bucks — the ones the old-timers call "rock eaters" — appear on the steep rutting slopes of winter, drawn by the timeless urge to mate. They are vulnerable, though the eyes of the alert does and the rugged terrain protect them well.

If you're a hard-core mule deer hunter, researching late season hunts is one of today's best trophy opportunities.

Given only one choice for as long as I'm physically up to the task, more than anything else, I would rather spend my deer bowhunting days somewhere up in the late summer high country, right next to the sky, looking for another big mule deer to stalk.

There is something about the mule deer and his summer home up there in the clouds that's special!

Taking A Mammoth Mule Deer Is As Much Luck As Following The Rules

THE SOUND of a loose rock sliding made me jerk my head around, throwing my eyes uphill. The big buck was standing at the top of the hill looking, it appeared, right at me. I was nine feet or so up the side of an eighteen-inch aspen that grew on a little bench below the crest of the hill. From the buck's vantage point, I was about as concealed as a bowling ball on a white sheet.

I don't normally hunt mule deer from tree stands, but this was a natural. In the three mornings I had perched there, no less than forty deer had filtered by, all of them passing along the bench that paralleled the ridge top where Mr. Big now stood. Not a single deer of any gender had approached from the top. Something about Murphy's Law flashed through my head, as I hugged the skinny aspen and swallowed rapidly in an effort to get my heart back down where it belonged.

For an eternity of a few seconds, the buck stared down into the aspen grove. Then, unbelievably, he started down, coming straight toward me.

Hunting mule deer with a bow is a challenge that has bested many a hearty soul who have dreamed of taking a trophy buck.

For the past ten days, I had been skulking around this lovely portion of northwestern Colorado and having the time of my life. I was hunting with Jay Verzuh, who runs an outfit named Colorado Elite. Jay's hunting country contains just the right mixture of habitat types to make it superb mule deer range. With its easy access from the upper elevations to the low country, the mule deer here had not suffered as severely during past harsh winters as had other herds. The results: lots of carry-over, lots of bucks.

I love to hunt mule deer. I cut my bowhunting teeth on muleys and consider them one of the most superb animals on God's earth. Now I was in some of the finest country on that same earth, and for the most part, I had been covered with bucks.

Unfortunately, I was greedy. I had come to Verzuh's in full knowledge of the quality of the bucks to be found in his area. I had made up my mind that for a change, for an entire hunt, it would be a real buster or nothing. For a good many years, I had been neglecting the muleys; chasing something else somewhere. Maybe I'd take a little buck in passing while concentrating on elk, most often not even bothering, or more likely missing when I decided to do one in. The time had come to rectify my delinquent attitude with a full-scale assault. I greedily locked the minimum of 165 Pope & Young points into my mind and proceeded accordingly.

Jay's hunting country sits on a little flat that overlooks a vast expanse of the mesa tight beneath a conifer-covered hill, the base of which gives birth to a pure, ice-cold spring. The main cabin's a rustic revamped relic of older, tougher days

Dougherty doesn't often hunt mule deer from a tree stand, but the thick aspens of northwestern Colorado were ideal for eyeing a passing parade of muleys. Then came Mr. Big!

Not the normal field tent, the Indian tipi proved warm and cozy for bowhunters seeking mulies in Colorado.

restored to a snug shelter possessing considerable charm. There were outlying wall tents for overflow sleeping beyond the cabin, that can comfortably house up to ten hunters.

The kitchen area constantly offers up tantalizing smells mixed with a base of freshly brewed coffee supervised by a lovely Louisianan, a Cajun lady named Jeanne. She has the neatest accent you have ever heard and a talent for making magic in a covey of huge kettles.

Verzuh organizes the hunting with the tactical approach of a professional who knows every inch of his hunting area and has an extremely thorough knowledge of the habits of the game. You can do it any way you want, but his most consistent success comes from the strategically placed stands he has scattered about, each one placed by application of his personal expertise.

When it comes to mule deer, I'm a walking-sneaking sort

Sure enough, just when you've positioned yourself for the best shot, you're visited from the off side by curious deer.

of hunter. I enjoy covering country, figuring it out, and I get the biggest kick in the world out of managing to get within close range of a critter that possesses some of the finest eyes to be found among our big-game animals.

In camp were two old friends who like to do it the same way: G. Fred Asbell from Colorado, then president of the Pope & Young Club and Bob Pitt from Indiana. Long-time running buddies, these two are among the finest mule deer hunters who ever nocked an arrow.

There was a fine bunch of Texans in camp, an old acquaintance from Alabama, a new friend from Wisconsin and a Yankee lawyer from New York who had his hands full with all the Rebels. There were experienced mule deer hunters and some who had never seen one. Quite a few had been here before, and everyone was primed, cocked and ready.

As so often happens in September throughout the Rockies, the weather can dampen you, freeze you or burn you up, as the unsettling effects of the equinox begin. My first morning of sneaking about became a sodden affair, beginning with a light drizzle just after daylight when I spotted a pair of nice bucks polishing their antlers on a scruffy little oak bush. It turned into a deluge that made them impossible to see at one hundred yards through my binoculars.

Small stands of aspen offer little cover from a full-blown thundershower. I retired from the field with everything dampened but my spirits. Then came the wind, surging from the south, just short of a gale force. While I detest wind for almost everything but waterfowl shooting and kite flying, it does provide a superb opportunity to practice the game of still-hunting.

Sooner or later, even when the wind is blowing, the deer will get up to feed. Even when bedded, they can be located if you carefully hunt the right sort of cover. The wind covers the noise of your approach. You do not have the swirling, unpredictable effects of calmer days and blowing leaves punctuated intermittently with falling branches, giving the slow-moving hunter additional cover. If you are careful, you can get close as Asbell did, and shoot a nice three-by-four in its bed at close range. That, my friends, is satisfying.

Rudy Wilkinson from Texas has great affection for hunting at Verzuh's, but he doesn't get in much time at it. On his last hunt, he killed a buster of a buck on the first morning in the first minutes. This day, the afternoon of his first, he did it again with a fine, heavily beamed old-timer that piled up within sight. Ah well, there were always chores he could do around camp while everyone else continued hunting.

At this time of the year, the bucks are still fairly well bunched up. It is not uncommon to see fifteen or twenty easing along together; it is routine to see five or six. Earlier, before the antler rubbing begins, Jay Verzuh has seen thirty to forty-five bucks traveling along pretty much together, their velvet-cased antlers looking three times the real size. I was somewhat disappointed that all the velvet was gone. Mule deer in velvet just have a look about them that fascinates me. It's deceptive though, if one wants to really look bucks over and try to accurately estimate the scoring potential. Hard horns are better.

Earlier-season velvet bucks can be easier to hunt, however, primarily because they are easier to locate during this period.

I was seeing plenty of bucks. I still-hunted and I plunked my butt in some of the stands. The first morning I sat in a stand that was stunning. It was like one of those John Ford Westerns

Fred Asbell (left) and Rudy Wilkinson took these fine high-county mule deer during the Colorado hunt. Habitat and heredity contribute to producing the excellent high antlers which are typical for the mule deer that thrive in northwestern Colorado.

where The Duke is standing there all squinty-eyed, staring off at the horizon with his Winchester dangling from his hand and his Stetson pulled low. Suddenly 400,000 Comanches crest the horizon all at once to glare down at Wayne and his beleaguered party of pilgrims.

I was in a tree stand just below the crest of a sage-studded flat. It was sort of an awkward spot, because the stand placed me just below eye level with the horizon, but there was cover and the place was stiff with sign. I had taken my eyes off the horizon to look elsewhere, and upon casting them back, I nearly died as a sea of antlers from left to right hove into view. I was carrying a Hoyt/Easton compound and wondered fleetingly if it would switch to full-automatic.

There were several nice bucks in that band. They filtered off the flat, slipping by me on all sides, while I tried to sort through them, doing some geometric spinning on the platform at half-draw.

It was incredible. It was stupid. I was suffering from a case of the goofies. There were some bucks in that bunch; several into the 150s and what am I doing but sitting up there like a dodo thinking I'm Teddy Trophy Hunter. Well, I had bitten this ridiculous bullet and my teeth were really hurtin'.

This went on frequently. I was keeping track. In the first eight days, I counted ninety-seven bucks. Sure, I saw some of them over again, but the point is, I was sighting more than twelve bucks a day. Most of them were, nice, respectable, four-point bucks. That is exciting!

The weather yo-yo'd around like it was more confused than I. The aspens went mostly from green to gold and the cover fell

in those ten days. A few hold-outs in the draws maintained a fragile hold on a life already ended. Fall was coming quickly now. We had spitting snow and freezing rain, but the bucks were cooperating.

There was some mighty fine venison accumulating on the camp meat pole. It was a happy camp with good cooking, good people. Pitt's Bloody Marys eased the kinks in worn-out joints and no one was getting too upset, because they hadn't scored while someone else had. Jeanne smiled every morning at 4 a.m., while Arnie Gurule, Verzuh's right-hand man, never missed a lick, having everything ready to go. Jay Verzuh organized some drives during midday lulls that turned out to be real Wild West shows. Larry Hazen from Wisconsin nailed one of the prettiest, big three-by-threes you ever saw.

It was somewhat along toward the tenth day or so that fate finally threw me and a big old rock-eater together and I got my chance. At the top of a long aspen-choked draw, there was a small sage flat tucked in a corner where another timberline intersects the draw. Slipping along slowly, just inside the trees where I could watch down the draw as well as the little flat, I noticed something in the sage that was not just not quite right. Through the glasses, I could see it was part of a deer with its head down. When the head came up, I knew I was onto a good one.

It was a perfect stalking situation, the wind blowing briskly straight into my face, with plenty of cover for me. The buck, actively feeding in the high sage, had his vision obscured most of the time. He was an honest-to-God Big-Big with plenty of width, length and mass; all the good stuff in all the right places.

Things progressed well up to about forty-five yards, Then a doe stood up to stare at me halfway between us. I was getting that up-and-down head-jerking action, the one that goes with those mincing little half-steps in your direction, designed to make you prove you're something bad up to no good.

The buck eased into an opening, becoming all at once aware of the doe and her problem. He watched her intently and I decided to shoot him where he stood.

There is a moment when you release an arrow that you feel everything is going to be right. At the mid-range trajectory, your brain signals *touchdown*. At that point, the apex of the yellow-fletched shaft's flight, at that precise spot where it starts to dip down into the target area of the chest, I said "gotcha" to myself. But the shaft did not fall off that last little remaining bit. It just sustained itself lazily along a path that, with a little puff of hair, told me I had just touched the buck's back.

He stopped at the edge of the distant woodline, maybe eighty yards away, to give his back trail a look to see what had startled the Billyhell out of him. I came to full draw again, held, trying to sort out the proper feel, then let down.

That night, I had several Bloody Marys. To make me feel worse, the buck had run up over the mountain to where Verzuh was driving down the ridge. He figured this one with his practiced eye as about 175 inches of record book entry.

I have missed more big mule deer than any other ten people you may know or have heard of. I'm getting used to it, but it does not make it easier.

The chase continued. I frequented the little sage flat several evenings, hoping we would cross trails again. We did, but I could never get within sixty-five yards. I don't like to shoot at them that far.

Bob Pitt and Fred Asbell departed. Pitt willed me an area he was hunting just over the ridge where the flats started to drop off into major canyon country.

It was here I found that little bench where the deer were coming around the mountain to their bedding ground on the canyon sidehill. I slipped in there one morning and saw twelve bucks in one bunch; three were dandies.

It was a natural for a portable stand, so Verzuh and I eased back in there midday to put one up. There were six bucks there when we arrived. This was *the* place. Deer came by me beginning at first light the next morning. By 8:15, the parade was pretty much over.

On this, the fourth morning, I had passed on three little bucks, a pair of little three-bys and a so-so four-point that might have gone 135. I had, however, lowered my sworn-to minimum by at least ten inches. I am only human and can subject myself to only so much abuse.

It was now that the big buck was coming off the hill while I tried to bury myself in the aspen. As he came lower and closer, each step bringing him into a more completely level position, I couldn't even move my hand to the bow handle just inches away. Then he stopped to pick around some snowberry brush, just fiddling about, looking for some last-minute pre-nap snack. I got my hand on my bow, gently easing it up off the little branch stump that was holding it with the arrow already nocked. He turned and looked right toward me, it seemed. It was terrible. Bows, even lightweight, sweet little bows, weigh heavily under such conditions. Nothing goes as smoothly as it should. You know the deer can see your eyes and read your thoughts. You absolutely *know* that he can hear your breathing and sense your trembling muscles.

Then he dropped his head and took a few more ambling steps to a point that was just about level-perfect with my stand. He spied another tasty morsel, just slightly uphill. He had to have it. To get to it, he fully extended himself, turning slightly in a way that threw open wide the doors to the old twenty ring.

I don't know how far away he was; not very. He was an almost perfectly formed, high-reaching, typical mule deer with sufficient mass to indicate maturity and a rolling walk that promised lots of steaks. He was in my pocket and I was about to get in his. He was history.

All that was left to do was lean my weight out against my rope and bust him with my eyes closed. That's exactly what I did. Almost.

I thought for a minute the bow had broken. The arrow went straight up, I think. The three remaining broadheads in my quiver clattered down, along with the arrow that had the rubber blunt and my right arm felt like it was broken. The buck jumped straight up, swapped ends and saw me when he landed facing me. His eyes just got bigger and bigger, then he left.

One limb, that stuck out above my head at right angles to the tree for a foot or so before it turned up, had this little tiny bump on it, right at the bend. Picture a wart on your elbow and you have the picture. Picture your bow quiver slamming into the little wart and you have the entire picture. It was not pretty.

It was not the deer's fault, nor was it the weather's fault. Certainly, it was not Jay Verzuh's fault. It was probably my fault that I didn't leave the Colorado Elite with a trophy mule deer, but I prefer to think the blame lies elsewhere.

I looked through my little field notebook and noticed an entry that says, "Saw twenty-three deer this morning, eleven bucks. Had a really nice four-by-four at ten yards, maybe 145 inches. Probably should have shot him."

Well, I probably should have tried.

Incidentally, Jay Verzuh can be contacted at Colorado Elite, 658 Young Street, Grand Junction, CO 81505.

Outfitter Jay Verzuh knows his hunting area and runs an excellent operation for bowhunters looking for trophy deer.

CHAPTER 11

THE EXCITING WHITETAIL

This Species Sets The Heart Thumping For A Nation Of Bowhunters!

Discovering the location and daily movements of whitetails is part of the excitement of bowhunting.

Many bowhunters dream of tagging a trophy whitetail. This beauty was taken in the wild country of Montana.

WHITETAIL DEER come in a wide variety of sizes, ranging from the huge specimens of Canada and our north central states to the diminutive little critter found in the Florida Keys. They are found over almost all of the entire United States. Alaska doesn't have any, nor do Utah, California or Nevada, though, at the rate they are expanding their range that is liable to change in time.

I have seen whitetails in southern Mexico where they are not very big but are common, and subspecies exist deep into South America. Many states that had little or none twenty-five years ago have outstanding whitetail hunting today. Restocking and good management programs are largely responsible, though the deer itself is pushing out strongly from much of its historical range.

Unlike the mule deer, whitetails thrive in proximity to man's agricultural efforts and can survive handily in a restricted environment. I have hunted them in places of vast, lonely emptiness, and last season I shot a buck at the edge of an industrial complex where I heard a guy answer a phone from my stand.

The Pope & Young Club lumps all of the whitetail subspecies into one category, except for the Coues. The same is true of the Boone & Crockett Club, although Safari Club International (SCI) has made an attempt to differentiate them on a rather sketchy geographic basis. This has taken place over the years — one state trading deer to another for turkeys, for example — subspecies purity goes out the window. I suspect the way it's being done by Pope & Young is best. It's cleaner, certainly, and easier to manage.

It is possible to live and hunt in an area where the chance for a record class buck is almost nonexistent. It takes two

The business end of the arrow must be razor sharp. Some hunters use blade inserts to ensure a proper cutting edge.

ing cicadas is about two steps from driving me nuts. I want summer to be over; gone. I wish for an early winter, but not a harsh one. Early winter means early fall, open windows with real air and the passing of summer's squalling bugs. I think about cool fall days, autumn leaves, hunting strategies and whitetail places a lot as the summer wears me down. The fun and the promise come just in time.

Early-season whitetail hunting in Oklahoma, like most places probably, is not exactly what we have been day-dreaming about. The weather is still warm, though the mornings and evenings will be getting cooler. You know true fall is coming, it's just not here yet. Late summer scouting has put you in touch with some bucks. If you are lucky, you might have a good one figured out. If you do, your chances of killing him on an early-season pattern are perhaps the best you will have.

In early October, bucks are still hanging out in bachelor bands. These can be mixed herds consisting of several age classes. Usually, in my experience, the bigger, older bucks keep together in small batches of two to five, while younger deer wander in larger groups.

Last season, in early October, I had one gang of thirteen bucks ranging from little fork-horns to mediocre eight-pointers all located in my hunting area. These deer were almost

Dougherty has studied the habits of deer. Knowing the food source for whitetail can give a bowhunter an edge. Here's Dougherty with a respectable buck. This whitetail is not big enough for the record book, but it is big enough.

things to make big bucks: genetics and age. A healthy diet helps, too. There are many places with excellent deer populations where these elements — collectively or in part — simply do not exist, or do not exist at a level that will generate record class heads meeting minimum scores of 100, 125, or in the case of B&C, 170 points. If you are unaware, 170 is huge!

This is the basic reason SCI attempted to break down the whitetail record-keeping structure into minimum score elements that seem to fit geographic potential.

All in all, it strikes me as rather a mess. No one is interested in shooting big whitetails more than I, but I do not treat it as an obsession. I am simply obsessed with deer hunting and having a helluva lot of fun doing it.

Most of us who live in whitetail country today are blessed with extremely liberal archery seasons, some running as long as four months; most are on the long side of two. When we compare our hunting time to the average gun season, bowhunters are fortunate indeed.

In my mind, I think about the coming season and break it down into thirds. Within those thirds, from October through December, the whitetails we hunt will change personalities and habits several times.

THE FIRST THIRD

By the time fall arrives, summer has completely lost what little appeal it has for me. Generally, the fish have quit biting some time ago and it's too hot and sticky to find out if they've changed their minds. The incessant hum of compressors spewing synthetically chilled air in poor harmony with screech-

Even a beginning bowhunter should be able to recognize that the bark of this sapling was removed by a rubbing buck. Such signs help a bowhunter locate whitetail activity and stand sites. Then comes the tough part of whitetail hunting: waiting.

always together. Occasionally, I would see only some of them, five or six, but the entire band was never too far apart.

As fall pressed closer and early signs of breeding activity began to show, these deer began to scatter. The four smallest bucks, identical forked-horns, stayed together through mid-November, when I'm sure they all were taken during gun season.

My strategy for early season is based almost entirely on food sources. This is a time of voracious feeding for bucks intent on bulking up before the rutting period. My stands are either along direct routes to and from primary feeding grounds or smack-dab in the middle of heavy sources of deer groceries. Deer are quite predictable at this time of year. The thirteen bucks were systematic in their movement, passing over the same route in a punctual, careless routine. There were five eight-points in the band; I could have killed any one of them. I did shoot one. It didn't alter their routine in the slightest. They were all back on schedule the following day.

If acorns are the prime food source, I prefer to hunt mast concentrations. There is usually good cover for stand locations among the leafy oaks. Deer rummaging for acorns are extremely intent while searching for nuts buried in the clutter of leaves and ground cover. This occupation increases their vulnerability. The scuffling, snuffling quest among the leaves is quite noisy, often alerting me to their arrival before I see them. The gentlest breeze rattles oak leaves with a clattering rustle that causes the forest canopy to move and shake, providing cover for any slight movement or noise required to shoot.

Early-season deer are not difficult to locate, feeding in open meadows. Agricultural plots of wheat, soybeans or alfalfa draw them like nails to a magnet.

They can be spotted with regularity approaching these locations in the evening. Sometimes, if you are early enough, you will catch them still in the open in the morning. If you stay late and have good binoculars, you might see some large bucks step out just as the last glow of sundown ebbs and the day dies.

A bowhunter can shoot a lot of whitetails in the vicinity of cultivated crops. They love 'em and will not forsake them even as hunting pressure hardens. What they will do is change their feeding timetable, becoming nocturnal in their visits.

When this happens, hunting the immediate perimeters in hopes of downing a good buck is mostly wishful thinking. For sure, does, fawns and naive juvenile bucks will still make legal-shooting-hour appearances, but not the big guys. You can find them there, though.

If spotlighting is legal for checking on deer in your area, go back two hours after dark and take a look. They will be there then, out in the middle, chowing down, standing stark in the light with their eyes glowing hot blue-green. They are easy pickings for the outlaws with lights and rifles. Too often they are shot where they stand, staring back, never hearing the fatal crack of the high-power. We lose too many big bucks, too many deer that way.

If bigger bucks are what you are after, stay back from the perimeters of the croplands. Studied scouting, not casual strolls, will reveal the prime runs from distant bedding grounds — sometimes surprisingly distant — to these feeding areas.

Locating whitetails usually means first locating their signs. Here, fresh droppings are mixed with those of a cottontail. A hunter will note the difference in size, shape and color.

Afternoon stands placed well back on these trails are better bets for collecting hunter-wise bucks that will not often step into the open in the full light of day.

MID-SEASON — THE WILD TIME

Along about the first of November, no matter where you are in whitetail country, folks start to look and talk a little different. By now, there has been a frost or two kicking loose a golden barrage of falling leaves that swirl in rattling gusts through the woods, pushed around by the winds that are becoming more and more oriented from the north.

The talk is now of rubs and scrapes, of the buster of a buck no one has seen yet that tears up cedars as big as a man's leg. The rut is upon us, and nothing else fires the whitetail hunter's imagination quite as much.

Rattling antlers are pulled from cool storage closets. Old-timers prefer real antlers and give them a ritual soaking to make them less brittle. I have a friend who claims nothing less than three days is adequate.

If there is one decent piece of advice I can offer about hunting whitetails in the rut, it's easily summed up in two words: patient persistence or persistent patience. Take your pick.

If you believe in a place, one that has everything in the way of sign and gut feel tells you, "This is it!" stick with it. I'm a poor one to be handing out such advice, because I don't do it well myself, though there have been some notable exceptions.

Once, in a place I thought was very good — a Bois D' Arc thicket along a creek bottom that was literally torn to pieces and held the biggest scrape area I have ever seen — I made up my mind to hunt it all day. I saw a few deer early, but nothing very good. At 10:20 a.m., I missed a decent ten-point, because

When a well used whitetail travel route is located, it often leads to a suitable location for a tree stand or ground blind.

I clipped a hanging branch. At 3 p.m., I shot one of the best whitetails of my life. When the rut is on, and the girls are in full bloom, bucks can be looking for them all day long. Your chances of shooting the buck of your life are just as good at high noon as they are in the first dim light of morning. In fact, data collected on the subject indicates chances might even be better.

There's an old theory about whitetails that suggests they live and die within small perimeters. I have seen and read repeatedly that this life and death is confined to a square mile. There are probably some places today, surrounded by civilization, where this is perhaps true, but states like Kansas, Iowa, Nebraska, South Dakota and my own state of Oklahoma, to mention a few, have whitetails who count their range in terms of square sections, not just one. And a whitetail buck in the rut will follow his nose and instincts anywhere he thinks there's action. When bucks are moving, it may be fairly easy to find the place to hunt them. Predicting the time he'll be there is the hard part. Being there at the right time ain't easy. The best results boil down to patient persistence!

WIND

If we bowhunters who have to reduce the distance to our quarry to well under fifty yards have one adversary to contend

Dougherty is a successful bowhunter because he knows deer — their regular habits and how they react during the different hunting season phases. Here, he's taken a nice doe. Good deer management requires a doe harvest for proper herd balance.

with, one element that most consistently thwarts our efforts, what would you say that was? This question, often, is a major topic of conversation among the folks I hunt with, because they have come to fully understand the problem. But at speaking engagements and seminars, I seldom get what I consider the be the correct answer.

The most common response seems never to identify the problem properly. Instead, the answers are based on elements that are far too human: the inability to get off a shot when the chance comes around, for instance. My reference is to the cause for those countless hours when no chance is provided, the frustration after the anticipation, time spent that goes for naught, no chance being offered.

To what do we most often fail to pay proper attention? What element is always there after we have properly practiced, carefully scouted and endlessly dreamed?

The wind!

For relative newcomers, there is some excuse. Inexperience and the bombardment of advertising statements and testimonials that speak of colossal breakthroughs in product innovation lead us to believe that a deer's nose, the most effective defense mechanism in the animal kingdom, can be rendered ineffective. No way. Until one has the experience of many days afield, it is difficult, almost impossible, to understand fully just how good those noses are.

No commercial scent makes a deer's nose ineffective. Good ones play on this superb sense, and properly used, will give a hunter an edge. The only thing that can work against a deer's nose is the wind. On occasion, it can confuse it. But even the strongest of winds is no guarantee.

In the pursuit of deer we can get away with a few things from time to time. A bit too much noise, perhaps, or some slight movement may not blow a hunt. We do not always have to be camouflaged from head to toe. And even the wrong wind sometimes will confuse a young deer into a moment of fatal hesitation.

But the wind, for old deer, is a different matter. Working it right is more important than you can possibly imagine. If you do it wrong, you might not even know about it. A mature deer can smell you at an unbelievable distance, and if it does, it will simply go away. An old doe might blow an alarm; you'll hear it in the distance and wonder what spooked it without realizing it was you. At such a signal, a wise, old buck will simply disappear.

One thing I have found to be very important in sorting out the wind is a puff bottle of fine powder. Cigarette lighters are much in use, but they only show you direction up close. A puff of powder will show you exactly where the wind goes. Does it lift or drop? Does it swirl, taking a hard right angle thirty feet away? You will be surprised how often it does. Thistle down is good, too. Anything that will let you watch how the wind is truly tracking will work.

The wind is the whitetail's number one security check. Always keep that in mind.

Big Whitetails Abound In Some Corners Of The Canadian Wilds

Dougherty (right) took this whitetail on a hunt in Canada with Dave Richardson (left). The deer is large compared to the whitetail sub-species that Dougherty hunts in Oklahoma.

IN SPRING and summer, the canopy would be closed by mature trees. Even in the fall, with all the leaves carpeting the wood lot, there was the impression of a well defined, cathedral-shaped tunnel through the timber. If a person were casting about, looking for a place a whitetail would walk, he would look closely at this natural corridor.

It was one of a couple of inspiring locations my friend, Dave Richardson, and I found the first day we scouted Terry Raymond's place not too far north of Calgary, Alberta. It was the kind of place that would keep you from getting a good night's sleep.

The western border of the woodlot fell into a long north-south bottom that was thickly choked with willow, poplars and some spruce. To the north, it was bordered by a quarter-section pasture that at night, when your headlights swung across it in driving out, reflected enough bright green eyes to indicate the whitetails were having a convention. Behind the patch — which might be two hundred acres — the land fell off gently to the southeast, made up of intermittent openings and continuing patches of heavier woods. There were but a few small conifers that didn't look like a buck had beaten them up, and all the little first-growth thickets had the perimeters rubbed raw. There was an electricity to the area that generated the firm conviction that something was liable to happen.

Alberta is noted for big deer, both muleys and whitetails. With the intense hullabaloo over whitetails sweeping the land, that species seems to get the majority interest. Canadian outfitters in whitetail areas have been capitalizing on big bucks in recent years, and they have made a lot of hunters happy in the process. Alberta has been giving up good numbers of trophy bucks. While Boone & Crockett bucks are never common, they are being encountered with enough regularity to turn starry-eyed whitetail devotees down the path of eternal optimism.

Dave Richardson's not an outfitter but a really fine friend

Here's a whitetail and a shot opportunity that will excite the most seasoned bowhunter.

with whom I have shared some campfires and frequent companionship in more civilized surroundings.

It started back in '71 when I had an Alberta bighorn permit and Dave an idea where we might find one. We saw quite a few rams, some of them dandies, while climbing no small amount of vertical country under quite brisk November conditions. I never got a shot at a ram, but it was mostly my fault.

According to Richardson, the area he hunted most frequently was stiff with both whitetails and mule deer. A non-resident could purchase a tag for one of each, for $150 Canadian apiece; about $135 U.S., depending on how the exchange flows. We agreed that I would join him in Calgary.

With the sun setting in the last day of the first half of the Oklahoma season, I gathered up my gear for the northern trip. My wife observed the careful packing, even assisted by folding the Pendletons, all the while wearing that interesting blend of expression, somewhere between pinched and pained, she reserves solely for me. She knows all about it, she might even understand it, but she simply cannot believe it.

Calgary is a beautiful city. It sparkled under a stark blue sky when I arrived on that crisp fall day with the temperature in the mid-fifties. Circumstances surrounding Calgary make it ideal for a bowhunter. This wide radius is classified as a Bow Zone, one of three such in the province. Hunting in these zones is for archers only.

Alberta's big game season begins in September and runs through the end of November. Beginning in '84, almost all the province had archery pre-seasons for the various big-game hunts. Regulations should be reviewed closely. Back then, some animals and areas required a licensed guide for non-residents. In other cases, hunting with an Alberta resident was sufficient.

It should be pointed out that, since Richardson and I hunted this area, the Alberta deer hunting laws have changed. A non-resident hunter now must be accompanied by a licensed guide/outfitter. I guess that proves good things never last forever.

In addition to deer, Alberta offers elk, bighorn sheep, moose and black bear. There are grizzlies for residents only in the southern part of the province and some antelope hunting.

Headquarters for Neil Harvie's Glenbow Ranches, Ltd. sit on a bench overlooking the shimmering ribbon of the Bow River. The river valley here is broad; the flood plain perhaps a mile wide in places. On the eastern side, the hills leap up quickly, steep and severe. To the west, they rise somewhat gently and undulate off into infinity.

Harvie has a vast ranching enterprise nicely laid out and beautifully kept. It's testimony to a man's pride in a successful effort to win a living from the land. Harvie allows bowhunting under a sensible set of conditions that provide opportunity and a quality environment for a hunter to pursue his ambitions. He divides the land on which he allows hunting into spacious zones on a reservation basis. Prior to the season he interviews those who wish to use his land, providing future trespass rights based on his evaluation of their character. There is a protocol for "signing in," and how and where you will go has applied conditions which are necessary to a rancher, and he expects you to adhere to these conditions; not stringent, only practical.

At distance, it appears too open, almost dull, but as you enter into it the land bucks and heaves, forming steep ridges, deep draws, major canyons and subtle pockets. There are grass hillsides dotted with tightly clumped willow thickets. There is big timber, spruce mostly, on the northern exposures and fine stands of poplar in the shallower draws. It is primarily mule deer country, but I was to find it not uncommon to bounce a whitetail out of a draw into which I had just followed a mule deer. Mule deer are there in numbers and sizes that will hold your complete, undivided attention.

Terry Raymond's place — he's Harvie's son-in-law and a bowhunter — where we found the corridor, is inland several miles from the river valley at a higher elevation. The habitat there is prime whitetail cover; one sees a mule deer here but rarely.

We opted to concentrate on whitetails first. The rut was in full swing, the weather just ideal: clear, crisp, invigorating.

I rattled up three bucks the first morning we hunted, but not in the corridor. The wind was behaving badly, so I decided to try a spot at the opposite end of the woods. One buck was a dandy, the other two not bad. None of them got into a position that would allow me to shoot. I also saw five does and two fawns. The fawns were about the size of an average southwestern adult; the adults looked like moose compared to what I had been chasing at home.

At mid-day, I went back and checked the corridor. The entire area seemed to have been thoroughly run over by a herd of love-struck bucks. I have never seen anything quite so good. I suppose this is what often gets called a primary area, a bordello for bucks. There was a perfect tree in exactly the right place, a lovely old spruce with scads of cover, built for comfort.

I put up my stand with a minimum of effort, low enough to give me a nice, not steep, angle to shoot from, amidst enough cover to hide Robin Hood and all the Merry Men.

I headed for the pasture to meet Richardson for lunch. While we sat in the truck sipping Dave's special blend of tea and conversing around mouthfuls, a buck that would score 140 if he measured an inch, charged out of the woods, crossed the road and headed for the corridor. I watched him through my Bausch & Lomb Compacs. As best I could tell, he passed within ten yards of the spruce.

It was not at all difficult to spend the rest of the day in the comfortable old spruce. During those last moments of evening, as the sky fell deeper and deeper into purple, I expected a big buck at any second. Nothing. I blamed it on the increasing wind, which was why I hadn't tried rattling. One has to be there at the right time.

To the left of the spruce, the corridor runs into a little indentation, like a cove in the wood-line that cuts back from the fence and ends. The perimeter of this opening was full of those little scrapes you expect to find in such spots, every six or seven yards. At the back end was a huge scrape which put it about twenty-five yards off my left shoulder, but out of play because of the intervening trees. The other major scrape was ten yards off my right shoulder in the center of the corridor, perfect for my left-handed set up. The trail between these two primary scrapes had lesser ones about every four steps. From the base of the spruce to the center of this trail was five steps.

I entered the area the following morning by making a wide sweep through the pasture to step over the barbwire fence at the center of the little opening. I stopped there to douse up the soles of my fleece-lined moccasins with a generous dollop of Scrape-Mate, cut through the opening bisecting the middle of a scrape that had been enlarged significantly overnight, then proceeded down the trail to the spruce. The morning seemed perfect. A nice breeze blew straight in from the pasture, pushing my scent behind the main travel lines to the corridor.

It was turning to gray dawn by the time I got settled. I

Dougherty took his Canadian whitetail from this stand. The tree, though bare, was thick enough to break up his outline.

already had shot four or five arrows into a bank by the truck in the dark, but I pulled the bow six or seven more times to stay loose. I hung the slim recurve with an arrow already nocked on the convenient peg. The rattling antlers were just as easily accessible. With dawn coming on quickly, the woods began to take shape. It was promising to be an overcast blustery day, the kind that could turn into something serious with the weather fidgeting ahead of a minor front. It was the sort of morning in which I have come to have a great deal of confidence.

I saw the deer's thick, blocky outline about twenty minutes later on the far side of the little opening. It was the kind of silhouette you knew was a buck before you ever saw his head. His head was down as though he was trying to sort out the trail of a lost lady friend, but his line of travel was angling away. I

Dave Richardson (left) needed help getting his Canadian whitetail back to ranch headquarters. The whitetails of Canada and the north central states of the U.S. are huge compared to those found in other parts of the United States, especially Florida.

grabbed up the rattling horns and gave them a pair of serious whacks, paused and did it again.

With one giant spring, the buck was at the clearing's edge, standing poised to go in any direction. He searched the woods carefully for a moment before moving forward with a stiff-legged, pugnacious walk that carried him right to the scrape I had passed coming in. Head down, nose extended, he took up the scent line laid by the moccasins with a brisk, purposeful walk that had him almost on me before I could lift off the bow without looking, or breathing, and get set.

I have shot quite a few deer in my life and a reasonable assortment of other critters. In more that thirty years, I have not become complacent. I tend to get pretty excited about it and trust this emotion will continue until I quit, which is not in my immediate future plans.

This buck appeared monstrous to a fellow who sulks through the Oklahoma blackjacks after a different sub-species. He was not the sort to generate complacency. My arrow put him down within short yards of the tree. I'm unsure as to how it happened, but my exit from the spruce possessed an alacrity that would have stunned a squirrel. In the process, it rent a severe gash in a pair of not-in-the-least-cheap imported pants. The rip ran from the vicinity of the right knee to an area I delicately refer to as the "upper right cheek."

Sitting in the woods, admiring the buck had been a satisfying experience. He had a fine big frame, deceptively deep-chested, with the rut-swollen neck and a deep, thick coat of heavy hair. He was what most whitetail hunters call a ten-point, but he would be termed a five-point in my province. I was born and raised in the Western style which means one totals up the side with the most points and forevermore refers

to that beast accordingly. Since moving eastward, I have become accustomed to the phrasing that considers everything "big enough to hang a ring on." I have come to the conclusion that reporting the taking of a twelve-or thirteen-pointer makes sense and sounds infinitely more impressive.

There is a column on the right side of a Pope & Young Club whitetail score sheet wherein *Differences* are noted. This column is used to reflect the numerical score, one-eighth-inch increments for balancing the symmetry of one point of measurement versus a similar measurement on the opposite antler. Symmetry, it should be pointed out, is a major objective in *typical* heads.

Also in this column is space to detail the accumulative scoring value of *abnormal* points, which means simply those little — or large — protuberances that are not where they are supposed to be. These little darlings, which I seem to have a propensity for finding on the better whitetails I've shot, will get you. This Alberta buck was, in reality, an eight-point — four-point for you cowboys — with what we shall refer to as "forked eye guards," or if you want to be technically correct, *abnormal points in G-1*. My somewhat practiced eye told me I was in trouble. I should have expected no less.

The bottom line is that this buck didn't matter at all, except that it kept my record intact. If I finally should collect a record book whitetail, I will not live long enough to do it twice, which would simply add to the frustration. With the whitetail segment of Alberta out of the way, there were still several days to devote to those long, timbered ridges and mysterious willow pockets of the mule deer range above the Bow River. It simply required changing the moccasins for more sturdy footwear.

CHAPTER 12

EXCITING COLUMBIAN BLACKTAILS

For Columbian blacktails, you need to hunt the northwest. These trophies are exhibited at Oregon's National Blacktail Hunt.

Not The Largest Of Deer, This One Does Its Best To Outwit Hunters

DURING THE first decade or so of my formative bowhunting years, we sincerely believed the deer we hunted in southern California were Columbian blacktails (*O.h. columbianus*). That perspective seemed correct, since they did have black tails. Technically, we were wrong.

The range parameters of the true Columbian blacktail deer were a matter of some concern and discussion over the years with record-keeping bodies such as Boone & Crockett, and Pope & Young, and what B&C does most usually has been followed by P&Y.

I shot several nice bucks along the coast in upper central California years ago that probably were true Columbian blacktails, as far as boundary line geographics were concerned, but that was before any of us had any knowledge of such things. In fact, the Pope & Young Club was little more than an embryo then, and most of us were not aware of what was going on.

Over the years, boundary lines were re-drawn and reduced in an attempt to keep clean borders between blacktails and encroaching mule deer bloodlines. None of this makes a helluva lot of difference today, but had I been on my toes record-wise years ago, before the boundary changes, perhaps I could now say I had a couple of "book" blacktails. As it is, they're just a couple of sub-minimum California mule deer. I haven't lost any sleep over it, but I fully intend to correct the matter with Larry Jones somewhere in Oregon in the near future.

If one is serious about blacktail deer in terms of being sure species-wise, it's best to focus on far northern California, Oregon or Washington for the effort. Columbian blacktails seem to be a transitional mid-point development between the Sitka blacktails and the Rocky Mountain mule deer (*O.h. hemionus*). There are some specific character differences, though the two do interbreed, mostly along the eastern edges of their range. Both the Columbian and Sitka blacktails have long, full black tails. The mule deer's tail also is black, though not as full or long-haired and it is interspersed with more white strands. The muley has a large, distinctive rump patch as opposed to the blacktail that has none or hardly any. Both species have similar bifurcated antler formations, as does the Sitka. The antlers become wider, longer tined and more massive in the Rocky Mountain guys that, in addition to being altogether larger from head gear to body size, have a much wider spread of geographic range.

From coastal northern California, where the blacktail seems at home in warm climates and open-timbered oak terrain, to the jungle-like, steep rain forests of Washington, and even dense high country of California's Trinity Alps, he seems an adaptable cuss that might be relatively easy to take in one place and almost impossible to find in another.

For sure-fire tough hunting, some of the places I have seen in Oregon — with the fog and rain to make matters worse — are nothing less than a full-time challenge. On the other hand, friends like Doug Walker knock 'em off with casual regularity on large private ranches along the California coast.

My impressions have been that coastal California blacktails, overall, are smallish deer compared to the heavier and stockier residents of Oregon and Washington. This is doubtlessly true, for as the sub-species developed, moving southward to become the California mule deer (*O.h. californicus*), then downward to Baja California in Mexico, they definitely became runtier in size and quite different in color, losing the sharper, more delineated markings of their northern cousins.

Strangely, though not far inland, along the Colorado River, where the Rocky Mountain and desert mule deer ranges sort of overlap, these mule deer species become significantly larger in what appears to me to be equally harsh living conditions.

I have seen quite a few of every sub-species from central Baja (*O.h. peninsulae*) inland and upward along the Colorado River and all over California. In fact, I think I have probably seen all the mule deer sub-species in every state and the three Canadian provinces where they are found, and have hunted successfully in most of them.

While I would have to say all of these deer are pretty, I tend to look upon the two blacktails — Sitka and Columbian — as being on a somewhat higher plane in the features department. It is rather interesting that, with science recognizing seven mule deer sub-species and upwards of thirty whitetail variants — some of which have very distinct differences — Boone & Crockett and Pope & Young, the record keepers, recognize three of the mule deer family and only two from the whitetail. As mentioned elsewhere, Safari Club International (SCI) is wrestling with that same issue.

None of that really is very important, unless you are intent on amassing a species list. What we have today in terms of recording big-game animal categories is more than adequate. Besides, I think the records thing is rapidly losing the foundation of its intent — recognizing outstanding animals for what they are rather than a platform for individual egos.

That there is a degree of difficulty in collecting a Columbian blacktail good enough for the record book is evidenced in part with the amount of total entries in the Pope & Young Club's records through the eighteenth recording period. Put another way, this is the total for over thirty years of compiling those records.

By comparison, there are 1149 typical mule deer, not counting non-typical and velvet entry categories, in the P&Y records. I suppose, if you use these numbers as a base, the Sitka blacktail — with only 150 in the records — would jump right out as being even more difficult.

Scouting major trails for the presence of blacktails is the first step in locating a good position for a blind or stand.

Premier bowhunter Dwight Schuh uses rattling antlers to call in trophy blacktails. He's dressed for the northwest.

Not true. By comparison, the remote Sitkas receive little hunting pressure, and your chances of taking a record class Sitka is the easiest among the deer.

Hunting techniques for blacktails follow normal mule deer rules over much of their range. Early and late day spot-and-stalk is a preferred method by my friends in California who take a lot of them. Stands over water sources comprise another prime method, as some of the California hunts take place during hot, dry weather when water is a fundamental necessity for both hunter and hunted.

No matter where you are, the geography of the country and the types of habitat dictate much of your hunting plan. It is difficult, if not impossible, to stalk through much of the blacktail's impossibly thick home range, without alerting it long before you have a chance for a shot. Ambush techniques favor the bowhunter here just as they do for whitetails where the same problems exist.

Tree stands have become a favored method with many bowhunters I know in Washington and Oregon, though all of these with whitetail experience state it is more difficult to pattern blacktails, and my most recent experience in Oregon supports their conclusions. The country is awfully big and the deers' travel routes vary as they move in a meandering manner.

For several years, the Oregon Bowhunters Association has been hosting Oregon's National Blacktail Hunt, which was organized primarily to expose and promote the joys of bowhunting blacktail deer in Oregon and, to an extent, Oregon

itself. This hunt is not a contest really, but a well run educational and social event that draws more and more folks annually. The nicest part about it is the help accorded newcomers to Oregon. The hunt coordinators want everybody to have a good time, along with a chance to see, and

This nice Columbian blacktail fell to Steve Jones' arrow. The deer has a stocky build and, as usual, a northwestern wet coat.

maybe even shoot at a deer.

In this regard, they are not skimpy with their information and provide a lot of solid assistance. Information on this annual event can be obtained from Neil Summers at Bowhunting Safari Consultants, P.O. Box 23906, Eugene, OR 97402.

I spent a week hunting blacktails during this event with Larry Jones, who operates Wilderness Sound Productions from his Oregon-based plant. Jones, a first-rate bowhunter, is no slouch in the blacktail department.

Joining us at Larry's base-camp home was Dwight Schuh, an eminent bowhunter, and his partner Doug Chase, another widely experienced bowman.

Schuh's past participation at this event suggests to me that it should truly be renamed the Dwight Schuh Blacktail Symposium, for in those two attempts, he downed a pair of record-class dandies.

I hunted with Jones and his camera crew in attempts to film the demise of a blacktail coming to rattling antlers. Film production, on the best day ever, is a royal pain in the butt. Encumbered as we were, our actual hunting time was restricted, though we did have some encounters and a great deal of fun amid the work.

I even shot a blacktail on that trip, albeit a lady deer in the very last hour of the final morning. It was a quick downhill shot through a nifty passage in the timber at forty yards. Even Jones, who likes to rag on me as much as I like to work him over, was forced to admit it was a handy piece of work.

I hunted from a tree stand on a couple of soggy afternoons. This was in a little glade where not one but two Boone and Crockett blacktails reportedly had met their fates. In the last dying light of evening, several does and a spike buck made wraithlike appearances, weaving in and out through the moss-covered timber on absolutely silent feet. A smallish fork-horn came when it was right down to the wire for shooting light.

I elected not to shoot because of the conditions, as well as having several more hunting days ahead of me. Later, as I looked over the chunky doe, I thought fleetingly that perhaps I should have busted the forkie, but the choice was the right one. The forkie got a chance to grow into a mature deer, and harvesting a mature doe rather than an immature buck makes much better sense.

I mentioned that Jones and I were trying to rattle up a blacktail buck. It's interesting to me, a life-long game-calling addict, that both the Sitka and Columbian critters are sound susceptible, while their big-eared cousins — the mule deer — will hardly give you a toss. Even the closer cousins to the south basically ignore rattling or grunt calls, while true blacktails respond quite well.

Calling the Columbians is becoming the thing to do. As a matter of fact, both of the big bucks Schuh collected were rattled up. Larry Jones did rattle up a couple of bucks while I was with him. I just couldn't get a decent shot.

The trouble with filming is that you might have the shot, but if the cameraman doesn't have the action framed to his liking, you have to start all over. I have made several bowhunting films and videos, and I suppose it beats working for a living, even if it is so frustrating.

Bleat calls work well on blacktails, and have been the instrument of a long-time technique on Sitkas. Here again, we see a similarity in the behavior of the Columbian and the Sitka. I think one of the reasons has to do with the close-knit cover both of them frequent.

As a comparison, I have found it easier to rattle whitetails in tight cover, at least drawing them close enough for a bow shot. In more open terrain, whitetails simply don't see what they expect to see and hold up.

With blacktails in the steep forested terrain of Oregon and Washington, where short-range visibility is a fact of life, the deer's penchant to investigate natural sound becomes a reliable trait that the hunter can use to advantage, though terrain elements are always against him and the close-range requirements of his bow.

Both Jones and Schuh rattle vigorously at the onset, and stay in place for a longish period of time. Where whitetails usually come in hard and fast, the blacktail is more of a sneaking procrastinator. In this regard, it is much like calling bobcats as compared to coyotes.

Given the tight quarters often associated with rattling blacktails, I believe the ultimate bowhunting approach would

Doug Chase's Columbian blacktail has heavy forked antlers. It will be close to making the record book.

be to do it from an elevated tree stand position, and that's something I intend to focus on the next time a chance comes along to join Larry Jones in Oregon.

A standard technique for spotting blacktails is to look for them along the edges of timber-cutting operations, which are frequent in the Pacific Northwest. Old burns and second-growth areas probably are even better, but the deer are quite difficult to spot and traversing that stuff with its millions of rotting board feet of slash lying helter-skelter beneath waist-high ferns is tough.

I tried it on a good buck one morning, and had I been able to move faster, having the edge on him in wind and elevation, it might have been a different story. Moving efficiently was impossible, as the meandering buck, a real dandy, simply walked out of my life. All this pointed out that Jones' theory of refining the art of calling the deer rather than stumbling after them, or waiting in ambush from stands or blinds, may be the real way to go.

One of the keys Jones showed me for locating blacktail bucks was rubs. We were hunting during the rut, of course, in order to capitalize on antler rattling as the way to get a shot. Jones had picked out his areas after scouting them for evidence of buck activity in the form of rubbed trees.

The country was a patchwork of freshly timbered land criss-crossed with myriad logging roads. In addition to scouting on foot, Jones and his son, Steve, a young bowhunter with experience beyond his years, cruised the roads bisecting heavy virgin timber that was adjacent to the clear-cuts. Looking for rubs, they checked these locations off on a topo map so they could develop a clear picture of buck concentrations.

Close inspection of the size of the rubbed trees and tracks can give one a good idea as to the size of the deer. It's an excellent method of narrowing down bowhunting hot spots in a broad area where simply wandering blind is akin to seeking the legendary needle in the haystack.

It doesn't take a mega-buck to make the record book. With a minimum of ninety points, most mature three- or four-pointers will do it, and I'm aware of a couple of extra-big fork-horns that score 90. It will, however, take a true monster to top the world record established in 1969 by B.G. Shurtleff at 172 2/8. The same hunter, incidentally, has the the number two buck at 163 7/8.

Take that as a severe challenge if you're really looking for something interesting to do. As for me, I have no such aspirations. I'll be really happy just to get into the Northwest again and mix it up with those slick deer in their remarkable country with good friends. Something around 95 would suit me just fine.

Dougherty took this blacktail during an Oregon hunt. It's not a buck, but after a long hunt, Dougherty was glad to fill his tag.

In Seeking The Columbian Blacktail, Settle On The Technique That Works For You!

"I SPOTTED a doe fifty yards away. Blacktail deer are quick to detect danger and she bounced over a log and disappeared into a vine maple thicket. It didn't matter that she had seen me. I was committed to taking a blacktail buck on video," Larry Jones recalls.

"A mile from where I'd just set up my tree stand, the cameraman and my son, Steven, were trying to get a kill shot on video. I had chosen a tree that overlooked a spot where two trails crossed. The mud in both trails was cut and gouged with deer tracks. The bucks were in rut and there was plenty of deer movement. Now that my stand was in place, as soon as Steven, my son, bagged his buck, I'd be ready."

Larry D. Jones probably knows as much about the Columbian blacktail deer as any man alive. A resident of Springfield, Oregon, he grew up in the foothills of the Cascade Mountain Range, and from childhood has had great respect for the wilderness and the wildlife that inhabits it. At 11 years old, Jones harvested his first deer with a rifle. At 20 years old, he bagged a deer just two weeks after buying his first bow.

Bowhunting since 1961, Larry Jones has taken twenty-five Roosevelt and Rocky Mountain elk in Oregon. He also has hunted in Africa, taking five game species with a bow. More importantly, perhaps, he has developed skill in calling many types of animals. Over the years, he has called in badger, bobcat, bear, deer, fox, turkey, elk, moose, wolf and coyote. In addition to the Columbian blacktail deer, he has cougar, elk, mule deer, Rocky Mountain goat and moose entered in the Pope & Young Club record book.

Larry Jones is chairman of the Oregon Foundation for Blacktail Deer, as well as a member of five state bowhunting associations. He is lucky in that he has been able to tie his livelihood to his hunting pursuits. He is president of Wilderness Sound Productions, which produces calling videos and cassettes. He also presents a series of sixteen different seminars on North American wildlife to groups across the nation.

With that sort of background, I figured Larry D. Jones was the one to outline some of the likely — and less likely — situations he has seen or experienced while in pursuit of the wily Columbian blacktail.

Jones carefully eased each foot down as he moved toward the spot where the doe had bounced out of sight. He pushed some broken fern aside and eased in front of a huge stump. He slowly scanned the vine maple thickets that skirted the old-growth timber. He saw a leg move and a doe appeared. She weaved right, then left, moving like a dancer as she made her way through the vine maples. She smoothly dipped under a windfall and walked onto the open timber trail.

"I noticed his gray muzzle first, as a buck followed. He was hot on her heels, head low, nostrils flaring, sucking in her scent. It would've been an easy shot. They walked within ten yards of me. His three-by-three rack would have easily made the minimum for the Pope & Young Club record book," Jones recalls.

"I was really enjoying this. It was a typical cool, moist November Oregon morning. A gray mist drifted through the

In the dense woods of the blacktail habitat, rattling from a tree stand provides the bowhunter with better visibility.

huge old-growth firs. Dew dripped from their crossed and intermingled branches. Lime green moss was in sharp contrast with the evergreen canopy, as it waved in the breeze like strands of uncombed hair. This was a beautiful stand of untouched timber, but I knew by the blue and pink ribbons dangling from low brush and limbs it would soon be cut and logged."

Jones had just figured out the travel routes of these blacktails. Once the timber was logged, he would have to change his area or his strategy. This had happened before and, because the habitat had changed and sometimes hunting pressure increased, Jones had to use a variety of strategies to

Dwight Schuh attracts bucks by rattling antlers. He adds to the commotion by thumping the ground with the antlers.

hunt blacktails.

When he swapped stories with other hunters during Oregon's recent National Blacktail Hunt, he found they had used different tactics and strategies to bag blacktails. In fact, a whopping forty-one percent of the hunters who entered the hunt took deer.

Randy Spanfellner of Molalla, Oregon, took a Boone and Crockett Club-qualifying buck that green-scored 132 3/8. Spanfellner took his buck by rattling antlers. He was walking an old skid road that he knew eventually would lead him into a super blacktail area.

He decided to conceal himself among the trees along the road and try rattling antlers. He smeared some Buck Stop doe lure onto his hat and clashèd the antlers together. Moving only his eyes, Spanfellner watched for a few minutes, then rattled again. The monster buck appeared and Spanfellner was able to hit him squarely from only eighteen yards.

Neil Summers, the hunt director for Oregon's National Blacktail Hunt, reports use of a different hunting strategy to bag a four-by-five Pope & Young record book blacktail.

Summers waited for fresh snow to blanket the upper peaks, then drove logging roads looking for concentrations of blacktails. He drove until he found an area that had a lot of deer tracks. He even saw a couple of bucks cross the road, so he was sure it was a super spot. Summers then used the melting snow falling from tree branches to cover his sound. He moved slowly through the area, carefully watching for deer.

Within an hour, he spotted a big-bodied buck courting a doe. Summers crept to thirty-five yards, then decided to use the "Summers shooting strategy." He nocked an Easton 2317 camo shaft, tipped with a Thunderhead 125 broadhead, drew his eighty-five-pound compound bow — and launched his arrow into the snow under the buck. Summers claims he does this to give the animal a chance. Most other hunters thought he just missed.

Summers must be lucky or good, because the buck didn't even flinch and gave him the second shot. His arrow struck home and, after a short tracking job, he tagged his trophy blacktail.

Another Oregon bowhunter, John Higgins, uses trees in his ambush tactics, but he doesn't use a tree stand. He uses forty feet of nylon rope, a safety belt, climbing spurs and a folding wood saw. He carries these items in his pack, and when he finds some trails that are cut up with deer tracks, he considers the direction of the wind, selects a tree and climbs up.

Once in the tree, Higgins attaches his safety belt and pulls up his bow and pack with the nylon rope. This rope also can be criss-crossed and woven between trees for a place to sit. He removes limbs with his saw so he will have a clear shot. He has experienced great success using this system.

Higgins states, "The reason I'm successful is that I don't make a lot of racket putting up a tree stand and I can climb a tree quietly without disturbing deer. If I see deer using a nearby trail, I just untie my rope, climb down and change trees."

Higgins' system works, but not everyone wants to sit on a limb all day. Higgins toughs it out and, during two successive years, proved his strategy on blacktails by bagging a buck each year.

Tom Crowe and many other hunters use the spot-and-stalk method to fill their tags. Crowe bagged a pure albino blacktail buck on a November, 1988 bowhunt. He was on the Pearson Spoilers team and was hunting the Evans Creek unit. Their team's strategy was to drive logging roads and glass the edges of timber and clearcuts. Once they spotted a buck, they would stalk it for a shot.

Crowe said he first thought the albino blacktail was a goat. His partner, Curt Mendenhall, looked it over with his binoculars and decided it was a deer. They moved closer, and after they were positive it was a deer, Crowe made a careful,

Steve Jones adjusts the reed on a blacktail deer call. The call is manufactured by Wilderness Sound Productions.

deliberate stalk, which ended in a thirty-yard shot. Crowe took his trophy on his birthday, and is having his spike buck mounted, because it's rare to find a pure albino of any species.

Ted Peterson, who comes to Oregon from Arizona to hunt the wily blacktail, enjoys calling game. He studied deer calling and the first morning on his hunt, he made the sound of a fawn bawling to bring a two-by-two buck to within fifteen yards of his tree stand. Peterson, a good friend, was on Larry Jones' team.

"I told Ted the contest wasn't important. What was important was having a good time hunting blacktail deer. Peterson passed up the forked horn, and during his hunt, called in several more deer," Jones reports.

"One day, Peterson sat next to an opening in some bushes. He used a deer call to make fawn bawls and rattled antlers. After several sequences, he called in a doe with a three-point buck in hot pursuit. Good luck was in the buck's favor, though. Peterson never got a shot at him.

"I did a lot of calling myself and, two days in a row, I called deer to my tree stand," Jones recalls. "On both days, a doe

came in with bucks following.

"Several years ago, Bob McGuire and I were hunting whitetail deer in Ohio. McGuire is an excellent whitetail hunter and he has used his voice to call in does and bucks.

"McGuire said, 'You can't call in a buck when he's tending a doe.'"

Jones made a simple suggestion. "Why don't you call in the doe? The buck will follow."

McGuire got a big grin on his face and said. "Why didn't I think of that?"

"I guess it's too simple," was Jones' response.

Larry Jones later found the same calling strategy works on blacktails.

"My son, Steven, uses tree stands, rattling and grunting to call in bucks successfully. Steven and I find that rattling from a tree is the most successful way of taking a blacktail buck as he comes to our call. Otherwise, the thick brush allows the buck to detect us before we see him. The height of our stand lets us see the buck sooner, and we can quietly wait for the right

Larry Jones sets a tree stand for a blacktail hunt. Note the heavy moss and lichen, an indication of extensive rainfall.

opportunity for our shots" Jones explains.

Several years ago Jones' friend, Dwight Schuh, took the biggest blacktail buck during the Oregon Bowhunters' first National Blacktail Hunt. Schuh used a deer call and rattling to bring in several bucks, but because of the brush, he wasn't able to get a shot.

The next day, Schuh located an area that had tree rubs and lots of deer tracks. He set up his tree stand, climbed in and waited an hour before rattling and calling. Schuh felt if he waited, any buck within hearing would forget the noise he had made while setting up his stand. He called and rattled several times.

After and hour-and-a-half, Schuh saw a big-bodied, heavy-antlered buck approaching and quietly waited. The buck stopped broadside twenty-five yards away. Schuh's shot sent the arrow through both lungs for a quick kill.

Hunting blacktails is challenging. When choosing a hunting strategy, pick one that will work for you. If you can't sneak quietly through brush, use a tree stand. If you like to glass for bucks, you can spot and stalk. If you like to fool them by calling and rattling, try that. Whatever strategy you choose, you're going to have a super time when hunting blacktail deer.

Larry Jones locates Columbian blacktail bucks by scouting for rubs. Bucks use their antlers to rub the bark from trees.

The father and son team of Steve (left) and Larry Jones has mastered the challenging game of hunting blacktails.

CHAPTER 13

THE UNUSUAL SITKA

Don't Let Its Diminutive Size Convince You It Is Not A Demanding Trophy

SEVERAL YEARS ago I hunted whitetail deer on Anticosti Island, which sits in the St. Lawrence Seaway, far north in the province of Quebec. It is the most distant known reach of the whitetail's range, though the deer — imported in 1917 — is not native to the island.

Both the habitat and the deer are unique, the deer having evolved handily to meet the specialized environment. I couldn't help but think, as I held the short stubby antlers of my first Anticosti buck— a deer of 180 pounds in spite of its miniature rack — that perhaps it should be classified among the deer hunters of the world as a separate species, for it is truly unique.

I was constantly reminded of the Sitka blacktail, as I pondered that thought.

Hunting Sitka blacktails has become one of the things to do if you're a serious deer hunter, though this phenomenon among the trophy collectors of the world is a relatively recent development. This is especially true among bowhunters.

Resident Alaskan bowhunters of my acquaintance mentioned the Sitka rather casually in passing. Hunting them was a sort of a lark, and the big bears in the same areas tend to make it rather exciting, they said. Their real reason was to gather a freezer-load of meat, of course. With bag limits of five or six deer, Alaskan hunters could gather up a pile. The bears, who eat the Sitkas, too, added to the fun. The Alaskans of my acquaintance always have had an odd perspective of fun!

The Sitka is a deer with special characteristics, like the stubby whitetails of Anticostis which have short, well marked faces and extra-long legs to carry them through deep winter snow. These legs are on a disproportionately short skeletal structure covered by extra-long guard hair, along with the highest body fat content to be found in the whitetail species.

Sitka deer are sort of like that. With distinctive body shapes and vividly marked, they are perhaps the prettiest of our deer and certainly a product of their special environment. And, like the Anticosti deer, the Sitka is the product of relocation transplants on much of their current range.

It has been my plan now for several seasons to make a major Sitka deer hunting trip. I have backed off, because reports indicate their numbers are down. As you might imagine, winter weather along the coast of Alaska and her offshore islands can be unbelievably harsh. Deer subjected to extremely hard winters oftentimes are impacted severely. What happens when this occurs in any deer herd is a higher mortality rate on mature bucks that are run down physically, as a result of heavy breeding activity, or because of the normal tendency in the mule deer sub-species to stay at the higher elevations — sometimes until it is too late.

The bottom line for the last few seasons: Sitka herds have

Sitka have an unusual appeal despite the small antlers that top even the largest of bucks.

been down, big bucks in particular. While I do not run around looking for world records, I do try to hedge my bets on major excursions in hopes that something respectable will come my way. As a result of this glum news, I have put off the assault temporarily.

I have a number of friends who have hunted Sitkas extensively, the most knowledgeable being Danny Moore of Kalispell, Montana. Chuck Adams, Bill Krenz, George Moerlein and Bob Robb all are Sitka hunters of note, and several of them have shot what probably would be a truck load. In-depth conversations with them all, taking into account the various ways and time to go about it, indicate a Sitka campaign can be the deer hunt of a lifetime.

A bit of the fun, as indicated earlier, depends on how much you like bears. Some pretty hairy stories come out of Alaska every year dealing with Sitka hunter's encounters with big, bad brown bears.

Chuck Adams told me of the strategy he used. Hunting the bucks up high in the summer pretty well got around the bear problem, and it was a perfect spot-and-stalk hunting situation at which Adams thrives. The days were long, with tough hauls

up and back, especially so with a pack full of venison, cape and antlers. However, the bears were lower, hunting the streams and chasing salmon. In the winter months, when the salmon are gone, bears start thinking about eating Sitka blacktails again.

Charlie Kroll, a long-time acquaintance, had a pair of bears take away his late-season bow kill, putting him up a tree in the process. Kroll watched as the two bears fought over the carcass, literally pulling it in half. Then each bear loped off with its hard-won portion.

Fortunately, Charlie Kroll was able to reclaim his trophy antlers later, and was pleased to retire to his Florida fly-tying bench where, I should add, he's expert.

Bill Krenz, one I consider to be among the best all-around bowhunters in the land, played out a Dirty Harry scenario with a hungry bear that wanted Bill's superb buck almost as much as Bill was determined to keep it.

Krenz played some serious music over the brown bruin's head at close range with his .44 magnum backup revolver before finally convincing it to retire.

"It was," he said, "getting down to the wire."

All in all, when conditions are good — no bears, for example, and the weather doesn't kick your butt — collecting a couple of good Sitkas on a carefully planned trip apparently is not difficult.

In winter months — usually December — the deer are down low. They are on the beaches or close to them, concentrated, and in the rut. This is a superb time to hunt them with the promise of some serious action.

Weather conditions, though, can be fragile. Drop-ins for self-camping are available by plane or boat from a host of services, or you can go through an outfitter. Some offer excellent facilities aboard offshore-anchored base camp ships. This has special appeal for me. Being an old blue water kind of guy, I like sleeping on boats.

However, most of the fellows I know who hunt Sitka deer do it on an on-their-own basis. It's not much different than any camp-out style hunt, though there are a considerable number of details to take into account in arranging the logistics.

Most of the bowhunting with which I'm familiar takes place on Kodiak Island — a name that rightfully conjures up visions of huge bears — and I know some who have done well on Afognak Island. Recently, emphasis has increased relative to Prince of Wales Island. This interest is among some of my bowhunting acquaintances who probably would prefer I didn't mention it. They tell me this is an almost totally do-it-yourself hunt, but the bucks are good. The bears are the smaller blacks, not browns, though of good size for their species.

The rack of a good Sitka blacktail probably won't make your heart stop, if you're used to better-than-average mule deer or whitetails. They are close-cropped, compact, stubby things, though above average in mass for their size.

As a Pope & Young panel measurer for many bi-annual competitions, I have had the opportunity to hold the very best of the best in my hands. There is truly something extra-special about the way they are built. Add that to the striking contrast of rich brown, thick black and the stark white of their capes, it's easy to see why this very special deer has won the hearts and interest of many of America's deer hunters.

Though the Sitka may seem far away — which they are for most of us — hunting the species offers a unique, reasonably affordable chance at a superb trophy deer. Care should be taken to plan a trip that follows several seasons of relatively mild winters. It is probably safe to say that hunting Sitka blacktails, even under the best of conditions, will still be tough, both physically and mentally.

Alaskan weather is totally unpredictable. The later in the season you go, the more likely you will experience the best of deer hunting, but the more fickle the weather can be. No one ever should hunt Alaska, British Columbia or other provinces of Canada if they do not possess the temperament to handle uncontrollable down-time weather and delays. Bad weather contributes heavily to mental discomfort — anxiety, if you will — and until you experience it and learn to roll with the punches, you probably will have a totally miserable time. I know hunters who have been stuck on Sitka hunts for up to two weeks after the planned closing time. Pick your companions carefully. Enough said!

Sitkas reportedly are suckers for a low bleat call. If you get right down to it, the very first deer calls ever to hit the market — back before most of you were born — were patterned after the so-called "Alaskan deer call."

Rattling is claimed to be good for luring the Sitkas, and I'm sure it is. However, on the islands where the big bears live — the big brown kind — as much as I like to call, I believe I'd keep mine in my pocket. Alaskan browns come to the call, too.

Given all that, my plans for a major Sitka hunt are drawing close. But I think I'll take myself to that other place, the island where the bears are black!

When planning a Sitka hunt, plan on dealing with bear. Remember, bears hunting the tasty Sitka also answer to deer calls.

Here's A Misadventure That Resulted In A Damaged Trophy

Two Sitka deer roam a clearcut on Alaska's Afognak Island. This is the closest most bowhunters will get to the elusive Sitka.

A JOURNEY to the northwest Alaskan coast or the offshore islands of Prince William Sound and the Gulf of Alaska, takes you into the last region of our continent to be re-occupied by deer since the retreat of the great Pleistocene glaciers.

An old friend and occasional hunting companion, Charlie Kroll, has made that trip into the Alaskan winterlands several times. A veteran of more than half a century of serious bowhunting, he wanted a Pope & Young record-quality Sitka deer. His misadventures are worth retelling here:

"The little Sitka blacktails inhabiting this area are certainly not the most magnificent of our deer, but in my opinion, they are the prettiest. And a big bonus to the hunter is that they live in some of the loveliest land our continent contains," Kroll contends.

The North Pacific islands are dominated by a marine climate, with overcast days more than half the year, high precipitation from autumn to spring and a relatively short, dry summer season. Dense coniferous rain forests of Sitka spruce and western hemlock form a dense, moss-festooned canopy over much of the habitat. Severity of winters is the main controlling factor on deer numbers, the annual hunting harvest having essentially little impact.

Charlie Kroll had ventured north three years previously with high hopes for collecting a typical blacktail buck. The trophy provided by this deer is insignificant when compared with larger members of the deer family. Nonetheless, in form and symmetry the dainty rack of a typical four-point Sitka is as beautiful and desirable as the antlers of any of its larger cousins, and is highly prized by the bowman who takes a good one. Comparatively few are listed in the Pope & Young record book since its inclusion in 1979, but as time goes on this listing should grow.

"My first venture in 1982, made with bowhunting friends

A Sitka doe and fawn warm themselves in the rare rays of sunshine on the beautiful island of Afognak. The island is one of many off the coast of Alaska in the North Pacific.

Ed Russell, John Koldeway and Bill Hobbs of Anchorage, had resulted in a fine trip, but with no trophies to show for our efforts.

"Our camp on that trip had been set up near an arm of Seal Bay on the southeast coast of Afognak Island. In the six or seven preceding years that my companions had hunted this island, they never had failed to come out with nice deer.

"In 1980, Ed Russell had bagged what has been the record Sitka blacktail with a score of 91 7/8 (minimum P&Y score for the species is 65). But despite ten days of hard hunting, we had little to show for our efforts except some fine eating provided by of a couple does bagged for camp meat.

"Ask any Alaskan bowhunter what he thinks of blacktail venison. You'll find them nearly unanimous in declaring it to be finer eating than moose tenderloin, north slope caribou chops or the steaks of a high mountain ram. That is high praise, indeed, but well deserved.

"So it came to pass that I joined my Anchorage friends, Ed and Linda Russell, John and Tom Koldeway, and John's fiancee, Chris Richardson, in November, 1984, for a flight first to Kodiak Island, then by floatplane to Afognak. This may seem a late date for an Alaskan hunt, but winter weather is considerably milder on the offshore islands than on the mainland and November is the mating month for the black-tails.

This particular year, Ed Russell had chosen a bay nearer the southwestern end of the forty-by-thirty-mile island, where the group set up camp in a grove of spruce and hemlock near the mouth of a mountain stream. The year previously, these outdoorsman had hunted this area for the first time with great results. History was — almost — to be repeated on this latest venture.

"After establishing camp, we set up a big medicine ring beneath a small spruce in the campsite's center. This consisted of items found in our daily wanderings such as shed antlers, skull plates, eagle and raven feathers and other esoteric bits of natural left-overs. In doing this we were following the practice of the old Plains Indians who believe that such collections — properly displayed — brought good hunting luck," Kroll recalls.

The first three days of hunting, however, were rather fruitless. A few deer were seen, a couple shots taken, but with no fresh meat being added to the larder.

Again, the deer were seemingly conspicuous by their absence, although the signs and sightings were certainly better than they had been three years earlier.

"The fourth day, my luck changed, after a fashion. I set out at daylight, and after fording the stream, began ascending the east facing mountain slopes. The little blacktails are sun worshippers, soaking up what comparatively little sunlight

A visit by bears wasn't in Charlie Kroll's plans when he went hunting for a trophy Sitka. We now know Kroll can climb trees.

they get at any opportunity. As it was a clear morning, I figured the high slopes would be a drawing card once the peaks were bathed in light.

"I got careless," Kroll admits. "So naturally was caught unprepared. I was nearly to a hillside terrace or bench when two nice eight-point bucks came walking along its edge, some thirty-five yards above me. By the time I shucked off my glove and got an arrow nocked, it was too late.

"I spent some three-quarters of an hour following up, calling at intervals, and even doing a bit of rattling with a set

Dense forest and ground cover provide ideal habitat for the small Sitka. This deer blends into the surroundings.

of antlers I carried in my daypack, but with no response."

The bowhunter finally gave up hope of seeing the bucks again, and resumed his ascent of the slopes, pausing frequently to survey the surroundings through seven-power Bushnell binoculars — as essential a piece of equipment in this country as a bow — and occasionally to try the deer call or a bit of antler rattling.

After an hour or so, he had reached another bench fairly high up and between two clearcuts. Six years before, small sections in this part of the island had been logged, leaving openings that had grown up in berry brambles and other deer staples. The blacktails use these openings at night, retreating to the big timber tracts during the day.

"Leaning against a huge old hemlock, I was surveying the terrain through my binoculars when I suddenly picked up a movement down the slope and to my right. It was a blacktail doe and she was on a trail that, if she stayed on it, would angle up by my position at about thirty-five yards. I had plenty of time to get ready, and as she drew nearer, I was about to attempt a shot when she stopped and looked back sharply over her shoulder."

"Oh, oh," Kroll thought, "maybe she's got a suitor." He let her go on by. Sure enough, a moment later, a nice buck came up the same trail.

"Again I got all set, but for reasons best known to himself, the buck detoured behind a screen of salmonberry bushes that negated all chance for a clear shot. 'Damnit! Frustrated again,' I muttered. But before I could really feel sorry for myself, I once again caught movement downslope. Here came a second, larger buck."

This time, everything went Charlie Kroll's way for a change. The buck came by on Kroll's side of the brush and

Ed Russell has successfully hunted Sitka on Alaska's Afognak Island. He took this buck with a recurve during a 1983 hunt.

stopped to look away at thirty-five yards. He was quartering toward the bowhunter. A Bear Razorhead-tipped cedar arrow took him behind the shoulder blade, nicking a lung, passing through the diaphragm and liver, and exited just in front of his off-side hip.The buck whirled and dashed straight downhill, only to pile up against a big log on the next terrace.

"It was over so fast I could hardly believe it. Yet even more unbelievable events were yet to happen.

"I retrieved my arrow which was protruding from a huge clump of moss, then went down to where the buck lay. Putting aside my daypack and folding my sleeves back up to the elbow, I proceeded to field-dress the deer. Before I had progressed vary far, a gang of ravens assembled overhead to make all those weird noises that only ravens can. How they detected what had happened so soon I'll never understand."

Having finished the dressing, Kroll was about to position the buck for some picture-taking, before quartering it to pack out, but a throaty grumbling noise caused him to look up.

"I suddenly felt the hair on the back of my neck rise up. Over the end of the bench, less than a hundred yards away and coming directly toward me, was a large Kodiak bear. And a few paces behind him was a second, slightly smaller and darker-colored bear!

"Evidently they had been close enough to be attracted by the raven talk, then had smelled the fresh meat and were determined to get it. Argue with the two of them? Not this child!"

A nearby spruce with moss-draped limbs nearly to the ground beckoned and, without further ado, Kroll scrambled up some twenty feet into what proved to be a rough-barked retreat.

When they came in, the first bear walked right over to the spruce where Kroll hunkered. The big bruin rose up on his hind legs with forelimbs against the tree trunk, and rocked it with a series of stiff-armed shoves, accompanied by a most unsettling growling and teeth clicking. The bowhunter's attention was fully on this apparition below, but he did remember afterwards hearing the sound of crunching bone in the background. The other bear was into the goodies.

"Suddenly, the bear beneath me realized he was being left

out of a feast. He forgot about me, and turning, charged back to the other bear, swatting at him as he got there.

"The smaller bear hadn't wasted any time. He had not only torn off one front leg, but also the head and half the neck of the buck. After backing him off, the larger bear picked up the carcass in his mouth and made off with it, as easily as you'd carry a six-pack. Shortly, he disappeared back over the rise, his companion complainingly bringing up the rear."

Except for the ravens overhead, quiet once more settled over the forest. After another five minutes, Charlie Kroll cautiously descended from his mossy perch, picked up his bow and arrows and made off down the mountain. However, after traveling a few hundred yards, he stopped for a breather and realized suddenly he had left behind his daypack with its contents and attached quiver behind. Shook up? Just a bit!

Nothing to do but backtrack. There was no life in evidence other than the ravens busily working on the leavings. "I retrieved my pack and quiver, picked up the detached head of the buck by an antler and once again retreated down the mountain, this time putting a half-mile between me and the encounter site before stopping."

The big Kodiaks had robbed the bowhunter of hard-earned venison, but by a quirk of fate he had a salvaged trophy to show for the experience. He took a couple photos of what was left, then used a small bone saw to remove the rack and skull plate.

There was no use trying to save the cape. What was left of it was ripped to shreds.

Hunting picked up for the group in the next few days. Tom Koldeway called in and collected another fine eight-point buck, after missing chances at a couple of others. John Koldeway had some shooting, with arrow deflection robbing him of his quarry. Russell kept the group supplied in camp meat with a doe and a button buck bagged on successive days. Kroll saw a few more deer but had no further shooting.

"Then the coastal weather turned nasty with gale-force winds that kept us marooned for several days. This, however, proved no hardship, as we had a snug camp and plenty to eat.

"The difficult part was returning to the confines of civilization and adjusting to its occupational schedules and restrictions. After two weeks in the bush, one begins to feel he is part of the natural environment; one with the raven, the deer and the forest. Atavistic instincts begin to overshadow the pretensions of modern culture and a quiet peace begins to seep into the soul. Such respite is one many people never get to experience or understand, but those of us who do have our lives greatly enriched as a result."

As the late Dr. Saxton Pope stated: "We who have hunted thus, trod the forest trails, climbed the lofty peaks, breathed the magic air, and viewed the endless roll of mountain ridges, blue in the distance, have been blessed by the Gods."

Charlie Kroll props on a log what is left of his Sitka after the untimely visit by two bears. This is a hunt Kroll will not forget.

CHAPTER 14

THE ELUSIVE COUES

One Can Spend More Time Finding This Species Than It Takes To Down One

The Coues deer roams the inhospitable plains and mountains of the Southwest. Finding the small deer is the major challenge.

High-powered optics are a must for searching the rugged countryside for Coues deer. The small deer hides easily.

I KNOW enough about Coues deer to appreciate fully that they constitute an unusually different and difficult bowhunting challenge. Discussion on which are the most difficult deer to bowhunt is often a lively topic between whitetail and mule deer guys. Coues deer hunters seldom get involved in such conversations. They believe they already know. If you happen to wind up in a bar stool conversation, say on a Friday night in a cantina somewhere in southern Arizona, you will find their opinions to be emphatically biased.

I read somewhere that an army officer back in the Indian war days originally identified and classified as a new species, the deer that today bears his name (correctly pronounced "cows" rather than what it looks like). It certainly must have seemed to be a new species at the time, given its almost miniature physical difference compared to the then more familiar Eastern whitetail variety, as well as its harsh, unforgiving habitat. Certainly, these were not forest or woodlot whitetails.

Some folks feel that according this one particular whitetail deer individual recording status among trophy hunters is inequitable, considering there are around twenty whitetail

subspecies roaming North America from Canada to mid-Mexico, some with equally distinct differences that have been all lumped together.

It's a valid argument if you want to be picky. The other subspecies do generate more hunting attention, and never mind the sub-tropical deer of the same family farther to the south that get hardly any consideration.

However, having spent a great deal of time roaming the often inhospitable country of the Coues deer, I can agree that separate recognition seems warranted, though I would make the same case for the whitetails of Anticosti Island in Canada as a similar evolutionary product with uniquely different characteristics.

For a bowhunter, the Coues may well be the most difficult deer to hunt, even though putting one in the records is proportionately easier than a mule deer. That might seem a contradiction, but it is so. When you take something as uncannily careful about its self-preservation as a whitetail, then put it in country that is as different as any a bowhunter can find in which to play his close-range game, you have the epitome of the expression: A stacked deck!

Thus far, in the thirty-plus years of recording big-game trophies taken with a bow and arrow, only seventy-eight Coues deer have been entered in the Pope & Young records. Sure, not all trophy deer are entered, but I believe that, as a percent of the total of the successful big buck busters who do take trophy deer, more of them will enter a Coues, or a Sitka blacktail, than any whitetail, blacktail or mule deer, simply because that's what most of the folks that go to the trouble of trying for one are after.

So, if you accept that, seventy-eight is a little tiny number today though I would bet that by the time the 18th recording period for the Pope & Young Club is over on December 31, 1992, the century mark for Coues entries will be in close sight, as more and more bowhunters are taking up the chase.

I have seen a lot of Coues deer. I used to hunt the land in which they live extensively in my heavy-duty varmint-calling days. There also were my many sojourns for javelina in Arizona, ranging from the mid-part of the state around Roosevelt Lake and the San Carlos Apache Reservation, all the way to the Mexican border and beyond.

To be frank, we never paid the Coues deer much attention. They were just some little deer that lived there, and we didn't hunt them. Arizona's deer seasons then were not the same as they are today, with opportunity for a combination javelina and deer hunt, but I am sure, there were several we could have shot easily. Compared even to our smallish local mule deer we chased at home, the Coues were dwarfish! We looked at them with only casual passing interest and I feel they perceived our lack of evil intent with docile appreciation. Sometimes things go that way. They were really rather unimpressive by our perception then, and not nearly so mouth watering as the much bigger desert mule deer we ran across on the same range in January hunting pigs, or later, into February when we were literally thrashing the coyotes.

I was well into my bowhunting career, just developing an eye of interest toward different species, or thinking about trophy class animals before I realized that they were really something unique, and considered precious as rare jewels by those who understood.

I recall a javelina trip I made on a private ranch near Nogales on the Mexican border in the late 1960s. It was a

Every hunter of Coues deer realizes, sooner or later, it may take hours of patient glassing before a Coues deer is spotted.

tightly controlled multiple thousand-acre tract of private land where a friend of mine, a guy with a glib tongue and some vague local ties, gained us access. The property was generally lazy, rolling hills dotted with prickly pear, cholla and ocotillo cactus. This terrain angled up gradually, as it ran to the north for many miles before jerking up onto higher ground. They were not really mountain peaks, though they lifted quickly enough into steep mini-canyon draws between rounded knobs scattered with short, stubby, thick stands of oak.

The oaks were the drawing card. An unusually lush mast crop had pulled the normally widely scattered groups of javelina to these higher places to forage and fatten on tons of the marble-like fruit littering the ground. Looking back, I recall it as the most abundant "easy groceries" drawing card for wildlife I have encountered. Mearns and Gambles' quail were there in great numbers, choking down the round, brownish-green nuts as big as their heads with amazing ease. It was no problem to spot javelina from any high vantage point all day long. Oftentimes they were foraging side by side with the little gray whitetails, a good mix of the blockier, darker-hued desert mulies — and we spotted a bear, too.

In the course of my carefully plotted stalks that led finally to arrowing a large javelina boar, I encountered many Coues deer at close range. I am sure, had I been hunting them — without being too trophy selective — I could have had great shot opportunities at several bucks.

Hunting conditions were excellent. There had been several recent days of rain, leaving the ground as quiet underfoot as

that landscape ever will get, along with cool weather and consistent, reliable day-long breezes. I never have seen anything since close to such prime bowhunting conditions in that environment. Unfortunately, access to that prime, vast rancho has slipped way over the decades.

Coues are petite deer. The second smallest of North American subspecies, they are slick and dainty without nearly the markings of most other whitetails. Color-wise they are bland compared with a northern whitetail from say, Alberta or Wisconsin, though they are not a great deal different in color from the deer of the south Texas bush. There is not as much contrasting white save for the ever-present flagging tail.

The majority of the Coues deer range in the oak and pine belts above the low desert, though I have encountered many, as I said, in the grasslands where we hunted coyotes adjacent to dry creek beds with heavy mesquite thickets and occasional clumps of cottonwood. There, stand hunting would be a good way to tag one near a water source such as a cattle tank, for the country can be very dry with water a premium item.

With better deer habitat, more deer exist in the upper ranges with oak being the major drawing card. Here, with some pine and juniper mixed with more broken country, there is much better stalking cover as well as the angles required to glass for deer.

Most of the hunters I know have one common ground when it comes to essential equipment for hunting these ghostly little deer: high quality, powerful optics. Spot-and-stalk is the preferred technique with emphasis on spotting. Far more time

It may seem a bit small when compared to more-hunted deer, but this Coues deer, taken by Bill Krenz, is an authentic trophy.

can be spent glassing for the hard-to-spot Coues deer than ever is spent actually hunting one down. First, a buck has to be located that's big enough to turn your crank. Next, it has to be in an approachable position. Long hours spent using binoculars are hard on eyes that will recoil from the strain with inferior glasses, too low in power and offering poor resolution. Nothing less than ten-power is considered adequate to the majority of experienced, serious Coues hunters who prefer tripod mounted glasses ranging from twenty to even sixty-power. Tripods are important to ease the strain of long periods of hand holding and to sweep every inch of the area under observation carefully without jiggling.

As a point of reference, his midget frame has a chest depth that measures around fifteen inches, with a small head atop a skinny neck. It can be hard to imagine a deer with an outside spread of twelve or thirteen inches as being a really good trophy buck. Today, though, there is one listed that exceeds the minimum score of sixty-five inches with an inside spread of 8 6/8 inches. They really are miniatures!

Compared to other good whitetail habitat today, one of the best things about hunting the little desert whitetails is the accessibility of good country in which to look for one. Today's climate of leased hunting lands and wealthy private retreats makes it more and more difficult for hunters — especially those close to large cities — to find good or affordable conditions. On the other hand, Coues deer are abundant on public lands in Arizona and the eastern portion of their range in New Mexico. In Mexico proper, where they likewise abound primarily in the state of Sonora, hunting is more rigidly controlled by government red tape.

Most all of those I know who have been hunting these deer lately have opted for the January season in Arizona for several reasons. First, many of them go, because the time of year is a good get-away period, and is really attractive if they happen to live in the eastern Snow Belt. Arizona in January can be spring-like and lovely during the day, with extremely cold nights. I have been there when it snowed or blew freezing rain, too, but all in all, one can expect nice weather.

Secondly — and this is probably what really draws bowhunters — is the dual-hunt opportunity. Javelina are one of the neatest animals to bowhunt and the seasons coincide. Quail shooting is widely available in the same habitat, varmint calling is at its best and there are mule deer.

Also of major interest to the serious deer hunter is the fact that both deer species are in the rut. I have heard of a few minor successes in rattling on Coues deer, but nothing nearly as positive as blacktails, however. Generally, guys with in-depth experience don't lay any value on calling these deer. However, Tom Hoffman, the noted trophy chasing bowhunter from New York tells me that last season ('91) he had excellent success with grunt calls in Arizona during the rut. Like all whitetails, mature bucks become more active, therefore more visible at this time of year. This may make sighting them easier, but more difficult to stalk. I'm told it's easier to pattern the Coues buck before the breeding activity heats up, which makes them pretty much like whitetails anywhere.

The Coues Deer, Not The Javelina, Is The True Gray Ghost Of The Arizona Desert Country

Dave Snyder displays his world record non-typical Coues deer. It scored 112 4/8 in the Pope & Young record book.

"MY SMALLEST trophy deer was the one that was the toughest to take," admits Dave Snyder. When he makes this admission, he is referring to the world record non-typical Coues deer he took in southern Arizona in 1984. The Pope and Young score on this buck was 112 4/8 inches, a petty measurement in mule deer circles, by comparison, but mammoth for this sub-species.

Dave Snyder is a retired firefighter, who spent nearly twenty-nine years with Nevada's Las Vegas Fire Department. A native of Nevada, he has been bowhunting since 1960. In the years since being introduced to the sport, he has carried his bowhunting tackle over parts of Alaska, Mexico and a batch

No matter how tough the bowhunter, the Coues deer is tougher. It hides well in the rugged, scrub-covered desert of Arizona.

of Western states. A member of the Precision Shooting Equipment advisory staff, he used a PSE Mach II bow in taking his record Coues. Doing the deed was a three-blade Brute broadhead on the forward end of a twenty-eight-inch 2215 Easton aluminum shaft.

Dave Snyder has been bowhunting out of Tucson for decades, but it wasn't until he had been hunting the area for a dozen or more years that he really began to concentrate on the Coues whitetail. January always has been a good month for Arizona javelina and 1983 was good for Bill Hardy and Snyder, as they each bagged a nice record class, Coues whitetail after success on javelina.

Dave Snyder has been hunting with Bill Hardy for a decade and Snyder considers the Tucson native the local authority on Coues deer, where to find and how to hunt them.

In the construction business, Hardy was a rifle hunter originally and had taken many of the diminutive desert bucks with that tool before he switched to a bow.

"The most time in hunting Coues deer is spent in glassing, if one really wants to find them," Hardy contends. "Glassing is the name of the game for Coues and it's more important than it is for the sheep hunter. Everyone around here calls the javelina the gray ghost, but that's a misnomer. The real gray ghost is the Coues deer."

"The next year — 1984 — we wanted to improve our trophy score and Bill Hardy spent endless hours prescouting for respectable bucks. He told me upon my arrival in Tucson he had located at least five bucks that might exceed a hundred inches each. This renewed my excitement for the hunt."

"We had hunted for three days, seeing deer each day before

Bill glassed up a nice buck that was hiding under a mesquite tree. After some debate, I planned a stalk and went after him," Snyder recalls. The stalk was useful, as it pointed out an error in Snyder's program.

"I made my approach, but the deer knew I was there long before I got within bow range," Snyder concedes. "After reevaluating the plan, I came to the conclusion that I would have been much more successful had I circled above the animal and worked my way down. With this valuable lesson, we continued on with the hunt."

The two hunted and glassed several different areas over the following few days. They always saw deer but nothing in the size range that dreams are made of. Finally they went back to an area they had glassed previously. This was one of Hardy's favorite tracts, and he knew there had to be good bucks somewhere in hiding.

The two sat there for nearly three hours glassing, then all at once Bill Hardy said, "I got him! There's a new world record Coues!" Hardy walked the Nevada hunter in on the deer, which proved to be a magnificent animal.

"We watched him for at least an hour and, with Bill's 15x60s, his trained eye, and experience, he believed the deer would go anywhere from 106 to 112 inches. We were hoping the deer would bed so I could plan a stalk, but with the rut in full swing, the big buck kept chasing a doe around the whole canyon.

"After some deliberation, we thought that, if I worked my way down into an area where these animals had crossed a couple of times, I could be in an ambush situation. I hurried down the hill to a prominent landmark hoping to be there

If a bowhunter doesn't have the patience to glass for long periods of time, he'd better acquire it if he's going after Coues deer.

before the animals arrived," Snyder recalls.

"I approached the area, arrow ready, sneaking, listening and looking for any movement. Suddenly, without warning, approximately thirty-five yards dead ahead of me was a doe that had me pinned. I froze, only my eyes moving, looking for the buck. My presence was too much. The doe turned and trotted off.

"I stood motionless for a minute or two, hoping the big buck would show himself. I could see nothing, and took two steps in the direction taken by the doe. There, to my immediate right, at about thirty-five yards, the big buck stood, watching me. As I hesitated, he bolted

"Had I only had the ability to wait him out, I would have had a nice shot, but impatience had overtaken my common sense. I returned to Bill's lookout from where he had been able to watch the whole show."

The two returned to that same area the next day, but could not relocate the buck. Bill Hardy had taken only a week's vacation and had to return to work. Dave Snyder was now on his own! Hardy no longer would be there to give signals from behind the glasses or to help analyze the stalk plan.

There is no doubt that Dave Snyder considers Bill Hardy the ultimate guide, when it comes to see-and-sneak tactics for Coues. Their meeting came about after a fellow Las Vegas firefighter kept talking to Snyder of his hard-hunting cousin. The cousin turned out to be Bill Hardy, who insists that glassing game at a distance is probably the most important — and often the most demanding — part of a serious hunt on North American big-game. And the larger and more powerful your binoculars or spotting scope, the better your chances of coming home with a trophy, Hardy insists.

More than forty years ago, Bill Hardy was rabbit hunting with a single-shot rimfire rifle on the south side of the Santa Catalina Mountains near Tucson, when a big animal jumped

out of the brush and took off. That was the first bighorn sheep he had ever seen. Today, he admits he's just as excited at spotting a bighorn through his binoculars as he was in that first experience as a teenager.

Some two decades later, the same Bill Hardy was hunting antelope, using a tripod-mounted spotting scope to help determine trophy value of the animals.

"I had a pair of 9x36 binoculars hanging on a strap around my neck," he recalls. "They kept clanking against the metal tripod, and just to get them out of the way, I rested them on top of my scope. I had picked up a buck antelope and was trying to determine just how large its horns were. By accident more than plan, I took a look through the binoculars. I was amazed at how clear and sharp the animal looked. The binoculars had only half the power of the scope, but I was sold in that moment on the idea of using binoculars with a tripod."

Bill Hardy decided he needed a more powerful set of binoculars and ordered Zeiss' 15x60s through his then employer, Jensen's Custom Ammunition. The price at that time was $1400 retail. Someone from the U.S. distributorship that handled the German manufacturer's products called and asked whether Hardy had not made a mistake in ordering.

"The man on the other end of the line told me the only people who used binoculars that powerful were whalers," Hardy recalls. "And for the first couple of years, I had a lot of trouble convincing hunters they'd be much better off using big binoculars on a tripod to find game animals. They insisted big binoculars were too heavy and nobody wanted to carry a tripod."

Over the next decade, however, most of the Jensen employees who hunt, as well as Hardy's other hunting friends, went to high-power binoculars and tripods. Eventually, it became something of a ritual for Hardy and his friends to show up at the Arizona Game and Fish Department catchment on the

Bill Hardy is considered the ultimate Coues deer guide. He uses tripod-mounted Zeiss 15x60 binoculars to glass the desert.

north side of Pusch Peak to conduct what they called a "glass-off." One of the hunters who became hooked on the use of big binoculars and a tripod was Bill Hardy's son, Tracy.

"He never had a chance," the senior Hardy contends. "As a youngster, I made him carry my tripod. With everyone else, I had to use persuasion, but Tracy had no choice. He had to carry the tripod and use it. He's my best pupil and he can hold his own with the best, when it comes to spotting game animals that're way, way out there."

As a result of Bill Hardy's continuing campaign, most of the state game wardens in the Tucson area now use 15x60 binoculars. Eddie Cocking, wildlife manager for the Catalina Mountain area, was the first member of the Arizona Game & Fish Department to become convinced and buy a pair, but others soon followed. Cocking now even teaches a class on how to use the big glass.

With Bill Hardy's help, Dave Snyder killed five Coues deer with his bow in five hunts. In each instance, Hardy's big glasses and tripod helped find the trophy animal. After that, of course, it was up to the hunter.

"I'm not a guide," Hardy explains. "I don't want to be a licensed guide. For me, finding the game animal is fun. I don't want to make it a lot of work. That would take the fun out of it."

However, legends are in the making over his abilities at finding the ever-elusive bighorn sheep. He has helped a number of hunters kill trophy rams in the Catalinas. One was Jack Ross, two-time president of the Tucson Rod & Gun Club.

"Jack Ross called me and told me he'd been hunting for five days and hadn't seen a single bighorn," Bill Hardy recalls. "I told him we'd find a ram the next morning. When we started to glass, I saw right away why he couldn't find sheep. He had a pair of those tiny, lightweight field glasses. They may be good for something, but not to find bighorn sheep. He killed his ram that first morning."

Bill Hardy spends a good deal of time helping Pete Shepley, head honcho of PSE, make bowhunting videos which are used in sales promotions of the archery products Shepley's company produces.

"It's really challenging," Hardy admits. "We've made a couple of videos on sheep and javelina. Now we're working on one about bowhunting coyotes. Calling in a coyote is the easy part. Getting him to stand still while a bowhunter gets into camera range is something else."

The same obviously can be said for the Coues deer. Shepley and his camera crew have been trying to make a video on hunting this type of deer for five years. They have a vault full of background shots, but they have yet to score a kill on a

Coues deer for the cameras.

"I'm totally spoiled by the big binoculars," Hardy explains. "The light-gathering quality of the 60mm lenses is really remarkable. As an example, I can be glassing a slope in the early evening and see quite well while others who are with me have given up, because they feel it is too dark."

With a lot of cheap binoculars, the outside edges of the field of vision is fuzzy. In this situation, at least a quarter of the field of view cannot be used properly. But there is more to it than that.

"When I have the big binoculars set up on my tripod, I have what is best called a dead field of vision. That means the glasses are perfectly steady and there is no movement as would be the case were the binoculars hand-held or if I was using a stick or even a tree limb for support. If anything moves out there, I'm able to see it the moment it happens."

In glassing an area, Hardy also feels comfort is another important factor. "If you're sitting there and have your knees pulled up and your elbows braced on your knees, there always will be a bit of movement," he contends. "And the longer the individual sits there, the more intense the movement becomes, because this person is growing tired from maintaining that awkward position. The tripod helps solve that problem, of course."

When moving from place to place, especially in cold weather, Hardy keeps the big binoculars inside his jacket or shirt. They are hung from his neck by a strap. Having the binoculars close to his body keeps them relatively warm and the lenses are less likely to fog up when he starts to glass an area.

When glassing a segment of wilderness real estate, Bill Hardy tends to scan the tops of the ridges and the other high areas first. He has found these to be the places where the animals are most likely to be in the early morning where sunlight strikes. Hardy uses a sort of mental grid pattern and glasses the slope laterally.

Hardy offers a knowing smile when told that there now are some two hundred different models of big binoculars that apparently have been developed primarily for observing wildlife. Some, of course, are good; others are not.

But he insists that one doesn't have to spend up to $1700 for a set of binoculars. He has found that the 10x50 glasses marketed by Bushnell are more than adequate for finding game on a distant slope. They retail for less than $300.

This was the type of help Dave Snyder knew he would be lacking when Bill Hardy returned to his job and this hunter found himself on his own. However, he also realized he had not run all those hills with Hardy for a decade without learning much of what the glassing expert had to offer.

"I felt perhaps we had put too much pressure on the canyon, so I tried another spot we had hunted the previous season. I found deer and pigs, but nothing in the class I wanted," Snyder says.

'I kept thinking about the big buck, remembering the thickness of his rack, so the next day I returned to the canyon where we'd seen him. I had been glassing for about ten minutes when I spotted two does across the canyon. They were being followed by a small buck, then a nice massive five-pointer appeared. I watched his every move for about thirty minutes — until he disappeared behind some trees. I looked the area over for further movement but finding none, came to

the conclusion my buck had bedded."

Making a decision, Snyder tried to pinpoint the big buck's location. Picking up his bow, he chose a route that would allow him to circle above the buck, then work his way down. It took the bowhunter about an hour and a half to circle to his predetermined goal.

"Stopping to glass the area, I knew I had to be careful after I spotted the smaller buck and doe, both of them bedded down. I certainly did not want to spook them as I had the day before.

"I worked my way to a point where I finally felt it was safe to come down into the area. I had plenty of time, so I was extremely careful in my movements."

After another hour, Dave Snyder found himself at a point from which he could see the bedded doe only fifty yards away. She lay there, chewing her cud, unaware of his presence. "The smaller buck was out of sight, but I had last seen him approximately fifty yards beyond the doe. I remained still about ten minutes wondering whether to try to wait out the deer, hoping when they got up they would mill around to give me a good shot.

"I could see the doe lying down, plus the area to my left, but I was unable to see the terrain to my right without exposing myself. I looked hard but still could not find the big buck."

Laying his bow down, Snyder crawled four feet or so to where he could survey the ground to his right. He knew the buck was there, but still could not locate him. He lay there, watching the doe for about fifteen minutes, then caught some movement directly to his left.

Coming out from underneath a bushy tree at fifteen yards, was what had become his dream buck. The animal stopped, looked around, then slowly walked toward the doe. Snyder had two choices — reach for his bow and try a hurried shot, or let the buck walk out of sight, then retrieve his bow.

"I can't remember ever before being more excited or impressed by a single animal, even though the Coues deer are small in comparison to other big-game animals. That massive

Bill Hardy (left) and Dave Snyder recount the day's events that led to the taking of the world record non-typical Coues.

Dave Snyder used a PSE compound to take his world-record Coues whitetail. The second arrow he nocked wasn't necessary.

five-point rack had me shaking. As soon as he reached the doe, she got up, and they walked behind some trees, still unaware of my presence. I immediately grabbed my bow, and snuck after them. I could hear them walking, then came a snort. I froze! Standing there, I waited for some indication of their location. Nothing!"

Snyder decided not to push his luck. He crept back and returned to his original vantage point, still hoping to locate his prize. Still nothing, and, after a couple hours, he returned to Bill Hardy's house to report on his day of frustration.

"I returned to the same area for five consecutive days," the bowhunter reports. "Glassing the buck daily, I attempted stalk after stalk without success.

"On the fifth morning, I found myself at the same spot earlier than usual, and after glassing for only a a short time, I found the big five-point. But this morning, instead of two or three deer with him, I counted a trio of four-pointers, two with three points each and three does. I could hardly believe my eyes. I watched for about an hour, wondering what they were going to do. It seemed to me they were working their way up the mountain, and if they continued to do so, they probably would drop into the next canyon."

Unlike the previous days, when Snyder let the deer bed, he decided to go after the big buck. Instead of being deliberately slow and quiet, he hurried to make a large circle that would bring him to the top of the ridge before the deer.

"In doing so, I lost sight of the animals, and arriving on the ridge, could not find any deer. I was not sure whether they had gone over the crest or were still below me.

"I moved along carefully, checking the terrain below me. I thought I was too late, but going another forty-five yards, I heard a loud snort. I stopped quickly, thinking I had spooked them. The snorting continued, accompanied by hooves hitting the ground.

"Still not seeing anything, I carefully moved a bit farther and saw the four-point and the much larger five-pointer facing one another, the other deer watching this display. I stalked about ten yards closer before a small deer, hidden to my left, jumped up and ran straight away from me.

"At that moment, I thought they would all disappear. Instead, the two big bucks, apparently confused, came toward me, the four-point leading the way. As he walked past at approximately thirty yards. I drew my bow, anticipating shooting this animal. However, I caught the larger Coues buck's movement, as he followed at about fifty yards behind the four-point. I took one last look at the latter, realizing he

Snyder stands next to his record-book Coues. Though taken in 1984, the much-admired whitetail is still a world-record.

was at least a one hundred-point-plus buck.

"Still at full draw, I turned my attention to Mister Five-by-Five. Walking quickly, he somehow sensed my presence, and began to angle away as I released my arrow.

"The buck exploded down the mountain, disappearing behind a large tree about thirty yards from where I had hit him. I watched and did not see any movement behind the tree. I nocked another arrow on my bowstring and slowly began to edge forward. A few feet later, I saw the little, but nonetheless magnificent trophy.

"It took nearly four hours to field dress the animal and get off the mountain with one thought bouncing about in my mind. This, my smallest trophy ever, had turned out to be the toughest to take."

CHAPTER 15

UPS & DOWNS OF DEER-TAKING

I'M NOT sure what possessed me to climb the tree. It was nothing I had ever done before. In fact, I don't believe I had ever heard of anyone doing such a thing. It used to be, when we went deer hunting, a bunch of us got together and just went. In the beginning, these outings were little more than armed walks along the firebreak roads that meandered through the foothills. Once in a great while, someone would see a deer peeking from a shadowed opening in the head-high brush. There were lots of deer. The foothills were full of them, but they were difficult to spot.

Being eagerly young and persistent, I made these early morning and late evening walks on a regular basis, probably because it was so convenient. I could be at most of my parking spots in fifteen or twenty minutes, patrol the firebreaks for an hour or so and, maybe, see a deer.

Every now and then someone might actually get a bow shot. Word of that event would spread to fire our furnaces of optimism. It was pretty tough hunting, and what turned everything around was the brush fires.

Once unbelievably thick brushland was opened up by the racing infernos that periodically plague California. The results were great deer spots where we actually could see them. They loved the burns and so did we.

On one particular morning, near the bottom of a big draw that some might call a canyon, I climbed out on to the almost level limb of a huge live oak just to sit and do some looking. The limb, sticking out over the sidehill, put me above a major deer trail cut into the opposite hillside fifteen yards away.

I hadn't been there five minutes when a buck appeared, wandering along the trail on a course that would put him in a highly vulnerable position. I was jittery as hell, shaking like the proverbial leaf, as he got to a spot perfect for my sitting posture in the tree. Somehow I managed to jerk back the strings of my fifty-pound recurve and shoot him.

Successful tree stand bowhunting requires more than just perching in a tree. A hunter must blend with background and have enough camouflage to break up the foreground.

Whether Perched In A Tree Or A Hole In The Turf, Some Basics Must Be Observed

Modern tree stands are light and compact enough to be easily carried to hunting area.

My best buck to that point in my life, also was my first ever from a tree.

TREE STANDS

If we were to give recognition where it's due, the tree stand has had more impact on bowhunter triumphs over whitetail deer than almost all the rest of the equipment we use combined.

The accolade can be extended in growing terms to include elk, mule deer and Columbian blacktails as excellent species for tree stand tactics. Without the elevated stand or, simply, a tree's lofty branches, hardly anyone would bowshoot many whitetails. Today, bowhunters take thousands upon thousands of whitetails annually. Take away the tree stand, the ladder or the tripod, and those figures would drop dramatically.

I can remember when tree stands were illegal across much of the land. The first time I hunted whitetails with Fred Bear in Michigan, any elevated tactic was a no-no. We hunted from ground blinds, and Fred, of course, shot a nice buck! In Michigan today, one can use tree stands and set them up over piles of carrots and sugar beets. "Bait stations," they call them. Times and philosophies change.

When I first hunted whitetails in Oklahoma — this was before commercial stands were much in evidence — experienced folks carried around various lengths of one-by-twelve boards with notches cut at each end; "crotch stands" they were called. Simply wedged between two near vertical limbs at the desired height in an accommodating tree, they provided an elevated shooting platform. They are still much in use around the country today.

However, it's not the same anymore. Man's ingenuity has spawned literally hundreds of tree stand devices and what amounts to a significant industry. As elevated stands became legal and safe, lightweight portables hit the market; deer hunters of all persuasions embraced them. Simple-to-use tree stands and exploding whitetail populations resulted in a hunting boom that has not slowed since.

Tree stand styles and applications today are almost as varied as tree types, but they can be broken down into three specific categories: climbers, portables and permanents.

Simply defined, the climbers require a nearly straight tree with no large, interfering branches below the desired height location. Small twig-like branches can be trimmed to make way for the stand's climbing motion.

This type of stand is particularly popular in the Southern "piney woods" states. The climber is attached to the tree — it is in two sections — and the hunter actually ratchets himself up the tree.

Portables are lightweight, collapsible stands, easy to carry and quick to install. The stand must be carried to the desired height in the tree and attached with the hook-up of chain, rope or nylon webbing belts. There are a number of hook-up styles, most quite easy to handle.

Permanent tree stands are exactly what the term implies. Most consist of cross brace two-by-fours with plywood flooring, though one can find any number of construction procedures. Permanents are allowed legally only on private lands.

Old permanent stands can be extremely dangerous. Never use one without carefully checking it out. Some of the most severe injuries, even fatalities, with which I'm familiar, occurred with old, weather-beaten permanents.

The portable is the runaway leader in popularity. I believe

A lone hunter will often be worn out just from installing a tree stand. Teamwork makes the job a lot easier and faster.

I probably have used every conceivable style and found them most satisfactory. Recent changes in most designs have raised the scat on those that have one built-in, which has added a great deal to their comfort. Long hours in a too-low seat uncomfortably affects your efficiency, as well as your enjoyment.

No matter what stand style I use, I try to position it so I can shoot from a sitting position. This eliminates unnecessary movement and helps keep my arrow impact area low on the target.

I do take into consideration my shooting lanes from a standing position out of the same stand in case standing is necessary for a shot — the best laid plans do go astray. No matter what type of stand, I always position it as low as I can possibly get away with depending on cover and the wind. In areas I hunt frequently, I position two for shifts in prevailing winds. I keep my stands low in order to get as close to a flat broadside angle as possible, which increases my odds for double lung hits, complete penetration, and good blood trails, by providing a larger vital target area. This is important.

Keep background cover in mind when in a tree stand. If necessary, import some greenery from surrounding trees, and consider how the stand will appear later in the season, as cover diminishes. Take the sun's position into account. Will it be in your eyes? Set the stand so the sun will be in the deer's eyes, and watch how its position affects your shadow on the ground. Avoid casting shadows where you expect to have deer.

I try to set my stands where the shot will be close, but still provide enough visibility to get set before they get too close. The perfect scenario is for the deer to be where you want it and you are at full draw, ready when it gets there. No motion, no squeaking arrow rest, no fluttering heart to spook it.

It was Barry Wensel, I believe, who said, in effect, "Put the stand where you can kill the deer, not where you can see the most deer." I love to watch them, but when I want to shoot, I want to see my fifteen-yard pin settling in dead-solid. That deer will go in the truck.

Always make certain the stand is positioned solidly, and check it every time before you get on it. Nuts, bolts or moving parts can come loose, perhaps caused by contraction or expansion from weather changes that affect the tree. These loose mechanisms can squeak, groan, click or squeal; all are sounds that have spared many a whitetail's life. Tree stands have made the woods a dangerous place for an uncautious deer, and they can be an equally dangerous situation for those who use them. They are the number one cause of deer hunter injury today. Use them in careful confidence; do not get complacent.

SAFETY BELTS

Before discussing other styles of stands, let's concentrate for a bit on the subject of safety belts. I know guys — and so do you — who eschew their use in some sort of hairy-legged flood of assured self-immortality. I knew one who is now dead!

I have a few stands where a belt isn't necessary, maybe, but there's still a belt there. There are two sound reasons of equal value for their use.

First, obviously, is safety itself. Second, a safety belt or the newer harnesses can provide one with a shooting area of maneuverability of almost 360 degrees. Adjusted to the right length, one can lean out, turn and swing in almost any direction. I have killed a lot of deer, because I could take advantage of the unexpected. Deer do not always come to you

Even the largest South Texas mesquite is too weak for tree stands. A single pole, lashed to the frail tree, holds this seat.

where they are supposed to.

As a visiting fireman in hunting areas around the land, I have been offered a host's favorite stand on more than one occasion. A postage stamp-sized platform at dizzying altitude...with no safety belt.

"Aaah, we don't use 'em heah!" is the usual comment. My ever-present, always-packed compact safety belt is a welcome friend on such outings.

I am not yet old or enfeebled. I believe I can and will bowhunt for a long time to come. My chances are doubled, because I will not take stupid chances by playing around in places God truly only intended for birds and squirrels. Anyone can make a mistake, anyone can slip. Anyone.

Deer habitat dictates how deer are hunted. The evolution of elevated stands has been oriented geographically. I believe it was Jim Baker who truly pioneered the tree stand market. The

Baker stands were climbers, designed for the Southern piney woods habitat with little understory, few branched trees, a world of straight pines and the need to get above line of sight.

Portables, of course, were more adaptable to varied habitat tree types. Permanents, with time to build them in desired locations, always have been part of the hunter's arsenal. I have seen old stands in place on private land that I guarantee were in use long before the technique was considered proper.

When I think of a stand type that has been designed especially to meet a specific habitat type, I cannot help thinking of Texas and the tripod. I had real cause for such reflection less than two weeks ago, on the broad vistas of south Texas. In that white brush and mesquite country, huge numbers of whitetails abound in numbers greater than in any other state. It's remarkably flat country, and one is hard-pressed to see any sort of tree that might safely hold a portable stand by itself, much less loaded down with a hunter.

The fragile mesquite, a rather pretty tree in my estimation, tops out for uncounted miles in the vicinity of six to eight feet. Three-legged stands are the product of necessity here, being high enough to provide visibility in the extremely dense brush and hopefully high enough to evade the wind. They are remarkably effective even though, while in one, you cannot help but feel nakedly exposed, certain you stand out like the proverbial sore thumb.

Actually, in such heavy, low cover, a tripod is a unique concept with widespread applications. We have taken to using them in the low, second-growth oak brush in Oklahoma. I have hunted from them regularly in Texas and more recently in tight cover in Missouri. They work. They are comfortable for long sitting spells, and offer 360-degree swivel seat coverage of the shooting area. I shot a deer out of that last tripod I was in. Thick brush and six-foot mesquite provided me with only broken twenty-yard visibility intervals at the junction of five heavily traveled trails. I caught brief glimpses of rain-soaked gray/black deer hide traveling a downwind track and had a perfect thirteen-yard shot when the deer stepped into full view.

Placed anywhere in the country with good background cover and available in heights up to twelve feet, the tripod is an extremely good elevated stand. Much the same can be said for the ladder stand which is rapidly gaining nationwide popularity.

Admittedly, because it is not free standing like the tripod, its position locations are more limited. However, in place against a solid support, the easy-to-move, lightweight ladder stands of today offer interesting possibilities. They are easy to get into. No safer than any stand, they require equal caution when mounted. Most require that one stands while atop its platform, which surely suggests a safety belt. I have several lightweight ladder stands that have been the undoing of a passle of whitetails.

Position with any stand is key. The flexibility of tripods and ladders often lets one place a stand where no proper tree is found, exactly where you want to hunt. With portable stands, finding a good hunting location — never too hard — we are restricted to finding that location with a proper tree. Sometimes that is difficult. The flexible versatility of ladders or tripods can make the difference in being able to set up exactly where you want rather than just close to where you want.

All of the foregoing suggests that to be a complete stand-type deer hunter, several stands are required if you want to play the game effectively. That's not true, but it's close.

If I have to pick one tree stand style that will offer me the most opportunities wherever I might hunt, the lightweight portable would get the call. Coupled with a half-dozen steps, I always can find a suitable location. I prefer, though, to have as many options at my fingertips as possible. I am, after all, no different than anyone else when it comes to possessing a garage full of life's real necessities. So I have a wide variety of stands, ranging from portables to ladders. I take some comfort in the adage: He who dies with the most toys wins!

STAND ACCESSORIES

In order to put up a tree stand of any type with ease, several items can make the task a great deal more simple. A good limb saw is required to cut away interfering branches around the stand and to clear out good shooting lanes. Pruning clippers

The folding limb saw is a necessary part of the tree stand hunter's accessory pack. It is used frequently.

These simple screw-in steps make climbing in and out of tree stands easier where legal. Check often for safety.

are also handy and those on extension poles allow clearing of hard-to-reach twigs that obstruct not only shooting lanes but visibility.

A bow hanger on a close-at-hand branch or a bow holder that attaches to the stand to hold the bow in the "ready" position, plus a comfortable seat cushion — can make long vigils much more pleasant.

I use a bow hanger, keeping it positioned where I can reach the handle riser with a minimum of movement. My son, Kelly,

Here's a way to take camouflage with you. Insure there is enough space inside the blind to freely operate your bow.

always sets his stands for a full standing position and always holds his bow. He holds it for hours, but he's young and tough. I trust he'll learn to sit in time.

A cord or rope is necessary to raise and lower your bow, as climbing with them can be both difficult and dangerous. Tree steps are super. On private land, screw-in models usually are legal, depending upon the landowner. Public lands require another style such as rope blocks or rope ladders. I hate rope ladders, but rope-style steps work fine.

The list of possible accoutrements includes a variety of seats for stands that do not have built-ins, umbrellas for rainy

With a climbing type stand the hunter actually ratchets up the tree. They are ideal for mature pine woods.

days — not a dumb idea, really — bow quiver hooks and attachable shelves for thermos bottles. Beyond a point, it's up to you, though I suggest it is possible to have too many toys.

Bottom line: An elevated stand is the bowhunter's best friend, and their impact on whitetails is the most significantly effective tool we use. In recent years, using such stands to take mule deer and elk has met with resounding success on trails, at water holes, wallows and feed grounds. We use the same tactics we employ for whitetails. Of course, bear hunters have understood their value for years.

I've been bouncing around the country quite a bit of late, somehow or another managing to spend more time in various deer camps than on more practical or commercial pursuits. I didn't say more important, I said *practical.*

I haven't shot much, but I've seen a lot of game and some pretty country and have met an awful lot of really good people with less than the usual amount of nerds. That has been refreshing. Usually, there is always one far-out idiot about in every camp to make being polite tedious.

The camps so far this season have been short on nerds; all but one. He was weird enough to cause us to believe we were going to get a whole year's supply wrapped up in a single camo suit around one campfire.

This guy was an expert. I know, because he told me so repeatedly. He told me a lot of things I had never heard before. Usually, such information is welcome; there's a lot of things I have never heard of before. But most of these tidbits were refinements on things I had heard about already. How high to get in a tree, for instance, if you're hunting whitetails, which we were.

I never knew, for instance, that you should never be lower than thirty feet. Honest, I really didn't. Nor did I know that higher was better! Because that gives a perfect angle on the deer's spine. I really should have known that, I guess.

I suppose my ignorance was based on a couple of errors; the first being somewhat geographic, so I'm not totally at fault. In the country I hunt most, Oklahoma, we're pretty hard pressed to find trees thirty feet high in good deer country. The second error was the most glaring. I have not been brought along over these last thirty or so years of serious bowhunting—nor have any of those of my acquaintance—to purposely set up my hunting strategy for spine shots. Those that do occur obtain spectacular results and are accidents.

Thirty to fifty feet and spine shots! Well, everyone has to march to his own drum beat and I suspect this guy's course will eventually lead him to the Funny Farm or his family burial plot. If the truth were known, he's probably harmless as far as depleting wildlife resources is concerned. He left camp empty-handed, not having seen any game, which I found surprising. From his lofty perch he could see the whole state. How in the world can a grown person come up with such a scatter-brained notion, then proceed to hunt accordingly?

It's been my opinion that people have a tendency to want to get too high in stands, anyhow. Admittedly, it offers better visibility under some conditions; less under others, I might add. It will certainly aid in scent dispersal, but too high is not good.

Those of us who understand the principle behind the killing efficiency of an arrow, know that we kill by introducing our razor-sharp hunting head to the animal's vital organs. Those are forward in the chest, ahead of the diaphragm and in the lower half of the deer. That's where we want to concentrate on and where we want the shot to go. If we do that right, the animal's down quickly.

To do this requires the correct angle at close range, so we can minimize our mistakes. If the deer is ten yards from the base of your tree and you are thirty to forty feet in the air, how are you going to get the arrow in the correct area? You're not. You don't shoot straight down and "spine him." You wait until you have the right angle that allows you to tuck that arrow in snug behind a foreleg or drive it through his lungs. This means that the flatter the angle from your stand to the deer, the better able you are to see and hit the proper area. The steeper the angle, the smaller and more protected that area becomes.

We also want to maximize our chances for complete arrow penetration. We will have a high entry on the deer from any elevated shooting position. We want a low exit wound to generate the maximum in blood flow and facilitate tracking. The higher you are, the higher you are most likely to hit the deer. Shooting a tad high is a normal occurrence when you're shooting downward. The higher you hit 'em, the less likely your chances for that desired complete penetration angle.

We want to hit them in the right place and we want a blood trail to follow. I have hunted whitetails in parts of the country that were virtual jungles, the ground covered with knee-high grass. I don't care if the deer went only forty yards; in that kind of stuff, you have to have a trail to follow or you're going to be spending an awful lot of miserable, frustrating time trying to sort everything out.

A big old buck wanders through the woods looking at everything from an eye level of approximately thirty-six to forty-two inches. You do not have to be at nose-bleed elevation to escape his normal vision area. If he looks up, it is because something you did wrong made him look up.

There's an old tree on a creek bottom bend in Oklahoma from which I have killed five bucks. My feet are five feet off the ground in that tree. It is a perfect tree with lots of natural cover. Only one deer has ever seen me in that tree and he was already shot. I was trying to do it to him again and got a little flustered.

Day in, day out, somewhere about ten feet up is an ideal height. It will provide you with that best angle of attack and give you plenty of room to maneuver above the average sight

Building natural blinds can take a lot of work and they are useful only until the foliage begins to fall away. However, they are a way of putting you in the middle of the action.

line. If you also have plenty of cover, especially behind you, then you're just as high as you need to be.

GROUND BLINDS

Some of my fondest recollections in forty years of bowhunting are the days I was able to spend with Fred Bear. Even after tree stands were made legal, Fred preferred to hunt from the ground. In Michigan, where I hunted with him on several occasions, a ground blind was his idea of a good and proper way to ambush a whitetail.

I have to admit, the Michigan woods in the fall provide much more natural cover at ground level than most any other place I have hunted in the same seasonal period. Constructing a good ground blind from dog fennel and other low brush, where it would not appear out of place, made a great deal of sense.

When it came to doing things that made sense, being able to slip easily into the natural order of things, and understand all of the reasons of how and why, no one in my experience or opinion will ever equal Fred Bear. He was the man I consider to have been the world's foremost bowhunter.

Fred Bear smiled and told me once,"Ground blinds are more comfortable." He went on to suggest that, if you are more comfortable, you certainly are going to be more effective.

Portable ground blinds have become popular with today's bowhunters. Dougherty believes they work if left in place long enough for game to become accustomed to structure.

That's hard logic to argue. I believe he was right, and I know we do not employ the use of ground blinds today as often as we should.

There are many hunting situations where a tree stand, tripod, ladder or whatever just won't work. Sagebrush country mule or prairie whitetails are good examples. Deer in these barren conditions can be patterned and the ground blind becomes the solution to getting close. I have taken quite a few mule deer from ground blinds.

Jack Howard, the famous bowyer from California, was a master at ground blind mule deer technique. John Lamicq, the well-known Colorado outfitter, had excellent ground blinds for his clients in the mule deer boom era of the late Sixties and early Seventies, and many a record book buck fell to their arrows.

Judd Cooney, my long-time hunting *companero* from Colorado, is a ground blind master. Actually, a more proper term would be "pit blind" master, as Judd perfected the technique of getting his hunters extremely low and well concealed. He has used pit blinds effectively for all forms of North American big game. Some ground blinds I've used actually were wooden sheds or camouflaged cloth tents. All

Ground pits can provide excellent concealment. Depending on location, their field-of-view can be extremely limited.

can work under the right conditions.

While there are exceptions, I think a ground blind of any style has to be in place well in advance of hunting season to allow deer to become familiar and comfortable with its presence. Pit blinds, placed well below silhouette level, seem to evade detection and resultant alarm.

Good ground blinds can be constructed as Fred Bear said, for comfort and designed for optimum concealment, while still allowing room for movement.

The tree stands' forte is its above-line-of-sight position, and for evading the wind. Ground blinds have to be placed with considerably more attention to wind than any other natural element. I have been in Texas where a portable blind, placed only hours before, went totally ignored. On the other hand, carefully constructed ground blinds that, to my eyes, blended perfectly with the terrain, have been studied by deer with suspicion from a distance for days.

Deer behavior varies greatly from one geographic location to another and depends largely on the amount of hunting pressure they have received over the generations, their daily proximity to man, feed and weather.

Given a choice, I would rather shoot at a deer from the ground than from a tree, simply because it offers better killing angles. Slapping a portable stand in a tree is much easier than constructing an efficient ground blind, but I am becoming more and more convinced that ground level tactics are the solution to an increasingly sophisticated brand of whitetail that is learning to favor the safety of open country and treeless visibility over timbered ridges and creek bottoms.

Being a consistently successful deer hunter requires imagination and flexibility. The ground blind is a valuable tool for the serious bowman.

Rope steps are easy to pack and safe to use. These steps are a must for public lands since screw-in steps are prohibited.

CHAPTER 16

CALLING THE WILD

Rattling Antlers Or Using Mechanical Grunts, Cries Or Sighs Can Work For Bucks

SOUTH TEXAS in January should be cool. It's not supposed to be hot with the bugs still out. But it was a hot eighty degrees under a bright, white sun at 11 a.m., and here was a buck bearing down on us like it was a cold, wintery, peak-rut December day.

Altogether, it seemed ridiculous with the little puffs of dust flying up every time the buck's hooves smacked the ground; not at all right for January. I don't argue with what doesn't seem right. I take what happens and wonder about it later.

Robert Louis Murphy, one of the premier guides at the Kenedy Ranch, way, way down in Texas where the humongous holdings of the ranch end and the Gulf of Mexico begins, clattered the antlers again, then lay down flat on his back.

The spot was a narrow oak mott finger jutting out for two hundred yards from a thicker copse of trees where the cover tightened up. It was, thought Murphy, a good place to rattle even though it was hot, late in the day, late in the season and very, very late in my hunt. He had had a hunch.

It's all a matter of opinion. In mine, nothing compares with the intriguing potential of calling up any kind of animal. Somehow, taking hold of a situation by imitating sounds that motivate game to approach for whatever reason is hunting in its purest sense. I admit to being partial to elk when they are lovestruck, rut-charging hot for the maximum in adrenaline rushes with North American big game, though there is something about a longbeard tom turkey in the spring that makes my mouth just as dry.

I have called up at least 3000 coyotes. Their galloping, sideways gait never ceases to fire me up. For sure, nothing is the same as the last turn on an upwind leg, when a bunch of Canada geese believe what you are saying, like your spread, drop their feet and commit. There is, of course, a similarity to all of these scenes. There is the thrill of watching, lying in wait, primed and ready, as the reward of practice and study are about to be realized. There is a feel of accomplishment attached to

Dougherty considers Brad Harris of Missouri one of the nation's top deer callers. Brad is using a Lohman grunt call.

calling in game that no other hunting technique can match.

The biggest story on the big game scene today is calling whitetail bucks. Nothing on this continent has as many hunters so totally wrapped up in their pursuit. Whitetail bucks of any size captivate us, while our passionate search for record-class bucks has become an almost uncontrollable obsession. By comparison, Lancelot's search for the Holy Grail was a casual scavenger hunt.

In today's bowhunting circles there are two prime themes of conversation: which bow is fastest and big whitetails. No other subjects come close. While the former puts me to sleep as being largely immaterial, the second is of immeasurable interest.

Truly, this preoccupation with whitetails, big ones in particular, has taken on all the proportions of a major cult. I admit to being a member. Big whitetails occupy a major portion of my thoughts. I dream of them with intensity, and pursue them with vigor. In the matter of collecting a truly big one I fall short.

I am optimistic that I will succeed someday, and I am confident that when it happens, calling, in some form, will likely be the determining factor.

There is nothing new about calling whitetails. Rattling bucks has been an established technique in the Southwest for as long as I can remember reading and hearing about hunting them. For years, the notion seemed to exist that the technique was only effective on the broad, flat vistas of Texas where whitetails exist in almost unbelievable numbers, but while the technique may have been developed there, the patent has long since run out.

Time and experimentation has proved that whitetail bucks can be rattled successfully wherever they exist from Texas' *senderos* to the Missouri River breaks.

It's a long ways from Texas to Alberta, Canada, where I took one of my best whitetails, a 212-pounder that nearly ran me down. Rattling may always be better in Texas simply because they have so damn many deer, but your chances are also exceedingly good in upper New York State.

There are two simple reasons for this. First, we have more whitetails today than ever before in this continent's history. Availability certainly generates interest and raises the odds for success.

Second, this population boom has spawned an explosion of theories, techniques and "revolutionary new products," new ones appearing almost daily, that will enable us (they claim) to improve our odds in the successful pursuit of big whitetail deer. In no short supply, in addition to the above, are the *experts*. To all of these, calling in a variety of forms is preeminent, though scents still get a great deal of attention.

Recently, the greatest emphasis has been placed on "vocalization." Whitetails do communicate with one another through a range of grunts, bleats, snorts and whines that mean something. We have known for years that deer are capable of sound. The blowing snort or the bawl of young deer in distress are familiar noises.

For years, in the spring, I have had does — both whitetail and mule deer — come hard to a varmint call, which is nothing less than a universal distress cry among mammals. During Western mule deer seasons, opening as early as August, where does still have young fawns, they will rally vigorously if you blow anything resembling a distress call.

But such events, while interesting, are not what most

Armed with a snort call, grunt call, bleat call plus a pair of lightweight "ticklers," Jody Hogle is set to call whitetails.

hunters seek. Calling and shooting protective mother deer doesn't fit the goals of anyone of my acquaintance. The same applies throughout whitetail range where archery seasons open early. Deer will respond to a distress bleat, and this, occasionally, will include a young buck.

As a practical matter, distress bleats are not going to be a significant factor in helping you collect a buck. There are exceptions. Larry Jones uses a bleat call to some extent when rattling and grunting for blacktail deer. He uses the call at the end of a series when, for all practical purposes, he is done.

It seems to be an "Oh-what-the-hell" approach from my observation, but he does get some bucks to show up. The only finite thing about calling is that it ain't, so I can't fault Larry's logic or technique. He's too successful a caller.

The big story today for calling whitetail bucks involves the grunt calls. There is no doubt they work. Sometimes the results will astound you. Personally, I think their effectiveness might be short-lived. It is difficult today to find a whitetail hunter who doesn't own a grunt call; a call he blows every time he sees a boy deer.

The first mistake is *when* these hunters use them. I listened to a guy where I hunt in Oklahoma last year lean on a grunt call so hard I thought he was high-balling mallards.

Coming to "the horns," this rattled-in buck offers tempting, deceptive shot. While he is in a good position, there is too much interfering clutter. It's quite a thrill to call-in a deer.

It was early October when he shinnied up a tree not too far from me. He didn't know I was there, and I didn't let him know. I figured I had him cut off from where the deer were coming from, so I didn't give it much thought. If something good came by, I'd shoot it, and he could help me get it to the truck. It would serve him right. He knew he was slipping into my area; he just didn't think I was around.

An hour later, four bucks showed up, feeding across a blackjack oak flat straight toward me. One was a medium eight-point; the others had promise, if they could hang on for three more years. I wasn't terribly interested in any of them, but my intruder was. When it was obvious they were not going to get near him, he started grunting.

At first, it was not too bad. It was okay, though after three or four blasts, the bucks started head bobbing. By the time it got intense they were flat, foot-stomping nervous. It suffices to say that, by the time the caller got into high gear, they were too, hauling tail!

It was too early in the season to grunt bucks. These youngsters were not gruntable, anyhow. In my opinion, all this hunter did was put a negative thought in their minds; one I am sure they still hold.

I was careful to walk up behind him quietly as he headed for his truck after dark. "Nice grunt job," I remarked. Quite startled, he went high in the air. I suppose I was wishing he'd break a leg coming down.

Conditions have to be right; no, perfect, to really rattle deer. I do not truly know how to tell you when they are perfect. I've been there too many times when it should have been perfect and wasn't, so I won't try to dazzle you with my knowledge.

I sincerely believe that, for antler rattling to be a super-effective hunting method, you have to be in an area with a lot of boy deer, all of them in a pre-rut, hot-pants mode. I do not believe, when you have an area with lots of girl deer and a

Learning to rattle-in deer takes practice and patience. Sharing techniques with others adds to each bowhunter's skills and can make the overall hunt a lot more successful, enjoyable.

Deer calling events test a bowhunter's technique and they can be a lot of fun. However, the real test takes place in the field. The winner is the one who calls in and takes a deer.

small ratio buck-to-doe herd mix, that rattling will be nearly as good.

None of this means you shouldn't try. Early on, when the rut is just beginning, I believe bucks can be rattled in herds of moderate buck/doe mix simply because they are curious.

Later, if you are able to pinpoint the area of a dominant buck —difficult when they are traveling widely in search of does—rattling might be the key to bringing him close enough for a shot. He's the type of brawler who resents intrusion.

In spite of the fact that it's being overdone, a grunt call has more potential in my mind when bucks are vigorously chasing does. This is the sound of a buck who has some action, not a fight. It's the real thing, with giggles and candlelight; serious cause for investigation. Grunt calls work extremely well under such circumstances.

Taking Texas out of the equation, since that state has so many deer as to be almost obscene, I have grunted up many times more deer everywhere else I have been than I have rattled. In fact, last season— not counting Texas — I never rattled a single deer. In Texas, I rattled up seven bucks on the first five tries. Two of them were dandies, but that's another story.

Some say mule deer can be rattled and I believe that is so, though I have never done it myself. I have called in mule deer in the rut with what was a grunt call before we had grunt calls: a soft, guttural, almost sighing call on a modified duck call. This is the same sort of thing I used on whitetails twenty years ago, though I wasn't smart enough to perfect it, put it on the market and become a guru.

I grew up with mule deer and often heard them utter this rather low growl when tending does. But rutting mule deer were in the open, so we could stalk them. The call was sort of an incidental why-don't-we-try-this sort of thing.

It's not the same with whitetails. You can hardly stalk

them, but pulling them to you is a possibility. For some reason, the Sitka blacktail, the northernmost cousin of the mule deer whose heaviest concentrations are on the offshore islands and coast of Alaska, is highly vulnerable to a soft bleat, as well as a grunt-style call. The call also attracts brown bear who think highly of the chunky blacktails as a food source, something to keep in mind!

Columbian blacktails, those intermediate cousins that range over the Northwest —Washington, Oregon and down into near central California— also are touted as being callable, and certainly can be rattled.

As mentioned, Larry Jones has a good all-around track record with these guys. I used to call a lot of them when I lived in the West, though usually incidental to calling coyotes. All this proves is that they have something in their makeup that causes them to be sound-susceptible.

Once mule deer range is reached, things seem to change. The blocky big boys of the species (all three are closely related) truly don't seem to give a damn. It's my belief that a lot of it has to do with terrain and visibility. Habitat breeds different characteristics. The thicker the terrain, the better calling seems to work. I cannot prove it, but I certainly have come to believe it.

For what it's worth, my theory on rattling antlers has changed in recent years. I used to carry a rather mediocre set of antlers in terms of heft. I now believe that bigger is better. There's a pronounced difference in the resonance and they sound better when you beat them on the ground, or rake branches in a general attempt to raise a ruckus, all of which is more inclined to incite a buck to investigate.

Rattling on the ground, bow close at hand, is almost an exercise in futility, if shooting a deer is the intent. Teamwork —pairs or even a trio in thick cover is a better technique. Two to shoot, one to rattle, everyone at full cock. By yourself, you are much better off in an elevated position, though you cannot usually make quite the right and proper amount of commotion.

Recently, I have viewed several new videos dealing with the subject of whitetail calling. One introduces an entirely new technique of snorts, bleats and "whooshies." All of the videos are cut together amateurishly and certainly deal with captive deer in the supporting roles.

For sure, these guys will sell some product to a whole bunch of grasp-at-straws whitetail hunters, which only proves the point that the pursuit of whitetails, marvelously exciting and challenging as it is, would have been a Godsend to P.T. Barnum's theory: "There's a sucker born every minute."

Calling deer can be effective. It is, however, the frailest of techniques employed by deer hunters and subject to myriad variables ranging from weather to the whimsical attitude of the subject itself. I believe in it, though I won't bet much on it, and I'm as much a dyed-in-the-wool call kind of guy as you're ever likely to meet!

And what happened on that aforementioned late morning Texas setup, where Robert Louis Murphy had the hunch? A chunky eight-point, all hot and bothered, was in the wide, wide open. I shot him through both shoulders at forty yards and took him back to Oklahoma

A great deal closer to my home in Oklahoma, I had another experience that dealt with the use of a grunt call and its effectiveness. Or maybe I should say I experienced what happened to another bowhunter.

It was shortly after dark when I pulled off the dirt road to swing into camp. The headlights illuminated the lineup of campers in the radius of the turn. Several fires were beginning to burn brightly against the crisp night air. The row of independent little campers that made up our main camp was spotted intermittently with sputtering lanterns. There was a crowd down by Billy's tent camper which was tucked under a giant oak three spaces down from mine. With the engine cut, we could hear the murmer of voices. There was an excitement in the transmission confirmed by Billy's louder, more vivid than usual exclamations.

"Billy's onto something," remarked Darrall, his teeth flashing in the darkness of the cab. With his face painted darker than a minstrel, my youngest son was difficult to see. Darrall's into face paint; a real Judd Cooney disciple.

Billy Davis is, well, excitable, putting it as charitably as I can. Darrall just says he's "pretty much always wound up." Billy used to be our UPS driver, didn't know a bow from a box of rocks when he started picking up at our place. He became intrigued and we sort of adopted him.

He's a karate expert, complete with belts. A robber held up his truck one day and shot him; dinked him with a .22 pistol. Billy took him out. Once, I put a box on my head and he kicked it off before I could blink. I'm not too big, — five-foot ten barefoot — but I wear cowboy boots a lot, good for about another inch. You have to be some kind of wound up to kick boxes off five-foot ten heads, plus boots.

As we walked over to the gathering of our hunting buddies, it was apparent Billy was about to come apart.

"Jim, Jim, Jim... I got one, Jim! Grunted him up, Jim. Shot him real good... grunted him up with that Haydel call... Man, I think I smoked him... Jim, I mean I grunted that..."

Well, we gathered up some lanterns and headed for Bill's stand, with him jabbering all the way about this giant buck and how it had come to his grunting till he had him just right. We found his arrow and a blood trail you could almost follow without any light. At the end of it, which wasn't far, was a sleek whitetail buck about half the size we had been led to believe. He was a dandy, though, and Bill freaked out. Nobody blamed him at all.

Calling whitetails isn't all that new, but last season there were more deer-calling stories going around the country than in the last ten combined. It was crazy and I think ninety-five percent of the tales were true!

Why, all of the sudden? There are two reasons: First, I believe it's simply because more people were trying to call deer, thus the percentages for success have increased. Second, it's because there are some new calls on the market. Calls such as Eli Haydel's are exact in their duplication of whitetail acoustics, specifically the cohesive grunt.

In addition to Haydel's grunt call, several other excellent calls have been introduced. Wayne Carlton has a fine call that uses a diaphragm reed. It's a bit more difficult to master than a simple "blow call," but the tones are perfect. Roger Wyant introduced the Varitone Deer Call, which is a blow model with a top-mounted knob that allows the pitch to be adjusted fully from deep buck grunts to fawn bleats.

Haydell's call goes hand in glove with a tape cassette, *Acoustics of Whitetail Deer,* which was produced by biologist Larry Richardson. His paper delivered under the same title is considered the definitive work on the subject.

Richardson indentifies eight stereotypical sounds of the whitetail: Bleat, distress call, nursing whine, grunt, alert-

This hunter raps an antler on the ground to imitate a buck. It is tough for a lone hunter to call in deer with antlers and react fast enough with his bow. It's best to work in teams.

snort, foot stomp, short-wheeze, and aggressive snort. Richardson identified the grunt as the only call associated with both a dominant-subordinate grunt and the cohesive behavior emitted by both sexes older than 1 1/2 years.

While the two forms of grunt are alike phonetically, the dominant-subordinate grunt is generally uttered only once and is louder than the cohesive grunt. The cohesive grunt, given in a series, is the one that a hunter oftentimes hears in the woods during the rut as the bucks pursue the does. Year round, the female apparently will utilize the cohesive grunt more frequently than a buck, mostly in communication with its fawns. Dominant-subordinate grunts are common to bucks and does throughout the years, as they attempt to establish and maintain herd structure and social status.

While Richardson doesn't discuss it in his paper, I have, on many occasions, observed bucks chasing does, grunting with almost every step. The doe, bounding ahead of the buck, issued a series of soft, swooshing snorts, less violent than the alarm snort we have all heard. This I assume to be an application of the snort-wheeze.

Bill Harper, past president of Lohman Manufacturing, one of the country's foremost call companies, introduced a snort call several seasons ago. On the surface, it may have

A champion animal caller, Dougherty used a grunt tube to call in this 200-pound buck.

appeared impractical to suggest imitating snorts in the woods as they are the most frequently identified as alarm notes. However, blown in a soft series and, in some cases, in conjunction with a grunt call, they have proved effective with some hunters of acquaintance.

I have a personal method for using grunt calls that seems to work well enough, and it has been effective on occasion. I seldom use the call on unseen game or in "blind" situations. Occasionally, if I am hunting in extreme cover with limited visibility, I will try periodic calling. I have done this quite often just prior to rattling, but in those instances, I try to utter just an occasional aggressive snort seconds before the first clattering of antlers. I don't know much more about it than it feels right.

In most instances, we have established our hunting location based on where we expect the critters to be; ambush points, actually. These will be along known travel routes, in feeding areas or perhaps in scrape lines. If your luck runs like mine, the stand will be just out of range of the path the buck chooses to take. Obviously, if the deer is coming to you, there's little you need to do but get ready. That, in itself, can

be difficult. But there you are, with a buck slipping through the woods in that distinct posture that tells you he's looking for action, for girls.

Grunting at this point makes sense. First, I do not think you have a thing to lose. I have seen only rare instances when the grunt, or a little series of grunts, has alarmed a deer or spooked it to flight. I have seen them stop and listen, then go on unconcerned. There have been deer that seemingly could not care less. Then there are those that come on in like Billy's.

If there is one thing I would caution you on it is never to call to a deer within fifty yards and facing you. If he stops, wait him out until he turns to go. Let him get started before giving him another series. The woods of November are open and a deer can see a long way. He expects to see something. His abilities to pinpoint sound, to pick you out in your tree, are excellent. You have to try to confuse him as to location.

A big whitetail buck at the peak of the rut is more vulnerable than at any other time of his life, but vulnerable, not stupid. You can tease one to a call; sometimes you can make him mad, but you cannot rub his nose in it.

CHAPTER 17

FINDING TROPHY BUCKS

Statistics And Study Can Be A Major Aid

Before you can begin the final close-range stalk on a trophy buck, you have to first locate such critters. There are plenty of statistics available to the bowhunter; however, they are often as difficult to read as deer signs in hard-packed brush country.

While this 212-pound whitetail is not big enough for the record book, it's one of Dougherty's favorite deer trophies.

AS A RULE, statistics tend to put me to sleep. This is probably because, for the most part, the schedules of charts and tables I have had to peruse over the years have been roughly as interesting as watching a tree die.

I have studied data that was revealing, beneficial, good for my education, helpful in the decision-making process and unquestionably rewarding, but mostly it is pretty dull.

I have friends who put these tables and charts — data, if you will — together for a living, and I do not find them, generally, to be dull or uninteresting people. They do what they like and so do I. Without exception, they are all smarter than I, better organized and certainly better educated, probably because they were not quite so put to sleep with all the statistics we had to study in order to get better educated. That does not bother me and I am glad there are people to do it.

But on occasion, I come across statistics I find of extreme interest, information that deals with the subject matter at the core of my dreams. This form of data gets my attention.

In what I refer to as the "good old days," I would sit around those close hunting comrades with whom I chose to make major assaults, and we would discuss going *out-of-state*. The main reason for such a foray of course would be to hunt and collect big deer. We were talking Western mule deer hunting.

We were California-based and California was not — nor is now — one of your hot beds of trophy mule deer. To be sure, there were some big deer in California; there are probably a few still. There are also gold nuggets of golf-ball size still lodged in the unreached corners of some of the State's river bottoms. But they are not discovered with anything remotely resembling frequency. Big California bucks are harvested in the same proportion.

Thus, we would charge off to this place or that with not much more to go on than gut feeling, a need to go and perhaps the basis of some archery club gossip to set our course. It was fun and I wouldn't have changed it for the world.

Today's bowhunters can make far more realistic assessments before striking out, because now there is a batch of information available that, in those days, did not exist. The information of which I speak exists in the form of interesting statistics!

Oklahoma's open prairie means tough hunting. Dougherty took this buck off the skimpy tree line in the background.

Dougherty considers Oklahoman Harry Milican one of the best whitetail bowhunters he has ever met. This beautiful buck scored 151 4/8 points on the Pope & Young charts.

On the occasion of the Pope & Young Club's 1987 meeting in Tulsa, Oklahoma, the highlight was the presentation of the third edition of the club's record book. This volume, which is nothing less than a genuine treasure, received appropriate *ooohs* and *aahhs*, all of them richly deserved, as did the ninety trophies on display at the meetings. Included were nine new world records.

Also available at the meeting was a booklet prepared by David Boland of Chatfield, Minnesota. This is a work of no small proportion. When one considers the effort involved in tabulating, it can be accepted as nothing less than a labor of love.

What Boland had prepared was a statistical summary of every North American big-game animal recognized by the Pope & Young Club, in what state or Canadian province they were taken plus a break-down of proportions in tenth-inch increments as recognized for antlered or horned game. As it says up front, if you want to know where the big ones live, this will certainly get you pointed down the right highway to the right state.

While this booklet was presented at the fifteenth recording period (1985-1986), it encompassed the entire records of the club's archives. In other words, it covers all 10,241 entries! No matter which critter strikes your fancy, it's there.

What is of particular interest to most of us are the deer, mostly the whitetail. The data on muleys, blacktails, Coues and Sitkas is included too. For instance, there were 863 mule

deer listed in this third edition including a world record of 201 1/2 inches (*gasp!*). Of these, 288 were taken in Colorado, which makes it the number one producing state — no real surprise — with Utah second at 114 and Idaho in third place with seventy-nine trophies.

The state where I did most of my Western mule deer hunting when I lived in California was Arizona. With its famed Kaibab Plateau, this state is eighth with thirty-five. Want to know something interesting? Arizona ties Kansas at thirty-five. How many of you think about mule deer in Kansas? It doesn't matter anyhow, because you can't hunt them unless you live there. There are 111 non-typical muleys in the book with the same states placing in the same order.

For the 1985-1986 recording period, there were 1024 whitetails entered into the records. Not a single one of them was mine. I take solace in an unknown statistic in this regard. While more than a thousand bowhunters succeeded where I failed, I do not feel like I am alone.

What state produced the most whitetails in this recording period? Well, if you guessed Ohio, a state that gets a lot of bowhunting press, you would be wrong. Nor was it Montana, which has been much in the news in recent years. The number one producing state for king-size whitetails is Wisconsin. Most of them fall in the range of 125 to 140 points. Iowa and Kansas gather up the numbers for bucks over 155 points and

No matter where you decide to bowhunt, after studying all the data, it still all comes down to the basics of reading the signs and then getting close enough to assure a clean shot.

rank fifth and fourth respectively for overall book-quality harvest. Iowa, incidentally, had the most bucks listed in the 185 category. I am not sure that I ever have seen a whitetail in the 185 range. I have seen a few of those I honestly believe would score at around 170; on every occasion, my heart has stopped. Ohio produces a great many bucks — 237 entries — and does have an impressive spread across the board in terms of size above 135; the best is 177 3/8.

Illinois, the state that produced a world record that is now almost as old as dirt — 204 1/2 points — is third on the all-time list, but the real comers are Kansas and Iowa. Until 1989, Iowa had not allowed non-resident hunting. Today it's open to a limited number of out-of-staters.

Bowhunting Big Game Records Of North America, Third Edition, lists the entries according to numerical ranking. Included in the summary that details some of the particulars such as number of points, length of beams and spread on deer, is a column that lists, for the most part, the county of kill. With the information that Boland provides and a copy of the third edition, one can sit down and begin to decipher just where the big ones live. To do so is an interesting exercise, the type that fires the imagination and keeps the spirit alive.

One more thing: Boland also has developed charts that provide data on some equipment, shot distances and hunting methods. The information I found most interesting involved whitetails. There are more trophy bucks taken — by almost twice the number — between 4 and 6 p.m. than from sunrise until 10 in the morning.

I have been doing it all wrong, and intend to get more sleep this whitetail season.

While the broad overview provided by the Pope & Young record book is helpful, additional material is available nowadays through many state hunting organizations. It has become fashionable for state hunting associations or special-interest deer hunting groups to publish record books on a state-specific basis.

These can be real eye-openers. Not every big buck gets entered in the Pope & Young or Boone & Crockett records, though many qualifiers are recorded at the state level. I have a library full of state record books, and many of the outstanding trophies listed are not to be found in the larger, more acclaimed books.

Locating and studying available state listings is another step in pin-pointing potential big deer hot-spots. Another way — actually a support tactic after you have zeroed in on an area — is to embark on a long distance reconnoiter via telephone and letter. The phone, for me, is better. Personal contact with regional deer biologists is a fine way to narrow down the search. While it might seem like a lot of extra, rather tedious effort, pinning down the country with a track record for producing big deer is a necessary first step.

Another fine way to get a feel for locations is to visit one of the expanding number of so-called Deer Classics held around the country each year. Here you get to see mounts of the big bucks up close. The overwhelming numbers of mounted trophies will set your head spinning, and you'll have a chance to visit with other trophy hunters and outfitters. It's all part of the valuable information-gathering process that is essential to serious trophy hunting.

I have learned a great deal about potential hot-spots by attending a number of state bowhunting association meetings every year. New friendships have led to some marvelous deer hunts, adventures in new country which I have always found just as exciting as the prospect of a big deer. Deep down, all of us want a trophy deer. Knowing we are hunting where the potential for one exists is important.

It adds a bit of undeniable spice, but I've always felt that just being there hunting, is the deep down reason for all this.

Dougherty (right) shows the wear and tear of a strenuous hunt in high, rugged mountains. Bowhunting is a challenging sport.

Bowhunting in cold weather presents its own unique challenges. The cold is tough on equipment and the hunter. Coloradan Marv Clyncke answers the wintry challenge while holding to tradition. He took this mulie using a sleek, simplistic longbow.

While following the paper trail just described can give one a pretty definite idea as to the location of those big bucks that just might make the record books, there is a less statistics-oriented factor that also brings results.

This has to do with weather. In fact, it has to do with the days of deep winter. Early in the season, no self-respecting trophy buck is going to be showing off his antlers when the woods are full of hunters.

But a few weeks later, a plummeting thermometer can bring a new set of potentials.

Cold, really cold down to ten degrees with the wind blowing lightly form the north. Chill factor is about zero.

The time is mid-December. Christmas is just around the corner and most folks are thinking about the happy warmth of the holidays. There are some outdoor types still thinking ducks and geese and a few chasing rabbits in the snow, but not many are still perched in tree stands thinking deer. A tree stand in December can be as cold and lonely a place as you are likely to find, but big bucks make great Christmas presents; something you can get for yourself with a little extra effort.

By the end of November a majority of deer hunters have retired to the comfort of flickering fires in the den. It's a good time for reflecting on the season past. The sweet crisp days of fall are remembered fondly, in comfort. Almost everyone has quit; almost everyone.

Some of us can't.

It depends on the circumstances of the seasons available to you — most states have a late archery deer hunt — and it depends on your frame of mind. That's the important part. Some of the best deer hunting takes place late in the year when the weather is nasty, unpleasant, tough; when almost everyone else has put up the bows until next October.

Shooting a bow and arrow, regardless of the configuration, is not a lot of fun when the weather is really cold. Sitting for long spells on a stand, most often in elevated positions without any form of insulation or wind break for protection, can be a miserable undertaking. You have to want to hunt deer badly and you have to believe your odds for a buck, a really good buck, are excellent; maybe better than at any other time.

However, there is one nice thing about hunting at this time of year. Competition for the game and the good hunting places is virtually nonexistent. Those other guys sitting by the fire are missing a bet.

Some of the greatest odds for success in bowhunting are evident late in the season. Deer can be easier to pattern now; food sources and the need to feed at an accelerated pace work in the hunter's favor. Winter's white carpet makes reading signs a cinch and the rut may not be altogether over. Late blooming young ladies still stimulate the boys and some of the biggest bucks, the crafty survivors of fall's heavy bow and gun hunting pressure, magically reappear for a last charge at procreation. It's an interesting time, a neat time; you should think about it. There is nothing too terribly different about winter hunting as compared to fall except the weather, but there are a few things you need to think about and do that are not quite the same in cold weather.

First, you must have the proper equipment in terms of clothing to remain comfortable on stand. Shooting a bow requires a comfortable temperature to be effective. It's a muscle game, in a sense. Cold, shivering muscles do not respond properly to the call for sudden action.

There is a wide assortment of cold weather gear and clothing available today. The secret to using any of it is that you should not become overheated before setting up so that you can remain still for the duration of your hunt. Go to your hunting spot dressed as lightly as possible to avoid generating too much body heat. Simply walking in without a hat on helps a great deal. Take it easy while traveling, allow plenty of time; don't be in a hurry. Cool off a bit before putting on the cold weather clothing, then settle in with a few extra comforts. A thermos of tea, coffee or hot chocolate for a periodic shot helps you mentally as much as physically; so will some of your wife's high-calorie cookies.

It won't take long for the cold to begin working on you, but isometric exercises can keep you loose. On stand, I periodically lock my fingers together and pull quickly, repeatedly, with my arms straight across my chest working on the shoulders and the back muscles, the ones I use to draw the bow. It requires no game-alarming motion, but it keeps one tuned up and loose.

The feet seem to be the key for comfort on winter stands. Cover the stand's platform if you're using a permanent stand — with an insulating layer of soft, quiet carpet. Cover the carpet with plastic to protect it from snow and freezing frost when you're not on it. Take the plastic off when you hunt, replace it when you leave. It makes a big difference comfort-wise and it helps reduce noise in the woods.

Footwear for winter stands is a serious matter. Waterproof, felt-lined boots, such as those offered by Cabela's, Browning or LaCrosse are excellent. I have a pair of thickly lined fleece moccasins I had custom-made with a heavy hide outer shell that I keep heavily oiled and waxed. These moccasins are as good in the cold as anything I've found. They are soft, wear well and are quiet. I don't wear them to my hunting spot, but carry them in a day pack and change to dry socks and the moccasins before climbing in.

If my feet do get really cold, it is not pleasant. It's tough to stay long and tougher to remain still while there. You can not last long with cold feet. Starting out with dry feet gives one more time before the inevitable, but in winter, if you have plotted correctly, you don't have to stay too long.

Wear the quietest outer clothing you can for winter hunting; wool is excellent. Some days are so still, the slightest out-of-place sound will ruin your chance. The alarm factor of noise in the crisp stillness of winter is harder to conceal than during any other season. It can be so quiet, it's sometimes spooky. Nothing is left to rustle; there are no shuddering leaves to provide sound cover and only a few twigs rattle sporadically in the breeze.

You can almost relax in a wintertime tree stand. The naked woods offer superb visibility. Stands might have to be placed higher, but try to locate a good big tree for background cover, rather than getting too high. On winter days, you can see and hear a deer a long way off and you should have a better idea of where they are coming from and when. It's not like fall with heavier cover restricting visibility. In winter you have more time to get ready. You can do your exercises, take that shot of hot chocolate, flex up and down on tiptoes. It's not too bad, really.

I know guys who back off their bow weight a bit in winter. The lighter draw is just a little easier to manage when the cold is working against you. It makes sense, I suppose. After all, putting the arrow in the right place compensates for a slight loss of velocity. I know others who shoot a release in cold weather, but don't when it's warm. The same mentality, perhaps; it seems worth consideration.

As winter becomes severe, when the snow piles up on main travel routes, trails are easily distinguished under these conditions and are followed almost religiously by the deer. That occasional big buck running a late doe may deviate, but they, too, stay closer to established paths.

The easiest part of the late season hunting is figuring out the deer's movement pattern. The hardest part is staying there long enough to intercept it. Actual hunting has to be a carefully plotted, relaxed approach. The time spent on time frame of major movement is the key.

Winter hunting takes place during a time of incredible beauty. It can be lovely, a little painful and not without an element of physical danger. Take care not to get overheated when setting stands; cold weather changes your constitution. Take nothing for granted.

My personal preference for late season hunting leans strongly to the afternoon when daily conditions will be at their best. Afternoon patterns are reliable and afternoon hunting is less stressful on the individual.

All in all, winter hunting provides a chance to bowhunt under different, tough, but high-potential conditions.

I like to reflect on the season in front of the flickering fire, too, but I'm inclined to put off kickin' back as long as possible. It's a long ten months 'til next October.

CHAPTER 18

LEARNING TO DRIVE

One Of Man's Oldest Hunting Methods Is Still An Excellent Deer-Taking Technique

DRIVING GAME was probably man's first hunting technique. Considerable evidence exists in our native North Americans' history to indicate that the earliest primitive tribes drove herds of buffalo off steep precipices, the shaggy animals falling in blind, panicked confusion to their deaths. Natural cul de sacs such as blind canyons also were used, pushers driving game into these inescapable barriers where animals were stoned or speared for the cooking fire.

I have read of vast drives in which game was driven doggedly by tireless runners, sometimes for days, into carefully selected natural traps, My oldest son lives directly in the shadow of a sweeping, round rock formation in southern Idaho known as Deer Cliff. Old stories suggest that early Indians ran mule deer off the treacherous rim as a method of providing food, while others — less romantic — simply acknowledge that occasionally a deer slipped and fell the several hundred feet onto the Cub River below. In either telling, it was fatal for the deer.

Driving deer is an astonishingly effective way of hunting them. It is popular almost anywhere deer are hunted, though often treated more as a social event — a meat-gathering outing — than a trophy buck hunt.

Now don't get riled. With all due respect, I recognize that many deer drives are serious campaigns carried out with a close eye to detail and form. I have been on many such drives,

Mapping out a deer drive's strategy is important, even if it's done roughly in the dirt. Each hunter must know his role.

Glassing by an experienced bowhunter, like Dougherty, can reveal the best location for conducting a deer drive.

conducted with all the tactical brilliance of major armed forces assaults and considered every bit as serious. To tell the truth, I enjoyed them immensely.

I will clarify this, however, by stating I also have been on deer hunts — drives, if you will — conducted with the use of dogs. In every instance, those events sucked!

I just walked all over somebody's toes, I know. I mean no one any personal disrespect, but running deer with dogs is just not my thing!

If there is any common factor at all in mule deer hunting, it would be that the deer are always ahead of us. They are also usually above us, watching our feeble attempts to close the gap before they bounce off in that picturesque, pogo-stick, hopping gait so perfectly suited to their environment. This can be frustrating, but there are ways to even the odds.

I grew up hunting mule deer in a variety of prime areas throughout the western states back in the day when the herds were at their peak. Mostly, though, in the Good Old Days, we hunted them in the foothills of Southern California close to expanding residential areas. Those areas have since enlarged enormously, squeezing out most everything wild and natural, except for the coyotes that seem to be holding their own and may be getting even.

In this semi-rugged, close-to-home terrain of thick, brushy hillsides with stately live oak canyon bottoms, the mule deer were much smaller in size than the sturdy Rocky Mountain muleys we encountered in Nevada, Arizona, Utah and Colorado. Most of them field-dressed on the down side of one

hundred pounds, though occasionally we caught one that was bigger.

The largest buck I ever shot there was an old-timer who had a taste for pink camellia buds. The habit was one that incurred the indignant wrath of the camellias' owner, a retired surgeon who allowed us to park on his property to pursue our passion.

This was long before anti-hunting or "animal-rights" were fashionable. Depredating deer were a problem — it wasn't their fault, of course — which was the main reason a "special archery season" existed in the first place. Folks just weren't happy watching high-dollar foliage reduced to a pile of non-decorative pellets on their lawns.

There were few residences in the hills then, although the die already was cast, the air choked in the dust of the developers' bulldozers eating homesites out of habitat. It was sad, but we could do nothing about it except take advantage of the new access they provided. Dr. Kraft, the victimized surgeon, caught up with me one morning as I returned to my truck, advising me of this "huge buck" that was assaulting his yard every evening.

"Would you," he pleaded, "please try and shoot him?"

I grinned. "You bet!"

I scouted the "yard," a full two hundred yards long, that dropped off forming three carefully sculpted terraces and found a major deer trail entering at the bottom of the second bench. Some quick preparation fashioned a blind that would be cradled in the gloom of afternoon shadows, from where, I informed the good doctor, I would do in the vandalous buck.

Standers should be ready for action as soon as they are in position. Big bucks have been known to appear within a few minutes of the drive's start.

I returned the next evening where, true to prediction, the culprit sauntered into the yard at exactly the appointed hour, pausing at thirty feet distance to nip a succulent bud. At the shot, he crashed across the yard and off the down slope toward the winding drive where he collapsed precisely five steps from my truck. It was a tidy piece of work. The old boy weighed 146 pounds, a monster, though he only carried the heavy forked horn antlers so typical of those scrub brush deer.

Our tactics in those early mule deer days were more run-and-gun rather than spot-and-stalk. We had our preferred trails and ridges to work. The lay of the land dictated how we could proceed, so off we went. For the most part, we simply chased deer ahead of us. They would pause far above to observe our progress at safe range. That we succeeded at all, which we did with rather astonishing regularity, was simply because we were young, eagerly tough and above all persistent.

Experience breeds maturity, for as we evolved from our late teens and early twenties, we realized that hot pursuit, besides being extremely strenuous, wasn't the most effective way to hunt with our chosen tools. We settled down to more systematic game plans. We learned how to slow down and actually stalk. Binoculars suddenly became important to our strategies; we spent more time observing, less in aimless chasing about.

There were still a lot of eager beavers running the ridges, sending the bounding muleys to flight along escape routes that patient observation determined to be consistent patterns. We shot quite a few mule deer, courtesy of some distant, struggling bowhunter lumbering cross-country, whom we never

Such a sight can drive a bowhunter wild! Drivers must be alert when moving through thick brush. Bucks often double back.

met to thank. He wouldn't have appreciated it anyway.

We also learned, because we were spending more time watching, that there were key mid-day places to which we gave our own secret coded designations: The Flat Spot, Hill 101, the S-Curve. By mid-day, they would hold bedded deer. On 101 alone, George Wright and I took a dozen bucks after the early morning rushes subsided. We nearly died every time, packing them out the three miles to the truck.

Drives can be conducted with careful cunning or a simple, loose-knit plan. It all depends on the real estate under consideration and how well someone understands it. An intimate knowledge of the terrain and how the deer that live in it react to pressure is the key to a successful drive. The primary rule is not to push the deer too hard. This rule is not easy to follow.

Most drives with which I have been involved start out with a rather well thought-out plan. Standers are placed carefully and given enough lead time to comfortably get into their locations well before the drive starts. The drivers, who should really act as still hunters, set out at an appointed time to push the area. What commonly happens next is that everyone doing the pushing gets in too big a hurry.

In the late 1960s, I ran a deer camp for several falls in north central Pennsylvania. I say I ran it. I was working for Ben Pearson Archery then, and we maintained this camp for our sales representatives and clients as an "educational retreat."

I just happened to be the guy who got the dirty job of having to supervise things and hunt for two weeks in some of the most beautiful, fall-colored country God ever made. It was tough duty, but I managed!

It was there I met Ed McCarthy, a local lodge owner with a quaint, Norman Rockwell quality about him. McCarthy knew his woods intimately, and in the art of driving deer, was a master.

"We will start," he would address his drivers in a splendid, sonorous voice, "with the sun on our right shoulder just here." (He would point to just here).

"We will walk at a pace of exactly two miles per hour, enjoying as we go, the glory of the forest that God has chosen to show us, and always keeping the sun just so." (He would point again.) "At each one hundred yards, I will gently call out, 'Number one!' You will answer, in a like, soft-mannered voice with your own number, Number two, Number three, so on.

"This will keep us in line. No one will hurry. You ask why? Because we must not!"

Standers can get the chance for extremely close shots at trophy deer during drives.

McCarthy supervised many mid-day drives for me during those seasons. I will forever remember his chiseled face and wild, white hair, as he strode with carefully measured pace through his beloved woods, his pauses to marvel at a shaft of sunlight splashing a crimson leaf and his call, "Numberrr Onnne!"

McCarthy's drives worked. I believe they worked for a reason. Controlled pace moves deer in a loose, unhurried manner compared to tight pressure that sends them scampering as though the devil is biting their tails. McCarthy's theory in his woods — mature woods with little understory, hardly any brambles or thickets — was to let the deer know you were coming while still a long way off. Most often, these drives were at least a mile long.

In thicker cover, I believe an even slower and quieter approach — without the sound of human voices — is better.

I do not believe you can force deer to a predictable spot in a drive with too fast a pace. Deer under heavy pursuit go where their survival instinct tells them to go. Big bucks under pressure seldom go where you want them to go. Often, they don't move ahead at all, but circle to stay inside the very cover being driven. A slow, measured pace has a better chance of moving deer into a trap than a fast one. Drivers frequently get too far apart. The way to compensate for this is to move in a weaving pattern, not a consistent line.

Within a gap of seventy-five to one hundred feet, a human-wise, mature deer, with amazingly little cover to work with, will allow drivers to slide by rather than bolt ahead. With few exceptions, the majority of the whitetails I have seen taken on drives have been young deer. With mule deer, the ratio of older, bigger deer has been just a tad better.

Standers always should have the wind in their faces. Drivers should keep it at their backs or work into a cross-wind, another reason for them not to hurry. A distant whiff of human scent will cause deer to move out easily at an unbelievable distance. The closer, hot human scent will prod the lollygaggers into a more speedy gear.

Unless food — the lack of it, actually — forces deer to return to a specific area, it is easy to force them from it permanently with too much pressure. In my experience, whitetails are more apt to return to a preferred home zone after pressure than are mule deer to whom things over the next hill are close enough to what they left to keep them happy. Driving any area too frequently either will move deer out permanently or make them so skittish that the next drive has little chance for success. The big deer simply won't be there.

The philosophy attached to the drive technique — which takes as much careful scouting for positive results as placing a stand — is that deer under pressure will follow natural lines of cover. These are points, long fingers of scattered timber,

A wintery drive in Colorado pushed this muley through a narrow mountain pass right into Dougherty's position.

If the terrain is open (below), standers can use optics to good advantage to spot deer.

creek bottom trails, saddles, skimpy brushlines and so forth. The philosophy involved often proves true, but I have seen the biggest deer on more drives than you can imagine completely ignore these sure-fire natural routes, settling instead for high-balling escapes across open land or speedy wild-eyed dashes out the back door after the drivers have passed.

I believe such deer are veterans. Older and wiser, they have been involved in push tactics before. As youngsters, they followed the course of natural cover and encountered danger. I do not give deer credit for the capacity to reason, but I do credit them fully with an ability to retain threatening memories and react accordingly. The survival instinct is refined through experience.

Nevertheless, a deer drive usually will move some deer to some standers, and as I mentioned, they are frequently conducted with an any-legal-deer attitude, and there's always the chance that the biggest buck in the county will run right up to someone's grandmother who'll whack it with a borrowed bow.

Set up right, the standers on these operations will perhaps be offered some of the best deer shooting opportunities of the season. The most important thing is to get set up comfortably in what you feel is the right place and stay ready from the onset.

There is a cardinal rule here that needs to be mentioned. If

Veteran deer will not always react to a drive as expected. Sometimes, instead of using natural cover and the terrain to escape oncoming drivers, they'll bolt across open fields.

you are participating in an organized drive, especially if you have been placed in a spot by the team leader, you *stay* in that exact spot! Again, older, wiser deer catching a distant scent of man will move instantly and show up much earlier than one might expect. The stander's best opportunity for a good buck may well be in the very first minutes of a drive.

Several seasons past, Judd Cooney and I — standers on a drive — were positioned in scattered timber and high grass at the head of a shallow draw. Perfectly camouflaged and at the ready, Judd shot a dandy eight-point whitetail at twenty feet when it stopped to look back toward distant drivers who had barely begun their downwind walk.

The size of the land area being driven dictates the number of people that need to be involved. Frankly, having seen drives conducted under a wide variety of conditions, I have come to the conclusion that the common tendency is to bite off more than can be chewed. I really believe the best drives are those dealing with smaller pieces of cover involving fewer people; those who know exactly what they are doing.

Hunters who draw the lot of drivers should think about getting a shot, too. More than one deer has been shot while circling away from a pusher and looking for the back door.

Never discount the factor of luck. The most successful hunters I know are eternally optimistic, and always ready. George Wright, my life-long hunting buddy, and I have pushed innumerable deer and other game to each other on two-man mini-drives simply by playing the wind and terrain between us. Two guys who think alike can be a tough

combination to beat.

Oftentimes it can be unbelievably difficult to move deer from cover. This is particularly true with whitetails. In Oklahoma, for example, we have areas dotted with smallish patches of thick sumac sometimes standing from six to eight feet. These patches will be interlaced with deer trails that a man can barely negotiate, often having to resort to hands and knees passage.

In the late fall, the sumac grows deceptively open, being nothing more than close-packed thin stalks that seldom are more than two inches in circumference. Yet, on repeated occasions, I have watched deer circle hunters inside these sparse thickets continuously and never break from cover. Acreages of high grass, briar thickets, sumac or scrub oak, for example, are hard places to drive. More open country seems to provide the best results for moving deer on a planned course. In heavy cover, they often never move unless almost stepped on, then simply circle inside. There is safety in the thickets and they know it.

On more than one occasion in open whitetail woods or mature stands of western aspen with its park-like glades, for example, I have seen shot, or shot myself, deer sneaking out the back door.

In the old days we called this the "drag-line." Drag-lining is an excellent technique that often is overlooked.

Here's how it works: A couple of hunters remain well behind the pushers and move at a snail's pace, staying to the side of the major trails and close to whatever cover is available.

Dougherty shot this South Dakota mule deer during a drive as it tried to use a creek bottom to slip away.

A cross-wind is desirable and sitting for long minutes is recommended.

The wind is the biggest problem, which is why one should parallel the trails. This technique works best on unsettled days with a squirrely, confusing wind. You will see more deer than you thought possible trying to use the double-back exit routine. One of the best mule deer I ever saw taken was killed by a drag-liner while it was slipping out the rear end of a Nevada aspen patch. The sidehill patch was less than an acre in size, but the deer slipped out between five pushers.

Frequently, you can utilize the efforts of other hunters' activities to set up your own private drive. In the Midwest, a procession of pheasant hunters often will bust tight-lying whitetails from cover. I have a friend in Iowa who has taken two Pope & Young bucks by hunting well ahead of bird hunters along known escape routes. George Wright and I have tagged many a mule deer simply by hunting far ahead and above wandering hillside ramblers whose hunting technique worked far better for us than it did them.

Drives provide excellent additional opportunities to punch your tag, especially when conducted during mid-day bedding

Drivers will often move too far apart when moving through heavily wooded areas. By moving in a zig-zag line, the drivers reduce the chance that a savvy deer will slip away.

Standers must remain in their assigned position, mask their outline and stay alert! Driven deer may appear immediately.

periods when you might otherwise be taking a nap.

Of all the ways I have hunted mule deer for almost forty years, the still-hunt/drive combination is one of the best. In a sense, that's what we were doing back in those early California days. Our group of long-time buddies was evolving into smarter, or at least better, bowhunters: We became pretty sophisticated in a technique that proved effective in many places, especially on that fabled plateau known as the Kaibab North, on the edge of the Grand Canyon, Arizona.

In those by-gone days when we traveled to the Kaibab, its deer herd was legendary for both the size of its bucks and the pure quantity of its deer. The quantity part interested us at that point in our lives as much as any other. We were just deer hunters then, and any we could claim was considered a prize. The Kaibab then — I haven't seen it for years — was old growth, larger timber with limited understory. There were some good stands of aspen mixed with Douglas, white and alpine fir, some spruce and vast expanses of towering, old Ponderosa pine.

My deepest impressions of the Kaibab still are hunting all day in a thick carpet of pine needles — in soft moccasins you could move as quietly as a wispy breeze — and how sleek and smooth-looking its deer were. But it was a clean forest and many times they spotted up before we could close those last few important yards. We spooked a lot of them, but there were lots to spook. We just pressed on.

Our best tactic became the "subtle push," a still-hunting sort of drive designed in a sweeping pincer movement with a few blockers in key positions at the end. The country was laced with logging roads. A quadrant for the attack would be picked with the use of a map. The blockers were placed in position, usually not the best draw due to their upwind position, while the balance of the troop, spaced usually seventy-five to two hundred yards apart in a huge, shallow V.

At the appointed time, they would begin to still-hunt in a common — we hoped — pace in the direction of the blockers. The area covered might well be larger than a square mile. In a sense, each of us was hunting individually at a careful pace. Most deer were shot circling away from one stalker and running into another, although quite a few collected their deer as a result of a direct stalk. Carefully coordinated and paced, this tactic could take half a day, but it was effective.

I have shot quite a few and seen a lot of other mule deer taken on drives. The tactic simply involves knowing the country, where the deer are and where they are likely to go. The nastier it is, the easier it is to pick out the key ambush points along the easiest to use deer escape routes. Shots offered should be within easy bow range; chances are, the deer will be moving. Keeping the movement to an unhurried pace — walking is just fine — should be dictated by the pace of the drivers. Slow and relaxed is the proper battle order.

Pushers on drives always should be in a mode to expect the

These bowhunters take a break after a demanding drive. The standers and drivers will then switch roles for another drive.

unexpected. Big bucks may slip out well ahead. That means the standers should be in place long before the push begins. But some will lie tight, sometimes coming up almost underfoot. Mule deer do it just like whitetails. Big bucks can be awfully cool.

I have seen many a muley sneak out behind a driver who passed within mere feet. I have also seen several big bucks shot by hunters in a secondary line of drivers sneaking carefully along fifty yards or more to the rear of the main drive line. All of them came out of aspen patches you would bet couldn't hide a cottontail.

The last mule deer I shot was during the same South Dakota hunt with Judd Cooney. We were having a lively week of mixed-bag hunting. The hunt was fun-filled with pheasants, whitetails and muleys boiling out of winding, tight little creek bottoms and the wider ravines the Dakotas call *coulees*. The mule deer bounced while the whitetails screeched by like rockets. There are lots of both in this country where a deer was

unheard of when my dad, a native South Dakotan, grew up there.

I had three chances at red fox, and missed them all! The fall sky was alive with migrating waterfowl. It was filled with the constant yammering of sandhill cranes, white-fronted geese; Canada's snows and blues. Dad had grown up with that and we had seen it together. It was good to see it again.

The muley was a chunky three-by-three, blocky of build in full, dark winter coat. I shot him at forty yards as he crossed a creek attempting to side-slip the drivers. Three whitetail does passed by within feet.

There are many ways to hunt deer. The best is any way for which you can find the time. The best time to go is when you can. Some may look down on tree stands, while others feel stalking is the only true measure of the game. As a practical matter, being flexible in your approach offers the best odds for success. Trying to push a few deer around comes with no guarantee, but it's a real good bet.

CHAPTER 19

LET'S WALK A STALK

More Is Involved Than Just Being Sneaky!

THE PLACE was the northern rim of Arizona's legendary Kiabab Plateau, at the time a fabulous stronghold for a vast mule deer herd. Many of the bucks were true trophy class, but, alas, this area was near the end of its spectacular era.

The buck I was after wasn't quite in that class except to me, which was all that mattered. He was bedded in the shadows of a scruffy thicket of immature pines at the head of a subtle draw at some seventy-five yards and slightly below me. It was late in the morning, about ten o' clock, on a warm September day, with nothing between us but a few scattered lodge pole pines. A smooth carpet of bone-dry, crackly pine needles covered the ground. It was the first time I ever took off my hunting shoes to begin a stalk.

In stocking feet, I began inching carefully from one ten-inch tree trunk to another. The wind was blowing in sighing gusts through the pines, waving them enough to pepper the forest with a skitter-scatter of broken shadows that certainly helped break up my slow-stepping approach.

He was a lazy buck. I stopped to watch him every few yards through my binoculars. His eyes appeared sleepily narrowed, though he repeatedly flipped his ears at flies, and twice they came to full alert as some distant sound intruded on his semi-nap. I was at his three o' clock, the wind was at his tail blowing from his six, his visual defense focused downhill, the nose sifting out anything from behind.

The stalk took about an hour, and I shot him in his bed at close to thirty feet. That incident remains today a memory of one of the most satisfying stalks of my life.

There is a difference between stalking and still-hunting, though the latter often begets the former. The stalking hunter most often isolates his target at a distance and plans a careful but hasty approach before commencing the last leg of his tedious stalk at a snail's pace.

Dougherty keeps his profile low and bow at the ready as he closes on a bedded deer. Moving slowly is important.

Remaining perfectly still is probably the biggest challenge for bowhunters. It is often best to wait instead of pushing forward.

The still-hunter is, instead, a sneaker who moves along on routes he feels will coincide with game movement to and from bedding areas inside of primary feed zones, or perhaps he sneaks directly into late morning bedding areas in hopes of spotting his game in an unsuspecting posture at close range. The difference is subtle, but it is a difference.

Still-hunting mule deer, one on one, is my favorite bowhunting pastime. I don't seem to find enough time to do it as much anymore, a circumstance I have vowed to correct after this year. Attempting to slip up on a bedded buck is about as neat a dry-mouthed experience as you can have with a bow in your hand. Getting close, if you're careful, pretty good and lucky, isn't the hard part. Getting a good shot is the problem. If I had a dime for every buck I have crept close to, but, was unable to shoot, or missed in the explosion of scratched gravel and flying sage brush, I would have a large pile of ten-cent pieces.

Teamwork among hunting partners is a super-effective way to stalk mule deer. The spotters remain in place while the hunter circles to a position of advantage, typically above the deer. Binoculars are important for all the players. We use a simple, easy-to-send and receive signal system for the hunter: Left, right, up or down, relative distance in terms of yards and a signal for stop and sit down. Signal teamwork can put the stalker right on target. Quiet clothing and footwear are vital in this game, as is a pocketful of rocks carried to lob over the bedded buck. Hopefully, this will make him casually stand in order to check out the disturbance, while looking the other way. Sometimes it works.

Once I crawled up on a really nice Nevada buck — maybe a Pope & Young Club score of 160, but they always look bigger in velvet — that was bedded in the shadowy shade of a hillside with a forty-five-degree slope.

The going was easier than I imagined; soil dampened by rain allowed me to close quietly. My spotter's signal said, "Right there. Sit down." It took a while before I made out the buck's antlers that were practically in my lap. The steep sidehill protected all but the tips of his velvet-covered tines from my view in the snaggly sage.

Presented with his intimate proximity, my breath became at once ridiculously short. I manfully readied myself for the deed, grabbing up a tennis ball-size rock to lob it over his bedded position. It hit him at the base of his right antler. The volcanic explosion of his departure is forever etched in my mind. Nothing works all the time.

I prefer to hunt mule deer from the ground, particularly in the late afternoon, reveling in the cat-and-mouse game of sneaking around as they move out to feed. I feel that it's the epitome of bowhunting big game. The popularity of tree stands, however, has had a major impact on the sport. Mule deer, early on in the season, while still grouped in bachelor bands, some as high as fifty, can be effectively patterned for tree stand or ground blind hunting tactics.

Jack Howard, the well known bowmaker from California, was a legendary mule deer man when I was just cutting my teeth. Howard's favorite technique was, after a long, careful observation, to use the ground blind, mostly in feeding zones. Many outfitters of my acquaintance, who each season cater to

Dougherty glasses a bushy area for feeding deer. Once found, Dougherty will decide on a route and start his stalk.

an increasing number of first-time "Eastern" or "whitetail" hunters with little practical still-hunting/stalking experience, have scored big with tree stands on travel routes to or from feeding areas.

The technique is, after all, simply a matter of knowing the country and the habits of the game using it. All this really requires is available time and patience to establish patterns, something an outfitter does for you.

As premier mule deer hunter/outfitter, Coloradan Jay Verzuh states: "It is extremely important that you have undisturbed country in which to do it and that the stand area not be overhunted."

This is not to say that tree stands will not work in areas of high hunter density. They do, of course, although luck and the fates are more inclined to jiggle the odds in the wrong direction where too many people are involved. The last time I sat a tree stand on public land in Colorado, I had perfect chances at three other bowhunters and a cowboy. A singing cowboy, at that!

In spite of my many hunting seasons since moving to whitetail country where I sit and wait in the tried and true local hunting method, I have stalked and shot far more big-game animals than I have taken from a stand. Part of this has to do with hunting a mixed variety of game, mostly it has to do with the fact that stalking or still-hunting are far and away what I would rather do. It all started with rabbits.

When I was a kid, a bow-shot cottontail or jackrabbit was a major trophy. It didn't take long to learn that slow, careful walking on silent feet was what produced good shots. It was really still-hunting, though sometimes a planned stalk was in order, primarily on the long-legged jackrabbits.

We used to glass prickly pear cactus patches for the location of a sunning cottontail or to pick out the tips of a blacktailed jack's ear, peeking up over some sagebrush before trying to stalk close enough for a shot. In those days, with the equipment we used, *close* was the watchword. What we were learning was how to walk. If you learn how to walk in the woods, you can learn how to stalk. Stalking is a game played in country open enough to allow you to locate the target first from a distance, design a plan, then make a silent downwind approach.

The savvy still-hunter moves in tighter cover without benefit of having located the target first. He relies on his instinctive knowledge of what the animals are doing within his hunting zone. Either way, each hunter is putting himself in a more direct confrontation attitude with his quarry. This is eyeball-to-eyeball stuff at ground zero where everything truly becomes a more equal match-up. In my opinion, the entire skill is based on carefully controlled, as close to humanely possible silent, near motionless movement.

That first time I took off my boots something inside my head told me that, no matter how soft the pine needles were, they would still crunch underfoot and make my approach difficult. In my stocking feet, I could feel each footstep subconsciously, and work my feet one by one without diverting my attention from the tell-tale position of the buck's head.

Several necessary ingredients contributed to this and the many other stalking successes I have experienced or witnessed. The first was having an advantage over the animal in terms of terrain. In the case of the deer under discussion, I was above him and he faced downhill. The second was the solid cross-wind and even though cover was at a minimum, I had a relaxed animal in a permanent bedded position providing that most important element — time — in which to make the approach.

Match your camouflage clothing and gear to the terrain and take advantage of natural cover. Glass often to keep track of the deer and to receive instructions from your spotter.

walk-away situation. One should move out to establish room to maneuver, cut the angle if possible, then close for a shot. If you do it right it will work with amazing consistency.

I would much prefer to close in on an animal that is still up on his feet than one bedded at mid-day. Even when you know exactly where the deer lies, it can be darned difficult to see. Invariably, you are in a poor position for a good shooting angle. A bedded deer does not often present a picture book shot at his vitals. Instead, his shoulders will be pushed back over his chest. He will be low to the ground surrounded by rocks, twigs, grass or light brush, all of which can deflect an arrow off target, or worse, into a non-vital body area.

I have come across a few imbeciles who, under such conditions, will elect to take a shot at the head. That is a completely unconscionable behavior.

More often than not, after having closed to within good bow range, you will find yourself figuratively handcuffed by a deer in this position. A common mistake is pressing the issue, trying to jockey for a shooting position. Moving too close most often will alert the deer to your presence. While it might stand up for a look, chances are it will come out running, offering a shot with lousy odds.

My strategy almost always has been to try to cause the deer to stand up out of mild concern or curiosity. First, I seek a good comfortable shooting position, preferring to be on my knees in order to reduce my silhouette. If it's late in the afternoon, I might consider waiting the critter out. It has to get up eventually. Even at mid-day, if it's hot, a deer frequently will stand and stretch before moving slightly to adjust his position in the shade.

Normally, having reached this point in the contest, it seems finding a good spot to settle in for a wait isn't in the cards. To

The key here was not to get in a hurry. Altogether, patience is the most solid virtue any deer hunter can possess, be it waiting on a stand or taking the deliberate time necessary to close on foot. The most frequent tendency among stalkers is to hurry in trying to get close enough for a shot. Haste is the most common cause of any hunting failure.

The most common stalking mistake is attempting to play catch-up with a meandering animal that's in plain sight. A deer moving with casual, comfortable grace through familiar country is a deer in his living room. If you enter that living room in a clumsy manner, the deer will know you are there, just as you become aware of a foreign noise in the sanctuary of your own home. Real or imagined, that sound will make you sit straight up and take notice. The deer is no different.

It is impossible for a human to slip through any type of deer habitat in total silence, but you can move through it in a natural, unalarming manner provided you exercise control over the impulse to hurry. The problem is, if you slow to a controlled, unalarming pace, you probably will not catch up. The best technique is not to try.

I know several fighter pilots, some with combat experience. None of them have talked much about good opportunities to flat-out run down their quarry — though one has. They tend to think more in terms of tactics, approaching from above or below, or the advantages achieved by angles of attack. These angles are provided by — in terms to which we can relate best — the technique of circling to engage. The last is exactly what a stalking bowhunter should attempt to do in a

Padded soles and soft uppers like these slip-over stalking shoes from Bears Feet are important in eliminating noise.

This bowhunter glasses ahead during a stalk. However, his camo outfit, while fashionable, doesn't blend with the area and his hands should be covered with camo gloves or paint.

wait, you have to be comfortable with enough room to maneuver your equipment noiselessly. In this case, we're talking about a bow with an arrow nocked and ready that either has to be held continually or laid down where it's readily available without any interference.

Further, I guess I feel that the longer I'm there in close proximity, the more apt things are to turn sour. Once I knelt in scattered sagebrush, not twenty yards from a good California buck I had slipped up on while he fed. Waiting for a broadside angle, I shifted the position of my knees, sort of digging them in for a good grip. The movement set off the unmistakable, high-decible buzz of a Pacific Coast diamondback very close at hand. I left that particular scene with a rolling leap and have no knowledge whatever of what happened to that deer.

Venomous snakes, incidentally, are something to keep in mind while skulking around the brush. I have had entirely too many encounters with them over the years and know full well that automatically a portion of my peripheral vision is constantly searching the ground as I slip along. I'm not scared of them, just carefully aware. You only have to be struck at a few times to learn the habit.

But back to bedded deer. The best way to make one stand is to toss something over him off to his tail side; nothing too big; no softball sized rocks; just something large enough to get him up.

One thing you always should have while stalking is a good pair of compact binoculars. Use them frequently in your approach to carefully study the surrounding area as well as where you expect a bedded or upright deer. Look for parts of deer, antler tips, the sheen of a patch of sunlit hide, the flick of a tail or ear. Always keep a lookout for other deer that may be in the area near your intended target. Don't concentrate totally on the spot where your deer is, because chances are it's not alone.

I use 7x24s for this. They are easy to hold with one hand and have more than enough power to sort things out under these rather close-quarter conditions.

There are umpteen variables that will aid or adversely affect a stalk. The primary one is wind — or the lack of it. I much prefer a rather sporadic day on the ragged edge of good weather such as approaching fronts provide. The wind is

A methodical stalk can be disturbed by other critters. This diamondback easily diverted the attention of this stalker.

reliable and shakes up the cover, moving sage, aspen, pine, tall grass or falling leaves. This helps immeasurably in breaking up the movement of the prowling human silhouette. In addition, it covers a lot of noise-making missteps.

I have an affinity for stalking on slightly nasty days with wind and misty rain. It deadens any sound I might make short of a major collision and definitely aids in scent suppression. No matter what you might want to believe — Madison Avenue hype or "expert" testimonials to the contrary — the only thing that beats a deer's nose is his nose itself for which his guardian angel, Mother Nature, is solely responsible. If she jerks him around by making the weather and wind tough, she just dealt you an inside straight.

But don't get too cocky. Most deer walk through life packing a full house, aces high! The glorious stalking days of early fall in the high country for mule deer are the most fragile from morning to mid-day when the winds are "soft and variable," as the weathermen like to say. The thermals will be pretty predictable, though, and must be taken to account. There will be reversals from downdraft to updraft, as night chill wears off, and the heat begins to rise. For this reason, the best stalking time — anywhere — is late morning through afternoon when, having circled from a distance to gain altitude, you can approach a bedded deer with that fighter pilot technique.

I seldom ever worry too much about being totally camouflaged, especially with gooey face paint or head nets when I am hunting from a tree stand. However, as cover diminishes in the late season, it does become an issue.

On the ground it is different. This is eye to eye, and blending in to reduce the perception a deer has to the human form calls for a more thorough evaluation of camouflage, head to toe.

I grew up hunting ducks and geese in what was some of the finest winter waterfowl habitat in the Lower Forty-eight. The most important thing I learned, the first thing anyone ever told me when the first flight of sleek pintails I ever saw made a pass was: "Keep your head down!"

Why? Because your face, no matter who might love it for whatever reason, is a glaring, out-of-place alarm signal to anything furred or feathered we humans pursue with deadly purpose.

I used to think a drake pintail could tell the color of my eyes at 2000 feet. I know a turkey can tell the color at twenty-five yards, but, with my eyes being the only thing showing, at that point he's in a world of hurt.

A full face, clean and bright from a pre-hunt shower and shave is probably visible to a whitetail or mule deer at ground level from, oh, about fifty-five miles if the sun is shining, a bit less on a dull day! Exaggerated? Sure, but just enough to make you pay attention. Your face, in its naturally beautiful state, is as out-of-place in the woods as a Christmas tree on Halloween.

Simple solution: If you're stalking, cover it up. Blend it with body camo that matches the terrain, patterns that aid in breaking up the blocky, upright shape of the human form. But most of all, if you are going to try to be a sneak-around sort of guy, wear something that is quiet.

Wool never has been equalled for the way it wears, its soft natural sound against brush and for its ability to retain warmth when wet. Certainly, today we have synthetics that do an admirable job, in some cases — keeping one dry, for example.

Materials such as the recently popular fleece products are extremely quiet, but not warm when rain-soaked.

Many times, I have worn rain gear under fleece or cotton materials when conditions got uncomfortably soggy. It works well enough in keeping one dry, while eliminating much of the nerve-wracking, scratching sounds generated by waterproof clothing worn externally.

Fleece-like gaiters have become popular with stalking bowhunters recently. These knee-high leg coverings help measurably in subduing the scrape of brush across lower legs, but are no help when interfering shrubbery is thigh high or above. Bears Feet, an innovative fleece upper, thick-padded soft lower overshoe offers a quick fix for slipping on over boots rather than removing them. Altogether, they seem quite effective, though nothing is quite as good as the total feel one gets in the almost barefoot mode of stocking feet.

All in all, the most important things to remember about stalking are to take plenty of time, watch the wind and avoid placing yourself in a skylined or wide-open position. Keeping the body in a low posture is much less alarming to any game than the upright human form.

I also suggest that it is best to throw the rock over the deer, rather than at it.

The pack to the truck doesn't seem as tough when you have successfully stalked one of nature's most savvy animals.

CHAPTER 20

...AND AFTER THE SHOT?

Finding Downed Game Sometimes Can Be The Greater Challenge!

FROM MY own experience — and that of a lot of other knowledgeable bowhunters — getting a shot at a deer, regardless of species, may not be the most difficult part of the hunt. Recovering the creature that was arrowed can sometimes be the real challenge.

Unlike the gun hunter, the bowhunter has a special set of problems all his own when it comes to the recovery of game. Bullets tend to knock animals down where they stand. This is not always true, of course, but an animal that is hit well with an adequate bullet usually does not travel far, even though it may not drop in its tracks. After all, the bullet is a high-velocity missile that brings thousands of pounds of energy in the form of knock-down power, thus creating extreme shock in the game animal.

The hunting arrow, on the other hand, moves much more slowly, regardless of the claims made by some advertising whiz who is promoting bow speed, an arrow shaft or a broadhead to the extreme. In my experience, a large percentage of those writing advertising copy today know nothing practical about bowhunting. Some of their claims verge on the ridiculous. The real surprise, in some cases, is that the client — the maker of bowhunting equipment — will accept such advertising when he *knows* the claims are misleading. But enough from that soapbox!

The broadhead seldom kills by means of shock. It kills by hemorrhage. The broadhead hunting arrow is just as humane and effective as a bullet, but because the arrow and broadhead create only a minimal degree of shock, the animal that has been hit by a bowhunter usually will run some indefinite distance before dropping.

This is where that difference between rifle hunters and bowmen shows itself. The latter almost always has to follow the game animal — in this telling, deer — to recover it after the shot.

This follow-up procedure is sometimes easy, but other times, is tricky and difficult. Let me say here, though, that properly placed broadheads kill even the largest game with unbelievable speed. Tracking problems are the result of a poor hit, overeager pursuit or occasional pure stupidity.

Over the course of a lot of years of tracking my own game and assisting others — or by being assisted — I have developed some personal procedures in handling what sometimes can be an extremely delicate situation. This includes elements of the actual tracking routine, and in some instances, the selection of equipment that will aid in the recovery process.

Take arrow fletching, for example. I believe in camouflaging the body, painting the face if it will help hide from wary game, using a camouflaged bow and even loading my bow quiver with a set of camouflage-anodized XX75 arrows. But in the matter of fletching, I want to see color; bright color, in fact.

For my own hunting, I prefer yellow fletching and I like a fluorescent nock on the rear end of my hunting arrow. The reason, I think, is pretty obvious: I want to be able to see where my arrows go. It is a help to my aging eyes, if you will, but I thought it was just as important back in the days when my eyes were not so old.

I think most of us with any experience at all have come to realize the fact that for most of the game we're after — and this includes deer, of course — the time we hunt most is when the

A hunter puts in lot of work before he can release an arrow at a deer. But the work isn't done. Now, the deer must be found. Here, Kelly Dougherty is ready to dress out his buck after a careful tracking job.

light conditions are what can be described best as "marginal." This, of course, means hunting at dawn and at dusk.

Under such dim-light circumstances, I tend to lose sight of dark-colored fletching at about the same instant the arrow leaves my bow. In talking to hordes of fellow bowhunters over the years, I find I am not alone. It is a universal problem.

At the other extreme, if my arrows are equipped with bright yellow fletching, I usually can follow the arrow's flight all the way to the target. Coupled with the reaction of the animal, this tends to tell me whether I have scored a hit, and where.

There is a technique that follows this phase. I literally freeze in my follow-through of the shot, watching closely. When game flees, it usually is lost from sight quickly, but one can hear what is happening out there in the bush. Concentrating on reading sign with the ears can tell one the direction in which the animal is moving, the tempo and the approximate

distance. This can be as important as what you see. Even when my vision is obscured, I try to sound-mark the course of the animal flight, marking trees or bushes that can serve as points of reference along its path.

Such close listening pays off in recovered game . Hunting from tree stands, I have heard many a deer fall out of sight in the brush. It's a satisfying sound, believe me. It means I'm not going to have to track it clear to the Continental Divide in the dark!

In that seemingly endless period during which I am listening, I try to run the sequence through my mind; sort of an instant replay with the mind as a screen. I review the shot, try to picture the arrow flight and exactly what I saw at the moment of impact. I attempt to recall in a mental flashback exactly what the animal did and where it went.

The instant mental rerun is audiovisual in nature. Arrows

Reading the blood signs on an arrow provides valuable insight into where the arrow hit and the damaged it caused. This helps the bowhunter determine his tracking strategy.

hit with distinct impact sounds. A volley of arrows striking indoor range targets hit with the soft pitter-patter pattern of raindrops. The 3-D targets give up a solid *thunk!*

Hits on animals have varied impact sounds that aid in getting a quick-fix. Experience is the best teacher, which means if you have it, you might be eighty percent right. There always are variables.

Here are some sound clues that should help in determining whether what you saw matches what you heard. Chuck Adams has often described a solid chest hit as "a ripe watermelon plunk!" I love it, the perfect description to which we all can relate. Defining the dreaded paunch shot is tougher. There is some substance to the resulting sound. You will know you made contact, but it has no real grit, sounding sort of squishy at the same time.

Shoulder bones and shoulder blades are not where you want your broadhead to hit, even though the edges can be penetrated with proper tackle. Such hits play back as a solid, meaty whack at impact. You know you hit bone, but not major bone. Hits below the shoulder blade that catch the knuckle (ball socket) or the upper leg bone can be positioned over the heart and lung area, depending on the deer's posture. These are large, heavy bones that can stop arrows, and even some bullets, instantly.

Not counting the spine, which has some weak points, these

are the strongest bones in a deer's body. Arrows hit them with a major exclamation point. Similar sound occurs on any solid bone such as the spine, neck vertebrae, hip, pelvis or rear leg bones.

Putting the sound together with the deer's physical reaction at impact helps fill in the replay scenario. The hit with the watermelon plunk most often produces a reaction reminding me of the quick head-down thrashing action of a bucking bronco. Instantly bucking, they come up running hard, fast and almost blindly, going through rather than around any obstacles in their paths.

That happens most of the time, but not always. Nothing happens always. Anyone who tells you this or that always happens when a deer is hit has only been there once!

Hit from a quartering forward angle — one that enters behind the rib cage, driving forward into the chest — often produces a hard dash punctuated by a series of running-in-place stutter steps. Every time I see that sort of hit, even though the sound is not real "plunky," I'm sure it will be a short tracking job.

The loud cracking bone hits almost always result in hard-running flight save for the ones that are instantly followed by a crash.

Spine hits — which really are accidents — can anchor deer on the spot. A few years ago, I was involved in a television outdoor show featuring bowhunting for elk which aired on ESPN. I stalked and shot a bull elk through the chest at thirty-five yards. The bull trotted off — elk don't act like deer — and stopped at somewhere around sixty yards where all I could see was his neck and head. With nothing to lose, I turned another arrow loose that severed his vertebrae, resulting in an instant and really spectacular crash.

There are two points to be made here. My mission was to get another arrow into the bull. Whenever you have a chance to do that — deer, elk or whatever — it's what you should do. Two hits are always four times better than one.

The second point: Luck was on my side, trying to bow-shoot spines and necks on purpose is stupid, and rarely seems to work. In this case, I was simply trying to get in another hit and got lucky.

A few drops of blood in the impact area announces some good news — there was a hit! It's now time to start trailing.

A map and compass are vital tools for a bowhunter. Blood and other signs may lead you to a downed deer, but you may get lost in the process. Always know where you are!

The paunch shot is the one that has the most consistently recognizable reaction. An initial jump is followed by what I can best describe as reaction to a low blow. If a hit is forward in the paunch area, along the edge of the diaphragm it's quite possible the liver also has been hit.

Liver hits and straight-through paunch shots generate almost identical reactions. With the liver hit, there is almost instant trauma. In both cases, the animal will move off slowly, usually humped up, its tail clamped down and the head carried rather low. If the liver has been hit, the animal will die quite soon.

One of the greatest mistakes any bowhunter can make is to follow up too soon. This happens most frequently among those new to this type of hunting.

When this over-eager bowhunter does happen upon his animal, it may be spooked and take off. I've seen this happen with animals that were standing, heads down, dead on their feet, ready to drop. In spite of this, the deer's natural instinct is to escape what amounts to an attacker. Its efforts powered primarily by adrenaline, the buck may — and sometimes does — escape to die unrecovered.

I learned this early in my hunting career, and unless I actually hear the creature fall out there in the woods, I try to stay in place for no less than half an hour. This little display

of patience saves a lot of wear and tear on my body and nerves, I've found. That gets more important, as I grow older.

In most whitetail hunting instances, I have made my shot from a tree stand. If that's the case, there is no real reason to mark the spot from which the arrow was launched. However, as suggested earlier, while waiting out the animal, I sit there and note the landmarks that will be useful in guiding me to the location of my downed deer once I climb down to the ground.

If my shot was made from ground level, it becomes a whole different story. While waiting, I mark the spot from which the arrow was launched. I always carry a roll of fluorescent red surveyor's tape in my daypack. If the ground cover is thick, I tear off a strip of this and use it to mark the site from which the shot was made. If the country in which one is hunting is unfamiliar, it can be a good idea to take a compass bearing. This helps to fix in mind the direction in which the deer has gone, as well as to establish your own position.

In most instances, if it doesn't hit a bone or is otherwise deflected, a well sharpened broadhead will go completely through the body of a deer, leaving your arrow stuck in the ground out there somewhere in the brush. Unless the shot was at extremely close range, I don't launch a search for my arrow until that waiting period has ended.

A few years back, I listened for sounds of the deer I had shot, then climbed down from my tree stand too soon to look

High grass makes tracking difficult. It easily hides signs. A bowhunter must progress slowly, searching thoroughly.

When a deer is shot, things happen fast. Deep scuff marks or "jump tracks" are usually located where the deer was hit.

for my arrow. The whitetail buck had stopped no more than twenty-five yards from my tree! We saw each other at the same time. In spite of the fact that he was weaving, on his last legs really, he bolted.

In this instance, my impatience did not create a major problem, because this buck was finished. However, that final dash took him into the bottom of a deep, steep draw. The result was that it took me the entire day to get my deer out of this ravine. I had no one else to blame, however, because I had allowed impatience to cloud my common sense. I did know better; I don't do that any more.

Then comes the matter of tracking. This is a skill that is acquired. No one is born with it. It is learned through experience, although some admittedly become better at tracking than others.

The most critical factors in learning to track are to take your time and to look closely. One must know what it is he is trying to see. Tracking really is a simple matter of close observation. We might call it a search for evidence.

The first piece of evidence, of course, is your own arrow. When I recover an arrow that has been used on a deer — assuming I have had complete pass-through — I seek any indication that the arrow penetrated behind the animal's lung area. Both arrow shaft and fletching are inspected closely for material that could have come from the deer's stomach or intestinal tract. I look for greenish-brown smears or off-colored blood.

If such evidence is found, whether I feel my arrow penetrated the chest cavity at one angle or another entering or exiting, I extend the waiting period. At the same time, I try to get another bowhunter to help me with the tracking. If the arrow is coated liberally with blood and the fletching — when feathers are used — is matted down, there is reason to hope finding the deer will not become a major project. Clean, red blood indicates that solid muscle and vital organs have been penetrated by the arrow.

Then there are those times when you don't find your arrow. It may still be in the animal or it may have been driven into the

forest floor and is lost forever. I always look for the arrow with a high degree of diligence, but once it becomes obvious I'm not likely to find it quickly, I know it's time to look for other bits of telltale evidence. It is time for serious tracking to get under way.

Since I have made every effort to watch the deer's line of flight, I start my follow-up in that direction. In so doing, I use the bushes, trees, boulders and other reference points I had noted from the tree stand or from wherever on the ground I made the shot.

One should be able to locate the deer's jump tracks at the site of the hit or very close to it. These usually are relatively easy to spot somewhere within the distance it took the wounded deer to make several jumps. Even better is, if the arrow scored a good, solid hit, we should find evidence of blood within twenty-five yards.

One has to keep in mind, of course, that a panicked deer,

Mark blood trails well. Arrows and fluorescent tape make perfect flags. Trails must be followed slowly and carefully.

Study even the smallest signs without disturbing the trail. It's also vital to keep "helpers" off the trail, out of the way.

Wounded game animals do what they feel like doing at the moment. Anyone who wants to hunt by hard and fast rules in this regard had better learn to accept a lot of disappointments.

Another point: If you are looking for indicators for blood trailing just on the ground, chances are you are missing some important evidence. Arterial spraying or spurting of blood from a lung shot can mark trees and shrubs at the approximate height of the wound. When you see this type of bleeding, you can feel confident this is not going to be a lengthy search.

In situations where there is not complete penetration and resultant exit of the arrow, some wounds do not tend to produce great amounts of outward bleeding. This makes it tough to follow a blood trail, of course. Over the years, I've come up with my own rule of thumb relative to the ratio of internal and external bleeding in big-game animals. I have come to believe there is at least four times as much blood going into the animal's body cavity as there is being pumped out of the wound to form a blood trail. That is the projected ratio, I feel, when there is a body hit that does not result in a total pass-through of the arrow.

Different types of critters — long-haired animals such as bears, for instance — tend to absorb the blood in their body hair which restricts free-flowing trails sometimes, but we don't have that particular problem with any of the North American species of deer.

If we use the human IQ as a basis, it would be difficult to

when it explodes to head for other stretches of geography, can cover as much as ten or more yards with a single leap. If there is going to be blood sign, it probably will start where the deer lands in that initial frightened leap.

Over the years of trailing my own deer and helping others find theirs, I have learned that, on the ground, blood often is found in what I call a spaced pattern. These are the spaces between blood sign, depending on the pace of the deer. The greater the distance between the specks or splashes of fresh blood, the faster the deer has to be traveling.

In the moment after I find that first blood sign, I mark it with some of that fluorescent surveyor's tape. If the trail is easy, one that is steady and seen readily, I just follow it with a slow, even pace, taking care to walk to the side of the actual blood trail. That way, the existing sign is preserved should I lose the trail and have to backtrack to pick it up.

On what we tend to designate as marginal trails, one should flag the blood sign on a regular basis. This can be an aid in determining the line or pattern the animal may be favoring.

Incidentally, there are any number of error-stricken fables regarding wounded game. For example, there are those — some of them experienced bowhunters — who will tell you in all seriousness that a wounded animal *never* will move uphill. Don't ever believe that. I have seen any number of hard-hit deer and other animals angle steeply upward. True, it may not be the expected pattern, but it does happen. I once had an elk that was shot through the heart run straight up the side of a mountain, leaping over blowdowns.

As a further contribution to fable-bashing, let me add that wounded game will not *always* head for heavy timber and wounded whitetails do not necessarily run away with their tails down. Over several decades of in-the-field observation, I have come up with one conclusion, unscientific as it may be:

Tracking a wounded, panicky deer during the day is a real challenge — at night it requires extra patience and skill.

Night tracking deer requires good lighting, experience and a careful pace. It is also a lot easier to get lost. Stay alert!

course is the logical line is something we humans tend to do, not necessarily a wounded animal. Following this line of reasoning oftentimes gets us off the proper course. It causes us to tend to hurry, something an experienced tracker has learned not to do!

If a trail appears to have been lost, the best technique I have learned is to circle tightly from the last sign, covering at least a fifty-yard radius. If that doesn't produce results, back up and do it again. If this doesn't help, cast forward on the travel line and go through the whole procedure again. When a situation like this develops, it's best to have some help.

I learned early on to pay attention to the birds. I have found many downed game animals due to the racket created by crows and ravens. In several instances, I have seen arrow-wounded mule deer and one elk found, because golden eagles were circling over them, looking for free vittles. For what it may be worth in the way of such oddities, except in Africa, I never have located any downed animal with the help of circling vultures or buzzards, although they are extremely common in most of the places I hunt.

Given any choice at all, I would rather not have to track a wounded deer — or any other critter — at night.

If the weather is cool and crisp and I'm certain there are no predators to contend with in the immediate area, I'll vote every time to wait until morning rather than to attempt to follow an animal that was hit late in the evening. However, the likelihood of this combination being in force isn't too likely. Where you have deer, you invariably have predators.

For example, in the area of Oklahoma where I hunt a good deal, there are masses of coyotes. I have witnessed these so-

suggest a deer is really smart, but I prefer to think he can be, if for no other reason than all the times a big buck outsmarts me. What is really an incredible survival instinct on balance with a suspicious nature tends to make us accord deer more credit for actual brainwork that they are capable of.

All that notwithstanding, I have seen them pull off some pretty smooth tricks. Often a deer can confound us and make trailing all the more difficult by circling to watch its backtrail — a frequent tactic with a paunch shot — actually circling back over its own trail to confuse the original sign. This is an inherent instinctive reaction to millions of years of being pursued by scenting predators such as wolves and wild dogs.

As an example of what I'm trying to get across, a year or so back, I had a whitetail buck — hard-hit though he was — circle back over his own trail five times. And would you accept the fact that the animal managed to do this all within a dense thicket twenty square yards in area? That mess would have had a bloodhound howling in frustration!

It is normal for us to assume wounded deer always will follow the path of least resistance, but they don't. As mentioned earlier, a hard-hit, fatally wounded deer will run blindly sometimes for what seems an exceptional distance. Such deer do not follow the easy path.

A wounded deer is confused, too, and will do erratic things. Assuming always that the most pronounced trail or easiest

For tracking at night, it is best to use a strong flashlight to pinpoint sign and a gas lantern for illuminating wide areas.

Opinions are useful as long as the group doesn't disturb the trail. These hunters take care to remain behind the signs.

called desert wolves trail a wounded deer and devour it within a matter of a few hours.

If the weather is warm, you are committed to spending some of the night in the tullies. The warmth can lead to spoilage of venison in a matter of only a few hours. In most instances, one can't wait for daylight.

Only the most inexperienced bowhunter goes into a hunting camp without a good flashlight. There invariably are plenty of them around, if one has to trail a wounded buck in the dark. However, I prefer portable gas lanterns of the type Coleman markets. They seem to cast better, brighter light over a broader area.

As mentioned, one should protect the blood trail. and not walk on it inadvertently. This is perhaps more important in the darkness than during daylight hours. Another care should be to watch out for snakes on warm autumn nights. I have found myself literally standing atop rattlesnakes, cottonmouths and copperheads on some of my night tracking excursions. Exciting, maybe, but definitely not fun!

The greatest cause for poor blood trails, as you may suspect, has to be poor shot selections, bad arrow placement or a combination of the two. While a tree stand is an excellent means of getting close to a deer, steep angles, as I've discussed elsewhere, can be poor bets for full penetration. Bad angles on the animal at either ground level or from stands, movement that causes deer to bolt, a squeaky arrow rest, any number of things can contribute to a bad hit and a poor blood trail.

It is unfortunate, but no matter how patient we might be, how careful we are in taking the best shot or how good a shot we are, sometimes things will go wrong. Oftentimes, too, a hit isn't as good as we think it is. That's one of the main reasons for sitting patiently, unwinding and reviewing what happened.

It provides some time especially for poor hits for the arrow to do its job.

A clean hit in the boiler room puts any animal down fast. A hit through the hams, if it hits the femoral artery in one leg or two, will kill a deer within seconds. Hits that do not catch these arteries are fatal, too, but it will take longer. Liver and paunch shots, with the animal reacting as mentioned — the slow, walking off — are fatal, too, but are not nearly as fast.

Waiting, then reviewing the evidence carefully sets the stage for how fast you should follow-up. The key is not to push a wounded deer. Once you do, your problems no doubt will multiply dramatically. Sometimes it can't be helped. An apparent good hit and blood trail leads you 150 yards, then suddenly the deer is up and running.

In almost every instance where I have seen that happen, the best advice would be to back off and wait. Here are some common scenarios and how I would suggest they be handled:

BLOOD TRAILS

Let's start this off by saying that, even though we have always described the killing capacity of an arrow — a broadhead, actually — as that of creating hemorrhage. This is called profuse bleeding in medical jargon, which I won't belabor you with in depth, because I am not at all qualified. However, it is much more involved than reflected by this simple layman's term.

Oxygen is the real key. Oxygen is supplied to the system through the blood, with the heart acting as the prime pump. This keeps the blood, thus the oxygen, moving throughout the system. Blood-rich organs such as the liver, heart or lungs are the primary way stations in that system. When they are destroyed, the break-down in oxygen supply lines are devas-

When the trail grows weak, one person should explore forward for additional signs while others stay to the side.

tating and death is swift; lesser organs, vein or capillary damage produce the same result at a slower pace.

This is the key as to how an arrowhead works, but, it does not obviate the fact that bleeding — hemorrhage — in whatever quantity, is what helps us in the recovery effort known as "blood trailing."

To the inexperienced, a little bit of blood often looks like a lot. To the experienced, there is never too much. Producing the maximum amount of blood is the sole responsibility of the broadhead. It does this best when it is so sharp it makes even you nervous. It should be made of good, solid steel, in a multiple-blade configuration and with as wide and smooth-surfaced a cutting edge, as your bow/arrow setup can handle.

The mission is to slice deep and effectively, the broadhead preferably clear through to produce both entry and exit wounds to generate hemorrhage.

This action induces both blood to trail by, and the loss of oxygen which kills. That's how it works, and anybody you ever heard about that is consistently successful — Fred Asbell, Gene Wensel, Chuck Adams, Judd Cooney, Myles Keller, Dwight Schuh, ad infinitum, and even myself — know that and shoot nothing but broadheads that generate these results.

Blood trails can be misleading. The only thing one need know about any of them is that they have to be followed. I hear, for instance, of blood trails "full of bubbles, obviously lung shots" that ran out. Lung shots run out at the end of the trail with the deer lying there. Lung shots are fatal! Show me

a guy who scored a lung shot "with bright, red, bubbly blood," but didn't punch his tag, and I'll show you someone who doesn't know what he's talking about!

Any blood can have bubbles in it occasionally, because the blood contains oxygen. Blood that flies through the air to hit and splash can and will contain air bubbles. Lung blood is expelled from the mouth and nose as well as from the entry and exit wound. Lung blood, at the most, is a two hundred-yard problem.

Hits in the heart, dorsal aorta along the spine, femoral in the rear legs or caratoid in the neck produce sufficient blood trail for a blind person. Severing one of these is akin to slashing the garden hose with a machete while you are watering the yard. Everything goes: blood, oxygen, hydraulics, and you have another easy-to-follow problem of less than two hundred yards.

With the pyloric, the only mid-section artery that runs through the paunch area, blood trails are much more skimpy and mixed with other materials that make them difficult to follow.

A pure paunch shot can be a trailing nightmare. There is little blood, but a paunch shot deer normally will not travel far before lying down. In the length of time it takes one to expire, the deer often will get up and move several times, frequently in an attempt to get to water. The circling technique described earlier locates a lot of gut-shot deer. If such a deer is lost, closely reconnoiter any water sources in the vicinity.

At last! A successful night of tedious tracking ends when a fine whitetail buck is found.

Dougherty shot this whitetail (below) from a tree stand at 10 yards. But it required some persistent tracking before the hunt was happily completed.

TRAILING

If you have bounced a wounded deer, the first thing to do is wait. When tracking is resumed, try to follow with the wind in your favor. Always follow slowly, paying serious attention to what is out in front in hopes of seeing the deer before it bolts, again. In such a situation, I am always assuming it will do that. If you find it stone dead along the trail, perfect.

Planning for the other eventuality is the smart move, though. Whenever possible, I like to have someone circle wide outside the suspected line in the hope of spotting the deer which, if alive, doubtlessly will be watching its back trail. Such deer will hold tight for as long as possible, providing an opportunity for a second shot, if approached carefully.

Binoculars are invaluable for this. Having someone hopscotch ahead on a trail can save time once a line is established. Sometimes even good hits can be difficult to follow, because something is retarding external bleeding. It may be the size of the wound — a common problem with small broadheads, and two blade designs — that allows layers of hide, muscle and fat to restrict it. Many times I have seen angled hits that were deadly, but were clogged with stomach contents that almost totally staunched external bleeding.

Not many hunters would choose to trail game at night. But the difficult task often adds to the satisfaction of the hunt.

Cut, which is a superb four-blade head, in my opinion, and it was truly sharp. Don't ask me how or why the deer didn't drop immediately. I don't know. I do know we didn't give up!

Here's another strange one. Darrall, my youngest son, shot a buck late last season that wheeled when he shot. His analysis, when he reported to camp, was that it didn't look good. "High in the neck, in front of the shoulder," he thought.

Here's what happens with neck hits. If they are above the vertebrae, you can figure it's a superficial wound that will bleed awhile, then stop. The deer will recover easily. Shooting a little lower, you hit the spine. All you need to know now is how to gut it. Or you can sever the caratoid (jugular vein) and skip down the blood trail, while reaching for your knife.

Possibly you could cut the wind pipe which will generate little or no blood and the deer undoubtedly will escape.

Nature's hunters can be helpful in tracking. Look for birds circling downed game. They'll often be raising a ruckus.

Scouting ahead can save valuable time. There are many variables, but the one thing you should never do is give up too soon. Last season, my son, Kelly, shot a nice eight-point from the ground while still-hunting. He was sure he had hit the deer well, and was able to watch it go fifty yards, where it stopped, then walked out of sight. Kelly looked for a sign, but found nothing but a handful of hair which appeared to be from the area tight and low behind the deer's shoulder.

We cast about for blood on the line he had marked. He backed up and positioned me as close to the spot where the deer had last been seen. Nothing. It was a tough place with really high blue-stem prairie grass that can hide a fallen deer easily and swallow up blood trails completely.

We took several natural lines along deer trails, which seemed logical, since the deer had simply walked out of sight. Nothing. We fishtailed across a grassy opening in figure eights and found the buck stone dead in a pool of blood on the other side.

The buck was heart shot, and as far as I can tell, never bled a drop externally until he fell. Kelly shot him with a Hoyt Top

High grass made it virtually impossible to blood trail this heart-shot buck. Kelly Dougherty located him by circling carefully.

Incidentally, I have seen several instances of such hits from which the deer fully recovered.

Darrall and I started out on the trail, spotting some blood soon, then his arrow without the broadhead, again a four blade design. The trail was sketchy, because the deer really had been hauling tail downhill. The blood trail became quite faint, and we were rapidly loosing heart when suddenly there was blood splashed everywhere, leading us twenty five yards to where that nice eight-point was piled up.

Here's what happened. The broadhead had hit about where Darrall had predicted, actually touching the top of the verte-bra. This impact knocked out the auxiliary blade, honed razor-sharp. The free-floating blade cut the jugular probably during the deer's leaping downhill dash.

Superficial hits are responsible for a lot of misconceptions. These are muscle (meat) hits of a non-vital nature that happen most in the shoulder or the high back area. A razor-honed head induces a great deal of initial bleeding after passing through these muscle zones, but there really is nothing major there in terms of arteries or major veins to pump out any significant amount of blood.

In relatively short order, this blood flow slows by clotting and the blood trail diminishes to nearly nothing, then ends completely. As I said, a little blood can look like a lot and a couple of hundred yards of it — perhaps a steady drip-drip type of trail — convinces the inexperienced bowhunter that he has killed a deer that couldn't be found.

Actually, the initial trauma is shaken off by the deer, as the damaged tissue strives to restore itself. The same thing happens with a cut on your hand for instance. These are clean wounds with little or no tissue damage to which any wild animal's dynamic recuperative powers respond quickly. Unlike the bullet that destroys magnum amounts of tissue as it delivers its shock load, arrows in nonvital areas do only slight damage. No carefully carried-out survey ever has proved that arrows result in more lost game than other methods, as is so often suggested by animal rights fanatics. I'm convinced that the recovery rate of animals wounded with arrows is much higher than in any other type of hunting.

Following up a shot requires nothing more than patient observation and a good pair of eyes. Getting in a big hurry, a normal enough reaction, is counter-productive. Experience is the best teacher, so whenever you have a chance to help on a tracking mission take it and learn.

The woods of fall are full of misleading little tidbits of color that can often be mistaken for blood, particularly dried blood. I'd suggest you keep handy a bottle of the tracking aid solutions available today. It will identify blood instantly from other material.

Some people have an incredible knack for tracking both in terms of reading sign such as bent grass or twigs to identifying part of an individual track. The more you can learn about tracking the better off you are, and it's fun. Grab any opportunity to perfect these skills.

CHAPTER 21

A STUDY IN EXOTICA

Importation Of Foreign Species Gives The Bowhunter Opportunities For Other Trophies

I F WE CONDUCT some serious research on the deer of the world, we learn quickly that science holds to the theory our North American deer have foreign roots. It is believed that the deer, like most of our other big-game species, migrated to this continent over the land bridge connecting Asia and North America somewhere around 15,000,000 years ago.

Not all of the deer species we have here today are descended from those that wandered over in that dim past to evolve into the current distinct variations. Some came later by more modern means. And somehow, most of these other breeds wound up in Texas.

Altogether, there is a broad spectrum — verging on endless — of deer in the world. Many of them only remotely resemble the creatures we love and respect so much. Beginning in Asia, where it is believed the deer of the world probably had their beginnings, we find today tiny specimens of the deer family, some not much larger than a jackrabbit. Some of them grow tusks rather than antlers.

The small axis from Asia are, like whitetails, spring-loaded. Their antlers are somewhat like an elk's with fewer points.

Dougherty took this fallow buck from a resident herd on private land. The antlers are superb. The eating was not.

In the evolutionary process, as the deer inched across Asia, eventually migrating to our continent, they became larger, developing their magnificent antlers in the process.

Slowly, some regressed back down the size scale to again become diminutive little fellows, as they moved deep into South America. These species did not regain tusks in the transition, though the antlers they carry are not much different than tusks in terms of size and shape.

With few exceptions, our North American deer are the most magnificent. Europe has its red deer, a close cousin of our elk. Asia has the axis, sambar and Barasingha. The fallow deer is widely scattered abroad. The interesting news is that, today, we have many of these species on our continent, some in a generally wild, free-roaming environment. These deer, products of early importation and mostly private land stockings, are referred to most commonly as "exotics."

With few exceptions, they are not truly "free-roaming," being confined largely to private lands behind gameproof fences.

Several times over the years, in the gorgeous fall season, I have hunted the lovely terrain of the Land Between the Lakes in Kentucky where fallow deer are considered fair game for archers during the whitetail season. My comrades on those hunts would point out fallow deer sign to me — not so unlike whitetail sign as to be very distinctive — and get quite excited at the prospect of someone bagging one. No one in my experience ever did, and I never laid eyes on one personally. Those deer, however, are truly a free-roaming herd.

I have hunted a great deal in Texas, a state I truly enjoy for its bowhunting variety and atmosphere; a state that has more exotic game than all the rest combined. I spent a week hunting axis deer there one time, slipping around on a rather closely held ranch, if 15,000 acres behind fence can be considered closely held. I never got a shot at a good buck, though I came close to almost drawing back several times.

There are a great many axis deer roaming Texas today, escapees from original imports that have spread and adapted well. Some biologists have told me that the axis' and fallow's

Hunting a sika is no easy task. The small deer is difficult to find in its favorite habitat: high grass and heavy brush.

in appearance. This was an invitational hunt hosted by a major corporation that, I am sure, was shafted on the deal as badly as I. The hunting environment was really quite good, but I never saw the deer again, and I understand the corporate folks still are trying to track down and resolve their differences with a rather unsavory "outfitter" whose whereabouts is still unknown.

Those things can happen easily in the pursuit of exotic game which many times is something much less than a true hunting experience. Far too many exotic deer, as well as other imported species, are kept on game ranches or hunting preserves of limited size where anything resembling fair chase went out the window the day they opened the gates.

This is not to say there are not excellent, pure hunting opportunities for exotic deer. There are to be sure. I suspect that for the axis and sika species in particular, the hunting will get even better.

The sika is a smallish deer that acts more like a 4-year-old, hard hunted cock pheasant than a four-legged critter. It loves heavy brush, high grass and thick cover, and collecting one is a tough ball game wherever the deer may be.

Axis deer are shy — acting like whitetails, actually — beautiful creatures with spotted coats, clean, lovely features and sort of elk-like antlers, but without as many points.

I have a special desire to go get an axis one day, but I would like to take it in Hawaii, on the island of Molokai where they have done extremely well and are quite wild. I have an invitation, and I will take my wife, thereby solving two major issues at once. Said issues involve around her increasingly pointed interest in Hawaii — "before we are too old to enjoy it "— and mine for this lovely deer.

Actually, my chances probabley would be better in Texas. However, Sue has no real desire to re-do the honeymoon in a south Texas brushland setting, big axis deer be damned! If you

A fallow buck has wonderful antlers, somewhat like those of a moose. These deer are white or brown, some almost black.

competition with the whitetail eventually could overpower the native deer and drive them to oblivion.

On one ranch I hunted in Texas, where a substantial pasture was set aside, fenced and stocked with both fallow and axis deer, the result was total decimation of the whitetails inside the perimeter within three years.

"Well, what the hell," as one guy said over a beer, "Texas has too damn many whitetails anyhow." While that may seem true, it's a shallow and dangerous way to look at the potential problem. In a sense, no matter where they might be in Texas, it would be hard to classify any exotic as truly free-roaming, considering the fact that the state is composed almost totally of private land. The exotics might not be behind a gameproof fence, but they certainly are held behind closely patrolled no trespass signs.

I have only hunted for and shot a couple of the exotics. Some time ago, I took a nice sika deer, sort of a miniature elk

Here's a rare glance at a sika in the open. Only serious bowhunters even attempt to hunt this small oriental deer.

are less second-honeymoon oriented and desire a big axis, the Lone Star State is really the place to check out.

I have shot one fallow deer which wasn't anything too special in the doing, though the deer itself was a Grade A dandy. I had read that the fallow species is high on the list of prime-tasting venison. The problem may have been with this specific fallow buck, but his meat was absolutely terrible on the table.

My Labrador — the finest hunting companion I'll ever know that wasn't two legged — wouldn't eat a chunk of broiled back strap and he would eat anything — up to then. My wife, who can cook a brick with enough pizzazz to make you cry, ordered it out of the house, and I, forsaking the Macho Provider position of: "I killed it, and will by God eat it," was only too happy to comply. On the other hand, I have eaten axis several times and it was wonderful.

I really like my fallow deer as a mount on the wall of my trophy room, though. Given some age, they have antlers with real character, heavily palmated, a very nice spread in his case with interesting points and funky bumps he is indeed an interesting deer antler-wise but I think in terms of pretty face-wise he isn't much compared to an axis, or a whitetail.

My fallow deer is white. They come in that color, or brown with spots sort of like an axis. and I have seen a few that were white-faced and shouldered running to a brown saddle. Some appear almost black, and there was one like that where I hunted mine that I had plans for, but he vanished. Word is he went down during the whitetail season which is generally acceptable anywhere they exist. Game departments usually look upon them as non-game, therefore are not their responsibility, during the deer season. I doubt strongly that I would ever shoot another fallow deer, but, if you are interested, again, Texas is the place I would look first for a quality hunt, though there are huntable fallow deer in other areas.

One of the nicest things about hunting these interesting deer is the timing. Generally uncontrolled by state regulations, year-round hunting is allowed in most areas where exotics exist. If I were to hunt in Texas, for instance, I would make plans for an early spring trip — probably March — before the brush rejuvenated itself from the rather lazy winters they have there. In late spring, Texas becomes uncomfortably, sometimes unmercifully hot.

This provides a fine break from the cabin fever syndrome of winter and is well suited to getting your juices flowing. After a few months of inactivity, it can be fine therapy.

Fallow bucks are onery during the rut. They gather large numbers of does and will fight viciously to protect their harems.

CHAPTER 22

FIELD TO FRYING PAN

Downing A Deer Is Only The Beginning For A Venison Feast!

This slick eight-point whitetail was one of 13 bucks Dougherty located feeding on early season acorns. After enjoying the satisfaction of a successful hunt, there comes the often demanding task of dressing the deer and quickly getting it to camp.

Dragging a buck by its antlers is a widely used method of removing deer from the field.

IT IS SAFE to say few people in the Lower Forty-eight states truly have to hunt in order to eat in today's society, though certainly some do. Recent polls among the middle-of-the road-elements of that same society — those who have no major conscientious bias regarding hunting, either seriously opposed or pro, the very folks who could one day decide hunting's fate — seem to feel hunting is sort of okay, if the game taken is destined for the table.

These same elements do not feel quite as liberal about "trophy hunting." Somehow, that seems understandable in today's climate, though it is not necessarily viable in terms of some game management concepts. Educating the general public regarding correct use of our natural wildlife resources is a difficult task these days.

Regardless of the fact that we do not need venison as food to survive, it still is a mainstay on the grocery list of millions of American households. When deer were close at hand and I was a young man with a growing family, collection of a deer was a financial advantage to our budget. Today, venison — deer meat — still constitutes a major portion of the protein for every member of my family.

This may not be a significant contribution to the family budget, for catching a deer costs quite a bit more now than in the "old days." However, that concept can arguably be offset by the fact that venison is a lot better for our health than most meat products of four-legged origin normally available at the super mart.

Venison, as far as I am concerned, is just plain good. How good it is depends largely on how well the carcass is handled after the scouting blends into the hunting, a clean shot is made and the tracking job is followed up to a successful conclusion. Proper care of game in the field is every bit as important to me as any of my abilities required to put a deer in a position requiring my knife.

Speaking of knives, it does not take something on the order of a sword to field dress a deer properly. To the contrary, something much smaller is a better tool than a ten- or-twelve-inch version of something Jim Bowie might have carried. I have dressed deer with pen knives. On more than one occasion, having found myself without a knife for some reason, I've done an adequate job with a sharp broadhead, though I felt a little foolish. I only own about four dozen knives!

Two years ago, I witnessed a remarkable job of field dressing a deer carried out by Robert Louis Murphy on the Kenedy Ranch in south Texas. Murphy, an accomplished

Here is one time Dougherty didn't have to carry or drag a deer out of the field. This Quad-Runner handled the tough work.

guide and woodsman, does it all with a small, razor-sharp hatchet. It was an object lesson in expertise.

Simply described — because you have to be dying to know — Murphy opens the deer with the blade from sternum to crotch with a perfectly executed cut that does not penetrate the stomach or intestinal wall. Reversing his angle, he splits the deer as far forward toward the upper chest as concerns for the taxidermy cape allow. He then rolls the blade of the hatchet through the upper chest around each wall to loosen the diaphragm. He gives the pelvis a gentle whack, while jerking up on the tail at the same time, to free the entire lower tract. He flops the deer over in a violent motion, and it's done. Neatest thing I ever saw.

"All in the wrists," he told me, though I felt the hatchet, easily as sharp as my most deadly broadhead, certainly helped.

Before we get into the actual matter of field dressing, let's discuss a few common, unnecessary mistakes frequently made by inexperienced — and sometimes even experienced — hunters, who happen to dote on old-time traditions.

The first has to do with the matter of cutting the animal's throat. I suppose this originated in early European times when stags were run to the hounds by royalty and brought to bay amidst great confusion at which time the royal huntsman was charged with terminating the critter by slashing its throat — probably with a royal sword!

Forgetting that, consider this in the context of bowhunting. The arrow that killed the deer did it by causing it to lose its vital life blood and oxygen. Slitting the throat — "bleeding the deer," if you will — makes no practical sense on arrow-shot game, or even gun-shot animals, for that matter. All it accomplishes is an unsightly mess.

Other archaic beliefs have to do with removing the deer's metatarsal glands, referred to as "hocks" by those who do it. These glands are found on the lower part of the rear legs. On rutting bucks, they appear enlarged and dark in color. You can go to the trouble, if you like, but it's totally unwarranted. Leaving them in place will not, as some old-timers I have run into claim, "taint the meat." Deer do not bleed after they are dead, until the chest cavity is opened, and external glands will not taint meat — unless you cut them loose and rub them vigorously and deliberately over the steaks!

The first step, once you have found your deer dead and are ready to get into field dressing, is to get the deer on its back, preferably on a slight slope with its head uphill.

If you are alone, with no one to help in keeping the deer in a steady belly-up position, shim it with rocks or fallen logs along each side to maintain the position. The downhill angle allows gravity to assist you.

Removing the entrails from a deer is a simple matter. The key to a clean job begins with the proper ringing of the anus region with a sharp knife. You need a blade length of no less than three inches to do the job right. The incision from the crotch to the brisket is a key operation. Not cutting too deep is the number one rule. A slight incision lets you slip a finger

Dougherty believes deer should be skinned as quickly as possible to allow the meat to cool. It makes for the best venison.

under the skin in such a way as to guide the point of the knife just under the skin without cutting into the layers of muscle tissue. Once enlarged, two fingers straddling the blade separate the tissue. As the stroke is moved upward to the base of the brisket, the finger pressure prevents cutting open the very core of the term, "guts."

At this point, the consideration is for the cape or head skin, if the deer is to be saved for a taxidermy bill. This incision is best terminated just short of the center of the brisket point. Full shoulder mounts require adequate cape material and taxidermists prefer to have way too much rather than not enough.

With deer or any game animal that is to be mounted, I remove the skin, uncut beyond the point of the brisket toward the throat. This measure in no way inhibits field dressing.

Actually, while still in the field, I prefer as small an abdominal opening as possible. It just keeps things cleaner while transporting the critter to the next step.

I also believe firmly in field dressing any game animal as quickly as possible. The primary reason for this is to allow the animal's body heat to escape and thus reduce the possibility of that heat spoiling meat, which it will do faster than all the metatarsal glands in the world!

The larger the animal, the greater the problem with internally trapped body heat. Elk comprise a prime example. With heavy hide and deep layers of fat and muscle, body heat is a major threat to internal deterioration, and it can happen with alarming speed in the early bow seasons of September when

mid-day temperatures are still at the upper end of the thermometer.

The best rule of thumb: The hotter the day, the faster you have to get to the job of field dressing and skinning.

There really are only two tricky parts to this exercise. The first involves slicing the diaphragm loose from the rib cage. The diaphragm separates the chest, organs, lungs and heart from the stomach, with the liver riding right on the fence. Simply run your knife along the inside of the rib cage from brisket to backbone and slice this material free. You will have to do it on both sides.

Once this is accomplished, reach up inside the chest cavity and grasp the wind pipe which will include the throat. Cut that off as far up as you can reach. With the diaphragm loose, the heart and lungs, plus the stomach and intestines, along with the reproductive tract coming through the pelvic channel, will pull loose in a complete unit.

This is where the initial ringing of the anal area plays through. If it has not been done with adequately deep cuts, that area can be torn apart at this point in the process. The danger here is in breaking open the bladder which might spill its contents on the meat. Should this happen, getting the deer to a place where it can be washed thoroughly as soon as possible is important.

Once the offal is removed, I separate the heart and liver and place them in the plastic bag carried in my day pack. For some reason, deer liver strikes my palate as okay, though I wouldn't

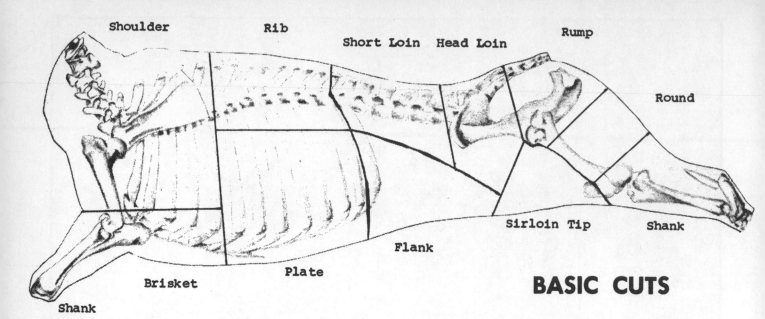

Shoulder　　　Rib　　　Short Loin　Head Loin　　　Rump　　　Round　　　Sirloin Tip　　Shank　　Flank　　Plate　　Brisket　　Shank

BASIC CUTS

These are the basic cuts for butchering a deer. The faster the animal is cut into sections the better the meat will be preserved.

walk across the street to the finest restaurant in Chicago for calves' liver and onions if the meal was free. Maybe it has something to do with gathering my own meat. I don't know, and it doesn't matter.

Deer heart is truly fine eating in the opinion of most of my hunting friends, though some will not eat liver in any form.

A point of caution here: Don't forget that the liver and heart are in your day pack, and get them out to soak in cold, salted water just as fast as you can.

If you are not used to this part of the bowhunting scene, several things will strike you as awesome when you field dress a bow-killed deer taken with a solid chest shot. The amount of blood inside the chest cavity will amaze you, and it may interfere slightly with what you are trying to do if you are not familiar with handling game. I mention this because of the important next step.

Once the animal is dressed, it should be flipped over and spread in such a manner as to allow it to drain thoroughly. I prefer to do this over a log or some sort of brush that allows air to flow under the deer, while I am figuring the next steps required in moving the deer. I already have split the pelvic bone which allows the rear legs to be spread wide, and facilitate perfect draining. This I do with my little folding saw, but it often can be done with a heavy knife. It all depends on the size of the animal.

The next step is to get the deer out of the woods where it can be handled properly. If this cannot be done in a reasonable amount of time, I make sure the deer is receiving good ventilation. I will cover it with a jacket or something carrying my human scent. A T-shirt works well to keep varmints such as coyotes at bay.

In warm weather, the possibility of meat spoiling obviously is magnified and extra steps are required. If you are in some remote back-country spot to which you might not be able to return in a matter of hours, the best move is to skin the deer, quarter it and hang the pieces in the shade. Flies can be a problem, but the "blows" from egg-layers can be cleaned off easily if done with in reasonable time.

I am a firm believer in removing the hide as soon as possible. This provides faster cooling and allows a hard glaze to form over the exposed outer carcass that serves as a protective barrier. In cool weather, I have kept deer hanging in camps with perfect results for up to a week.

During the day, keep the meat hanging in the coolest, most shady spot, hopefully with a breeze. Wrap the carcass with whatever you have that provides insulation. Oftentimes, I have used my sleeping bag.

At night, remove the covering and let the cooler temperatures work for you in chilling the carcass. Avoid letting it get wet. While I wash out many carcasses when I can, in an effort to flush out blood deposits, I also dry them right away to reduce the possibility of bacteria getting established.

Remove blood shot areas of meat as fast as possible. Trim them out, and discard the pieces away from where the carcass is hanging. This will reduce the chance of drawing pesky critters to the site as these particular pieces apparently have a strong attracting aroma for hungry varmints.

My preference in game bags does not include the commonly sold cheese cloth variety that will not impede blow flies or the gnawing of yellow jackets. Such bags fit the flesh too snugly and only serve to keep deer flies and other ravenous insects from getting inside the cavity. Roomy, light cotton bags that allow circulation, but do not touch the carcass work best.

A heavy coating of pepper long has been considered a protective measure in keeping meat. I have never found this to be adequate, however. To do it thoroughly requires a helluva lot more pepper than anyone ever has in camp, and it doesn't seem to help. Today, there is a new product on the market called Liquid Game Bag, which I'm told sets up a strong protective barrier against insects.

There will be times when getting a deer to the truck involves a great deal of labor. A mule deer adventure in Colorado's high country is a good example. After the glow of success has ebbed and the deer is properly dressed, you realize you are one mountain and two canyons from camp. A mature

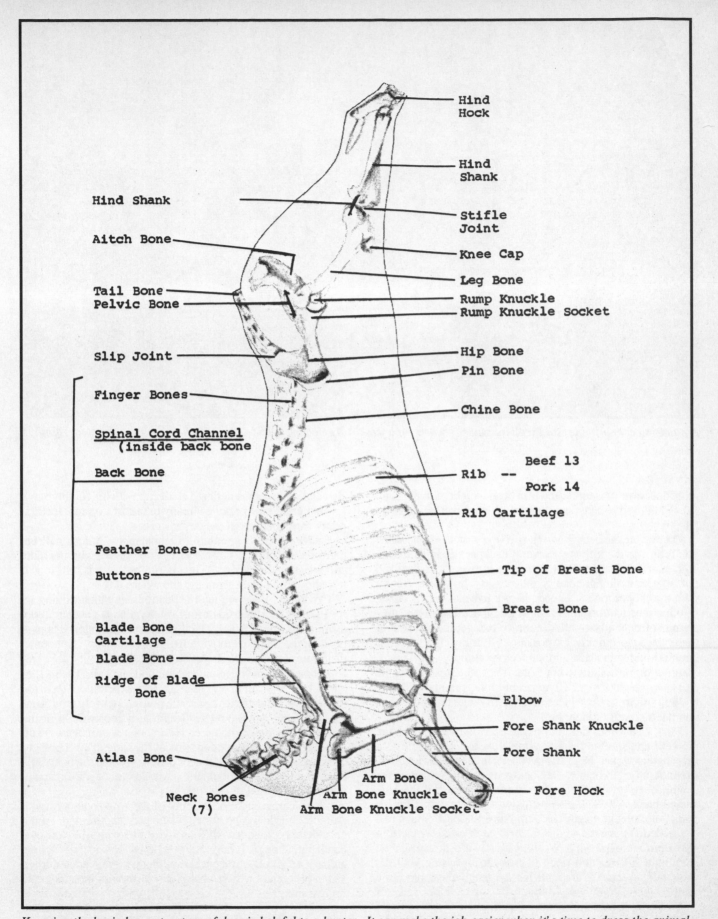

Hind
Hock

Hind
Shank

Hind Shank

Stifle
Joint

Aitch Bone

Knee Cap

Leg Bone

Tail Bone
Pelvic Bone

Rump Knuckle
Rump Knuckle Socket

Slip Joint

Hip Bone
Pin Bone

Finger Bones

Chine Bone

Spinal Cord Channel
(inside back bone

Rib -- Beef 13
Pork 14

Back Bone

Rib Cartilage

Feather Bones

Tip of Breast Bone

Buttons

Breast Bone

Blade Bone
Cartilage

Blade Bone

Ridge of Blade
Bone

Elbow

Fore Shank Knuckle

Fore Shank

Atlas Bone

Fore Hock

Neck Bones
(7)

Arm Bone
Arm Bone Knuckle
Arm Bone Knuckle Socket

Knowing the basic bone structure of deer is helpful to a hunter. It can make the job easier when it's time to dress the animal.

A handy stream provides an excellent place to wash out a freshly dressed deer. The water also helps to cool the meat rapidly.

mule deer now presents you with a dead weight problem of up to two hundred pounds; not something you slip in the old game bag.

Quartering the deer is one step, if you will have help when you return to the kill site. Several backpacks can be loaded with quarters that are divided equally for weight and walked out. Packing all that bone is unnecessary, however. Return with the proper tools — good sharp knives, a compact meat saw and some cotton bags. If plastic bags are used — and they are most frequently — after the walk-out, get the meat out of these bags as quickly as possible. Plastic eliminates air circulation, retains heat and induces spoiling.

It's a simple matter to bone out a deer, and thus reduce the carrying weight. Marv Clyncke, my long-time bowhunting buddy, shoots at lots of remote, high-country game. His approach is well thought out.

First, Marv does not gut out the deer. After enjoying the moment and shooting some suitable photos, Clyncke uses a reverse technique. He splits the deer's hide lengthwise down the back, along the spine. This also provides the proper cut for caping out a trophy headskin. Once opened and the hide peeled back — which also provides sort of a carpet for his work — Clyncke begins by removing the back straps and desirable neck meat. As this is done, each piece is placed in a position to cool and dry. Working downward, he can remove each hind quarter and bone it, then do the same with the shoulders. I have oversimplified the technique a bit in the telling, but it is quite easy to do.

When all is said and done, Marv Clyncke has a compact load of boned meat. The cape and head he often skins out on-site, and removes the antlered skull cap with his folding saw. Loaded in his backpack he's ready to return to camp, feeling pretty darn good about the day's work.

Under the most common circumstances, a deer will be delivered to camp or taken home in one piece, with the hide still intact on the carcass. The interim problem is how to get it to the chosen place from the site where it fell.

Obviously, there are many situations in which driving to the location in a pick-up or four-runner makes transportation a simple matter. Usually, though, we all find ourselves in a position that requires moving the deer physically over some distance.

Let me caution you about one method. I recall a time when a bunch of us — all in our younger, less experienced days — thought tying the deer to a suitable pole and carting it through the woods on our shoulders would be a cool way to do it. Someone, I suppose, had seen it done that way in a movie or possibly some sporting magazine of the time. Don't bother. The carcass swings and bounces on the pole and the bouncing pole destroys your shoulders. Altogether, it's a difficult, unpleasant method of transport.

I have carried a lot of deer out of the woods on my back. Admittedly, they were not real heavyweights, and I was considerably younger. It's an okay procedure, if you can handle it, though I only suggest it be considered during archery-only hunts, It's not something recommended during a high-power gun season when sight of a moving deer hide can bring a shot.

Dragging a downed deer is the most common method of removing one from the woods. It works well enough where

Deer hanging in camp should be skinned and cooled quickly. Keep them in the shade and protect them from flies and critters.

the terrain favors the dragger, but it is rather strenuous work complicated by the uncomfortable, stooped-over position that can be dangerous to the lower back. The older one gets the more such possibilities have to be taken into account.

If the deer is a buck, the usual technique is to grab an antler and go. It works, though it's terribly uncomfortable, and the deer can be difficult to control on anything other than level ground.

Remember that your body is in a precarious posture that can result in injury. Over the years, I have developed a method that aids in the dragging procedure which I use — if I can't find someone bigger, younger and tougher to help me. Getting help is a possibility that always should be considered, no matter what your age or physical condition.

If the deer is a buck, I look around until I find a stout piece of wood about two feet long. It should be two or three inches in diameter and not weathered or rotted. Cutting a green stick is best.

I lay this stick through the buck's antlers and place a foreleg over the stick on either side. Then I lock the legs and horns in place securely with the handy nylon rope I carry in my day pack.

This keeps the front legs from dragging and provides a carrying-type pull stick I can haul with my hands, or a center-tied pull rope that is looped, around my waist. This posture

This old fallow deer with its heavy palmated antlers meant a lot of work when it came time to remove it from the field.

Noted bowmaker Jack Howard collected numerous bowhunting trophies. Preserving the trophy was important to his success.

elevates the deer's head and the forward part of its body slightly, making it easier to drag and control. Dragging a deer on a sidehill is a major hassle, but over relatively level ground or smooth slopes, I've found this system to work quite well.

If the deer is a doe, I can harness it in the same way, though I have to secure the head under the pull stick, the forelegs on top and lash them even more securely. Bucks are better for dragging. As an old buddy once said, "They do come with handles."

There are several compact deer drags on today's market that are worth considering. These allow the drag-line to be positioned at hip height or even shoulder level, thereby eliminating the strain and danger of pulling from a bent-over position. The problem with these devices is that they do not elevate the animal's head very much. A buck's antlers invariably hook on every obstacle between you and the truck.

When dragging a deer happens to be the best or only solution, and you find yourself all alone and faced with the task, a word of caution is in order: Take your time. The weather likely will be cool and you probably will be wearing too many clothes. Eliminate some to keep from overheating,

then pace yourself. There's no real need to hurry; the deer is not going anywhere! Take the drag in comfortable increments. Rest frequently and enjoy the experience.

Dragging deer is a common cause of lower back injury among hunters of all ages and of heart attacks for those of us who never will see 40 again.

Just as soon as it is convenient, I remove the deer's hide in order or let the carcass cool. We usually wind up skinning our deer in camp after they have been elevated on a gambrel run though the tendons at the hocks.

I prefer to hang my deer head down. As an aid to skinning, I usually begin the task before the deer is elevated by freeing up the hide around the tendons and begin the peeling of the rear-leg quarters. It is just easier to get them started before the deer is hung.

As for the matter of head up or down, I believe the head down position allows body heat to dissipate more rapidly and provides better drainage once the head is removed.

One of the first steps after bringing the deer into camp is to see to the liver and heart properly. The second move is to remove the tenderloins, those small filets that lie next to the

Dougherty collects some nice, tender venison. Deer has been part of the Dougherty family's menu for more than 30 years.

spine just in front of the hips. These are delicate pieces that will dry out easily, ruining their texture. Deer tenderloin and eggs comprise one of my favorite in-camp breakfasts, incidentally.

Once the deer is skinned, take care to cut out and remove any bloodshot areas carefully. Chest shots frequently will cause what appears to be blood in the shoulders. Oftentimes, though, this is simply blood that has run through muscle layers. Soaking these portions in cool, salt-saturated water overnight will clean up a lot of it.

Shots that have penetrated the hams will appear to have ruined more meat than is truly the case, though there will be some significant damage. Again, cleaning and soaking can salvage a remarkable amount that is perfectly suitable for burger or sausage. After that, it's only a matter of personal preference in butchering.

Quite honestly, I have become accustomed to dropping the deer carcass off at a handy processor close to camp whenever possible, particularly if the weather is warm.

I like my meat to hang in a cold room for a least a week. If it's cold enough, I can hang it at home, and cut it at my convenience. Admittedly, I don't do nearly as expert a job as

a professional who also wraps the meat perfectly after cutting it to my specifications. He or she also is more properly set up to render the less desirable left-overs into burger or many forms of sausage. The average price for this service in my neck of the woods runs about $30 per deer.

I always specify that the steaks and chops be cut no less than three-fourths-inch thick. That seems to be just right when they are broiled or barbecued. Venison is a dry meat compared to beef, so thicker slices cook better and retain more moisture.

For some reason — because it's "wild," possibly — there is a universal tendency among the inexperienced to overcook wild game. While I always caution my butcher/processor, or take care to do it myself, there will be a certain amount of fat still attached. Beef fat can be tasty; whether it's good for you or not isn't the point. Deer fat is horrid and serves no benefit in the cooking. Remove all the fat you possibly can from venison when preparing it for the table.

If you treat venison properly, and prepare it as you would any prime beefsteak, you will enjoy its delicious flavor to the fullest.

Properly done, it's the perfect conclusion to a wonderful hunt.

CHAPTER 23

FAMOUS BOW FOLKS

Dougherty Has Had The Opportunity To Learn First-Hand From Some Of The Best!

Circa 1960, life-long friends Dougherty, George Wright and Doug Kittredge hunted Arizona's Kiabab Plateau. Recurve bows are Howard Gamematers. The novel broadhead Silent Stalker hip quivers were designed by Dougherty and Kittredge.

LOOKING BACK on forty years of bowhunting for deer — and not including the many other big game species I have been fortunate enough to hunt in many spectacular places around the globe — there is no question that I have had a truly good time, and have been lucky to have had the opportunities to do all this.

I feel fortunate to have become involved when bowhunting was just rolling into gear. Being active since my teenage years in the industry, and being involved in organizations dedicated to bowhunting provided me the opportunity to know and share hunting experiences with the legends of our sport, both past and present. Let me tell you about some of them.

I think I should start with Doug Kittredge.

When I first wandered onto the scene, Doug was becoming a major force in the archery mail order business. In those days, there were only a few isolated pro shops scattered across the land, and for the most part these were subsidiaries of existing

Dougherty and Doug Kittredge hunted the Mojave Desert in 1956 for these jackrabbits. They used simple recurves.

In the Fifties, Tom Jennings made some of the first recurve bows. Today, his name is on modern, high-tech equipment.

mail order firms. If you needed some item of bowhunting tackle, there were precious few outlets that supplied it.

Most of the practicing archers of that time made the bulk of their own equipment. High-production laminated bows were relatively new and, for sure, significantly different than what we have today. Some archery products were listed in the mail order catalogs of Montgomery Ward and Sears & Roebuck. Serious stuff was available from Herter's, Robin Hood Archery in New Jersey, Anderson Archery in Michigan; Doug Easton was in California, along with Henry Bitzenburger and Hugh Rich. The big manufacturers were York, Stemmler, Bear and Ben Pearson. Earl Hoyt was making custom bows; Bob Lee hadn't started Wing Archery. Compounds hadn't been invented. Tom Jennings was making recurves with M. R. Smithwick, and Pete Shepley's ship was a long way on the other side of the horizon.

A lot of the custom bowyers still were working with self bows of yew and osage, though the fiberglass technology of Frank Eicholtz was certainly on the scene and things were changing rapidly. I've no doubt missed a few key players, as there were really quite a number, but I'm getting along a bit myself, so it's excusable.

Doug Kittredge started out making custom arrows and bowstrings in his garage. When I met him, he had just opened a full-fledged shop — about a hundred square feet — as the front portion of enlarged quarters. The place was in South Pasadena, California, and was called the Kittredge Bow Hut. It eventually became quite well known to archers around the

The amazing Howard Hill did a lot of the on-screen shooting for Hollywood productions. Here, he and Roy Rogers use longbows for a demonstration.

world. Many champions of the time shot Kittredge arrows.

Doug Kittredge and I actually learned about bowhunting deer together and shot our very first deer — he was first — only a few months apart. Not many people got a deer with a bow then, and it was considered quite a feat.

We shared a mutual passion for fly-fishing. Every summer, we would load two weeks of provisions up in our backpacks and cruise the High Sierra's with his wonderful wife, Sally, as our traveling companion. How that lady could walk!

Altogether, we covered most of the John Muir Trail and a hundred others less noted. We saw the Sierra's lengthwise and crosswise and caught I have no idea how many thousand trout — browns, rainbows, brookies and the Sierra's coveted jewel, the golden trout. I can still remember my first golden trout. I

wanted to hold it in my hand forever.

Kittredge was an accomplished woodsman. He read of interesting techniques, then went out and applied them. He and Sally were among the most adept outdoor people of my experience. Eventually a green-eyed brunette joined some of our escapades, though not any of the "death marches" to which Doug and I often subjected ourselves in searching for another high lake and a bigger golden.

The brunette and I baby-sat the Kittredge kids, she learned how to fish and even won a few archery tournaments herself before settling down to give us five sons, all of whom handle a bow with ease. Genetics, I suppose.

My favorite recollection of Doug Kittredge as a bowhunter is his dead-solid, serious attitude about the sport without missing a single moment of enjoying the experience. His attitude always has been one of purpose.

We learned about game calling together, too, and both won a handful of world, national and state titles. It was a helluva lot of fun. At one time Doug held both the Pope & Young world records for Yellowstone elk and for cougar. He always says I'll get my own world record one day, but that seems rather far-fetched at this late date.

It was Doug and a couple of his buddies who came up with the concept of gluing razor blades to broadheads. We didn't have razor insert-style heads, so it was all hand-sharpening.

It took a while to perfect the gluing process, but the results were great. We broke razor blades carefully on a jig and glued them to Bodkins, a three-blade broadside design that still is manufactured today by the L.C. Whiffen Company of Milwaukee.

Doug Kittredge and I came up with the first broadhead-carrying hip quiver. It was called the Silent Stalker. I hunted with an early prototype on one deer hunting trip we made to the Sierra's eastern slope. Doug then took the idea to Bob King at King Leather Goods and we hit the market a few weeks later. It was a real winner at the time.

PSE eventually bought King Leather and a similar quiver still exists in the line, as do other styles from Sagittarius and Chuck Adams.

Howard Hill's film, Tembo, *charged young Dougherty with even more excitement for the sport of bowhunting.*

Dougherty visits with bowyer Jerry Hill who is continuing the longbow traditions of his famous uncle, Howard Hill.

Doug Kittredge still bowhunts today, usually for elk which has always been his favorite. We remain close friends, and I'm asked about him often in my travels. I advise the inquirer that Doug and Sally probably are bouncing around somewhere on the Sea of Cortez where the water goes from blue to purple, and are hooked up hard to a marlin. Doug is a superb blue-water, light-tackle guy. I always lay claim to teaching him how to fish. He counters with his being responsible for any archery skill I possess.

My association with Kittredge opened the doors to a lot of friendships and experiences. One of those experiences was knowing the late Howard Hill.

My dad took me to see, *Tembo,* Howard's African hunting film, when it was playing at movie theaters across the land. Can you imagine what sort of reaction there would be today to a feature-length bowhunting show at the movies!? Gads! George Butler can't even get *In The Blood,* the finest pro-hunting film I have ever seen on cable television, but we can have dopers blowing each other away in explicit four-letter-worded four-color. But, let's not dwell on society's deterioration.

Imagine my enthusiastic response to *Tembo.* Close scrutiny today probably would reveal it was pretty Hollywoodish, but that didn't matter at the time. Its impact certainly was good for archery and the sport of bowhunting.

Glenn St. Charles and Dougherty have challenged the steep ridges of Catalina Island together in quest of elusive goats.

I got to know Howard Hill fairly well some years later. While I never hunted with him, I did shoot some archery exhibitions with him at the Los Angeles County Fair. On one occasion, I tossed coins for him during an exhibition. We started with half-dollars, worked down to quarters and wound up with dimes. On that day, he hit eleven straight dimes dead-center with his arrows at a distance of thirty feet. I still have one somewhere, center-crunched by the heavy blunts he favored.

Hill was an impressive man. He was deceptively big, extremely strong and obviously possessed remarkable hand-eye coordination. His shooting style was the product of the times, not unlike the styles of Ben Pearson or Fred Bear.

Howard Hill favored the longbow and didn't go for the newer recurve that was gaining favor. There is the story, reflecting upon his strength, which has to do with a visit to the shop of Tom Jennings in the early Sixties. At that time Tom was building custom recurves.

Howard spotted two of the custom bows standing in a corner and picked them up. For some reason, both bows were strung at the time. He asked about the draw weights and was told each of the bows had a one hundred-pound draw.

Clutching the handles of both bows in one big hand, Howard Hill grasped the twin strings and came to full draw with both of them. In effect, he was making a two hundred-pound draw!

In the matter of getting off a quiverful of arrows, Hill's speed was amazing, the accuracy dazzling. Howard was an entertaining man, great with stories and anecdotes, but that's what he was: an entertainer. It was he who did most of the trick

Ben Pearson and Dougherty inspect one of the first production Mercury Marauders, a bow Dougherty used for many years.

Ben Pearson took these extraordinary polar and grizzly bears using the Deadhead, a broadhead he designed in the Sixties.

Dougherty and Pearson were close friends both in business and in the field. Many memories were formed testing equipment.

shooting for Errol Flynn and others when the star made *Robin Hood* in the 1930s.

I used to go to meetings at Doug Easton's house in the days of Archery, Incorporated, an organization of folks in California's archery industry. Hill was often there, and we talked frequently of going to his favorite stomping grounds in the Simi Valley to hunt cottontails and ground squirrels, which I think he enjoyed as much as anything. We never got around to it before he moved back to his home country in Alabama, and I've always regretted that as much as the fact that some villain stole the bow, quiver and arrows Howard Hill gave me.

Hill was a great man. While Fred Bear justifiably earned the title, Father of Modern Bowhunting, Howard Hill was certainly one of its greatest pioneers. A passage from his classic book, *Hunting The Hard Way*, seems especially meaningful today.

"Hunting and studying the traits and habits of the various animals are what give the really lasting thrill to the chase. To me, the kill is merely the badge of merit one may expect on special occasions when he has learned to stalk well and shoot straight," Howard Hill worte.

"My advice to the archer who is just beginning to hunt is: Do not take the kill too seriously. To the true sportsman, the pleasure of the chase and the fellowship of one's hunting companions make deer hunting with the bow worthwhile, even though one never actually bags a buck."

I mentioned Doug Easton. At the time we met, his aluminum arrow shafts had begun to dominate the archery scene,

Roy Hoff got into the Pope & Young records with this buck. He took it from a tree stand, a hunting method he'd never used before. Hoff published, in Archery Magazine, *the first article Dougherty ever wrote.*

taking over from Port Orford cedar in a big way. There were some fiberglass shafts on the market then — Micro-Flites the most popular — but Easton's aluminum product was racing ahead.

Doug Easton was a true genius and gentleman. I used to get the biggest kick out of the fireplace in his huge den. It seemed to burn constantly year round. The only fuel, was Port Orford cedar!

Sadly, Doug Easton and Howard Hill passed away at about the same time. Today, Easton Aluminum, under the stewardship of Doug's son, Jim Easton, has become one of the largest, finest sporting goods companies in the world. Jim Easton is a long-time friend and an occasional hunting partner. His many contributions to archery and bowhunting are immeasurable.

In the mid-Sixties, I went to work for a sporting goods conglomerate that had acquired Ben Pearson Archery. I had met Ben previously on a hunting trip to Mexico, and we hit it off really well.

Ironically, with Ben, I shot my first whitetail in Oklahoma.

I told Ben Pearson how much I liked the country and the atmosphere — the pace was markedly different from California — and he said, "Well, maybe you ought to move here."

Fate is funny. I did move to Tulsa some years later as the result of a corporate acquisition, but by then, Ben was gone.

I became quite close to Ben Pearson in those last years of his life. He was one of those old-school, pure-instinctive shooters like Howard Hill, who was a close friend of his. His forte was moving shots. The old movies of him shooting ducks with arrows at Stuttgart, Arkansas, are poorly filmed, though many people I know remember Ben's true skill in shooting winged targets.

There must have been something to it. On a mule deer hunt in Colorado we made together, Ben Pearson agonized over missing two nice bucks, both standing, in one day.

The next morning, he drilled a nice buck that was on the dead run at forty yards.

"Maybe you ought to scare them for me first from now on," he suggested.

Ben Pearson was a mechanical genius. Some of the

Dougherty's long-time hunting buddy, Judd Cooney, shot this muley on a drive in the Sixties.

machines he invented for archery tackle manufacturing, as well as for other industries, were remarkable.

His Deadhead broadhead was designed primarily with turkeys in mind, though it became popular with big-game hunters. The Deadhead came in two sizes, both with very wide blades which Pearson felt were a necessity for bowhunting turkeys. He had a marvelous collection of side-by-side shotguns, mostly L.C. Smiths. "Better for turkeys," he once suggested, a point of view I continue to share.

Ben had an incredibly dry wit, though he was mostly a quiet person, an unassuming man who really didn't say much. During a spring bear hunt in Canada, one of the guides had a girly book which he quickly tried to hide when Ben walked into the room.

"That's okay, son," Ben Pearson said, "we Baptists like women, too!"

We had made some serious hunting plans in mind when he died suddenly. I made one of the hunts later, in Africa. It would have been much better as Ben Pearson's partner.

Among my memories of extra-special people I had the opportunity to know and hunt with, I must tell you a bit about Roy Hoff.

Hoff was a one of the hardest working guys for bowhunting I've ever known. I met him the first time at a hearing before the California Fish & Game Commission, where we were fighting for our Los Angeles County special archery season. Roy was a strong orator, and I believe he saved the day then as well as many other times.

Roy Hoff published the first magazine article I ever wrote, or sold. He was the founder/owner of *Archery Magazine*, then

the official publication of the National Field Archery Association, and the major archery periodical of the time. Mr. Archery to thousands of us, Roy Hoff loved to be with people who shared his enthusiasm.

In the company of his wife, Frieda, Hoff could be found anywhere something archery-wise was going on. I remember the evening he shot the best mule deer of his life. It was on the Roan Creek Plateau in Colorado at John Lamicq's place, then as good a big buck pasture as any in the West.

Lamicq had spotted the deer frequenting a certain favored feeding ground, and had built a permanent stand in a mighty pine. Roy was reluctant to hunt him that way. Stands or blinds were not his thing, as he was a spot-and-stalk bowhunter. I recall his personal attitude about shooting bears or cougars from a tree. He didn't hold it against anyone who did it, but it was nothing that held any interest for him.

Well, Lamicq virtually pleaded to get Hoff to hunt that stand, and finally, he did. As luck had it, the big buck made an appearance, and as Roy was fond of saying, "I made a perfect one for twenty on the critter." He admitted the deer had him completely shook up. There was considerable pandemonium in camp when Roy Hoff allowed this tree stand stuff wasn't so bad.

"I don't think I have ever been as excited as I was watching the old boy come along," he said.

As soon as the required sixty days for drying had passed. I drove out to his home in Palm Springs to score the buck. It went in to the Pope & Young records at 164 1/8. Taken in 1968, it remains a tribute to one of a great man's happiest hours.

Fred Bear had a genuine, infectious sense of humor. He liked to laugh and share stories. This picture was taken in the woods of Allegan, Michigan in 1944. Fred Bear was the father of modern bowhunting.

Over the years, I have shared a lot of campfires with some of the greatest bowhunting guys in the world. I have celebrated big bucks by drinking something too strong with Fred Asbell; climbed some too-high mountains and seriously discussed shooting an outfitter with Chuck Adams; and tracked a wide assortment of wild critters with Judd Cooney.

I have wandered over a whole lot of western real estate with Doug Walker, and when I thought I knew all there was to know about varmint calling, the Burnham brothers and Wayne Weems showed me new ways. I chased goats over the steep, prickly pear-studded ridges of Catalina Island with Glenn St. Charles, fly-fished with Charlie Kroll and rumbled over Texas with guys like Bill Krenz, and M.R. James. All of them have their own memories of Fred Bear.

Fred Bear's passing left a hole in my life that can never be filled. A lot of people feel the same way. It's not as though we were bosom buddies, but we were good friends and I think

Fred cared about me and my well-being. In the thirty years I knew him, there were many indications along those lines. A lot of people can say the same thing. He was that kind of person; a nice man. I liked him a lot.

Fred Bear became my hero years ago, probably because he was *the* bowhunter, with deer and bear, tigers and such, who started it all. The sport just grew from there. He had all the right ingredients for a hero. He was tough, he was honest, incredibly likeable and powerful without arrogance. In the vernacular of the time, he was cool.

The man had to be strong and brilliant to accomplish all he did in his world and in his time. He always said he was "just lucky" and certainly, luck helped. But weak-willed folks do not rise to become giants, to pioneer an industry almost single-handedly or to evolve as legends. Such people make their own "luck." He was extremely capable and a superb bowhunter; we all know that. But, I wonder, just how many of today's

Fred Bear and Dougherty share a special moment in the field. Bear believed it was important to enjoy bowhunting.

"bowhunters" fully appreciate how he did it, or more importantly, what he did for them — for us? Take pause and think about it. We owe him.

Fred Bear was an honest-to-God legend in his own time. He earned the title and he carried it with measurable class. That is not an easy load; most people stumble under it. Fred Bear did not.

A charisma seemed to surround Fred. You instantly liked him and enjoyed his presence. You were glad he was the hero he was supposed to be. The role fit him so well and was so comfortable on him, because the man genuinely liked people. He was so tolerant of them that it just rubbed off and made everyone feel good. He gave a lot of himself and believed in paying back.

Ten years ago, Fred Bear was due in Tulsa as the guest speaker for the Pope & Young Club convention. That was no small commitment from a man in his eighties and not in the peak of health.

I had spent a week in his deer camp the previous fall. Among other more interesting topics we spoke of that week was business. It came out that I had opened a retail archery store as part of our operation in Tulsa. Prior to the convention, Fred called to ask if it would "be helpful to me if he came by the store for a few hours as sort of a promotional effort." It was a heckuva gesture, and he was not to be dissuaded.

We set him up at a table in a store packed solidly — wall to wall — with people. Fred said he wanted "a beer and a pretty blonde" to help him. He got a Budweiser and my daughter-in-law. He signed photos and bows, shook hands and told stories, until the last admiring soul had been accommodated.

He was tired from a long day of travel and a lot of years of doing it. You could see it if you knew, but he didn't want you to. Later, we went to my house for dinner and hunting stories with a few friends. It was a great evening. When it was time for my wife to take him to the hotel, he wanted to know if she had to be in by a certain time. I said, "Yes." Sue said, "No." Fred laughed and laughed. She and I can both still feel it.

In today's bowhunting community, we have a saturation of experts; folks who have all the answers. Fred Bear never pretended to know it all, but he knew more than any collective truck load of us ever will understand.

I recall a walk we took one day in Michigan twenty years ago. It was on one of my first whitetail hunts and colder than Billy Hell for a young guy from California who hunted mule deer mostly in the summer. I was wearing so many clothes I couldn't have shot the Goodyear blimp if it was tied down.

This was Fred Bear's realm, and he was comfortable in it. He showed me how to be comfortable and how to enjoy it. We just walked and talked about what was going on. Not just what the deer were doing, but what everything was doing, how it all

Fred Bear was a hero to Jim Dougherty. The bowhunting pioneer befriended a young Dougherty in the Fifties. The friendship lasted for 30 years.

came together, what it meant. The man was a superb naturalist and woodsman. It was not just a whitetail hunt, it was an exercise in appreciating the experience; the opportunity. It is my favorite recollection of times spent with him.

Fred shot a really nice eight-point buck on that excursion. It was no "book" buck, but he told me once, as we were looking at a collection of trophies someplace, that he had never seen a whitetail near the size of what we were viewing anyplace he had ever hunted. He said he didn't believe he had seen many that would make the "book." I said I had seen a few, but couldn't kill them. Then we went to a whitetail seminar. When it was over, he told me that now we knew all we needed. We just had to go hunting and take the bucks to the measurers!

We looked at each other, and he gave me that wonderful shoulder-shaking laugh.

What I remember the most about Fred Bear is not his many accomplishments, but his laughter and his stories. He found so much humor in life, and could laugh at himself with comfortable ease. Great people can do that. His shoulders would shake up and down, while those piercing eyes we will always remember glaring down an arrow became twinkling lights of gentle pleasure. It made you feel good.

Back in the Sixties, I asked Fred about a good place to hunt antelope. He said he had a place and would fix me up. He lined us up with Bill Maycock, a Gillette, Wyoming, rancher, with whom he had made some of his first bowhunting movies. We had to go there, he explained, because Maycock was such a great guy and told such wonderful stories; we would enjoy his company. Fred kept things in perspective.

Some years later, Maycock wrote a book titled, *Shoot "Em*

Again, an epic collection of stories encompassing thirty-two years of antelope and deer hunters visiting his ranch. Fred naturally got a chunk of ink in Maycock's book. Re-reading it points out how well Fred Bear meshed with folks wherever he went, and how much he could give and teach, without pressing.

Bill Maycock is gone, too. Fred sent those of us who knew him a note concerning his passing. On mine, he penned, "Jim — Trails run out. Take time to have some fun."

Now, as I remember a bit of Fred Bear, I am reminded of the last line in Bill Maycock's book. "So each and every one of you, unless I see you before, we hope to see you up in the Happy Hunting Grounds."

I bet they're having a ball.

All in all, I think I gained the truest insight to the proper philosophy and attitude about bowhunting from Fred Bear. It was his opinion that, in spite of all the pressures we place on ourselves to succeed, the real importance was to absorb and enjoy the experience: to have a good time.

Today's climate of big-buck mania seems charged with a competitive need for success that erodes the foundation of that premise. I like to think I'm not affected, though I freely admit to occasional envy of another's successes. In my business, which is really bowhunting-oriented, it helps to have your own triumphs from time to time — and I do on occasion.

But, as Fred Bear suggested, it is really most important to have fun doing it, which I certainly have. I bowhunt for deer, because hunting them with the people I choose to do it with is fun. I intend to keep it that way. Who knows? I might even catch another nice buck or two in the process!

CHAPTER 24

TROPHIES & YOUR TAXIDERMIST

These deer, taken by Jack Howard (left) and Doug Kittredge, represent two types of antlers: velvet (left) and hard horn.

How Well That Wallhanger Turns Out Depends A Lot On You!

IT IS EVERY deer hunter's ambition — dream, if you prefer, for surely we all dream — to collect a "wallhanger" for the den. Personally, I cannot think of any major expenditure that pleases me more than writing a check to my taxidermist.

Depending on the circumstances, how you handle your prospective trophy can be either a simple or complicated task. That also can make a simple or truly tough chore for your taxidermist. Many of our best bowhunting seasons take place in late summer or early fall when the weather usually is still quite warm. Caring for the meat, cape and hide poses a set of problems requiring special attention.

We already have discussed caring for the venison, itself, which has to be the first priority. Now let's talk about proper care for that cape and the antlers.

Few things in the world of deer hunting torque my crank more than the sight of a big, late-summer mule deer with his handsome, high rack fully covered in glistening velvet. Western seasons in states such as Utah, Nevada and Colorado, for example, offer archers a solid chance at harvesting one of these spectacular trophies through mid-September.

Around the middle of the month — perhaps a little sooner — the big deer will begin to remove the velvet by rubbing it off on small trees and brush.

This process does not take long at all. On one occasion, I was hunting a really good buck in the Colorado high country. He had a wide spread four-by-four rack in thick velvet that would score every bit of 170 Pope & Young points.

We played tag for three days. I never was able to get the right shot, but remained confident that time was on my side. He was frequenting the same steep hillside every morning until the sun pushed away the morning shadows.

On the fourth morning, this buck emerged from a tangle of scrub brush and lay down on the point of a ridge some distance below my hard-climbed vantage point. His antlers were stripped completely of velvet and glowed with a pinkish, bloody hue in the early morning sun.

Velvet is living tissue with a rich blood supply that nourishes the antlers through their five to six months of growth. As the antlers reach the end of their growing cycle, the velvet-like growth begins to dry. It is said that, at this point, it itches, which triggers the deer's urge to remove it by rubbing.

A proper trophy begins with how the deer is dressed. Care must be taken to preserve as much of the cape as possible.

Because the velvet is a living substance, it must be treated with care, if preserving it for mounting is the hunter's desire. The simplest step to accomplish this is by freezing the entire rack. However, this is not often a viable option either in terms of expediency or adequate room in the family freezer. However, if you can get the antlers to a taxidermist quickly, many of them have adequate freezing storage.

Generally, proper care is required in the field. One of the most commonly accepted methods of preserving velvet antlers is to inject them with what is called a Formyline solution. I have done this on many occasions, but I do not like working with the formaldehyde. I don't care at all for the odor, and it

While anthers are the usual trophy, a deer's hooves can be used for a unique mount.

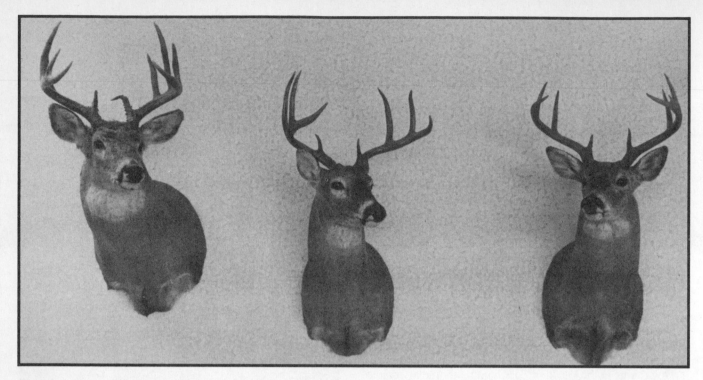

These excellent whitetail mounts preserve the natural beauty of the deer. The slightly turned heads add an element of dignity.

can be somewhat dangerous, as I have seen it squirt from antlers being injected, splashing the one using the needle. I would recommend some form of adequate eye protection as well as rubber gloves, if this process is being carried out.

Recently, other options have come along that my taxidermist prefers and claims is much better. Velvet Set is a name brand product that can be obtained through taxidermy supply houses or, perhaps, with some advance notice, your taxidermist can supply it before you head for the woods.

Injecting either material into the antlers is done through the series of prominent bloodlines or veins that feed the antlers. Start at the tips and work downward, injecting the solution at

The bowhunter who took this whitetail chose to have it mounted as it was moments before it came into bow range: responding to a grunt call.

Before: Here a trophy that has significantly deteriorated.

After: With a new cape, the trophy is restored to splendor.

intervals until you are certain the antlers are well saturated, then keep the rack in a cool, dry place until they can be transported.

Take care not to handle the antlers in any twisting motion that can loosen the velvet. A taxidermist can repair small rips; big ones are difficult.

If retaining the velvet is not a consideration, then it should be peeled from the antlers as soon as possible and the blood washed from them. Velvet will spoil quickly in hot weather, and it's nasty stuff when it goes bad.

For many years, the Pope & Young Club — following the tenants established by Boone & Crockett — did not recognize mule deer antlers in velvet. Over the years there has been considerable debate about this posture, all with valid points of view. However, it is a common fact that many outstanding deer are taken by early season bowhunters every year, and that many of these hunters were reluctant to strip the velvet, preferring to keep the antlers in their fuzzy state. Finally, the Pope & Young Club elected to form a separate category for velvet-antlered mule deer.

Prior to the decision to establish a separate place for these fine animals, a trial period was conducted with the provision calling for a deduction of five percent from the total score. No one thought this was a satisfactory solution, that particuler percentage being a random number that made no scientific sense.

Master taxidermist Michael Bates of Tulsa, Oklahoma has mounted a lot of trophies, including many for Dougherty.

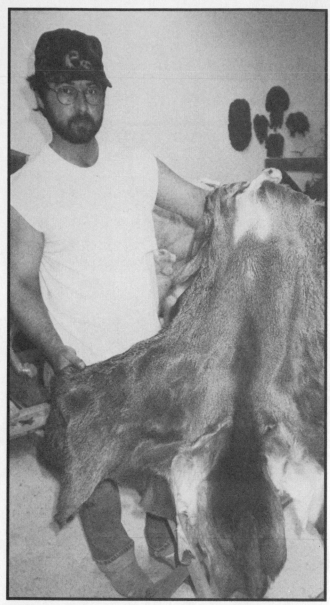

While a deer's antlers are most often the main attraction of a mount, a well-preserved cape is vital to accent its beauty.

Mule deer in velvet are unique trophies hunted mostly by bowhunters due to the timing of our seasons, and according them a place in the bowhunting records seems totally sensible to me. There is one catch to the decision, however. No velvet-covered trophy can be awarded world record status. The antlers would have to be stripped.

I tend to agree with this. Having a place for the fuzzy-horns, and recognizing them in the bi-annual celebrations of the Pope & Young Club seems like the perfect solution.

While velvet antlers require special care, hard "horns" really do not need any extra treatment other than ensuring that the skull plate or cap does not get broken, if the antlers are removed — a consideration for velvet heads, too.

This is only a problem if the head is of record-class size, for broken skull plates negate the trophy from consideration, a common rule wherever inside spread is considered in the scoring process.

Broken caps are the result of not cutting the antlers loose with enough bone left to hold them together. To ensure there is enough, the line of the saw cut should be from the center of the back of the head toward the center of the eyes. This cut line dimension is perfect for your taxidermist and just fine for simple plaque antler mounts.

Before the antlers can be removed — if mounting the head is the objective — the cape or headskin must be skinned out. For first-timers, this might appear a difficult task, but it is remarkably easy with the proper tools. I use a skinning knife and a short, stout-bladed pocketknife.

Begin with a V-shaped cut from the base of the back side of each antler to the centerline of the neck. This cut is approximately four inches and provides a flap of skin angling back from the antlers and forehead. Then continue the cut down the neck's centerline to a point equal to the top of the shoulders. The main thing to keep in mind is to leave enough cape material for a proper shoulder mount.

Using this cut as the beginning point, simply begin skinning the neck forward. You should encounter no problem area, until you reach the ears. Using the sharp, heavy-duty pocketknife, cut the skin free around the base — or burr — of the antlers. Sometimes a screwdriver can be helpful as a pry bar to push the hide loose, though a strong knife should be enough. Cut off the ears, keeping the knife as close as possible to the base. This area is all cartilage, and the line to cut is easy to identify.

From here, continue skinning out the side of the head as well as the forehead until the eyes are reached.

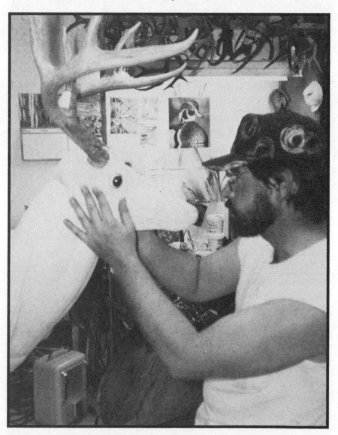

Bates closely examines this trophy's eyes which he has just positioned using modeling clay. The eyes must be natural.

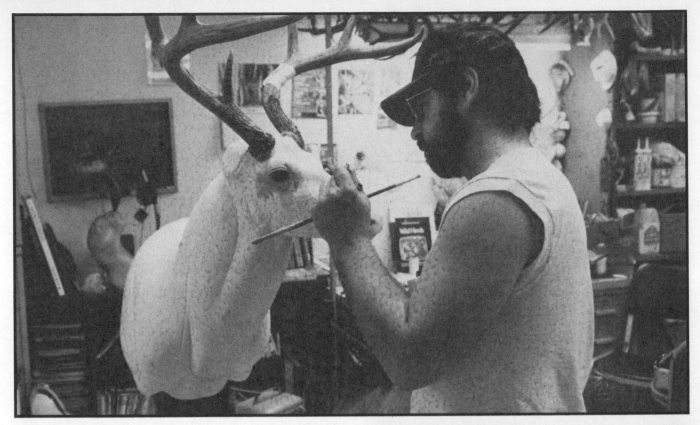

Bates paints around the deer's eyes to provide blending for the cape. Such touches add to the attractiveness of a trophy.

This is the trickiest part. Keep the knife extremely close to the bone, pull the eyelids upward from the outside, then cut carefully through the attaching membrane. At the front of the eye socket will be a tear duct; these must be skinned carefully deep inside the duct with a narrow-pointed, sharp knife.

From this point to the nose is easy. At the nose, cut it off well back down through that cartilage. Using a sharp knife, remove the skin around the mouth from the inside, cutting high above the gum line. Remember it is always better to have more material that needs fleshing off than getting too close to the surface and cutting through the skin. Always work with careful, short strokes.

If you do cut through the skin, don't panic. A skilled taxidermist can repair any minor cut and add an unbelievable assortment of big ones. Once the cape is removed, the antlers can be sawed from the skull.

Now it is necessary to flesh all meat, fat and cartilage from the skin. The importance of this is intensified, if warm weather is a factor. Begin with the ears, carefully skinning them with delicate strokes on each side to separate the interior cartilage. Once this is accomplished, you can turn them completely inside out.

Proceed to the lips and turn them, too, making sure you leave plenty of the actual skin from inside the mouth intact but fleshed. Remove all other meat from the hide with flat strokes. Do the same with the nose.

Removing all this material will let the salt you are going to use next go to work to draw moisture from the hide and

The head is now ready for the cape. A quaility-mounted trophy is no small investment, but it can provide years of fond memories of a special moment in bowhunting.

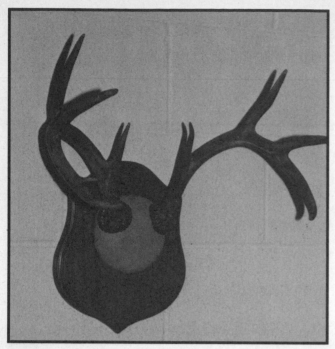

Simple wall plaques also are a fine way to display a pair of antlers. They takes less space and are a lot less expensive.

preserve it. Use plenty of salt and rub it into the hide and all the crevices thoroughly. If you don't have salt readily available, keep the hide in a cool, dry place where it can drain, free from blow flies. I place mine in a deer bag for this purpose and hang it. However, get to some salt and treat the cape as soon as possible or, better yet, get it into a freezer as quickly as you can.

Setting aside for a minute our interest in a head mount, there are a great many uses for various deer parts that can be crafted into interesting memorabilia as well as some that are functionally useful.

If the deer has been caped for a trophy mount, the back skin can be tanned for leather or left with the hair attached for perhaps fashioning a decorative shoulder quiver for the den. The feet with hooves make nice bow, gun or clothes racks. Smaller antlers also can be converted to various racks or cut cross-ways for attractive buttons. All of these and other uses can be discussed with your taxidermist, or accomplished as home projects with little effort. I save all my whitetail tails as well as some of the hair to use in tying fishing flies such as streamers and bass bugs.

Today's taxidermy techniques — and the skills of the taxidermists, themselves — are a far cry from the short-necked, bug-eyed creations crafted years ago. These are ones you see hanging around in old,out-of-the-way stores and bars. The antlers usually are attached to some monstrous buck taken in the Thirties by the owner's great grandmother firing from the back porch with a .30-30 Winchester.

Good taxidermists are true artists, able to recreate a perfectly life-like specimen from the battered messes they often receive. If you take proper care of your trophy in the field, he'll love you for it.

I like to spend time browsing in a taxidermy studio whenever I get the chance. The innovative guys have displays that may give me a new idea for my trophy room. One can analyze the various techniques and make up his own mind as to style and taste.

It has been my experience that each taxidermist seemingly has a specialty; one or two species of game with which he really excels. In many cases, of course, this will be one member or another of the deer family.

In today's market, good taxidermists are busy, so don't expect them to turn your deer around over the weekend. Average delivery from a quality taxidermist is around one year. Lead times have to be considered for the best time to send

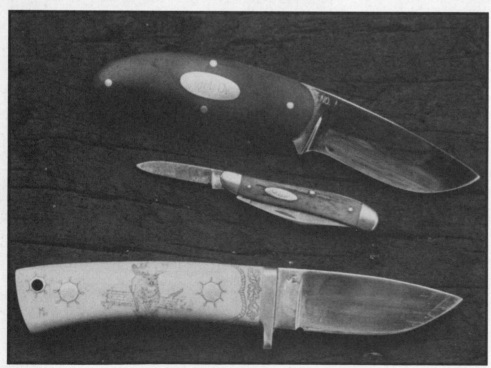

These are Dougherty's skinning and caping knives. It takes practice to properly dress a deer while preserving its cape.

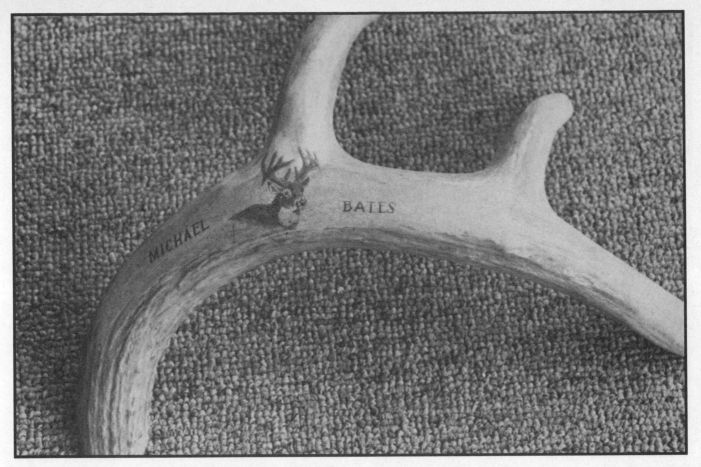

Antlers don't always have to be mounted to be displayed. This antler desk sign adds a nice touch to Bates taxidermist's shop.

Trophies also can be worn. A section of an antler provides a frame for a bear. Antler tips add a nice touch to this bolo.

their capes to specific tanneries for processing. Taxidermists who promise quick turn-around are not very busy. Often they produce poor-quality, home brew-tanned capes that will not hold up over time, and they do not produce high-class, artistic work. They are usually less expensive; solid support of the you-get-what-you-pay-for mentality.

I like good taxidermists who are busy and have adequate display rooms that let me judge style and price to my satisfaction. A deer head mount today is an investment as well as a trophy you want to cherish as a reminder of a special event. On the average today, a high-quality mount will range from $225 to $300. This is no small amount of money — enough to throw the wives of several of my acquaintances into orbit, in fact — and it should be spent only with a taxidermist in whom you have confidence.

Speaking of this, let me offer up a tidbit. For some unknown reason, in recent years, I have been made aware of more and more quality deer heads that have "disappeared" while waiting to be mounted in taxidermy shops across the land.

Further, there is an increasing number of mounted heads that are stolen. None of this makes any sense to me, but the fact is, there is a market out there among the nerds for good deer racks.

Get a signed, dated receipt for anything you leave with a taxidermist complete with a full description. And as a back-up, have a photo file of the antlers for yourself.

It is highly unlikely anything would ever go wrong, but Murphy didn't make that law just to practice *juris prudence!*

CHAPTER 25

START 'EM YOUNG, START 'EM RIGHT

The Future Of All Hunting Sports Rests On The Shoulders Of Your Children

WHO TOOK you hunting for the first time? For most of us it was probably our fathers or a close relative; perhaps a combination of both.

My dad's father didn't hunt, so someone else started him. I don't know who it was, but I'm grateful he did. He began by hunting pheasants in his native South Dakota, so bird hunting always was Dad's thing; mine too, right up there with bowhunting and fishing.

There are fewer parents who hunt or fish today than when I grew up, though I know a lot of people who say "they used to." There probably will be fewer in another decade. It seems, though that youngsters — especially boys — still are born with the interest. Maybe it's instinctive. Unfortunately, that instinct can ebb away simply from lack of exposure. Hunting isn't convenient in a big city environment, and interests are affected by life's survival patterns. With the rural atmosphere vanishing, it's a sad sort of condition that suggests a questionable future for wildlife, its habitat and certainly hunting.

My fondest memories as a child are of hunting and fishing

Backyard practice is a Dougherty family tradition. Son Jim, after a lot of teaching from his dad, has since taken seven species of North American big game with a bow.

Kelly Dougherty's first buck as a pre-teen was a big step in his education that has lead him to dozens of larger deer.

with my father and his friends. They were good teachers, and I was an interested student. They were bird guys whose shotguns rode in the crooks of their arms as comfortably as the socks on their feet. My earliest hunting impressions are of sultry September mornings with the tangy smell of dove weed, plowed ground and the pungent blue smoke of gunpowder from the old, paper-hulled shotshells that don't smell the same anymore.

I tagged along for many years before I had a shotgun of my own. By the time I did, I understood the rules. Deer hunting wasn't much on the minds of those men. My uncle was sort of a big-game hunter. He brought a deer by once, a fork horn. I felt a bit sorry for it — more sorry that it wasn't my dad who got it — and got charged with the notion that someday I was going to get one myself. Altogether, it wasn't too many years before I did.

Going hunting was easy then. There wasn't any red tape involved. When you were big enough, and wise enough, you got to go. When you reached a certain age, 14 in my case, you had to have a license — something you just went and bought.

The year I got my license I felt truly grown up. Today, it is not as simple. Nowadays young hunters have to pass an accredited Hunter Safety Course and be certified as competent before being licensed to take either a gun or bow into the field. Even adults born after a certain date face the same requirement.

I certainly don't have a problem with this, though it often can be troublesome to find a convenient course. I do have a problem with the inconsistencies that exist between states as to what is required and suggest that any of you who plan on an out-of-state expedition — especially with young hunters — research the legal requirements carefully. Recently some states, Montana for example, have dictated that bowhunters must have proof of passing a National Bowhunter Education Program course, too. A regular hunter safety card, by itself, isn't sufficient.

Besides the obvious training, I see several additional values to hunter education programs. First, it answers a need for non-hunting parents to see that their child is trained properly in conduct, safety and game management philosophy.

I see a lot of single parents today — women mostly with a young son or daughter — who are willing to support their

outdoor interests even though they might not echo their own. I take heart in these examples, though I suspect it's a more common occurrence here in Oklahoma or Nebraska than one perhaps would find in California or New York!

Further, there is a substantial value to these courses in terms of hunter image. There is something about taking a mandatory course for the licensing of anything that adds a degree of credibility to the matter. Society seems inclined to accept such regulated things. Of course, none of this is meant to obviate the strength of the instruction itself. It does produce responsible attitudes and understanding.

Some of the greatest pleasure I have had as an adult and father have been the outdoor adventures shared with my sons. As they grew and showed a strong interest in the outdoors, I could not wait to teach them the ways of it.

In the time period in which my own five boys were raised, they were not required to take any established course — they didn't exist then. What they learned initially, they learned from me, their grandfathers and some of my closest friends. Eventually they had to have the hunter safety cards to go other places. By then, passing was a piece of cake.

In the beginning, hunting has to be fun. It cannot be too much work. I have seen the interest of some children squelched completely by men who pushed their kids as hard as they did themselves. It doesn't work very well.

Whenever possible. I took my kids along to see how things were done. They learned by observation before they fully participated. The exposure was designed to be fun. You can have a great time showing a kid the difference between a deer and coyote track, where a trout will lie in a stream, how a fox

Dougherty permitted his children to hunt small game on their own. It instilled confidence in the young bowhunters.

Sometimes the outdoors was brought into the Dougherty home. As a youngster, Dougherty's oldest son spent a lot of time training a coyote pup. It was a great education.

Dougherty, an expert, has called varmints and javelina for his sons. It provided them with excellent field experience.

deadly capabilities of their hunting tools came first. Once that was grasped, the rest was easy — as long as it was fun. I never force-fed them; the interest had to be natural. I have seen some kids in deer camps that were rather miserable; either intimidated, or just plain uninterested.

One of my sons never was very interested. He shoots a bow well and enjoys it, though I doubt he would walk across the street to shoot a really large deer. Life for him has other objectives. He was always invited, the choice was his. I hold his decisions and different interests in the highest respect.

Small-game hunting — cottontails, for example — bowfishing and varmint calling are ideal training grounds for young bowhunters. It's something you can almost turn them loose on by themselves, and observe from a distance as they make their own way. It helps them develop a self-confidence that will serve them well in all elements of life.

Archery equipment geared for youngsters of all ages is readily available today, ranging from low-cost fiberglass recurves to some rather high dollar compounds; miniature replicas of adult models. Some of them shoot with awesome performance. Backyard archery training is good family fun, and it can become as involved cost-wise as you choose to make it. I have seen a child as young as 3 shooting with amazing competence, though admittedly that's a rare case. Usually it takes a few more years before they grasp the manual fundamentals as well as a capacity for the draw weight. Compound bows for little tykes are becoming better and more affordable. However, it usually requires a draw length of at least eighteen inches to make such a bow work. Twenty-inch draw lengths seem to be where the geometry of the mechanics and the little person come together best on inexpensive models. However,

squirrel builds a nest, which plants, such as poison ivy, are best avoided.

I took my kids fishing a lot, and they witnessed a lot of bird shooting, just as I did, and got in a lot of practice with both bows and guns before they got the green light.

Still, there were a few mistakes that required attention. An example: It was opening day of the dove season and son Jim had a 20-gauge autoloader. He was around 11 at the time and had shot quite well for several years. It was a hot field with lots of birds scorching the air lanes, echoing with constant popping stacatto of light field loads.

Jim ran over to my location and knelt down next to me as a trio of birds whipped by. I glanced at him, then at his gun. Second nature. I could see the red line on his cross-bolt safety. It was off.

"Is your safety off?" He looked down, it was off, his face drained a bit

"Unload your gun right now," I ordered. "Take it to the truck and case it. You are through for the day !"

The facial drain was complete. It was a stern move. Opening day is a hallowed event in my family, and this looked like a really good one. I felt badly about it, but I'd have felt worse had his gun gone off accidentally. Jim never forgot. He wasn't supposed to. Bows and arrows can be as dangerous as guns.

Each and every one of my kids and their peers among my friends went through a lot of patient explanations on how equipment was to be treated as well as used. Understanding the

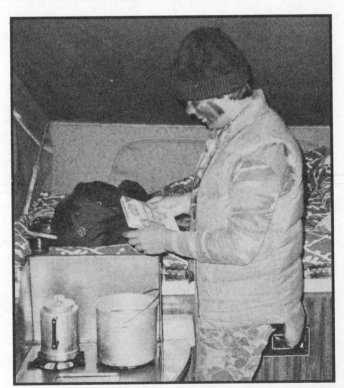
Early years spent in camp teach youngsters how to pitch in to help. The experience helps them become self-sufficient.

Dougherty (left) enjoys the time he spends bowhunting with his sons. Here, three of them, (left to right) Holt, Darrall and Kelly, share a successful deer hunting weekend with Dad. He knows they share his concern for the future of bowhunting.

if you're willing to to put up somewhere around $175 dollars, you can get an extra-short-draw compound.

The down side of buying a high-priced bow for short-draw children is the use expectancy — how long it will last a fast-growing kid who's draw could run off the bow's specs. Some can be converted to larger wheels. These things should be checked at a pro shop when you're considering the purchase. For kids in the 5- to 10-year range, depending on their physical size, I frequently recommend a short, fiberglass recurve bow as the best choice. As the child grows, they can increase the bow's efficiency simply by drawing a longer arrow. The cost is less — around $30 — and the enjoyment factor certainly is equal.

It takes some age and training for a youngster to work into the forty-pound legal requirement for deer hunting in most states, though some states have a better gauge — the bow's ability to cast a hunting arrow a specific distance as a mark of efficiency.

I do not really believe in a minimum arrow weight as the legal criteria to hunt. I know that a thirty-five-pound bow with the proper arrow and broadhead will shoot an arrow clear through a deer struck in the right spot. Hits in the wrong area are a problem with any equipment match-up.

While the compound had made meeting weight requirements a bit easier for young shooters and some women, the effort required to break it over requires some size and muscle, as well as training.

There is certainly a mixture of emotions when you put one of your children into a whitetail deer stand for the first time on his own. Of course, he thinks he understands it all. Yes, he will keep the safety belt on, do all the little things you have gone over a thousand times; things they have seen done before. You trust he will not get down and wander off, but you tell him again to stay put.

But kids have always been kids. I recall when son Holt was really quite young; his first year actually hunting. We put him in a low, safe stand just off the road near the camp. We figured he would be safe and happy there. Maybe he'd see a rabbit or a squirrel.

One signal we had established should anyone need help was to honk the truck horn. Jim headed north of camp, while I walked Kelly through the woods to his spot, then cut off a few hundred yards to reach my stand. I was just pulling my bow up into the tree stand when a long blast from the horn, followed by others more frantic, shattered the quiet fall afternoon.

Fearing, as parents will do, that disaster had struck, I scrambled from the tree to begin the three-quarter-mile dash through the creek bottom briars and brambles. The horn never let up. As I broke from cover, I could see both Jim and Kelly converging on me as we reached the truck. Holt was wild-eyed, tattered and dirty, his fist still pounding the horn. I figured he'd fallen from his stand somehow.

"What's wrong?" I gasped.

It came out in a stuttered squeak. "I just shot a deer!"

Bowfishing (above) is great training for young bowhunters. When a young hunter takes a buck it's a real milestone. Darrall Dougherty (right) took this deer when he was 12.

Sure enough, he had killed a young doe. It wasn't much larger than he was, but Holt had launched his arrow with his diminutive bow and done his old dad proud. I like to think young Holt had copied my style and technique.

The hardest thing to teach any kid, I think, is patience. They tend to display remarkable talent for the patience required to hunt or fish. It seems they are the eternal optimists in the matter of waiting for a fish to bite or a deer to wander along. It's a characteristic that does not necessarily cross over to other things.

Adults are like that, too. We are more patient doing what we want to be doing than we are doing what we should be doing. As I have said before, bowhunting is a matter of patient perseverance. Displaying it in the matter of training our new hunters is an important factor.

Our youth — your kids and the children of your friends, my grandchildren and the kid across the street — are the future of this country. Their involvement and future decisions will chart the course of America politically, economically and in all matters governing the land and its resources. Many of them will choose to hunt and fish. They must be taught and trained in the proper codes of doing it, and made aware that it will have to be their mission to preserve it.

If we get them set on the right course, I'm optimistic that they will succeed.

Bowhunting is too often taken for granted, but it could be only a part of history if left to some groups. Bowhunting organizations ensure youngsters will have a place to hunt.

CHAPTER 26

LET'S GET ORGANIZED!

Bowhunter Organizations Are More Than Social Clubs; They Can Have Political Clout

I JUST returned from a gathering of bowhunters in Missouri. The drive home took about six hours. It's early spring and the country is taking on a refreshing pastel glow, lime-tinted with splashes of red bud, which are really magenta, and stark white plum.

The low spots — creek bottoms and valleys — are turning emerald with new grass, but the hardwood ridges are still open, dull and covered with last fall's leaves.

As usual, I found myself watching for wildlife, and was rewarded several times by spotting three coyotes, a group of seven turkeys and several bands of the rapidly expanding giant Canada goose Missouri and Oklahoma have been propagating. There was an endless assortment of non-game birds, many of them just arrived from wintering grounds farther south.

I have another habit beyond this built-in thing I do on highways and that's to study — for the few seconds provided — the occupants of the vehicles I pass or that pass me. I suppose it's something we all do. Today, I gave the studying thing a little extra care, because I was thinking about people pretty hard. I was thinking about how much I enjoyed watching the country, looking into it as best I could in order to maybe see one more of its secrets, like those coyotes.

The folks in the other cars never saw the geese or noticed the turkeys. Maybe they noticed that spring was coming on hard. That probably meant more to the folks in the mini-van with the Minnesota license plate.

I wondered, while whizzing southward, just how many of these people really and truly give an honest hoot about such things. Probably they would rise to the defense of the geese they never saw, if we happened to be just visiting and I mentioned in passing that, in the fall, with the proper chance, I probably would shoot one or two of them for dinner.

I suspect that nine out of ten of these individuals would have a jerking fit over such a plan. They wouldn't understand that I have a deep-seated personal interest in the geese. I have paid money for their restoration and well being in the form of

Fred Bear made hundreds of public appearances to promote bowhunting. He was often joined by Dougherty (in white coat). Their efforts have helped preserve bowhunter's rights.

Bowhunters are proud of their trophies and they're concerned citizens. A lot of their money goes into conservation efforts.

various contributions, some occasional hard labor and in the purchase of my state and federal waterfowl stamps. Those contributions and efforts are not just so I can shoot one every once in a while — though, certainly that's part of it — but to make sure those geese are here forever! That gives me a strong feeling of entitlement, and until an opponent of my perspective has made his own contributions to conservation, I don't think he or she has a thing to say about it.

But back to the convention of bowhunters I mentioned. The occasion was the annual meeting of the Professional Bowhunters Society. For those who do not know of this organization, it is not a "professional" group such as a gathering of certified engineers or accountants. Instead, it is a collection of men and women who happen to be bowhunters and subscribe to a code of professional conduct — the ethical pursuit of hunting, along with the well being of our wildlife resources.

Admittedly, there are members of the society who can be classified as "professionals," for some derive all or a portion of their livelihoods from bowhunting in one form or another. Most do not, so the name of the organization might be a tad misleading. What is not misleading is the commitment of the members.

In the course of the weekend, this relatively small group raised almost $100,000 that was earmarked for conservation projects, as well as the support of their right — and yours — to hunt. I would bet no small amount of what few hard earned bucks I have managed to salt away over the years that the collective contribution for like causes of all the non-seeing occupants of all the cars just discussed wouldn't fill a shoe box. Yet — and this is the tough part — the lion's share of those I observed would vote us and our bows — or guns — out

of the woods in a heartbeat, given the opportunity such as a ballot decision in a general election. It would not necessarily be because they don't like us, but because they do not know or understand what or how much good we do. They simply do not know the truth. The truth is being carefully camouflaged and withheld from them.

The future of the wildlife resources we cherish — in particular the game birds and animals we pursue — is in trouble. This is not the kind of trouble brought on by shrinking habitat or pesticides which all sportsmen and conservationists have been concerned with for years, but by our fellow man — or woman — who are adamantly, hysterically and irrationally opposed to our consumptive use of those resources. They are the animal rights activists. They are zealots, terrorists and, I think, mostly, they are nuts. From those who simply oppose hunting, which I can almost understand, they evolve to the radicals whose position is that any life, from that of a fly to a zebra, is as meaningful as any human's — your wife or son, your mother, daughter, or the next-door neighbor. Their promise is that no white rat should be confined to a laboratory in a search for any cure, be it AIDS or heart disease. No deer should be harvested as a sound solution to over-population and starvation. No tuna should be swept from the sea, or beef slain to feed a hungry family. A statement I read recently said in essence: "I would rather that they (the deer) were not even here than to know one was killed by a hunter."

"So what. They are nothing but crazies. They will go away. No one can stop me from hunting. It's my birthright. I buy my license, so the game department will settle this." These all are common responses to obvious fruit cake mentality. Common responses. Wrong answers!

These forces are not by even the slightest wishful thread of

Bowhunting organizations draw large crowds to hear hunters share techniques. Conservation responsibilities also are stressed.

your imagination going to go away. While the PBS raised a hundred thousand bucks on a weekend, animal rights groups somewhere else raised five times that. Somehow, where our defenders have accumulated budgets that can only be measured in single digit millions, the animal-rights activists have accrued bank roles in the millions. I know it doesn't seem right, but we are getting our butts kicked and it is very, very unnerving.

Why? Because only two things seem to talk in today's society: Money is one. The only other factor involves votes. And money has a lot to do with vote gathering, too. Sportsmen in today's world are being outgunned. financially big-time, and completely out-maneuvered in the media. Our grade schools are being penetrated with ridiculously unsound, anthropomorphic material that gives our children a completely unbalanced look at real life, courtesy of People for the Ethical Treatment of Animals (PETA), to name only one source. While that propaganda is countered to some extent with correctly structured efforts such as those from Project WILD and others disseminating honest information, these organizations seem to be met with increasing bias among educators, a contradiction to their mandate to teach the truth.

The problem here is twofold: Some educators simply do not know the truth, while others prefer to support animal rights philosophy rather than proper science. To an increasing extent, we see the same mentality infiltrating our state and federal agencies, though I think animals rights motives are less an issue than irresponsible preservationists ideals, though I am becoming less sure of that.

As late as March, 1992, a Gallup Youth Survey reported that teenagers are highly supportive of efforts to protect animal species that are endangered. We all agree there is nothing wrong with wanting to protect endangered species.

However, Gallup adds that a majority of the nation's teenagers also say they support the "animal rights movement," even if it would mean the end of laboratory and medical tests that use animals.

Nearly nine teenagers in ten say they support protecting endangered animal species even if it would cost a lot of money. Those of us involved in conservation already know how much such protection costs, as we've backed many such protective efforts.

However, two out of three teenagers say they support the animal rights movement. According to Putting People First, a Washington, D.C. organization, "A plurality of forty-one percent support the movement very much, and are joined by twenty-six percent who say they are somewhat in favor of it. Among the responding teens, eighteen percent say they are somewhat opposed to animal rights, fourteen percent are very much opposed and three percent have no opinion about the movement.

"Young women (forty-six percent) are more likely than young men (thirty-five percent) to be very much in support of the animal rights movement. They also are slightly more likely to support the protection of endangered species by a margin of fifty-five to fifty-one percent."

In spite of what I have just detailed — only a tiny sampling of what's going down — the vast majority of America's outdoorsmen and women seem unconcerned. My estimate is that somewhere around eighty percent feel it's not really a problem!

Let's take it a bit further. Save for a few editorials on the outdoor pages, seldom will you find anything in any major newspaper that doesn't either subtly or blatantly malign hunt-

Experienced bowhunters from throughout the country share their expertise at the Anderson Archery Clinic each year.

ers. With a few exceptions, most nature programs cunningly infer that any problem for any creature on this planet is hunter-caused. In the language of today's press, poachers are "hunters." Only rarely is there a distinction separating one as being honestly fair, the other half a thief. We are all lumped in a common pot. Seal clubbers are "hunters," in the vernacular of today's media.

Some celebrity — usually seeking publicity — classifies a whitetail hunter in the same category with a seal clubber, an eagle killer with a duck hunter, and rarely acknowledges the good we do such as restoring the wild turkey. No matter what, these people condemn us for chasing a whitetail. Regardless of what act of fate might befall an eagle, hunters will be charged with its demise directly or by innuendo. I can recite such dishonest allegations forever.

I'm going to use Arizona as an example of how sharp the animal rights followers are, and, second, because by the time this book is out, there might still be an opportunity for you to react.

Arizona is an outdoor-oriented state. There was a time when I thought it was perhaps the perfect place for a guy like me to live. It is eighty-seven percent public land, rich in wildlife, diverse in life zones and cultures. However, as of right now, animal rights activists have gathered enough signatures to place an initiative (Proposition 200) designed ostensibly to ban trapping on public lands — that 87 percent — on the ballot in November, 1992. Such a trapping law, in and of itself, might easily pass in a general election given today's climate. But here's what it really says under Section I (B) "Declaration of Policy":

It is the intention and desire of the people of Arizona to make our public lands safe and humane for all creatures found on Arizona public lands.

We desire to manage our wildlife and protect our property by humane and non-lethal methods.

This initiative concisely disallows the use of everything from fishhooks to mouse traps, shotguns, bows and arrows, boomerangs and obviously traps, against any form of wildlife whatsoever. This, incidentally, is brought to you by the same folks that would eliminate the use of seeing eye dogs or white rat research.

Arizona is a pending battlefield. The lines are drawn and each opposing force is digging in. The anti's can dig in deeper; remember the difference I mentioned in the depth of our pockets versus theirs. What happens in Arizona will absolutely set the stage. The future well being of our wildlife resources is at stake. Who do these people think are going to take care of the wildlife? There will not be any fish and game agencies, biologists, foresters, fisheries experts, Pittman-Robertson funds or enforcement personnel, unless the bunny-huggers plan on ponying up the bucks to cover the slack created by the loss of sportsmen's dollar contributions. And not very likely, since these followers seem to live in a Disney-esque dream world.

The previous paragraphs have been less than you bargained for, if picking up this book just to read about deer hunting was the motive. But what you are reading now is deer hunting; the future of deer hunting. If you don't pay attention, there won't be any hunting for deer or anything else. All of us guys who have done a whole lot of it will spend the rest of our days telling our kids how it was. I'd much rather they learn first-hand.

All of this brings me back to people in cars who don't see the forest for the trees. Groups like the Professional Bowhunters Society and the efforts of the Pope & Young Club have raised many thousands of dollars, as well as many other fine organizations. The most damnable fact remains that roughly eighty percent of the folks who hunt and fish aren't helping a bit.

We all have to make a contribution to tomorrow, if there's to be a tomorrow. I believe every bowhunter should belong to his state organization. If that was put on a ballot tomorrow, as a requirement, I'd be the first to vote yes. Fortunately, though, forcing people isn't the American way — or is it? The antis are trying to force us to their collective will!

The involvement of joining an organization would certainly be a help to the problem of political clout. It gripes my soul when a state association leader stands at a podium in a public hearing to represent a membership of only 2000 bowhunters, when 50,000 bowhunters use the seasons he's trying to protect!

While joining up certainly would help, there is another way that can be even more beneficial: Contributions.

America's sportsmen and women have been blessed in recent years by the efforts of an organization dedicated solely to the preservation of our rights: The Wildlife Legislative Fund of America (WLFA). More importantly, WLFA has spearheaded the Bowhunters Defense Coalition which counts among its membership every national archery organization and many related private corporations, in addition to over fifty state associations. Simply put, WLFA and the BDC are the front-line forces designed and dedicated to saving our bacon. WLFA, the primary coordinator for the fight in Arizona, saved bear hunting in California, and the organization's track record of victories have been enviable. They know how to play the game, but they haven't won every time. The issue in Arizona has them deeply concerned. Joining the WLFA or the BDC is the one significant step we can take to preserve our rights and heritage. Contact them at WLFA, 801 Kingsmill Parkway, Columbus, OH 43229-1137.

Other strong bowhunting organizations that are working hard to protect your rights on a national level are:

BOWHUNTERS OF AMERICA
1030 W. Central,
Bismarck, ND 58501,
(701) 255-1631

POPE & YOUNG CLUB
P.O. Box 585,
Chatfield, MN 55923
(507) 867-4144

PROFESSIONAL BOWHUNTERS SOCIETY
P.O. Box 20066,
Charlotte, NC 28202
(704) 664-2534

If you don't do something now, you might as well be on the other side.

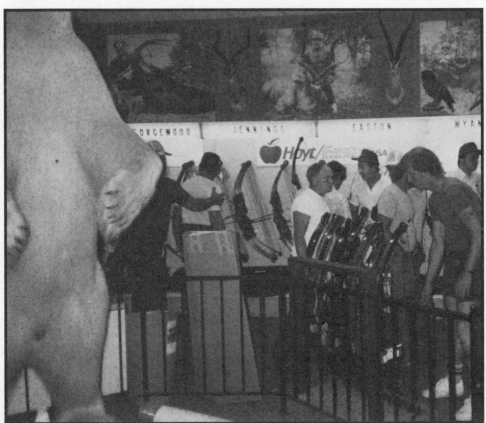

Organizational gatherings are a great place see new bow equipment and to learn from the country's top bowhunters.

DIANA WEARS CAMO

Roman Mythology's Goddess Of Hunting Often Was Pictured Following Dogs, Bow In Hand; Today's Lady Bowhunters No Doubt Take More Deer!

IF YOU'RE into Greek and Roman mythology, you probably recognize the fact that Diana was the Goddess of the Hunt; at least, she was for the Romans. If you were a Greek, a lady goddess called Artemis was supposed to cover things in the field and see to it that the hunter got his game.

I only see one problem with the myths as they have come down through a couple of thousand years of interpretation. Diana or Artemis, take your choice, often was pictured by artists of the day as chasing through the woods, bow in one hand and a leash in the other. Purpose of the leash was to control what appeared to be a couple of slavering Egyptian hounds!

Somehow, I get the feeling that the artists who came up

CHAPTER 27

with this interpretation didn't know much about bowhunting. Diana may have been a goddess and all that, but could she outrun a frightened buck that was working hard at leaving the country? The billowing gown she was pictured as wearing couldn't have done much for her speed and chances are the dogs alerted the deer and the latter were way out in front from the day someone created the myth!

There are modern-day Dianas in the woods, but these lady bowhunters are a lot more realistic than a goddess might be and what they may lack in mystical powers, they obviously make up in numbers. As nearly as anyone has been able to determine, there are more than 100,000 of them in the country today.

Instead of the straight bow favored by Diana of the myth, most of them settle for compounds and aluminum arrows. Rather than the flowing gowns in which artists nearly always pictured their goddesses, these bowhunters are dressed in camouflage hunting clothes. They come from all sorts of climes and backgrounds, but they comprise a sisterhood with a common goal: To bowhunt!

Ann Clark Is Modern Archery's Senior Lady Bowhunter, An Honor She Tends To Ignore.

An early Ann Clark thrilled crowds with her amazing skill. Today, she is still drawing attention to the sport of archery.

FOR NEARLY forty years, Ann Clark has been promoting archery both on the target range and in the game fields. Named to the Archery Hall of Fame in 1984, after more than three decades of touring the country to promote archery, making friends for the sport and presenting demonstrations and seminars, she still is going strong.

In fact, it was Ann Clark who came up with the the idea for the series of all-women bowhunts which have drawn some of the best distaff archers in the country.

Ann Clark got into archery in 1953, learning the basics from her husband, Jack. Three months later, she won her first Ohio State field archery tournament, shooting instinctive. Her list of shooting and tournament accomplishments reads like an all-star list of amateur and professional archery tournaments across the nation.

In the last two decades, Ann Clark has appeared on numerous national television shows and has represented a host of major companies, using their products to introduce them to the archery-oriented public. She still is making her livelihood with bow and arrow, although some of her tournament bows now are on display at the Smithsonian in Washington, D.C., along with a bow used by her daughter, Debbie, to capture many of the same titles her mother had won earlier.

"Archery has been good to me," she is quick to state. "It has given me more than I could ever return."

As stated, she won her first tournament in 1953 shortly after entering the sport, but in less than four years — in 1957, to be exact — she was a member of the United States' archery team and took part in the World Championships in Prague, Czechoslovakia. She not only shot, but she won! Over the years, she

One of Clark's demonstrations involved hitting a target tossed into the air. She rarely missed.

has devoted a great deal of time in introducing archery to the handicapped and has taught numerous senior citizens — many in their eighties and nineties — to handle a bow. Some of the shows have drawn more than 20,000 people.

And the effort has not halted with this feisty competitor. She has long been a leader in the Junior Olympic Archery Development program. All of her children were archers in their younger years and Ann Clark has been instrumental in teaching three generations in her own family. Of her nine grandchildren, she has coached six of them. She also has nine great-grandchildren and is teaching them the rudiments of the sport.

Daughter Debbie with whom Ann Clark teamed for many a demonstration was the youngest member of the World Archery Team which was chosen a decade ago in Helsinki, Finland. Ann Clark's granddaughter, Debbie Sue Mets, was the 1978 cadet archery champion.

Okay, so you're asking what all this target stuff has to do with bowhunting for deer. Admittedly, Ann Clark cast a lot of arrows at paper than she ever leveled broadhead-tipped shafts at big game animals, but let's go back to November, 1969.

Ann Clark had been invited to take part in an annual bowhunt for deer that was sponsored each year by the Narrowsburg Chamber of Commerce in Pennsylvania. Not only had she been asked to demonstrate her talents and trick shooting at the celebration, but to take part in the actual deer hunt.

It had rained all the previous day and Ann Clark arrived in the hotel lobby wearing red coveralls and carrying a bowcase. It was 7 a.m. when she met Joe Purcell, a local who was going to guide her. Twenty minutes later, she had her deer.

Purcell explained it this way:

"There was the doe and there was Ann. I have never seen anyone quite so cool, calm and deliberate. She held the doe in her bowsight so long that I was in near panic for fear I'd yell at her to shoot.

"But I didn't, probably because she let that arrow go. It was then I saw something I'd never seen before. The doe dropped as though it has been poleaxed. It never moved."

Oddly, Ann Clark had been in a serious auto accident several months earlier, suffering a broken finger and whiplash. She had removed the neck brace only four days before the Pennsylvania deer hunt.

As for taking the doe, she explained that, "It was as fine a shot as I've ever made. I took all the time I could because of the alders between me and the deer. I felt sure one of them would deflect my shot, so I waited. I aimed at the shoulder and my hit was four inches off. It was in the neck. The deer

Dougherty, as president of the American Archery Council, inducted Ann Clark in to the Archery Hall of Fame in 1985.

dropped that way because the arrow had severed the jugular."

Not all of her shots came off that well even back then, she admits. She loves to tell of the time in her Ohio home when it was raining and she had to shoot inside. She was working on a tough trick shot and was shooting from the living room into the dining room, with her husband arranging the target on the dining table in front of the backstop. She was tiring and knew it, but decided to try just one more shot.

"My next arrow hit the edge of an aerosol can filled with red paint," she recalls. "The can began whirling around, spewing cerise daubs all over the room through the hole the arrowhead had cut. The room had just been refurnished, too."

In the early Fifties, bowhunting still was a sport practiced by a few ardent sportsmen who had been influenced by the writings of Howard Hill and Saxton Pope. But it was in those days that Michigan began to promote bowhunting. Whitetail deer were overpopulating the East Michigan forest lands and the bowhunters soon were allied with the conservation and tourism folks. A lady bowhunter, however, was unusual to say the least

"I was one of the oddities to be found in those forests," Ann Clark admits today. "I was less than five feet tall and weighed less than a hundred pounds. I was a mother of three daughters who dared to break into this specialized sport with my bow and arrow.

"But I learned to understand the woods, the birds and the animals. I learned to know the animals' signs, their bedding areas, the food they ate and the water areas. I learned to stalk game quietly, using all my senses. Patience was learned through those many hours in the woods.

"Sitting quietly in my blind, I watched nature come alive:

the tiny field mouse scurrying about in its search for food; a black squirrel, never still, forever cautious but darting from one tree to another with its perpetual chatter; a small, unknown insect crawling on a leaf. These things I experienced and learned to love," the lady from Ohio recalls on a nostalgic note.

Bowhunting brought Ann Clark a world of knowledge as she pitted her skills against the elusive whitetail. "It is amazing to observe him as he visits his scrapes, pawing the ground and flicking his tail for no apparent reason, then turning and bolting away, white tail flying.

"But just as fast as he bolted, he returns, cautiously walking his well traveled route, stopping at times, head up, staring, his eyes focused on my own. I dare not move. A flutter of my eyelash and once again, the white flag is up and the quarry lost. I damn myself for being careless. I wasn't totally ready. But I don't quit."

Minutes later — maybe even an hour — the buck suddenly appears again. "My heart begins to beat so loud I'm sure the whole forest is alerted. My body is shaking, my mouth is dry. But here he comes, sauntering into range!

"Ever so slowly I raise my bow, draw the arrow, then release. There is a thud and the Game Tracker runs off as though I have a giant fish on the end of the line. I sit transfixed, as I watch the line peel off rapidly. Then it stops."

The lady bowhunter forces herself to remain quiet and wait for what seems an eternity. Actually, it's forty minutes. Her heart continues its rapid beat and her body begins to shake more than ever. Finally, she follows the white Game Tracker line. It takes her a distance of 150 yards.

That event happened many years ago, according to Ann

Clark, and has been repeated countless times since. After all the hours of training, practice and patience, a well placed sharpened broadhead had hit its mark. She had mastered putting it all together at the right time, and, "for a change, was the victor. The freezer would be stocked with venison and the family would again enjoy the fruits of my efforts."

Back in those early days of her efforts, being the only woman in a deer camp wasn't always easy. "I always had to prove myself," Ann Clark recalls. The tree steps leading up to the stand always were too far apart for my short legs and I always was expected to do the so-called 'woman's work.' I guess I was a pioneer then without really realizing it. Now women are welcome as bowhunters."

Ann Clark's first bow was a laminated Ben Pearson lemonwood model with a twenty-five-pound draw. She had bought it for her husband's birthday. After he outgrew this bow, he had one custom-built for himself, then cut two inches off the lemonwood bow and presented it to her.

"He believed that, because I was so short, I needed a shorter bow," Ann Clark recalls today. "You can see how much either of us knew about archery back then. We never did put this short bow on a scale to measure draw weight, but it was stout." In her demonstrations and trick shooting routine, she still uses bows with light draws, but for hunting, she favors a fifty-pound compound and 1816 aluminum shafts.

The Clarks had become so involved in the sport that they opened an archery shop. "We bought a good deal of equipment from Bear Archery, and when Fred Bear learned we had taken up deer hunting, he invited my husband and me to come up to Grayling, Michigan, and hunt with him," Ann Clark says. "I suspect Fred was somewhat skeptical as to what kind of hunter I might be, and I am certain my first day in his camp did little to instill confidence in what I could do."

What it comes down to is that she forgot to shoot, literally! Several deer came within range, "but I was so fascinated with the sounds of the forest and the wildlife that I just plain forgot our purpose was to shoot deer. I was so involved that I almost left my tackle there when dark came and I went back to camp."

Before the hunt was over, Ann Clark had bagged her first whitetail with a bow and respect for her abilities was restored among the other hunters.

Occasionally, when hunting a new area where she is not known except by reputation — and that usually has to do with her target work — Ann Clark runs across those who doubt the capabilities of a woman bowhunter, but this no longer bothers her.

"I don't think any bowhunter should feel he — or she — has to prove anything to anyone," she contends today. "Individuals choose to bowhunt for many different reasons. In my own case, a prime reason is to attempt to place myself in closer harmony with God's other creatures and with nature.

"For those who have similar goals, our concern should be to enjoy the hunt and the harvesting of animals we find particularly challenging or which we enjoy eating. The only persons we should worry about proving our abilities to are ourselves. Based upon that philosophy, I have come to have pride in my ability to scout game, to plan an ambush that will work, to select and climb a tree and to set up a tree stand properly.

"I take pride, too, in the fact that I have the self-control to wait long hours and endure severe weather, if necessary. I'm pleased that I have learned to overcome emotions in order to

Clark, a grandmother by then, took this doe in Ohio during the state's annual Archery Hunt-Meet. Later the same day, she gave an archery exhibition, wowing crowds, as always.

execute a good shot. Knowing I can field dress my own game, drag it into camp if necessary and cook it for the enjoyment of myself and others gives me the ultimate pleasure, I'd say."

There also are some items that irritate Ann Clark. One is having someone ask about her biggest buck. "By some people's standards, my biggest buck was rather small," she explains. "Such questions tend to upset me, since I feel that any animal that has been taken with a bow and arrow is a trophy in its own right.

"Every time I shoot a deer, I think that animal is fantastic," she adds. Several years ago, when she shot a four-point buck in a West Virginia state forest, a gent named Joe Roy was close at hand. He was the forest manager, as I understand it.

"Joe, I don't understand why every time I get a deer, I get the same excitement," Ann Clark commented.

"Ann, when you lose that feeling, you'd better just quit hunting," was Joe Roy's reply. Ann Clark understood what he was saying.

This mule deer fell to Clark's arrow. While she shoots a fifty-pound bow, she only takes shots inside of twenty-five yards.

"Each time I go hunting and see a deer, my heart starts pounding again," Ann Clark insists. "I know I'm going to lose the shot because of my arrow clicking against my bow. Then, when I do draw and take careful aim, everything seems to get dead quiet. When I hear that thud of a broadhead hitting the deer, my heart starts pounding all over again."

In bowhunting of any kind — deer of all species included — Ann Clark feels the first requisite is to learn everything one can about the game. After that comes proper selection of equipment; learning its limitations, then the proper operation within these limitations.

"People talk a lot about using the heaviest equipment they can handle and I agree with this approach," Ann Clark says, "but there may be some confusion as to just what is meant.

"I hunt with a fifty-pound bow which is the heaviest I can shoot comfortably. However, because of the possibility of arrow deflection or movement by an animal, I try to restrict myself to twenty-yard shots in the woods. A good many of the deer I have harvested have been taken within twenty yards. One year, I got a nice four-pointer at only twelve yards."

In recent years, Ann Clark has been involved in the annual all-women's deer hunt. In 1991, it was sponsored by Horton Manufacturing, a firm that makes crossbows. Site of the hunt was the Horton Ranch in southeastern Ohio's Monroe County. Eight women from across the country were invited, with Ann Clark being designated as hunt master.

"Crossbows are somewhat controversial," she said at the time, "but so are women bowhunters, so we decided to put the two together.

"It used to be that women who came along on a deer hunt could expect to do the cooking and cleaning. But for this hunt, we had the guys around to do all the chores for the lady bowhunters. We were nice to them, of course, but they were our lackeys for that week, stringing our crossbows and even doing the cooking. The ladies where there to do the hunting.

"These all-woman bowhunts have taken us around the country," the Ohio native says. "The first year, we hunted whitetail in Michigan. The following fall, we headed for Colorado to try our hand at elk and mule deer.

"In 1990, we were in Texas for a hunt that I felt was much like going to Africa. You could hunt so may different kinds of game there." (Texas is noted for the exotic species that are raised on many of the ranches in the southern part of the Lone Star State.)

For the 1991 hunt, there was one major change. "A woman used to have to make do with her husband's hand-me-downs or shop in the boys' department for hunting clothes," Ann Clark explains. "But for this hunt, we all were wearing camouflage jumpsuits styled for women and made by an Oregon company. We looked good!"

But looking like a lady bowhunter apparently doesn't cut it in some social circles. "Some of my acquaintances are anti-hunter," Ann Clark states, adding, "This is basically because they don't understand what the modern world is all about.

They have visions of Bambi and that is all they want to see.

"We know we don't shoot sad-eyed little fawns, and I have attempted to educate a lot of these folks and explain to them the reasons why I feel the need to get out into the woods. I also attempt to explain that areas can become overpopulated with deer, which either means slow starvation or introduction of disease that can wipe out whole herds of undernourished animals.

"It's too bad we can't take these anti-hunters out and show them areas where proper conservation methods are not used, to see what happens to game animals in such a situation, then take them to an area where the money from our hunting licenses is used properly. If we could do this, a lot of these individuals probably would become hunters and would help in any way that they could to see that game animals are not subjected to starvation."

Ann Clark is quick to admit that such a happening is beyond the realm of reality. After all, some of her own friends tolerate her, she says, "only because they like me personally. They don't understand — and probably never will — that there is a great deal more to bowhunting than simply harvesting an animal.

"I am not a trophy hunter. I simply enjoy the hunt and the chance to be out there with nature even if I don't get my game. The truth is that I enjoy coming home and telling my children — and their children — how a deer or some other game animal has outfoxed me...and I've been outfoxed so many times most people wouldn't believe it!"

Ann Clark shakes her head when recalling some of her confrontations. "I learned long ago that one cannot argue with some anti-hunters. They deal in emotion and reason just isn't for them. They are ignorant of what is happening, they are

Clark shot this six-point whitetail during a snowy hunt near Marlington, West Virginia. She enjoys the hunt and shares her field experiences with her children and grandchildren.

ignorant of nature and her ways and they don't want to learn.

"Instead, they want things to be the way they think they should be, not the way they are. They fail to understand that we cannot argue with nature. As hunters, we face reality and recognize that without the fees from hunting, there would be little in the way of conservation. If we practice conservation, we are going to have deer and other animals."

And that's the way the lady from Ohio feels about it!

Judy Kovar Brings The Heritage Of Her Cheyenne Ancestors To Her Bowhunting

"I DON'T have any mystical secrets when it comes to bowhunting for Pope & Young record whitetails," Judy Kovar is quick to admit. "What it comes down to is that I try to think like a deer or as I imagine a deer would think. That means I have to be extra-careful with my own scent and constantly attempt to use wind direction to my advantage.

"I'm careful not to press or crowd a big buck too close. Instead, I try to let him come to me. And if whatever plan I've devised isn't working, I try to change it on the spot."

One cannot help but wonder how much of this hunting philosophy has been learned in the six years — as of this writing — that the Illinois woman has been bowhunting. Or is a lot of this knowledge of hunting and animal behavior drawn from her native American heritage? Judy Kovar is the daughter of a full-blooded Northern Plains Cheyenne Indian and the granddaughter of a Cheyenne medicine man. Her father was French Canadian.

Virtually from the time she was able to walk, Judy Kovar was raised in the Indian tradition. She followed the older Indian women in the woods and was taught the ways of the wilderness and the wild things that inhabit it. She learned to stalk animals in the forests, she learned to track and she learned

to read sign of all the animals that surrounded her. She absorbed all of these lessons well and grew up hunting and trapping. As a result, during her teen years, she consistently helped to put wild game on the family table and to prepare valuable furs for market.

With this sort of background, it may seem odd that the young lady had little or nothing to do with bows and arrows until 1985. That was when she met the man who was to become her husband, Herman Kovar. The meeting took place at a check station for wild turkey hunters. The place was Pere Marquette State Park, where Judy was employed by the State of Illinois to check hunters and to record information about their tagged birds.

Herman Kovar admits he was fascinated by the Indian girl with her flowing black hair and the camouflage clothing that she seemed to wear like a uniform. He had long been a collector of Indian artifacts, which gave them something to talk about. It wasn't long before he had learned Judy's mother had developed her Indian skills through her own father, Gray Wolf, a Cheyenne medicine man who lived in the sacred Black Hills of South Dakota.

The medicine man's daughter, in turn, passed on the Indian

Judy Kovar displays one of her Pope & Young record whitetails. During a hunt, she tries to imagine what a deer is thinking.

ways to her own daughter, Judy, who still gathers such herbs and roots as American ginseng, snakeroot, bloodroot, goldenseal and others from the fields near their home in Fieldon, Illinois. From this collection, Judy Kovar makes the medicine bags that have been used by the Plains tribes for countless generations to guard against illness.

All of the young Cheyenne's hunting had been with rifles, so her reaction wasn't exactly one of total enthrallment when Herman Kovar handed her a compound bow, a Darton model, plus a quiver holding a dozen arrows.

"I can't shoot one of those things!" she insisted.

"Sure you can," Herman Kovar assured her. The result was her first twenty-minute lecture and instruction period on bowhunting with the compound. Within half an hour, the lady was hitting a paper plate at fifteen yards — and from then on, she was hooked!

"I didn't realize I had created a monster," Herman Kovar jokes. "Every time I would stop by to visit, Judy would be out there in her backyard, flinging arrows at a target. Because of the way she had been raised, learning about wildlife and the woods, she was way out in front of most beginning bowhunters. She had the knowledge. All I did was supply the tools."

A bit later, Herman Kovar bought her a Martin DynaBo and fletched a couple of dozen Easton Gamegetter aluminum shafts. He chose hot pink feathers for the four-fletch job. A few weeks later, Judy took her first bowhunting trophy, a twenty-seven-pound turkey gobbler that sported an 11 1/2-inch beard. Since Illinois has a two-deer limit, she scored on a fat doe and a buck with a small rack that first fall of hunting.

Within four years, Judy Kovar had four whitetail bucks included in the Pope & Young record book. Her husband has two.

Herman Kovar is the traditional tree stand bowhunter, so it followed that he would introduce the lady to this type of ambushing. Judy took to the trees in the beginning, but today, she sticks with her Indian traditions and does her shooting from blinds that are firmly anchored to the ground.

The decision was made in 1987. The lady bowhunter had climbed into the tree where her tree stand was situated and the first thing she did was to strap on her safety belt. Then she stepped around the trunk of the tree and onto the stand. For some still undetermined reason, the stand shifted beneath her feet and Judy Kovar felt herself being launched into space.

Her flight came to an abrupt and painful end as she hit the end of the safety belt's anchor rope. She dangled head down for what she estimates to be twenty minutes before she was able to grab hold of the tree trunk and right herself. She knew she was hurt, as she unbuckled the safety belt and climbed down. It turned out she had three broken ribs. Since that day, she has been ground-bound — and prefers it that way!

In spite of the broken ribs, the Illinois bowhunter didn't let them interfere with her pursuits afield. Less than a week later — the ribs wrapped with tape but still painful — she had erected a blind among some old bales of hay that edged a picked field of corn. Feeding whitetails were a common sight in this field, so she was waiting silently as the sun faded into the grayness of coming night.

She was watching as a buck jumped the fence that separated the cornfield from a growth of timber, then walked past the pile of bales. Judy Kovar wasn't even certain she could draw the bow, but she gritted her teeth against the pain, drew the sixty-pound bow and let fly one of her pink-fletched Gamegetter arrows. The arrow caught the deer high in the spine, and a second shaft put him down for keeps.

"At first, I didn't know what to think. I guess I was a little surprised at how well everything had gone," Judy Kovar recalls. " I just stood there in the growing darkness looking down at my first trophy buck." Later, after the sixty-day official drying period, the big whitetail was found to measure 140 6/8 points for the Pope and Young scorings.

Things were pretty much status quo for the next year as far as Judy Kovar's bowhunting pursuits were concerned. Then, in December, 1988, she was hunting the edge of another picked cornfield when she spotted another high-racked whitetail buck moving cautiously through an adjoining brush-filled ravine.

Heart pumping with excitement, Judy Kovar ran the length of the ravine, bow and arrow quiver in hand. Pausing for breath, she found herself virtually staring the buck in the eye. Before she could do anything about the meeting, though, the big whitetail had turned and trotted into the trees.

"I took note of the direction the buck was traveling in, and I ran in a circle to try to get ahead of him again," the bowhuntress recalls. "I came to an old logging road and began to slip along it, looking and listening all the way. I knew that buck had to be close by."

And he was. The buck suddenly came out of the trees just ahead of her, pausing at the edge of the logging road to turn his head and check his backtrail. While the buck was thus occupied, Judy Kovar put one of her pink-fletched arrows into his heart/lung area at only fifteen yards.

"Try that from a tree stand!" she suggests with a mischievous grin. This particular buck had some thirteen inches of non-typical points, but still measured an even 148 at the end of the required drying period.

Hunting from the ground as she does has not been all that easy for the young lady in one regard. If she is going to sneak and snoop through the brush a la Indian, she has to wear camouflage clothing.

"And finding camouflage clothing that will fit a small woman is not an easy task. They don't make the stuff that way.

"I buy insulated camouflaged coveralls in a men's small size, but even when I'm wearing that size, the crotch hangs down around my knees. Try running through the brush rigged out like that, and you learn what a real challenge is!"

In December, 1989, almost a year to the day from the time she had taken the Pope & Young buck on the logging road, Judy Kovar took up a position in another blind fashioned from straw bales at the edge of a cornfield that had been picked and now was nothing but broken stalks. On the frozen ground, though, was a good deal of corn that had been missed by the mechanical picker. That free banquet always seemed to draw deer.

Judy had taken a respectable eight-pointer earlier in the season, but now she was looking for more record book entries. In this vicinity, she had seen a big non-typical buck several times. In fact, she had had one chance to take him earlier in the season, but had blown it. Now she was hoping for a second opportunity.

But to paraphrase the old saying, the best laid plans of mice and men sometimes get superseded. It was not her non-typical buck that moved out of the sundown shadows to feed. Instead, it was a big ten-point that she was certain would make the record books.

Kovar has studied nature and uses it to succeed in bowhunting. She watches birds which often help lead her to a downed deer.

The buck certainly had not grown that large by being stupid, and even as he fed, he was on his guard. He saw Judy Kovar just as she brought her DynaBo to full draw and he turned to run. The self-preservation move was a bit late, for Judy's arrow took the buck in the spine. The heavy Snuffer broadhead doing its job caused the big buck to drop in his tracks.

Between bowhunting seasons, Judy Kovar organizes programs that allow her to share her knowledge of Indian ways with the children in her area. She frequently brings these programs to Cahokia Mounds and Blackhawk State Park in Illinois and Angel Mounds in Indiana, demonstrating Indian ways and telling stories of her ancestors.

"Such story-telling is the way that the Indians maintained their family trees," the Cheyenne lady explains. "If your grandfather did a certain thing, this becomes a story and is passed down from generation to generation."

Integrated into her stories is an ability to mimic many of the animals with which she has come in contact both in her early years of trapping and more recently, bowhunting. She can reproduce the warning rattle of a rattlesnake or the call of a wild turkey. When hunting for turkey, she uses none of the commercially produced calls, but depends upon her own knowledge and ability to call in a big gobbler with her own vocal cords.

"The kids eat this stuff up," she declares. "When they walk in and see me in my elkhide dress, then have a chance to see and feel the bone tools and needles that my mother and my grandmother used, their eyes really light up!"

In keeping with her native American heritage, no part of the deer she takes goes to waste. She scrapes and tans the hides just as she was taught by her mother, employing the same bone scrapers that her mother and her grandmother used.

"Everything seemed to find a use," Mrs. Kovar insists. "They ate the meat, used the sinew as thread and used bits of sandstone to form the bone into needles and other tools."

As might be suspected, deer are much in evidence in the Kovars' home. Mounted deer heads line the walls and a lamp features a base fashioned from deer hooves. Indian arrowheads and other artifacts gathered by Judy and her husband are contained in a cabinet in a corner. Many of the arrowheads were picked up in their yard. According to local legend, the Kovar yard was the site of one of the larger Indian encampments in the area a century more ago.

Judy Kovar's fourth record-book buck fell to her expertise — and another of her pink-fletched shafts — in November, 1990. This was during a bowhunt in Pere Marquette State Park where she first met her husband.

The season in the park was only five days in length. For three of those days, Judy Kovar had been hanging in near a giant scrape she had located along a well traveled game trail that was situated atop a steep ridge. Each of those days had been spent in rattling antlers in an attempt to lure in the buck that had created that giant scrape.

On each of those three days, the lady bowhunter had been able to lure the buck close enough to determine that he was Pope & Young quality, but in none of these instances had she been able to draw him in close enough for a bow shot. Instead, the buck would hang back in the undergrowth, tearing up the brush and reacting the way one might expect of a buck that feels his domain has been invaded by a lesser light. But that was as close as he came.

Time was growing short — only two days left — so in that fourth dawning of the special season, Judy Kovar arrived at the scene early, packing her rattling antlers, her grunt call and, this time, the metatarsal glands from a buck she had killed earlier in the season. There are those bowhunters who feel that this particular gland doesn't really do much to lure in a big buck, but in the Cheyenne hunting lore, it does — and Judy Kovar was ready to pull out all the stops for a single shot at the buck.

"When I found that the buck already was there on the ridge top, working his scrape, I began to wonder if the gods of hunting were against me," the lady recalls. In spite of such wonderings, she waited until the buck had given a final pawing to the scrape, then moved off into the timber. Once he was out of sight, she moved in, hanging the tarsal gland in a tree, then set up close to the scrape.

"I gave a few grunts on the tube and that brought the big buck charging back, ready to take on any invader. His attention was on the scrape and nothing else at that point, and I put an arrow into him from less than ten yards away."

The arrow shaft went in between the buck's ribs, but the buck didn't simply run. According to Judy Kovar, he acted as though he thought the arrow was the antlers of another buck, thus causing pain. He whirled to face her.

"I really thought he was going to come after me," the Illinois huntress recalls, " and there was nothing between us but one skinny little tree."

Realizing that his opponent was not another buck, the deer turned and ran. That was the beginning of two weeks of frustration and, at moments, despair for Judy Kovar.

"My arrow had hit him a little farther back than I wanted," she recalls, "but I was certain I had scored a liver shot. I found a blood trail and was able to follow it, until the buck went out of the park and onto private land. When he jumped the fence that separated the two, he broke off the arrow — and that ended the blood trail."

The next step was to contact the landowner and obtain permission to search his property for the wounded buck. This required a bit of doing, but even after permission was granted, she was unable to find the animal. "I tried to figure where a wounded buck would go, but it didn't work," Judy Kovar acknowledges. "He just wasn't there."

With the help of Park Ranger Richard Niemeyer and her husband, Judy Kovar spent each day combing the park, searching, then covering the same ground again. She was certain the hit had been fatal.

On a hunch, she returned to the area where she had scored the hit with her arrow. Searching carefully, she found the big buck less than seventy-five yards from where it had been struck by her arrow. Apparently, he had traveled a wide circle to return to his home habitat. The buck had twelve points and went into the Pope & Young record book with 148 2/8 points.

The fact that Judy Kovar has taken all four of her Pope & Young bucks in Jersey County, Illinois, where she lives leads many people to figure that this area just across the Mississippi and a bit north of St. Louis, Missouri, has nothing but big, big bucks.

This is true to a point. The area is well known for big bucks — but there are a lot of lesser bucks there, too. Three of the record-book bucks, in fact, have been taken on the Kovar farm near Fieldon. Unlike many bowhunters who have to journey to game country, then travel areas with which they are not familiar, Judy Kovar has had years of getting to know the ground and the game in the area where she hunts. She is the first to admit that this familiarity is a help to knowing where to look for a big buck when the annual season opens.

"I bowhunt deer alone and on their territory. I hunt from the ground the way my grandfather, the Cheyenne medicine man, and my other Indian ancestors hunted."

Herman Kovar takes a stronger view of his wife's accomplishments. "All of the hunting techniques — the basic knowledge — have been there all along because of her breeding and the Indian environment in which Judy was raised. This has to be the reason why she has been able to accomplish so much in so short a time. After all, she got her start in life by trapping, hunting and digging roots with her people. A lot of what she learned is being used subconsciously now in locating big bucks. It has to be!"

"Luck is part of bowhunting," Judy Kovar philosophizes on a note that marks her as a true realist. "I may never take another buck that is good enough for the record books and I realize I may go through more than one season without being able to tag a big buck, but all of that's not too important. I hunt for me, Judy Kovar, and I enjoy what I do. After all, that's what it's all about."

Out of all this, however, Judy Kovar has made some observations that may prove to be of value to other bowhunters.

She is convinced, for example, that big bucks learn quickly and are able to pattern a bowhunter when they are pursued. She advises working the wind and using a lot of Scent Shield to keep from being scented. And perhaps the greatest problem for less experienced bowhunters is patience. "We all like to shoot at game," she admits, "but you don't make the record books by shooting at the first deer you see after the season opens."

She also feels that getting to know and understand your bowhunting tackle is an important element of hunting success. Confidence in your bow and, resultantly, your shooting abilities are primary factors. "Your bow," she insists, "should feel like an extension of your arm." Perhaps not so oddly, this is the same advice that is offered by top-ranked pistol shooters who say the handgun should seem to be an extension of the arm.

Judy Kovar knows and understands the Martin Cheetah DynaBo with which she took her first deer. She keeps it set at a sixty-pound draw, regardless of the type of game she is hunting. Her missile system is composed of 2018 Easton XX75 Gamegetter shafts and the Snuffer broadheads that she sharpens herself before ever using them. She has tried both plastic vanes and feathers and has come to favor the latter in a four-fletch configuration — always in hot pink — because they are, as she puts it, "more forgiving."

The first arrows she used for hunting were those with the hot pink fletching Herman Kovar gave her. She has continued to use the same color for fletching to the point that she considers it her trademark. However, there is more involved than simple ego.

"The pink feathers show up well in low-light situations and especially in heavy leaf cover. The combination has worked well for me from the start and I have confidence in what it can do. Why experiment?" Less subtly phrased, perhaps: "If it ain't broke, don't fix it!"

Her advice on how to locate a trophy buck is based upon her own personal experiences and techniques. Judy Kovar spends countless hours each year in scouting long before the season opens.

She feels that a serious hunter first needs to determine the general range in which a trophy deer lives. After that, it is necessary to determine the exact area he is likely to claim when the annual rut gets under way.

"This is difficult, I know, because the bowhunting world is full of people who work five or more days a week for a living. They just don't have the time to drive countless miles and spend endless hours in checking things out, simply observing game and the terrain. Even for those who have the time and are close enough to the hunting area, it takes a lot of time, but it's the only way I know of to increase the odds for taking a Pope & Young whitetail," she says.

The Illinois native begins her scouting early in January, not long after the regular season has ended. When snow is heavy, covering some foods, she seeks out the food sources that are available. Visual observation usually helps Judy Kovar to spot a big buck that has managed to get through the previous year's rifle and archery hunting seasons.

The Illinois archery season is three months long. In the month just prior to the season's opening, she spends long hours in early morning and late evening glassing corn and grain fields for signs of bucks that might have record-size racks.

Her first week of the season is spent in one of the ground blinds she has prepared earlier. She likes the idea of hay or straw bales stacked in a pattern that gives her cover, yet the room to maneuver her bow and openings through which observation of the likely terrain and possible routes of approach can be maintained.

"These bales should be arranged well in advance of the season opening so that the deer have a chance to get used to them being there," the lady cautions. "Putting up that kind of blind the day before the season opens will defeat the purpose."

Her observations have shown Judy Kovar that the whitetail rut in her part of the country usually is announced by the appearance of small rubs and scrapes made by smaller, younger bucks. A few days after these appear, the larger, older bucks — those likely to carry the big antlers she is seeking — will come out of hiding to begin making rubs on larger trees and pawing scrapes that are large and in proportion to their sizes.

This usually happens late in October and this is the time when Judy Kovar sets about attempting to determine the pattern the big buck will use, the route he is likely to follow in traveling to and from a major food source. She also does her best to establish the most vulnerable spot at which an old, wise, big-racked whitetail buck can be caught unawares.

Harking back to her heredity, hunting from a ground blind, one-on-one with the whitetail she wants is the real thrill for this huntress. Of course, some of her preference harks back to the unpleasant experience with the tree stand.

"My forefathers, the Northern Cheyenne, hunted from the ground for centuries. They often used nothing more than a clump of tall grass from which to launch an ambush. I think

Kovar uses all the hunting techniques to attract record-size deer to her bow. Here, she uses antlers to rattle in bucks.

all this breaks down to developing confidence in whatever style of bowhunting one comes to prefer," she says.

"I've found that ground blinds have several advantages when compared to tree stands," Judy Kovar adds. "First, the bowhunter has an unlimited number of places where a ground blind can be constructed. Also, I find that the angle of the arrow's trajectory is better for making a clean kill. Finally, if you stick to a ground blind, you don't have to know how to fly if you should doze off in the early morning sun. That's hardly the case with a tree stand."

Judy Kovar believes in keeping her ground blinds simple. Those she uses the most are the stacked hay bales or simply a small stand of unpicked field corn. In more than one instance, deer have walked right up to the blind to offer Judy a can't-miss shot.

While the blinds themselves are simple, placement gets a bit more involved. Let's take the unpicked corn, for example. Through some sort of pre-harvest agreement, an arrangement must be made with the farmer on whose land you are hunting to leave such a small area unpicked.

"I've found, though, that most of our Illinois grain farmers are willing to leave a bushel or two of corn standing in the field, if it will help to get rid of a crop-eating deer which can destroy several hundred dollars worth of grain of various types in the course of a year."

Arrangements also must be made with the landowner for bringing the bales of hay or straw onto the property and arranging them along fence rows, in soybean stubble or in picked cornfields.

When hunting season is over, the bales usually are badly

weathered and worth virtually nothing. Most farmers don't require that they be removed, if the bowhunter will tear them apart and scatter the straw so it can be plowed under the following spring.

However, heavy-duty plastic cord is used these days to tie most bales. This material can be injurious if eaten by livestock, so the plastic binding should be carried away by the bowhunter at the time the bales are torn down.

"Once the ground blind is in place, it will take a few days for the deer to accept it as just part of the terrain. After that, it becomes just a matter of choosing the right time of day and proper wind conditions to sit in the blind and wait," Judy Kovar has found.

"Bowhunters need to be alert to wind direction during each visit to the blind," the hunter warns. "Human scent and other unfamiliar odors cancel more opportunities to take trophy deer than any other element of a hunt."

She has found that if a buck she seeks to ambush pinpoints a blind as the hangout for a hunter just one time, she can forget that particular deer. Chances are the buck will leave and not return for the rest of that season, at least.

Once the rut is well under way, Judy Kovar usually comes out of her prepared blind and uses anything that will break up her outline — thick stands of saplings, brush, rocks — to ambush the buck she is after. During the rut, bucks, big and small, seem more interested in the lure of sex than in self-preservation.

Even in this situation, she is careful to wear the correct coloration in camouflage so that she will blend with the terrain. The other necessity is not to move a muscle so long as a buck can see you even with its peripheral vision. Only when she is sure the buck cannot see her will she draw her bow and send that pink-feathered shaft after venison.

And because it is not possible to know from what direction a buck is likely to approach, Judy Kovar uses a liquid odor remover, Scent Blaster, which is marketed by Buck Stop.

It's no great secret that rutting bucks are particularly vulnerable to horn rattling, but it doesn't always bring them close enough for a shot with an arrow. Judy Kovar feels her most trying experience to date was with the big twelve-point — her top-scoring Pope & Young trophy — that she was able to rattle in three days running, but not within bow range. This particular deer would approach to a certain point, then suddenly turn coy and try not to show himself.

The Cheyenne huntress drew upon her knowledge of the species and found the heavy scrapes that the wary old buck had made to mark off his territory. She made a series of false scrapes — equally as large and impressive as the real ones — then hung the metatarsal glands from a previous kill in the nearby trees.

The next morning, she crept into position well before dawn, but the record-quality whitetail buck was ahead of her and was angrily pawing at the mock scrapes she had left behind. Still quiet, she moved into position near one of the false scrapes and rattled her antlers. That brought the twelve-pointer charging in her direction, ready for a sparring match with an interloper. What he got was an arrow behind his shoulder at eight yards.

Today, a wall of the farmhouse where Judy and Herman Kovar live is filled with the six Pope & Young record trophies the two of them have garnered, as well as several lesser examples of whitetail beauty.

Judy Kovar never has lost any animal she has shot with a bow. That fact once again harks back to her Indian upbringing and the respect for nature that she was taught from infancy. She believes that every hunter should take only the shot that is a sure thing. If there is doubt, it should be passed up.

There will be another day and there will be another big buck. Those are the things Judy Kovar knows and believes.

Kovar is justly proud of her four Pope & Young record whitetails. Her husband, Herman, also holds Pope & Young records.

For Career Woman Charlie White, Shedding Her Business Suit In Favor Of Camo Means A Whole Different Way Of Living!

Charlie White is comfortable as a career woman with a corporation and as a successful bowhunter. Her home reflects her great love for the outdoors.

In 1989, White took part in Second Annual All Lady Bowhunt in Colorado. That was the year she was elected to the PSE Hall of Fame.

MEET CHARLIE White on the street or in her office and you'd probably say to yourself, "Now there goes a real career woman." And that is an accurate description of the Mississippi lady's daily business pursuits.

But here is another Charlie White, the one who isn't afraid to get her face dirty in trying to snooker a trophy buck. She isn't fearful, either, of getting her hands bloody when it comes to caring for the venison and the downed animal's cape.

A graduate of Mississippi State University with a degree in business administration, Charlie White is currently the human resources manager for the Atlas Roofing Corporation, a company with 520 employes. In her managerial post, she is responsible for overseeing two assistants and handling employee relations, recruitment, safety in all of the company's six plants spread across the South, as well as worker's compensation and employee benefits. If that isn't enough, government regulations requirements, department budget, training and development, a profit sharing program, public relations and labor relations also are among her responsibilities.

She has held this position since April, 1989. Prior to that, she spent some sixteen years as director of personnel for two different newspapers, one in Biloxi, Mississippi, and later the *Herald-Tribune* in Sarasota, Florida.

Does that sound like a true career woman? Well, let's take a long, hard look at the other side of the coin. Charlie White has been a bowhunter for more than fifteen years and has been named Bowhunter of the Year in so many situations that she has literally lost track.

The last time anyone counted, she had taken thirty-eight whitetail deer, four bears, two mountain lions — one qualified for Pope & Young honors — five caribou, with two of them P&Y record-book entries, and four pronghorn antelope. Other trophies include four javelina, five mule deer, a Sitka blacktail deer and two elk. One of the elk made the Pope & Young records by scoring 272 6/8 points.

That covers her North American hunting. She also has African trophies that include a pair of warthogs, two impalas and a gemsbok. She was selected as female Bowhunter of the Year by *North American Hunting* magazine and Precision Shooting Equipment each year from 1983 through 1988. In 1989, she was elected to the PSE Hall of Fame.

But it wasn't always this way. Before she began hunting seriously, Charlie White racked up some impressive wins on the tournament trail. Between 1982 and 1984, she won the following championships in Mississippi: overall women's state Necedah champion, 1982; overall women's state field champion, 1983; first place, Mississippi State indoor championships, 1983, and she was the overall state indoor champion in 1984.

Chances are your original vision of this comely lady as a hard-nosed business executive is starting to fuzz up a bit. Let me make it even foggier by pointing out that in 1987, when she left the newspaper business in Florida, Charlie White and her husband, Gary, decided it was time to put ambition on hold temporarily in favor of fun. The two of them took what they like to call a "sixteen-month sabbatical" and covered the North American continent for the express purpose of bowhunting and collecting an array of trophies.

Near their present home in Stonewall, Mississippi, Charlie took a pair of whitetail deer, then scored on another near Vicksburg. Just outside of Laredo, Texas, she and her husband

White has collected more than sixty bowhunting trophies in North America and Africa.

hunted and harvested javelina. Montrose, Colorado, was the scene of a successful elk hunt.

Moving northward, along the western slope of the Rockies, black bear was the target in Rifle, Colorado, then it was to Gillette, Wyoming for antelope. In Wisdom, Montana, Charlie took an elk and a mule deer before she and Gary White moved on to Prince of Wales Island, off the coast of Alaska,. There she hunted in a dozen days of rain before she scored on a Sitka blacktail deer. Clear across the expanses of Canada, in Schellfferville, Quebec, she took her pair of caribou.

"By then, we figured it was time either to go back to work or file for acute bankruptcy," she admits with a grin. It had been quite a year, for she had bagged thirteen animals, several of them under what can only be described as horrendous conditions.

Charlie White attributes her abilities and the trophies she has taken to good equipment and excellent training. She shoots a fifty-three-pound compound bow and uses Easton XX75 1916 aluminum arrow shafts. Her husband, incidentally, shoots a 70-pound compound, but often switches it for a recurve model he built for himself. Charlie White named it the Cherokee Hunter and the name has stuck. She has used a release from the time she first began shooting, while Gary favors a finger tab. There are some advantages to their

differences. One doesn't have to worry about a spouse borrowing equipment.

There are those bowhunters who tend to look down their noses at target archers. However, Charlie White insists that her early exposure to paper-punching has been a help in her hunting endeavors.

"I've found that when you compete with targets," she says, "this teaches you to follow through, pick your spot and become totally familiar with your equipment. And those 3-D shoots can be a big help in teaching one to judge distance to a target — or a deer!"

One can wonder how and why Charlie White became a bowhunter. It was not one of those things that just happened overnight. She had spent a good deal of time hunting and fishing with her father long before she ever picked up a bow. "I was the son he never had," she explains matter of factly.

Gary White is a construction man and had been an avid bowhunter long before he and Charlie met. He bought her a compound bow in 1977.

"I'll be the first to tell you I did not fall in love with that bow overnight," Charlie White says now. "It took months for me to build the strength in my arms and shoulders required to handle that bow with any degree of proficiency." The effort paid off, of course, for her total number of trophy animals

White studies the habits of deer, especially their feeding patterns. She then determines the best location to wait in ambush.

comes to more than sixty to date.

In more recent times, Charlie White has become deeply involved with the National Bowhunters Education Foundation and is a life member of the organization. She contends that organizations such as the NBEF keep the bowhunting sport alive.

"It is the job of those with more experience to educate and train the new and less experienced concerning the basics of bowhunting and their special responsibilities as hunters," Charlie White is quick to point out. "I firmly believe that the future of bowhunting depends on effective education of the bowhunter."

She feels the mountain goat is the toughest trophy to take, but her favorite is the whitetail deer.

"I don't think I'll ever tire of hunting the whitetail," she insists. "For me, a normal day of bowhunting for this particu-

lar species is spent perched on a portable stand fifteen feet above the ground. I usually arrive half an hour before daylight, then stay on the stand for about four hours."

After that stretch of inactivity — if that's the way it has been — she gets down from the tree, moves away from the area and has lunch and works the kinks out of her muscles. About 2 p.m., she gets back on the portable stand, hooks up her safety line and stays there until dark.

"I've had any number of women, including some who bowhunt, tell me that my system sounds like a real bore, but to me it's private time. It is my own personal way of getting rid of the pressures of business. Letting them go. During that private time, I'm able to clean some of the corners of my mind and get rid of a lot of tension build-up just by being with nature in surroundings I love."

That does not mean, however, that the lady simply sits in

the tree and depends upon luck to get a deer.

"Most non-bowhunters think we just go out in the woods, climb a tree and shoot a deer," she says. "They don't understand that the process actually starts many months earlier for the true, dedicated bowhunter. He — or she — will spend many hours practicing with the bow that will be used in the field. After all, plenty of us have gone all season and only gotten one shot. The bowhunter has to be physically and mentally ready to take that one shot and make it count."

Charlie White also knows that the true bowhunter spends countless hours out in those woods before the season opens. In looking for deer sign, one first must determine the area that has a good concentration of deer. Hopefully, this area will be somewhat isolated, because once the season opens, the woods will be full of other bowhunters who are walking around and spooking whatever deer are there.

"I try to study the area and determine just where the deer are feeding," Charlie White explains. "I want to know where they bed down and what trails they use to travel between bedding grounds and the food source.

"Deer tend to be creatures of habit unless there is too much hunting pressure on them. I try to study their habits and determine the best place to wait in ambush for that big buck I've seen flitting through the brush."

Charlie White is aware that deer like many different foods, but that acorns are high on their list. "From my own experience, the acorn from the white oak is the one most deer seem to prefer. Also, were I hunt in central Mississippi, we have discovered that persimmon trees and crab apple orchards make excellent places for erecting a tree stand. One year, I took an excellent whitetail buck that was working his scrape under two crab apple trees!"

In choosing a spot to erect her tree stand, Charlie White wants as much natural cover as possible to surround the stand and she wants it to be no less than fifteen feet high and she feels twenty feet is even better.

"It has become a joke in Mississippi deer camps that the deer now are looking up into the trees as they walk along their trails on the way to or from food," the Mississippi lady says, adding, "But it has become less and less a joke and more a case of reality with the passage of time. As bowhunters, we have perched in those stands for so many years that the deer seem to be looking for us in our tree stands."

Charlie White will admit that she initially fought the concept of a safety belt and harness. However, while hunting mule deer in Colorado, her husband insisted she wear one.

"I felt as though I was wearing a girdle and a kidney belt all at the same time," she recalls. "However, after two weeks of sitting in the swaying aspen trees there in Colorado, I learned to appreciate the darned thing.

"I now use safety gear whenever I get into a tree, especially if I'm more than fifteen feet into the tree. I gives me a greater feeling of security. I've noticed, though, that a lot of bowhunters wear just the safety belt and tend to ignore the harness. Whatever works for you is the name of the game, of course."

This lady bowhunter, incidentally, doesn't like to gamble on long shots. "The maximum range of most of my shots in the swamps and hardwood forests of Mississippi have to be between twenty-five and thirty yards," she explains. "Beyond that distance, you usually can't see enough of a whitetail to tell where you should hold.

"I don't think I ever have shot at a whitetail at over thirty yards and most of my deer have been taken at ranges of only fifteen to twenty yards."

She harks back to her days as a competitive target shooter, when she discusses archers who are just thinking of getting into bowhunting.

"The untried bowhunter should be able to group his hunting arrows reasonably well in order to know his maximum effective range, then not take any shots on game beyond that distance," is her time-tested advice.

"One also should have some knowledge of the actual anatomy of the animal that is to be hunted. One should know the location of the heart, liver, lungs and major arteries. It also is helpful to get a game target, then practice by shooting only at the areas I've listed."

In her own case, Charlie White tends to favor the lung shot, feeling, "It is the easiest, largest and most important vital area to hit. This type of shot usually results in heavy bleeding that leaves me a good blood trail to follow."

Charlie White and her husband, Gary, tend to be quite competitive — in a friendly way, of course.

"You have to remember that you never learn more or become smarter than your coach," she concedes. "When you do, you have a problem automatically, because a little knowledge can be dangerous. The one who teaches you the sport should always be the master, with the student continuing as the learning pupil."

In fact, Charlie White is convinced that bowhunting for a couple can bring them closer together, making them better friends and partners. "Some of the most enjoyable times of our being together have been when times got rough or even on those cold, cold mornings when it takes both of us to make sure we get out of bed. Having Gary remind me that I can't kill a record-book animal with my head under my pillow is enough to get me moving."

The lady from Mississippi has her own philosophy concerning her bowhunting efforts, and it's not unlike the feelings expressed by a lot of other bowhunters, male and female.

"I have worked at bowhunting just as hard as I have worked at my profession," Charlie White states. "Persistence, hard work in the field, digging down deep in order to go that extra mile, along with encouragement by my husband and other bowhunters have given me an edge, perhaps."

And as is true with many other bowhunters, Charlie White doesn't feel that her success should be counted in the number of animals she has taken over the course of the years.

"The main success and gratification for me has come from the animals I have had an opportunity to watch and the enjoyment I get by being involved in a vital part of nature. There is no experience like being perched in a tree deep in the woods at daybreak, seeing the forest awake with the coming of light and a new day.

"Bowhunting, for me, is a private experience. There are no crowds, no cheers, no spectators. It's just nature, my bow and me. If I take a deer, when I walk up and look down at this trophy, I cannot help but feel proud and a little sad at the same time. Before me lies a beautiful animal I have met in the woods. I have conducted a battle of wits with him, then taken him with a stick and a string.

"But I also know I cannot ever loose my respect for this animal or any other that I pursue. If that should happen, some of the peace I find out there alone in the woods would die."

And that's how she sees her other life.

From The Olympic Games To The Pope & Young Records Is Not That Long A Trip!

Denise Parker beams with pride in taking her first mule deer. Here Dad, Earl, and Mom, Valerie, seem pretty proud, too.

A S THIS is written, there seems little doubt that 18-year-old Denise Parker, a 1991 graduate of Bingham High School in Hildale, Utah, will be making her second appearance in the Olympic Games, this time in Barcelona. The trials for the U.S. Olympic archery team begin the same week this book goes to press. However, at this point, the young Miss Parker is leading all other women contestants.

At 14 years of age, this young lady was the youngest ever to compete in the Olympic Games as a member of the United States archery team. It was she who helped her team win the Bronze medal in 1988 in Seoul, South Korea. Denise Parker has more than enough trophies and medals to stock a trophy shop, and as recently as the 1991 Pan-American Games, she set several women's records in target events.

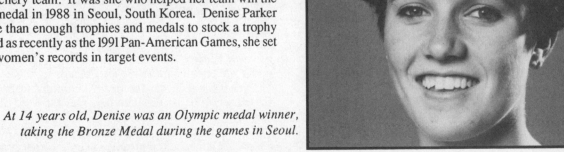

At 14 years old, Denise was an Olympic medal winner, taking the Bronze Medal during the games in Seoul.

Parker captured the women's division of the 1991 Junior World Championships. Vic Wunderle won the men's title.

In January, 1992, she won the women's limited event of the Professional Archery Association tournament and went home with a $1500 prize. Eighty of the top professional archers in the world were in Las Vegas, Nevada, to compete for some $30,000 in prize money. Among the newest members of the PAA were three Olympic archers: Jay Barrs, Rick McKinney — and Denise Parker. Amateurs now are allowed to compete as professionals under recent rule changes that have been approved by international archery organizations.

On the target range, Denise Parker shoots a sixty-six-inch recurve of the type required under the Olympic rules. Draw on this competition bow is thirty-two pounds with a twenty-six-inch draw. But when this young lady ventures into the mountains of her native Utah to hunt mule deer with her parents, Earl and Valerie Parker, all that changes.

Her bow becomes a compound with a forty-pound draw, her arrows are tipped with razor-sharp broadheads instead of target points, the ring-with-pin target sight she uses in competition is replaced by a peep-type sight and the all-white uniform affected by competition shooters around the world gives way to camouflage clothing.

Denise Parker was 14 years old when she represented the United States in the Seoul Olympic Games. She also was 14 years old, when she killed her first deer with that compound bow. She killed another mule deer the following year and has continued to combine hunting with competition ever since. She did not have the opportunity to hunt mule deer in 1991, however, because she was competing in — and winning — the world archery championships in Poland.

Even if she is chosen for the 1992 Olympic team, however, she expects to be in a deer hunting blind when the Utah season opens.

On that first deer hunt in 1988, Denise Parker learned one lesson that never had been taught in target archery sessions or by her Olympic coaches. That particular lesson had to do with patience.

Only minutes before, young Denise had crouched in her ground blind to send a broadhead-tipped shaft into the vitals of a three-by-four muley. As she had been taught, she did not pursue the arrowed animal immediately. Instead, she lay back in the blind to look up at the sky and feel the sun of late August warming her face. She would give the buck time to expire, then would track him down in the accepted fashion.

But the sound of crackling brush — dry in the summer heat — drew her out of her drowsy reveries, and she wondered whether the deer she had shot was still moving about, perhaps moving out.

Cautiously, the 18-year-old blonde sat up and peeked cautiously over the top of her blind. What she saw was a mammoth five-by-five buck. And it was standing broadside to her, only ten yards away!

"All I could do was stare at him and think about what might have been," Denise Parker recalls. "We were in a one-deer-only section and I already had taken my deer. If nothing else, I learned that day it does not always pay to draw on the first deer that comes close enough to ensure a good shot." This from a young lady who won the Gold medal at the Pan-American Games when she was only 13, the youngest archer ever to win the coveted first place award.

One would think an individual of Denise Parker's experience would be beyond an attack of buck fever, but she admits this big ten-pointer affected her that way. At the same time, she admits, there was a touch of remorse that she had not waited for this larger buck to come along.

The young lady plays on the girls' soccer and basketball teams in her home town of South Jordan, Utah, but archery is her major interest. She started shooting, with her parents' help and encouragement, at the age of 10. In the beginning, she shot left-handed, because she does everything else with her left hand. It was not long, however, before her parents discovered that her right eye was dominant. They got rid of their youngster's left-handed bow and started her shooting right-handed. The rest of what has happened on the target ranges of the world is pretty much recorded history.

While such contests as the national championships, the Olympic tryouts, the world indoor championships and a host of other target events can become pressure-building events, bowhunting in the Utah mountains can best be described as "down time" for the young lady. This is a time for her to spend with her two best friends, not worrying about anything beyond enjoying the surroundings of nature. Those two best friends are her parents, Earl and Valerie Parker, both avid bowhunters in their own right.

On that day when she shot the four-by-three deer, Denise Parker found it and was able to load the carcass into the family truck. She did it quietly, still thinking about the ten-point that had showed itself too late for her to do anything about it. Both of her parents were in stands close by and there always was the chance one of them might have a chance at taking that big one.

Two days earlier, Valerie Harper had killed her first deer and daughter Denise was thinking about this as she waited for her mother and father to come in from their stands.

"Dad and I were both thrilled that mom had gotten her first buck," the teenager recalls, "but that feeling was being eroded by my own competitive spirit. I suddenly felt the need to kill an even bigger deer. After all, I'm not used to being in second

The bow, the arrows and shooting style are different when Parker is in competition, but her winning spirit is the same.

place when it comes to things that can be done with a bow and a quiver full of arrows!"

In retrospect, Denise Parker feels that ten-pointer at which she couldn't take a legal shot might have scored larger than the buck taken by her mother, but it would have been close either way.

The four-by-four, in-the-velvet buck taken by Valerie Parker was green-scored at 173 points. Even after the required drying period, it qualified for the Pope & Young record book. According to the official measurers for the club, the dried measurement for the mule deer was 164.

Denise and her mother had taken up archery at the same time as a means of spending more time with Earl Parker.

"He had just taken up bowhunting," Valerie Parker explains, "and it was probably the best thing that ever happened to our family. We all eat, breathe and sleep archery these days. However, neither Earl nor I ever even considered the idea that our daughter would come to represent our country in the Olympic Games."

Mother and young daughter used to accompany Earl Parker into the field just to get into the wilderness, be able to enjoy the outdoors and to make it a family outing.

A moment Parker will never forget was when a 10-pointer stared at her from 10 yards away, and she'd already filled her tag with a smaller deer.

"In those days, Denise and I didn't even have broadheads on our arrows," Valerie Parker confides. "We carried arrows with field points.

"But that all changed the afternoon I was poking around in the brush and came face to face with a big buck muley. That evening, I asked Earl if he could put some of those tips you hunt with on our arrows. At that point, I didn't even know they were called broadheads." Valerie Parker had been hunting for seven years, when she scored on the Pope & Young qualifying four-by-four.

Earl Parker is convinced that the family's mutual love for archery has bonded them together more closely, but this particular hunt had become a pressure thing. His wife had scored on the third day and Denise had shot her deer on the fifth. "With only those few days left, I knew I had to score to uphold my bowhunter image," he half jokes.

Earl Parker settled in for the afternoon hunt not far from where daughter Denise had shot her muley, but he was less than confident that this was truly a good spot. By 8 p.m., with the shadows threatening to turn into night, he was even less certain. That was when the big buck with eight velvet-covered tines edged cautiously out of the brush.

"The deer seemed to take forever to come toward me. All I could see through the brush were those antlers, as he moved closer. Finally, he was only ten yards from me. When he stepped into the open, I had a clear shot.

"The circle was now complete," he adds. "The Parkers had scored one hundred percent on trophy mule deer."

With a bit of prodding, the head of the Parker household will admit that hunting with his wife and daughter now is a great deal more fun than it was when the the two started following him into the woods.

"Trying to bowhunt for deer with two people following along a few paces behind you leaves a bit to be desired," he notes diplomatically.

"Then we reached the point that Valerie was willing to go off on her own and try to find her own deer, while Denise went along with me. The next day, Denise would go with my wife and I'd hunt alone. Believe me, it's all a lot more productive now that Denise can go off and stalk her own deer."

The bowhunter, however, does feel strongly about the three of them following the same pursuits out of the same hunting camp. "We hunt each year with a group of people we know. It's as much a social event as a hunt," he explains. "But we run across some other guys out there who look at us a bit oddly. Actually, I think it's envy, because I feel deep down inside that each of them wishes he had the same relationship with his wife and daughter."

Of course, Denise Parker is now 18. In a few months, she will be headed for college, but her studies — possibly in the field of medicine — will keep her in Utah. And that's close enough for the Parker trio to share a lot more hunting seasons!

Peggy Barcak Sees Bowhunting As A Family Affair, Not A For-Men-Only Endeavor!

Bowhunting and enjoying the outdoors are important to Peggy Barcak. She is committed to preserving the rights of hunters.

A NATIVE Texan, Peggy Barcak is one who has managed to raise two children — with the aid of her husband, Gene — attend college, pursue careers at various times as a legal secretary, vice-president of a property investment firm and secretary to the vice president of an abstract company. She also has developed a devoted following with the stories she spins as a freelance writer, specializing in outdoor subjects, primarily bowhunting features.

Her objective in life, she states, is "to share my love of the outdoors with others and to work with diligence to protect the privilege of enjoying the outdoors."

In keeping with this aim, she has been — and is — involved with a number of outdoor and conservation groups. Since 1975, for example, she has been associated with the Lone Star Bowhunters Association, and at various times, has been the organization's vice-president, secretary/treasurer, programs chairman, legislative chairman and the association public relations chairman and representative.

She belongs to eleven different organizations that are devoted to protecting the rights of hunters and battling restrictive legislation that she feels is not in keeping with the best recognized and accepted conservation practices.

Another item also has been of continuing interest to Peggy Barcak down through the years since she traded in her rifle and began bowhunting in 1969. This has to do with women's acceptance in the sport of bowhunting.

"The fact that women can handle the responsibilities of the hunt are important to me," she explains. "A woman should not seek recognition in the field as a female, but as a hunter. Our love of the outdoors is a common bond that should be shared by everyone."

Over her more than two decades of serious bowhunting, Peggy Barcak has hunted in her native Texas, Alaska, Colorado, Utah, Wyoming, Alabama, South Dakota, Missouri and Saskatchewan. With her bows, she has harvested whitetail deer, mule deer, elk, pronghorn antelope, black bear, caribou, javelina, Russian boar and Rio Grande turkey, as well as a batch of Texas-bred exotics, small game and rough fish. In short, the lady knows what she's doing with a curved stick and string!

Peggy Barcak also is another of those bowhunters who considers the whitetail deer the ultimate challenge for testing her hunting skills.

She began hunting with a rifle while still attending high school in her hometown of Angleton, Texas, switching to bow and arrows shortly before her son, Lloyd, now 21, was born. A daughter, Andra, is 19 at the time of this writing.

"I've heard all this talk about how men take off for the wilds and the fellowship they'll find in a bowhunting camp, while women are expected to stay behind and make like housewives, mothers and keepers of the flame," Peggy Barcak says.

"Out of all that — if you are a confirmed soap opera fan —

Since 1969 when she began hunting with a bow, Barcak has encouraged a lot of women to become involved in the sport.

is supposed to come loneliness for thousands upon thousands of women. This seeming neglect is supposed to lead to anger, depression, alienation and all sorts of other family and personality problems.

"Today, though, that doesn't seem to be the way things happen — except in those television soapers. These days, when one walks into a bowhunting camp, among the first things most likely to be heard are the sounds of women's voices and their laughter. We have joined the ranks of bowhunters who are out to prove to the whitetail population that we are smarter than that big, old buck that's been dodging around the woods for years.

"Not only have women joined in the sport, but a lot of them are really good hunters," the Texas lady declares. "And if a woman enjoys hunting and would rather do that with her husband or boyfriend over staying home, there is a lot less problem in a deer hunting camp with that choice than there used to be. In fact, I've had a number of hunting wives tell me that the time spent bowhunting with their husbands actually has strengthened their relationship, as well as offering relaxation and the pleasure of hunting deer.

"Let's face it," the lady from Texas adds, "there has to be something of therapeutic value just in getting into the woods and being able to spend some time away from work-place pressures, the chores that constantly face the housewife — and never seem to get done — along with temporary escape from telephones, television, et cetera. I've always found that, after the hunt — even if I don't score — I can return to my usual routine with a fresh outlook on life."

Peggy Barcak admits many of her peers just can't seem to understand how she can have so much fun by simply disappearing into the woods for even a weekend.

"But the fact that I have fun and come back with an improved outlook on life and the world is intriguing to them. A lot of them, especially the women whose husbands hunt, have shown genuine interest and keep asking questions, wanting to know more about bowhunting. It's pretty obvious some of them, at least, would like to become proficient with a bow, and be able to share those hunts with their husbands and perhaps even the whole family."

How many of these women actually will become serious bowhunters is open to question, of course. "I believe the only real criteria for becoming a bowhunter — man or woman — is that one must have a real love affair with the outdoors," Peggy Barcak says.

"If one can truly enjoy sitting in a blind or a tree stand and

During an All-Lady Bowhunt in Colorado, Barcak demonstrated deer calling for Howard Heath (left) and Dee Williams.

observing wildlife and what goes on in the woods — including the splendor of a sunrise, even the sound of leaves falling through the trees — that individual has the makings of a bowhunter. At the other extreme, if the woman's idea of camping is the Hilton or Marriott, she isn't going to like bowhunting."

Peggy Barcak is quick to acknowledge that when she makes a killing shot on a good whitetail buck, she is excited, but she feels that just the time she can spend in the field is more important than the deer-harvesting process.

"People are starting to understand, I think, that men are not the only ones who need to escape the pressures of day-to-day life," she insists. "I think I can speak for a lot of other women bowhunters when I say that the hours we spend sitting in a tree stand, surrounded by the quiet of nature, goes a long way toward maintaining sanity."

One of the early objections — long ago dispelled in most quarters — was the contention that most women just did not have the strength required to draw a bow with sufficient poundage that would ensure a proper shot on deer-size game.

"That objection was heard often back in the days of the recurve's popularity," Peggy Barcak protests. "The minimum draw weight in most states for a hunting bow was forty pounds then. Most women, with a bit of practice, could learn to draw a bow of that weight. Today, the minimum draw weight for hunting still is forty pounds in virtually all states, but introduction of the compound has made drawing and holding that

weight even easier. One doesn't have to be six feet tall and weigh 180 pounds to be a bowhunter! Any woman archer can build her strength through practice. If she is disciplined and shoots enough, she will be able to increase her draw poundage to thirty-five pounds, then to the necessary forty."

Peggy Barcak insists draw weight is not the only factor that need be considered when one is selecting bowhunting equipment. Draw length is a critical factor in "breaking" the bow, holding the draw and shooting accurately.

"I noticed long ago that a woman who is not comfortable and confident in her equipment won't shoot. She'll hang the bow in the garage and take up something else. Also, shooting with a bow that puts too much stress on the individual can mean aches and pains that just never go away."

Based upon her own experience, Peggy Barcak suggests the neophyte visit an archery pro shop to have her draw length measured. At the same meeting, the beginner can discuss other needs such as the type of arrow to use, release aids, bow length, draw weight and what broadhead to install on her shafts.

Buying equipment is the most simple part of the process, according to Peggy Barcak. One has to learn to shoot properly and accurately. This requires finding a place to shoot and getting proper instruction. She suggests the new shooter ask the archery dealer from whom she bought her gear about local clubs where she can get instruction and other help. Equally important, Peggy Barcak feels, is a hunter education course.

Barcak took this South Texas whitetail during a 1986 hunt. It scored a 136 1/8 in the Pope & Young record book.

"Hunter education courses are important for learning safety rules and regulations," she points out. "They also help teach us when and where to place the arrow when we shoot at live game."

Nothing, though, can replace in-the-field training. In keeping with this, Peggy Barcak suggests that the woman new to bowhunting join her husband or others for scouting trips before the season opens. From this, she can learn to locate bedding and feeding zones, how to choose a proper tree stand site and how to read animal sign. This newcomer also can get in some stump shooting which will help her judge distances once she comes face to face with a big buck.

Getting back to the matter of draw weight, the Texas lady says, "All too often I have seen women try to pull their husband's bows that may have a draw weight of up to a

Continuing her top performance in 1986, Barcak took this Colorado antelope that hit a 68 2/8 Pope & Young score.

Bowhunting is an enjoyable part of Barcak's life. It's given her an opportunity to gain a greater appreciation for the outdoors.

hundred pounds. When these women find they can draw the string no more than an inch or two, they decide on the spot that bowhunting is not for them. Most figure that, if they wanted to build that sort of muscle, they'd be weightlifters!"

Instead, she suggests, inexperienced women who want to join their husbands in bowhunting should start with a compound bow that has a draw range of thirty to forty-five pounds. This type bow can be set at a higher let-off and can even be used on the target range.

In spite of the fact that most state fish and game departments now demand draw weight be at least forty pounds for

deer, Peggy Barcak feels draw weight is far less important than proper arrow placement.

"I have had no problem in harvesting deer — or any other type of game, for that matter — because of the draw weight of my bow. I have taken numerous big-game animals with lighter draw weights than I use now. I just worked on precision so I could make a well placed shot in a vital area."

Peggy Barcak is the first to follow her own advice in making bowhunting a social event. She always looks forward to sharing those autumn days with others who have the same aims — pun not intended — as she!

CHAPTER 28

JUST DEER HUNT'N

Smoke from a hunting camp fire provides a special setting for memories of friendships gained and families united.

There's More To To The Sport Than Setting Your Heart On A Record Book Trophy

Camps are a great place to relax, chat and enjoy life. Women, most of whom don't hunt, and children add a warmth to camp.

WHATEVER HAPPENED to just going deer hunting; just hunting one to eat? Nothing, probably, but it sure seems like it. I am as interested in licking branches, primary scrapes, estrus cycles, dominant/subordinate herd interaction, pre-rut, post-rut, moon-phase and barometric pressure as the next guy, but I think this preoccupation with trophies has spoiled something of the values of going deer hunting for hunting's sake. Being able to just go hunting is the important thing.

I have shot a few nice bucks, because I understand a little bit of it. That, plus thirty-some years of just going deer hunting means I get lucky once in awhile.

When you do score, you feel pretty much hot stuff. But I am willing to bet that as many nice bucks — the big, gnarly kind that cause grown men to suffer delirium — are shot by folks who are just out deer hunting, out for the pure pleasure of it, because it's time to go. That's great. It proves everyone has a chance, that it's not necessary to be an "expert," though admittedly expertise helps.

Really and truly, I go deer hunting to go deer hunting, because it's fun. It is tradition, a way of life necessary to those of us who have not forgotten what we are, where we came from and how to restore ourselves.

I can re-stoke my fires in the woods or on a trout stream; a day on the golf course doesn't get it. Mostly, though, it's a time of year to be spent in the companionship of close friends and family when important bonds are strengthened in the elixir of wood smoke and camp coffee. It is the time to teach new bowhunters — mostly the kids, the future generations who have to understand and protect this special time — what it is all about. That is as important as killing a big buck. The big bucks will be there to hunt tomorrow only if we set new hunters on the right path today.

Deer hunting is honestly more than just shooting a deer. But shooting a deer is, honestly, the reason we go. I like to eat venison. I would be unhappy at season's end with an empty freezer. I might not get a big buck, but I will, by God, try to get some steak. I won't go hungry, if I don't. It is not life or death, just vitally important.

It is fashionable today to speak in terms of "harvesting" game rather than killing it. I think I understand the reasoning behind the term, but I do not really like it. My farmer friends harvest their crops. I shoot deer on the land that eat the crops they grow. I do this as efficiently and neatly as I can. Excuse me, but I enjoy shooting at game. It is the reason I practice long and hard with my equipment, tear my hands up while placing tree stands and freeze my butt off sitting in them.

One of the greatest pleasures more than thirty years of deer hunting has given me has been watching the development of my children and the offspring of my friends evolve as hunters and as people. There are many lessons taught in a deer camp that go beyond hunting. Kids brought up in such an atmosphere seem to turn out pretty well.

I have enjoyed many camps in the close companionship of

There's something really special about the grin of a young bowhunter when he poses with his first deer. It's priceless!

good. When you pull into camp, someone always looks in the bed of the truck to see if you have one lying back there. Usually you don't. Either you haven't got one or it's too big to get out by yourself. It is nice when you can report that you "need a little help."

Usually you don't have one in the truck or still in the woods, but often someone else will. As you approach the core of the camp, you check out the surrounding trees illuminated by the flickering fire and hissing Colemans. Is there anything hanging? In the orange/yellow light, the reflection off a white underbelly turning slowly on a gambrel catches your eye. You search the faces for the successful one. It will be the one straining to be casual. If it's a kid, he'll look like he's about to blow up. I love it when the kids score, especially on their first ones.

Ice tinkles in your glass, blending comfortably with the murmur of a half-dozen hunting stories. You listen and congratulate the owner of the critter in the tree while passing on your report of a scoreless afternoon. When the gals are in deer camp, there will probably be *hors d' oeuvres,* good with the cocktail you really wanted that's just a tad too big.

Lantern-lit dinner talk is interrupted by big moths stranded,

Darrall Dougherty didn't take the time to remove the camo from his face before cooking a batch of delicious deer ribs.

one or two men. Most often these were "serious" hunts far away from home, carefully planned, important, expensive and good. Yet, I find more real pleasure in a camp of larger size, full with the presence of youthful enthusiasm and garnished with adult experience. They are the deer camps in which I spend most of the hunting time each fall. They are the ones I enjoy the most.

These are camps where women fit in quite nicely; some of them hunt, but most do not. When the weather of early fall is at its best, crisp with light morning frosts and pleasantly warm days, when the colors of autumn come on, the wives enjoy being there as much as the boys. When the weather sours, they stay home; they generally are smarter than we are.

Evenings are best. The return to camp from the afternoon hunt always fills me with anticipation; who got what, what stories will be told, what screw-ups will there be to laugh at, but not too hard. The screwer-upper never thinks it is quite as funny.

If the gals are in camp, the fire is crackling pretty well by dark and dinner will be under way. When the ladies stay home, we have to start from scratch. Dinner will be late and not as

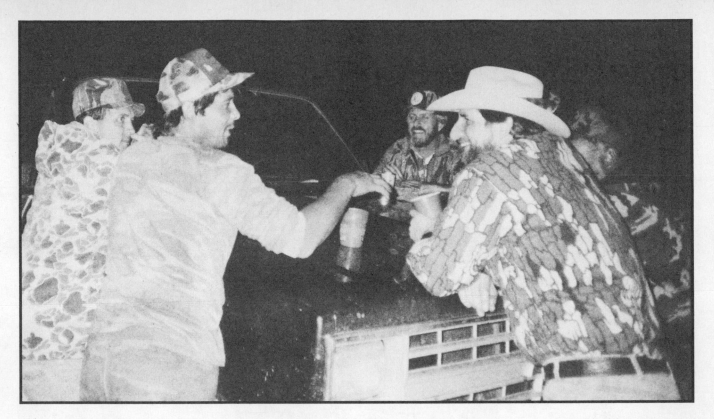

"Then, you should of seen this monster..." There's nothing like reliving, with friends and family, the adventures of the hunt.

fluttering hopelessly in the creamy salad dressing. Others plunge to a scalding end in steaming mugs. A large praying mantis gets stuck in the butter. Everyone tries to avoid eating a bug.

Most often the coyotes sing about an hour after dark; I like them for dinner music. If there is a problem with such camps, it is only that the evenings sometimes can run too long. Daylight, after all, comes early, but conversation and good stories are loathe to die and no one wants to go off to bed. We do, though, finally. We are reluctant to slip from warm clothes into a chilly bag that seems sub-zero. It is best, in cozy co-ed camps, to send the wives to the double bags first. Chauvinistic? Uh-huh. Smart too!

Sleep is instant, filled with the mind's impressions of the day played back through the VCR in your head. You close your eyes and the pictures are there. You dream about what has happened, but mostly about what might be; the good dream where the biggest buck in the woods is about to step into that perfect spot. You are at full draw when the alarm goes off.

I have perfected the technique of lighting the stove in my trailer from my bed; it requires some maneuvering, but it beats getting out. I see no sense to leaving the bag before the coffee is fully perked. The pot is there, primed, awaiting ignition. Non-hunting wives in deer camp don't get up to make the coffee. They arise at a more sane hour, the sun fully up, when the frost is off the pumpkin. No amount of discussion ever will change their position on the subject.

Barred owls squall and gargle at the pinkening east as the sounds of stirring, grumbling life increase around camp. I have a son who has perfected last-minute departure from bag to truck to an art form requiring no more than thirty seconds.

It takes me ten minutes to put on my boots. He is never up, but he is always ready. Engines cough, doors slam, someone is wandering about looking for his finger tab. He finds it where he left it — on his finger.

I can hear wild dogs or domestic mongrels that are loose running deer in the bottom below camp, as I go to start the truck. They are a problem here; everywhere, I think. We find where they have killed with alarming frequency. Wors than coyotes, the dogs seldom feed on their victims; kill and go, go and kill. They seem to be present everywhere I go these days.

One by one, the vehicles pull out. As usual, I try to handle the rutted road with one hand, the second cup of coffee splashing in the other. It never works. I throw most of it out rather than wear it. A doe and fawn skip through the headlights. We have lots of cottontails this year and they zig-zag down the road, confused by the brilliance. You have to be careful not to crunch them, but you mentally mark the areas with the most bunnies. You can come back when it snows and shoot some.

My youngest son wishes me good luck when I drop him off.

"Stick one," I tell him.

"Big time," he replies. He disappears into the dark, no longer a little boy who started bowhunting when he was 9. He's an adult now with a new son of his own. Driving off, I wish it otherwise, remembering each first deer; what a big deal it was, how cool they tried to be, how much they have come to love it. We have grandsons and granddaughters now, and I can start the training again in a few years.

We are there to hunt deer. It is still early in the season and there are lots of deer. Some of us will hold out. Antlers are always a priority. A "trophy" exists in the eyes of the

Dougherty has introduced his children to bowhunting. They are now grown with families of their own. He now has new students: his grandkids.

individual, a personal thing. For others, four legs will suffice. For the kids and other newcomers to the game, there is no greater lesson than the act of doing it. If you want it, shoot at it. Just because it is there, within range, is no guarantee.

You may do it five times or fifty during the season; hundreds or thousands of times in your life, but every morning when you climb into that tree stand, you know a new full-length feature is about to be played. This day happens only once. There are no re-runs, but there will be similarities. The scenery may vary from season to season, place to place, but the game is the same. Each hunter from your camp is doing the same thing, feeling many of the same emotions.

We are widely scattered across the area, each in a location determined — hopefully — to be right for this morning's hunt. From my stand in a sprawly, old oak, I watch a covey of bobwhites scurry like little wind-up toys through the oak leaf litter. Somewhere to the west I can hear — I strain to be sure — yeah, turkeys.

Deer filter through all morning. I never saw the first one until it was right underneath me; a little button buck with his nose in the leaves. I need to have my ears checked; he sounds like a tank. The doe and the buck's sister soon catch up. They are right there, ten yards away for a long time. There's not a deer that slips by that I don't fantasize about shooting: where, how and when I should do it, were I going to do it. Because I am not going to do it, they are all cinches. Nothing goes wrong until you are really going to do it.

I vacillate about a fat four-point. I can see him in the freezer with his parts properly labeled. I don't try and he goes on. I talk to myself about it. I am really in the mood to shoot one — or at one. I tell myself that if another buck that chunky comes by I'll do it. Nothing does.

My empty stomach is threatening by ten o'clock. I get down from the tree. The girls will be up, breakfast will be good.

I'll shoot one next weekend.

The Bowhunter's Trade Directory

BOW MANUFACTURERS

Alpine Archery, Inc.,
P.O. Box 319
Lewiston, ID 83501

Barnett International, Inc.
1967 Gunn Highway
P.O. Box 934
Odessa, FL 33556

Bear/Jennings Archery, Inc.
4600 S.W. 41st Blvd.
Gainesville, FL 32601

Black Widow Bow Co.
HCR 1, Box 357-1
Highlandville, MO 65669

Bows By Groves
116 Veranda N.W.
Albuquerque, NM 87107

Browning
Rt. 1
Morgan, UT 84050

J.K. Chastain
490 S. Queen St.
Lakewood, CO 80226

Darton Archery
3261 Flushing Rd.
Flint, MI 48504

Golden Circle Sports
Box 400
Koosklia, ID 83539

Golden Eagle Archery
111 Corporate Dr.
Farmington, NY 14425

High Country Archery
P.O. Box 1269
Dunlap, TN 37327

Howard Hill Archery
248 Canyon Creek Rd.
Hamilton, MT 59840

Jerry Hill Longbow Co.
231 McGowan Rd.
Wilsonville, AL 35186

Horton Manufacturing Co., Inc.
3100 Surrey Hill Lane
Stowe, OH 44224

Hoyt USA
475 N. Neil Armstrong Dr.
Salt Lake City, UT 84116

Indian Industries, Inc.
817 Maxwell Ave.
Evansville, IN 47711

Martin Archery, Inc.
Rt. 5, Box 127
Walla Walla, WA 99362

Oneida Labs, Inc.
235 Cortland Ave.
Syracuse, NY 13202

Oregon Bow Company
250 E. 10th Ave.
Junction City, OR 97448

Dick Palmer Archery
824 N. College Ave.
P.O. Box 1632
Fayettville, AR 72701

Ben Pearson, Inc.
P.O. Box 7465
Pine Bluff, AR 71611

**Precision Shooting
Equipment, Inc.**
P.O. Box 5487
Tucson, AZ 85703

Premier Archery Corp.
P.O. Box 132
Ocono Falls, WI 54154

Pro Line Co.
1675 Gun Lake Rd.
Hastings, MI 49058

Quillian's Archery Traditions
483 W. Cloverhurst Ave.
Athens, GA 30606

Rancho Safari
P.O. Box 691
Ramona, CA 92065

Sierra/SeaStar International
P.O. Box 806
Fort Smith, AR 72902

York Archery
P.O. Box 110
Independence, MO 64051

**Total Shooting Systems,
Inc.**
390 W. Rolling Meadows Dr.
Fond Du Lac, WI 54935

ARROWS & ARROW SUPPLIES

Acme Wood Products
P.O. Box 636
Myrtle Point, OR 97458

Aero Trak
P.O. Box 82158
Portland, OR 97202

AFC, Inc.
Hwy. 52 S.
Chatfield, MN 55923

Anderson Archery
P.O. Box 130
Grand Ledge, MI 48837

Archers-Ammo, Inc.
P.O. Box 821
Issaquah, WA 98027

Arizona Archery
P.O. Box 25387
2781 N. Valley View Dr.
Prescott Valley, AZ 86312

Arrow Tech, Inc.
8905 Glen Lake Dr.
Austin, TX 78730

Barrie Archery
2 Knoll Drive
Waseca, MN 56093

Beman Archery Corp.
3065 North Rockwell St.
Chicago, IL 60618

Bi-Delta Archery
25 Dempster
Buffalo, NY 14206

Bohning Col Ltd.
7361 N. Seven Mile Rd.
Lake City, MI 49651

**Custom Archery Equipment,
Inc.**
21529 Menlo Ave.
Torrance, CA 90502

Easton Aluminum, Inc.
5040 W. Harold Gatty Drive
Salt Lake City, UT 84116

**Forestline International,
Corp.**
775 Rt. 82
Hopewell Junction, NY 12533

F/S Discount Arrows
P.O. Box 8094
Fountain Valley, CA 92708

Godfrey Enterprises
1000 Goodlander Circle
Selah, WA 98942

Magnus Archery
P.O. Box 144
Otis, KS 67565

Mar-Den Co.
RR1, Box 744A
Willcox, AZ 85643

Muzzy Products Corp.
3705 S.W. 42nd Pl.
Gainesville, FL 32608

Nirk Archery Col
Rt. 1, Box 80
Potlatch, ID 83855

North Star Archery Products, Inc.
527 Elizabeth Ave.
Grand Rapids, MN 55744

Satellite Archery
1111 Corporate Dr.
Farmington, NY 14425

True Flight Arrow Co., Inc.
R.R. 5, Box 746
Monticello, IN 47960

WASP Archery Prod., Inc.
9 West Main St.
Plymouth, CT 06782

L.C. Whiffen
923 S. 16th St.
Milwaukee, WI 53204

Whitetail Disguise
P.O. Box 22187
Chattanooga, TN 37421

Zwickey Archery, Inc.
2571 E. 12th Ave.
St. Paul, MN 55109

ARCHER ACCESSORIES

Accra 300
805 S. 11th St.
Broken Arrow, OK 74012

Chuck Adams Bowhunting Co.
Box 228
Stevensville, MT 59870

Adventures In The Wild
3168 S. 108th E. Ave.
Tulsa, OK 74146

Aimpoint
203 Elder St.,
Herndon, VA 22070

Allen Co., Inc.
525 Burbank St.
Broomfield, CO 80020

Bob Allen Co.
Box 477
Des Moines, IA 50302

All Rite Products, Inc.
1001 W. Cedar Knolls S.
Cedar City, UT 84720

Americase
Box 271
Waxahachie, TX 75165

Ames Industries
3631 Interlake Ave. N.
Seattle, WA 98103

AMS, Inc.
411 W. Highway 29
Abbotsford, WI 54405

Archer's Advantage, Inc.
Box 7134
Marietta, GA 30065

Archery Center International (ACI)
15610 S. Telegraph Rd.
P.O. Box A
Monroe, MI 48161

Arizona Optical Case Co.
1015 S. 23rd St.
Phoenix, AZ 85034

Arizona Rim Country Products, Inc.
1035 South Vineyard
Mesa, AZ 85210

Arrowzona Products Mfg., Inc.
P.O. Box 50551
Tucson, AZ 85703

Autumn Tracker Design, Inc.
Box 658
Floodwood, MN 55736

Bagmaster Mfg., Inc.
3014 N. Lindbergh St.
St. Louis, MO 63074

E.W. Bateman & Co.
Box 751
Fischer, TX 78623

Benders No-Glov
Route 2, Box 609
Stoddard, WI 54658

B-K Archery Products, Inc.
P.O. Box 531
Mason, WV 25260

Black Sheep Brand
#220 W. Gentry Parkway
Tyler, TX 75702

Bowhunters Discount Wrhse., Inc.
Box 158, Zeigler Rd.
Wellsville, PA 17365

Bowhunters Supply, Inc.
1158-46th St.
P.O. Box 5010
Vienna, WV 26105-0010

Boyt Sporting Goods, Inc.
P.O. Drawer 668
Iowa Falls, IA 50126

BPE, Inc.
Rt. 3, Box 92
Emporia, KS 66801

Brauer Brothers Mfg. Co.
2020 Delmar Blvd.
St. Lewis, MO 63103

Brownell & Company
P.O. Box 362
Moodus, CT 06469

Brunsport, Inc.
Box 65
Aurora, IL 60507

BSI
Box 5010
Vienna, WV 26105

B-Square Co.
Box 11281
Fort Worth, TX 76110

Buckey Sports Supply
2655 Harrison Ave. S.W.
Canton, OH 44706

Bushmaster Cases
451 Alliance Ave.
Toronto, Ontario M6N 2J1
CANADA

Chek-It Products
Onalaska, WI 54650

Cobra Manufacturing Co., Inc.
P.O. Box 667
Bixby, OK 74008

Custom Chrono
5305 Reese Hill Rd.
Sumas, WA 98295

Deerslayer Gloves
Box 260
Chillicothe, MO 64601

Delta Industries, Inc.
117 E. Kenwood St.
Reinbeck, IA 50069

Diamond Machining Technology
85 Hayes Memorial Dr.
Marlborough, MA 01752

Doskocil Manufacturing Co.
P.O. Box 1246
Arlington, TX 76010

Jim Dougherty Archery, Inc.
4418 S. Mingo Rd.
Tulsa, OK 74146

Emerging Technologies, Inc.
Box 581
Little Rock, AR 72203

C.W. Erickson's Mfg.
Rt. 6, Box 202
Buffalo, MN 55313

Fast Fletch Archery
#92 Rt. 6
Columbia, CT 06237

Ferguson Adventure Archery
Hwy. 36 W.
Hartselle, AL 35640

Fine-Line, Inc.
11220 164th St. E.
Puyallup, WA 98374

Flex-Fetch Products
1840 Chandler Ave.
St. Paul, MN 55113

Foam Design
444 Transport Ct.
Lexington, KY 40581

Freeman's Animal Targets
111 S. Griswold Rd.
Indianapolis, IN 46234

Full Adjust Archery
2195A Old Philadelphia Pike
Lancaster, PA 17602

Game Tracker, Inc.
3476 Eastman Dr.
Flushing, MI 48433

Golden Key-Futura
14090-6100 Rd.
Montrose, CO 81401

Gordon Plastics, Inc.
2872 S. Santa Fe Ave.
San Marcos, CA 92069

Gorman's Design
P.O. Box 21102
Minneapolis, MN 55421

Granpa Specialty Co.
3304 Woodson Road
St Louis, MO 63114

Grayling Outdoor Products, Inc.
P.O. Box 192
Grayling, MI 49738

Gun-Ho Sports Cases
110 E. 10th St.
St. Paul, MN 55101

Hasmer Sales Co.
24550 Rosewood
Oak Park, MI 48237

Hawkeye Distributor
822 First Ave.
North Escanaba, MI 49829

HHA Sports, Inc.
6210 Wintergreen Dr.
White Rapids, WI 54494

Hilsport by Hilco, Inc.
2102 Fair Park Blvd.
Harlingen, TX 78550

Stanley Hips Targets
17585 Blanco Rd.
San Antonio, TX 78232

Horne Archery Mfg.
P.O. Box 1616
Pascagoola, MS 39567

Impact Industries, Inc.
333 Plumer St.
Wausau, WI 54401

Inventive Technology
120 W. 300 S.
American Fork, UT 84003

Kalispel Case Line
P.O. Box 267
Cusick, WA 99119

Kapul, Inc.
P.O. Box 9018
Trenton, NJ 08650

Keller Manufacturing
5628 Wrightsboro Rd.
Grovetown, GA 30813

King Archer Archery Prods.
Rt. 1, Box 895
North Wilkesboro, NC 28659

**Kinsey's Archery
Products, Inc.**
1660 Steel Way Drive
Mount Joy, PA 17552

Klasic Kase Products
9727-D Business Park Dr.
Sacramento, CA 95827

KLP Mfg.
278 Calvin Ave.
Holland, MI 49423

Kolpin Manufacturing, Inc.
123 S. Pearl St.
Berlin, WI 54923

Kwikee Kwiver
P.O. Box 130
Acme, MI 49610

Lakewood Products, Inc.
627 Coon St.
Rhinelander, WI 54501

Leals' Archery Sights
62 Liberty St.
E. Taunton, MA 02718

Lewis & Lewis Corp.
1013 Co. Hwy AA
Nekoosa, WI 54457

L.W. Lyons
1122 DeWitt Ave.
Niles, MI 49120

Maple Leaf Press
1215 Beach Tree St.
Grand Haven, MI 49417

Mason Manufacturing Co.
4115 Silverleaf cove
Memphis, TN 38115

McKenzie Supply
P.O. Box 480
Granite Quarry, NC 28072

MTM Molded Products
3370 Obco Ct.
Dayton, OH 45414

Neet Products, Inc.
Rt. 2
Sedalia, MO 65301

New Archery Products Corp.
6415 Stanley Ave.
Berwyn, IL 60402

Norman Archery Wholesale
132 N. Santa Fe
Norman, OK 73069

Northeast Products
3 Thompson Street
P.O. Box 8
Methuen, MA 01844

Okie Manufacturing, Inc.
Rt. 1, Box 155
Hendrix, OK 74741

"Ole" Norms
P.O. Box 966
Clemson, SC 29631

Ole Whiskers, Inc.
43 Rd. 3523
Flora Vista, NM 87415

Original Brite-Site
34 Kentwood Rd.
Succasunna, NJ 07876

Pape's Archery, Inc.
9115 Minors Lane
Louisville, KY 40219

Penguin Industries
Airport Industrial Mall
Coatesville, PA 19320

Potawatomi Products
16931 W. 6th Rd.
Plymouth, IN 46563

PP&S Archery Targets
P.O. Box 375
Raceland, LA 70394

Pride Plastics, Inc.
575 Glaspie
Oxford, MI 48051

Pro Release
P.O. Box 609
Utica, MI 48087

**Quillian's Archery
Traditions
Outdoor Edge Cutlery**
2888 Bluff St., Ste. 130
Boulder, CO 80301

Range-O-Matic Archery
35572 Strathcona Dr.
Mt. Clemens, MI 48043

Ranging, Inc.
Routes 5 & 20
East Bloomfield, NY 14443

Razor Edge Systems, Inc.
P.O. Box 150
Ely, MN 55731

Ridgewood Group
8909-19th St. W.
Rock Island, IL 61201

Sagittarius
9030 Carroll Way #5
San Diego, CA 92121

Saunders Archery Co.
Box 476
Columbus, NE 68601

Sight Master Bowsight
293 Hwy. 12 East
Townsend, MT 59644

Smith Whetstone Company
1500 Sleepy Valley Rd.
Hot Springs, AR 71901

Southern Archery
P.O. Box 204
Louisville, MS 39339

Stuart Products, Inc.
P.O. Box 1587
Easley, SC 29641

Target Systems
315 W. Sherman St.
Lebanon, OR 97355

**Timberline Archery
Products**
P.O. Box 333
Lewiston, ID 83501

Timberline Targets
P.O. Box 667
Williston, ND 58802

Tink's Safariland Corp.
Box 244
Madison, GA 30650

Toxonics
796 Hoff Rd.
O'Fallon, MO 63366

**Trautman's Outdoor
Creations**
2082 S. First
Hamilton, MT 59840

Trophy Glove Co.
Box 668
Albia, IA 52531

Tru-Fire Corporation
7355 State St.
N. Fond Du Lac, WI 54935

Tundra Targets
Box 683
Brandon, Manitoba R7A 5Z7
CANADA

Western Recreation, Inc.
3505 E. 39th Ave.
Denver, CO 80205

Whitewater Glove Co.
216 Main St.
Hingham, WI 53031

Wyandotte Leather
1811 6th St.
Wyandotte, MI 84192

Ziegal Engineering
2108 Lomina Ave.
Long Beach, CA 90815

TREE STANDS AND BLINDS

Action Products Co.
Box 100
Odessa, MO 64076

A&J Products
3560 Karen Court
Hart, MI 49420

Amacker Tree Stands
1212 Main St.
Delhi, LA 71232

Apache Products
2208 Mallory Place
Monroe, LA 71201

A.P.I. Outdoors, Inc.
602 Kimbrough Dr.
Tallulah, LA 71282

Basse Deer Blynds
3410 Belgium Lane
San Antonio, TX 78219

Brell Mar Products
5701 Hwy. 80 W.
Jackson, MS 39209

Camouflage Systems, Inc.
Box 1133
Thermopolis, WY 82443

Centaur Archery, Inc.
45 Hollinger Crescent, Unit 1
Kitchener, Ont. N2K 2Z1
CANADA

Deer Me Products
1208 Park St.
Anoka, MN 55303

Deerhunter Tree Stands
Box 1397D
Hickory, NC 28602

East Enterprises, Inc.
2208 Mallory Place
Monroe, LA 71201

Evans Sports
Hwy. 63 & B
Houston, MO 65483

Forrester Outdoor Products
3495 Marion Court
Buford, GA 30518

LOC-ON Company
1510 Holbrook St.
Greensboro, NC 27403

Loggy Bayou, Inc.
1615 Barton Drive
Shreveport, LA 71107

Lone Wolf, Inc.
3314 E. Grange Ave.
Cudahy, WI 53110

Ocmulgee Sales
Box 127
Eastman, GA 31023

Pack-A-Stand Mfg.
14920 Butternut St. N.W.
Anoka, MN 55304

Seat-A-Tree, Inc.
25450 Ryan Rd.
Warren, MI 48091

Silent Stalker, Inc.
RR.5, 4500 Rt. E.
Columbia, MO 65202

Sport Climbers, Inc.
2926 75th St.
Kenosha, WI 53140

Summit Specialties, Inc.
P.O. Box 786
Decatur, AL 35602

Thomas Tree Stand, Co.
905 East St.
Texarkana, AR 75502

Trailhawk Treestands
108 Clinton St.
La Crosse, WI 54603

**Warren & Sweat
Mfg. Co., Inc.**
P.O. Box 440
Grand Island, FL 32735

SCENTS AND LURES

Advanced Hunting Products
Box 9335
Spokane, WA 99206

Buck Stop Lure Co., Inc.
3600 Grow Rd. N.W.
Stanton, MI 48888

Cover Up Products, Inc.
RR 1, Box 66
Hill City, KS 67642

Cross River
W2649 Hillcrest Ave.
Nekoosa, WI 54457

Deer Run Products, Inc.
261 Ridgeview Terrace
Goshen, NY 10942

D&H Products, Inc.
465 Denny Rd.
Valencia, PA 16059

Dr. O's Products Ltd.
Box 111
Niverville, NY 12130

Foggy Mountain
Box 2009
Bangor, ME 04401

Glacier Valley Sporting Scents
210 W. Liberty St.
Evansville, WI 53536

Hunter's Specialties, Inc.
5285 Rockwell Dr. N.E.
Cedar Rapids, IA 52402

Johnson Labs, Inc.
Box 381
Troy, AL 36081

Milligan Brand
Rt. 1 Box 87
Chama, NM 87520

Outdoor Technologies
23179 Bear Run Rd.
Danville, OH 43014

Pete Rickard, Inc.
Rd. 1
Cobleskill, NY 12043

Robbins Scent, Inc.
Box 779
Connellsville, PA 15425

Robinson Laboratories
2833 15th Ave. South
St. Paul, MN 55407

**Tri-Lakes
Outdoor Products**
Box 1561
Kerrville, TX 78029

Ultimate Lures
Rt. 2, 9506 Hwy. Y
Sauk City, WI 53583

**Wildlife Research
Center, Inc.**
4345 157th Ave., N.W.
Anoka, MN 55304

Woodstream Corporation
Box 327
Lititz, PA 17543

HUNTING FOOTWEAR, APPAREL

Ace Sportswear, Inc.
700 Quality Rd.
Fayetteville, NC 28306

**All Weather
Outerwear Co., Inc.**
1270 Broadway
New York, NY 10001

B.C.B. Intl. Ltd.
Clydesmuir Road
Cardiff, CF2 2QS
GREAT BRITIAN

Bell Fatigue Co.
Box 14307
Augusta, GA 30919

**Brigade Quartermasters,
Ltd.**
1025 Cobb Intl. Blvd.
Kennesaw, GA 30144

Broner, Inc.
359 Robbins Dr.
Troy, MI 48083

Chippewa Shoe Co.
610 W. Daggett
Ft. Worth, TX 76113

Clarkfield Enterprises, Inc.
1032 10th Ave.
Clarkfield, MN 56223

Classic Designs Ltd.
Box 1064
Rockwall, TX 75087

Codet, Inc.
Box 440
Newport, VT 05855

Columbia Sportswear
6600 N. Baltimore St.
Portland, OR 97203

Commander Garment Co.
Box 659
Cambridge, MD 21613

Danner Shoe Co.
12722 N.E. Airport Way
Portland, OR 97230

Dunham Boot Co.
P.O. Box 813
Brattleboro, VT 05301

Duofold, Inc.
120 W. 45th St.
New York, NY 10036

Duxbak, Inc.
903 Woods Rd.
Cambridge, MD 21613

Empire Insulated Wear
114-120 Forrest St.
Brooklyn, NY 11206

Fabric Distributers, Inc.
1207 Boston Rd.
Greensboro, NC 27407

Famous Trails, Inc.
3804 Main St., Suite 1
Chula Vista, CA 92011

Fieldline
533 S. Los Angeles St.
Los Angeles, Ca 90013

C.C. Filson Co.
Box 34020
Seattle, WA 98124

**Bob Fratzke
Winona Camo**
625 Clarks Lane
Winona, MN 55987

Haas Outdoors, Inc.
200 E. Main
West Point, MS 39773

Herman Shoe Co.
1 Sound Shore Dr.
Greenwich, CT 06830

I.S.W.
Box 5492
Chico, CA

Kamik Footwear
554 Montee de Liesse
Montreal Quebec H4T 1P1
CANADA

Kaufman Footwear
410 King St. W.
Kitchener, Ontario N2G 4J8
CANADA

La Crosse Footwear, Inc.
P.O. Box 1328
La Crosse, WI 54602

Melton Shirt Co., Inc.
56 Harvester Ave.
Batavia, NY 14020

National Dye Works
Rt. 1, Box 3
Lynchburg, SC 29080

Pendleton Woolen Mills
218 S.W. Jefferson St.
Portland, OR 97201

Predator Marketing, Inc.
P.O. Box 2837
Sioux City, IA 51106

Quiet Wear
Box 563
Milwaukee, WI 53201

Ranger Mfg. Co., Inc.
P.O. Box 14069
Augusta, GA 30919-0069

Red Ball, Inc.
100 Factory Ct.
Nashua, NH 03060

Red Head Corp.
P.O. Box 7100
Springfield, MO 65801

Red Wing Shoe Co.
314 Main St.
Red Wing, MN 55066

Rocky Boots
45 Canal St.
Nelsonville, OH 45764

Skyline Camo
184 Ellicott Rd.
West Falls, NY 14170

Spartan - Realtree
1390 Box Circle
Columbus, GA 31907

10X
2915 LBJ Freeway, Ste. 133
Dallas, TX 75234

Tempo Glove Mfg.
3820 W. Wisconsin Ave.
Milwaukee, WI 53208

Timberland Co.
Box 5050
Hampton, NH 03842

Trebark Camouflage
3434 Buck Mountain Rd.
Roanoke, VA 24014

Vasque Hiking Boots
314 Main St.
Red Wing, MN 55066

Walls Industries
P.O. Box 98
Cleburne, TX 76033

Woolverine Boots
Courtland Dr.
Rockford, MI 49351

**Woolrich
Mill Street**
Woolrich, PA 17779

HUNTING KNIVES & ACCESSORIES

Barteaux Machete
Box 66464
Portland, OR 97266

Blue Grass Cutlery
304 W. 2nd St.
Manchester, OH 45144

Blue Ridge Knives
Rt. T, Box 185
Marion, VA 24354

Boker, USA., Inc.
14818 W. 6th Ave., #17A
Golden, CO 80401-5045

Buck Knives
P.O. Box 1267
El Cajon, CA 92022

Camillus Cutlery Co.
54 Main St.
Camillus, NY 13031

W.R. Case & Sons
Box 22724
Knoxville, TN 37933

Catoctin Cutlery
Box 188
Smithsburg, MD 21783

Coast Cutlery
609 S.E. Ankeny
Portland, OR 97214

Colonial Knife Co., Inc.
Box 3327
Providence, RI 02909

Compass Industries, Inc.
104 E. 25th St.
New York, NY 10010

Consolidated Cutlery
696 N.W. Sharpe St.
Port St. Lucie, FL 34983

Degan Knives, Inc.
1830 S. Robertson Blvd.
Los Angeles, CA 90035

Empire Cutlery Corp.
12 Kruger Court
Clifton, NJ 07013

Eze-Lap Diamond Products
15164 Weststate St.
Westminster, CA 92683

Gerber Legendary Blades
7811 West Stewart Ave.
Wausau, WI 54401

Gutmann Cutlery, Inc.
120 S. Columbus Ave.
Mt. Vernon, NY 10550

Imperial Schrade
99 Madison Ave.
New York, NY 10016

Ka-Bar Knives
31100 Solon Rd.
Solon, OH 44139

Kershaw Knives
25300 S.W. Parkway Ave.
Wilsonville, OR 97070

Leatherman Tool Group
P.O. Box 20595
Portland, OR 97220

Linder Solingen Knives
4401 Sentry Dr.
Tucker, GA 30084

Al Mar Knives
5755 S.W. Jean Rd.
Lake Oswego, OR 97035

Normark Corp.
1710 East 78th
Minneapolis, MN 55423

Outdoor Edge Cutlery Co.
2888 Bluff St.
Boulder, CO 80301

Parker Cutlery
Box 22724
Knoxville, TN 37933

Queen Cutlery Co.
Box 145
Franklinville, NY 14737

Sports Blades
447 E. Gardena Blvd.
Gardena, CA 90248

**Swiss Army
Brands, Ltd.**
Box 874
Shelton, CT 06484

Taylor Cutlery
Box 1638
Kingsport, TN 37662

Utica Cutlery Co.
820 Noyes St.
Utica, NY 13503

BINOCULARS AND SPOTTING SCOPES

Brunton USA
620 E. Monroe
Riverton, WY 82501

Bushnell
300 N. Lone Hill Ave.
San Dimas, CA 91773

Celestron Intl.
2835 Columbia St.
Torrance, CA 90503

Jason Empire
9200 Cody
Overland Park, KS 66214

Leica USA, Inc.
156 Ludlow Ave.
Northvale, NJ 07647

Leupold & Stevens, Inc.
Box 688
Beaverton, OR 97005

Minolta Corp.
101 Williams Dr.
Ramsey, NJ 07446

Nikon, Inc.
623 Stewart Ave.
Garden City, NY 11530

Pentax Corp.
35 Inverness Dr. E.
Englewood, CO 80112

Redfield
5800 E. Jewell Ave.
Denver, CO 80224

Simmons Outdoor Corp.
14530 Southwest 119th Ave.
Miami, FL 33186

Steiner Binoculars
216 Haddon Ave.
Westmart, NJ 08108

Swarovski Optik
2 Slater Rd.
Cranston, RI 02920

Swift Instruments, Inc.
952 Dorchester Ave.
Boston, MA 02125

GAME CALLS

Adventure Game Calls
R.D. #1
Leonard Rd.
Spencer, NY 14883

Ashby Turkey Calls
P.O. Box 65
Houston, MO 65483

Big River Game Calls
509 S. 4th St.
Dunlap, IL 61525

Burnham Bros.
Box 669
Marble Falls, TX 78654

Butski's Game Calls
453 79th St.
Niagara Falls, NY 14304

Cedar Hill Game Call Co.
Rt. 2, Box 236
Downsville, LA 71234

Faulk's Game Call Co., Inc.
616 18th St.
Lake Charles, LA 70601

Flow-Rite of Tennessee
Box 95
Bruceton, TN 38317

Haydel's Game Calls
5018 Hazel Jones Rd.
Bossier City, LA 71111

**Knight & Hale
Game Calls, Inc.**
Box 468
Cadiz, KY 42211

Lohman Manufacturing Co.
4500 Doniphan Drive
Neosho, MO 64850

Tasco Sales, Inc.
7600 N.W. 26 St.
Miami, FL 33122

Carl Zeiss Optical, Inc.
1015 Commerce St.
Petersburg, VA 23803

P.S. Olt Co.
Box 550
Pekin, IL 61554

Primos Wild Game Calls
P.O. Box 12785
Jackson, MS 39236

Quaker Boy, Inc.
5455 Webster Rd.
Orchard Park, NY 14127

E.J. Sceery Co.
1949 Osage Lane
Santa Fe, NM 87501

Scotch Game Calls Co., Inc.
6619 Oak Orchard Rd.
Elba, NY 14058

Stuart Products, Inc.
P.O. Box 1587
Easley, SC 29641

Sure-Shot Game Calls, Inc.
Box 816
Groves, TX 77619

U-nique Archery
Rt.2, Box 267
Hartselle, AL 35640

**Wilderness Sound
Productions, Inc.**
1105 Main St.
Springfield, OR 97477

Wildlife Calls, Inc.
Box 821
Cedar City, UT 84720

Woods Wise Products
100 Bowman Lane
Franklin, TN 37064

MISCELLANEOUS HUNTING EQUIPMENT

AA&E Leathercraft, Inc.
104 Hickey St.
Yoakum, TX 77995

Alpine Product Designs
#3 4th Ave. E.
Polson, MT 59860

**Wayne Carlton's Hunting
Accessories**
206 Lynch St.
Edgefield, SC 29844

CKY-Ber Enterprises
4189 Ember Lane
Stevensville, MT 59870

Cross Country
337 E. Penny Rd.
Wanatchee, WA 98801

E-Z Mount Corp.
Box 2599
San Angelo, TX 76903

Ezee Drag, Inc.
33057 Grossbeck
Fraser, MI 48026

Gryphon Engineering
P.O. Box 050407
Roseville, MI 48066

Knickerbocker Enterprises
15199 S. Maplelane Rd.
Oregon City, OR 97045

Outlaw Products
316 1st. ST. E.
Polson, MT 59860

San Angelo Mfg.
909 W. 14th St.
San Angelo, TX 76903

Trail Timer
P.O. Box 19722
St. Paul, MN 55119

NATIONAL ORGANIZATIONS

American Archery Council
604 Forest Ave.
Park Rapids, MN 56470

Archery Manufacturers Organization
2622 C-4 N.W. 43rd. St.
Gainesville, FL 32606

Archery Range and Retailers Organization
4609 Femrite Dr.
Madison, WI 53716

Booster's Club of America
200 Castlewood Dr.
North Palm Beach, FL 33408

Bowhunters Of America
1030 W. Central
Bismarck, ND 58501

Fred Bear Sports Club
4600 S.W. 41st Blvd.
Gainesville, FL 32601

International Bowhunting Organization of the U.S.
668 Raddant Rd.
Batavia, IL 60510

International Field Archery Association
31 Dengate Circle
London, Ontario
N5W 1V7 CANADA

National Archery Association
1750 E. Boulder St.
Colorado Springs, CO 80909

National Bowhunter Education Foundation
Box 1120
Piscataway, NJ 08854

National Field Archery Association
31407 Outer Highway 10
Redlands, CA 92373

Professional Archers Association
26 Lakeview Dr.
Stansbury Park, UT 84074

Professional Bowhunters Society
Box 20066
Charlotte, NC 28202

Pope & Young Club
P.O. Box 548
Chatfield, MN 55923

Safari Club International
11430 Stevens Dr.
Warren, MI 48089